CINEMA AND IRELAND

Irish Studies

Cinema and Ireland

Kevin Rockett, Luke Gibbons and John Hill

Syracuse University Press
Syracuse, New York

93 92 91 90 89 88   6 5 4 3 2 1

Published in the United States of America by
Syracuse University Press, Syracuse, New York 13244-5160,
by arrangement with Croom Helm Ltd., Publishers, England

Printed in Great Britain

Library of Congress Cataloging-in-Publication Data

Rockett, Kevin.
    Cinema and Ireland.

    (Irish studies)
    Bibliography: p.
    Includes index.
    1. Moving-pictures — Ireland — History. 2. Ireland
in motion pictures. I. Gibbons, Luke. II. Hill, John.
III. Title. IV. Series: Irish studies (Syracuse
University Press)
PN1993.5.I85R6 1987   791.43′09415   87-7121
ISBN 0-8156-2424-7

Contents

Acknowledgements   vii

Preface   viii

Part One: History, Politics and Irish Cinema
Kevin Rockett

1   The Silent Period   3
    Early exhibition   3
    Kalem   7
    Ireland a Nation   12
    Film Company of Ireland   16
    General Film Supply   32
    Irish Free State, 1922–30   38

2   1930s Fictions   51

3   Documentaries   71
    Ethnicity and landscape   71
    Fianna Fáil and political documentary   73
    Post-war modernisation and government films   80
    Versions of historical revision   86

4   An Irish Film Studio   95
    Early proposals   95
    Ardmore Studios   98
    Ardmore Studios and the Abbey Theatre   103
    Ardmore and international productions   111
    Irish Film Board   114

5   Breakthroughs   127
    Conclusion   142

Contents

Part Two: Representations of Ireland

6 Images of Violence   147
   John Hill

   Introduction   147
   Odd Man Out: 'We're all dying'   152
   The Gentle Gunman: 'Put away your guns'   160
   Shake Hands With the Devil and *A Terrible Beauty*:
        'It's just killing'   164
   The Violent Enemy: 'The violence is deep'   168
   Hennessy and *The Long Good Friday*: 'Mad Micks'
        and Englishmen   171
   Angel: 'We know where the madness is'   178
   Cal: 'What a fucking country'   181
   Conclusion   184

7 Romanticism, Realism and Irish Cinema   194
   Luke Gibbons

   Language, nature and Irish romanticism   203
   Landscape and character in Irish romantic melodrama   210
   Romanticism and Irish cinema   221
   Character, community and Irish cinema   234
   New departures: Irish cinema in the 1980s   241

Bibliography   258

Index   259

Acknowledgements

The authors wish to acknowledge the assistance of the following institutions and their staffs in the preparation of this book: Irish Film Institute; National Library of Ireland; Trinity College, Dublin; State Paper Office, Dublin Castle; Department of the Taoiseach; Bord Scannán na hÉireann/Irish Film Board; RTÉ Film Library; British Film Institute Library and National Film Archive.

Kevin Rockett would also like to thank Liam O'Leary, Donald Taylor Black, David Collins and Paddy Woodworth for their comments on sections of Part One. For her support and encouragement during the researching and writing of Part One, special thanks to Gina Moxley. Luke Gibbons is grateful to Dolores Gibbons for her comments and constant support and to Hylda Kelly for typing Chapter 7. John Hill wishes to thank Julie Barber for commenting on Chapter 6 and Noleen Kennedy for typing it. Thanks also to James Hickey and Lorraine Kennedy.

Preface

When it was first decided to undertake a study of the cinema and Ireland, it was expected, by friends and colleagues alike, that it would be a brief and undemanding exercise. The cinema and Ireland, it was suggested, was almost a contradiction in terms: a fit subject for a short paper, perhaps, but hardly likely to run to an entire volume. It was an understandable response. Not only have many Irish films been lost or destroyed but the literature on cinema in and about Ireland has been sparse: so sparse, indeed, that one commentator was moved to declare that the bibliography on the subject would not match that of a neglected nineteenth-century Irish poet! Researchers such as Liam O'Leary and Proinsias Ó Conluain have made important contributions to the study of Irish film history while Louis Marcus has provided a valuable analysis of the Irish film industry. Nonetheless, there is no doubt that, by comparison with other national cinemas, the cinema in Ireland remains relatively unexplored and it is with the intention of redressing some of this imbalance that the present volume is offered. It provides the first extended overview of film production in Ireland, charting the development of the cinema in Ireland from its beginnings through to the present day, as well as the first detailed analysis of key representations of the Irish on the cinema screen.

The initial impetus for such work was provided by the first major retrospective of film and Ireland, programmed by Kevin Rockett for the Project Cinema Club, Dublin, in 1978. The screenings and discussions which this involved paved the way for a number of similar events: the screenings and seminars at the National Film Theatre and Institute of Contemporary Arts, London, in 1980 as part of the 'A Sense of Ireland' Festival; the week-long summer school organised by the Irish Film Institute under the title 'Film Study and the Irish Context' (1980); and a major retrospective, 'The Green on the Screen', in Dublin (1984). In 1986 an Irish film festival toured six West German cities and in early 1987 the Cinématèque Française at the Pompidou Centre was host to a thirty film programme of Irish films. Organised by the Irish Film Institute, these festivals provided the occasion for the publication of German and French language publications on Irish cinema which placed the festivals in their historical and cultural contexts. All of these events not only made available a large number of relatively unknown films to a wider audience but also offered the occasion for argument and debate. Some of the work that appears in this volume was first presented at these events and all of the authors have benefited from the resulting public discussion.

Despite such events the lack of an Irish film archive has inevitably inhibited the research in this book. In the absence of some of the films, especially of the silent period, written testimony has had to be relied upon for information and critical appraisal. The research has also been made more difficult by the absence of a central information/documentation centre for the collection of written material on the cinema and Ireland. One of the hopes for this volume is to demonstrate the need and value of not only an Irish film archive but also a national body for the collection and preservation of material relevant to film which will be generally available to researchers and the general public alike. Following its organisation of 'The Green on the Screen Festival' the Irish Film Institute took an important step towards making these films available on a permanent basis in Ireland by seeking and receiving a grant from the Irish Film Board to research and write a report on an Irish film archive. It is hoped that its recent completion will prompt both state and private concerns alike to recognise the importance of preserving Ireland's cinematic heritage.

Despite these difficulties it has still been possible to view a large number of films and accumulate a large body of material. Indeed, such has been the extent of material generated by the research that it will require a further volume to make it all available. The work which follows, therefore, is not intended to be exhaustive. The first section, on Irish cinema, for example, concentrates on the history of film production and only makes passing reference to the details of film distribution and exhibition. In a peripheral capitalist economy such as Ireland's, exhibition and distribution policies have been largely determined in the metropolitan centres. In Ireland's case this has served to categorise the country as a provincial territory organised from the London offices of the main renters. In Ireland itself, though, exhibition has most often been seen, at least until the 1960s, through the moral prism of lay and religious conservatives campaigning for a more restrictive film censorship. However, these issues require their own social and economic study, and remain largely outside the concerns of this volume. Similarly, the second section on representations of Ireland on the cinema screen only deals with certain key sets of images and does not attempt to cover the whole range of Irish-theme films. Despite these qualifications, however, the book still presents the most comprehensive overview to date of films made in and about Ireland.

The history of indigenous film production which is outlined in Part One traces all aspects of film production since the beginning of the century. Cinema made its first appearance in Ireland in music hall programmes shortly after the first Paris and London screenings in the mid-1890s. This early primitive stage of cinema in Ireland lasted until 1909 when Ireland's first cinema was opened. The following year saw regular fiction film production begin. Film production by native and foreign film-makers in the silent period is the main concern of Chapter One. The close relationship between film-makers and the evolving nationalist movement at this time is traced, as is their frequent conflicts with the British authorities. Despite sustained film production during 1910–20, Independence in 1922 did not see a continuity of film activity by nationalists in their newly-acquired positions of power. It was not until the 1930s that more confident, but still irregular, indigenous film production resumed (Chapter Two). By then, however, the key government department concerned with film production, Industry and Commerce, had set its face against support for smaller scale indigenous projects. It sought instead to emulate Hollywood and Elstree by building an Irish film studio. For nearly twenty years, from the mid-1930s to the late 1950s, the Minister promoting this policy was Sean Lemass. He finally succeeded in his objective in 1958 when a privately-owned film studio at Ardmore, Co. Wicklow, was established with state support. But, these studios were to primarily benefit foreign film interests during the following 25 years (Chapter Four).

Despite the haphazard support given by Irish governments to indigenous film-makers, and with little or no private investment in film production until the 1980s, considerable achievements can still be recorded. Documentaries (Chapter Three) and fiction films continued to be produced often on minimal budgets. It is to the great credit of generations of Irish film-makers that they produced these films in spite of state policy. In recent years, however, the Irish state began to respond more favourably to the needs of Irish film-makers. Direct grants and loans were available through a statutory Irish Film Board and the 1987 Finance saw a significant breakthrough in tax relief for corporate investment in Irish films.

It is all the more depressing, therefore, to have to record that only a week after this tax concession was announced, the Taoiseach (Prime Minister) revealed that the Film Board was being wound up as part of the government's economic austerity programme.

The first part of this book, therefore, traces government policy and the history of indigenous film production. This latter activity is presented through each film's production context and thematic concerns. In the early period of film production these themes included questions of nationality and nationhood, the British presence in Ireland and life on the land. Quite often these issues were explored indirectly in historical rather than contemporary films. In the first decades after the founding of the state, a blander, less radical image of the past, especially of the War of Independence, came to the forefront. By the 1970s these themes had been largely discarded or re-interpreted by new generations of Irish film-makers. The catalysts for that development were the social and cultural changes brought about by the internationalisation of the Irish economy from the late 1950s onwards. Rather than displace all Ireland's wrongs onto the old enemy, England, as in the past, film-makers began to interrogate internal social and cultural divisions. This re-orientation has led not only to a cinematic investigation of new issues — class, family, religion, history, sexuality but also the adoption of new formal approaches, which are discussed in Chapter Five. Collectively these chapters serve as a background and complement to the discussions which follow on the dominant cinematic representations of Ireland.

Due to the Irish state's failure to provide for a native film industry, as identified in Part One, popular representations of Ireland on the screen have, with some notable exceptions, been left to the predominantly commercial designs of American and British film companies. What the consequences of this have been are identified in Part Two. Here, the focus is both the images of Ireland which have characteristically dominated the cinema screen, and the manner in which such images may, in turn, be seen to have 'set the agenda' for a popular understanding of the Irish. As with Ireland's troubled attempts to establish an indigenous film industry, it is difficult to separate these questions from the larger context of Ireland's subordinate status within the world economic and political order. As both Chapters Six and Seven make evident, Ireland's peripheral (and ex-colonial) status has not simply hampered the possibilities for a native film industry but, in its absence, has also made possible a set of cinematic representations which have tended to sustain a sense of cultural inferiority. For whether it be rural backwardness or a marked proclivity for violence, the film-producing nations of the metropolitan centre have been able to find in Ireland a set of characteristics which stand in contrast to the assumed virtues of their own particular culture.

The implications of this line of argument are followed through in detail in Chapter Six. By concentrating on a number of key British, and, to a lesser extent, American films, this chapter indicates how a recurring image of the Irish as inexplicably violent has lodged itself within the cinematic imagination and, indeed, continues to exert a hold upon film-makers, even those within Ireland itself. The attempt to elevate 'the Troubles' to the higher plane of 'the human condition' only succeeded in projecting an image of the Irish as a people trapped by Fate, Destiny, or, indeed, by the mythic 'Irish character'. By way of a contrast, the chapter concludes with a call for an Irish cinema which can get to grips with historical and political complexities and challenge, rather than merely support, dominant, taken-for-granted assumptions about Ireland and the Irish.

This is a point which is pursued in Chapter Seven. It is often assumed, for example, that the way to challenge the simplifications and stereotypes of the Irish, such as those identified in Chapter Six, is by recourse to realism. Misrepresentations of the Irish, it is argued, can be corrected by attending to authentic realities of Irish life. But as Chapter Seven indicates, this may not be the simple solution which it at first appears. What often passes as realism is often no more than a variant of romanticism, albeit a romanticism that attends to the darker and harsher aspects of social life. Indeed, the drive towards realism is often self-defeating, as the need to include endless authenticating details (as in the use of landscape for natural locations) leads to a form of 'visual excess' which overwhelms the narrative, destroying the credibility of the story. The most important strands in Irish romanticism thus contain a kind of inbuilt 'uncertainty principle'. It is in this sense that the most innovative films in contemporary Irish cinema seek not to disown the powerful romantic legacy but to prise open these fissures, exposing the ideological fault-lines in the landscape.

Even from such a short summary as this, it should be clear that the discussion found in Part Two is not of an entirely conventional order. It is not concerned with film personalities or the case-histories behind any individual film's production. Nor is it concerned to provide the conventional evaluations of film as 'good' or 'bad' art. This is not, of course, to suggest that these two chapters then dispense with critical judgements; quite clearly they both provide assessments of films which make their critical preferences clear. What is significant, however, is that these judgements are arrived at not on the basis of traditional conceptions of 'artistic quality' and 'cinematic merit' but, rather, according to the considerations of political complexity and formal and cultural self-consciousness. By this yardstick, many of those films which have been conventionally designated as 'classics' emerge a lot less favourably than they might normally, while films which have been denied the full weight of critical approval often appear more complex and engaging than is conventionally considered to be the case.

However, it is not only the received views of cinematic quality which this discussion puts into question. For it also casts doubt upon the conventional distinction, perhaps particularly predominant within Ireland, between the merits of high art, on the one hand, and the shortcomings of popular culture, on the other. Literature has always enjoyed a privileged place within Irish culture and, indeed, it may well have been the peculiar premium placed on the written word which was, in part, responsible for the shortage of enthusiasm for establishing a native film industry. Moreover, while it is popular culture which is frequently held responsible for a misleading image of the Irish, it is often literature which is looked to as the source of an effective counter balance. One of the main impulses behind the Literary Revival, it will be remembered, was precisely a desire to combat a history of misrepresentation as found in popular imagery.

Yet it is not always clear that popular images are on the side of the apes, while literature and 'serious' culture are on the side of the angels (to appropriate the title of a well known study of the Irish in Victorian caricature). For as Part Two of the discussion makes evident, many of the pervasive myths popularised by cinema, particularly in relation to political violence, have their echoes in the work of leading Irish literary figures. Conversely, some of the most interesting and complex attempts at reworking, or indeed challenging, dominant stereotypes are found in such marginal areas of Irish culture as Victorian melodrama and romantic fiction. It is to this often misunderstood prehistory of the Literary Revival that we must look in order to fully understand some of the more familiar images of Ireland on the screen.

Through its recurrent concern with landscape, violence, the past, community and sexuality, cinema is perhaps the best placed of all cultural forms to investigate critically what 'Irishness' means in the popular imagination.

In a sense, it is this very issue of 'Irishness' which runs through the book as a whole. What emerges clearly from Part One is that the establishment of an indigenous Irish film industry must always amount to more than simply the provision of a studio, equipment and trained personnel (important as these might be). For what is also of critical importance is the types of films which an Irish film industry produces — what issues they attend to, what formal approaches they adopt and what kind of cultural intervention they contribute. This is a point reinforced by the discussion in Part Two. While there may not have been any sustained output from a native Irish cinema, there has nonetheless been a considerable number of films, mainly from Britain and America, which have chosen Ireland as their subject matter and, in doing so, have furnished us with many of the most familiar and durable images of the Irish. It is a perennial temptation for Irish film-makers to simply adopt such images as a short-cut to commercial success, yet, as the growth of independent Irish film-making has so admirably demonstrated, it is also possible to re-work and challenge these same images without necessarily forfeiting international appeal. One of the ambitions of this book is to demonstrate the disabling effects of the dominant screen images of the Irish and thereby establish the importance of an Irish cinema which is concerned to render these problematic. Inevitably, this means that much of the book looks backward but it does so in order to go forward properly prepared. By putting on record the history of Irish film production and the issues which the resulting films raised, and by raising questions about how the Irish have been represented on the screen and with what political and cultural consequences, so it is intended that the book should be able to contribute to ongoing debates about the future direction of Irish film-making. Insofar as it assists the building of a revitalised indigenous Irish film culture the book may be deemed a success.

PART ONE:
History, Politics and Irish Cinema

1

The Silent Period

Kevin Rockett

Early exhibition

In *The Freeman's Journal* of 17 April 1896 Dan Lowrey's Star of Erin Theatre of Varieties (now the Olympia) announced 'the world's most scientific invention: The greatest, most amazing and grandest novelty ever presented in Dublin: The Cinématographe'. Three days later the cinema arrived in Ireland. Dublin's first screenings took place only four months after the Lumières' first public screenings in Paris on 28 December 1895 and exactly two months after London's first screenings on 20 February. Using the equipment and films from London's Empire Palace this first series of screenings lasted one week:

> Great pains were taken. Intense secrecy was maintained as to how this miracle worked. Stage hands and staff were under orders not to tell. A boxlike shelter was built to hide the Conjuror-Operator . . . and his machinery. Box office was excellent . . .[1]

But all that happened initially was some flickering which revealed a pair of prize-fighters. After a breakdown, an acrobat, fighting cats, a Scots dancer and a drummer became discernible.

Poor illumination was the problem and Lowrey went to London to seek a more effective show. This time he arranged for the Lumières' agent, Felicien Trewey, to bring his apparatus to the Star of Erin at a cost of £70 per week, £10 more than for the April showings and much cheaper than the £150 per week Trewey was being paid at the Empire Palace the previous March.[2] Trewey himself acted as Operator, ensuring a much more professional performance. The series began on 29 October and proved enormously successful. Seven thousand attended during the first week and the screenings continued, in tandem with the regular music hall acts, until 14 November. A new series of pictures was presented during the last week. As in Paris the Lumières' *Train Coming Into A Station* had an immediate impact. *The Freeman's Journal* reported:[3]

> This very wonderful instrument (the Cinématographe) produces with absolute correctness in every detail animated representations of scenes and incidents which are witnessed in everyday life. To those who witness the exhibition for the first time the effect is startling. The figures are thrown upon a screen erected in front of the audience and, taking one of the scenes depicted — that of a very busy Railway Terminus into which the locomotive and a number of carriages dash with great rapidity — the effect is so realistic that for the moment one is almost apt to forget that the representation is artificial. When the train comes to a standstill the passengers are seen hurrying out of the carriages, bearing their luggage, the greetings between themselves and their friends are all represented perfectly true to life and the scene is an exact reproduction of the life and the bustle and tumult to be witnessed at the great Railway depots of the world.
>
> The representation of Westminster Bridge was equally attractive. A representation of a Cavalry charge, in which every action of the galloping horses in the advancing line was distinctly marked, was a grand picture. The Wedding of H.R.H. Princess Maude of Wales and the Procession in St. James's Street after the ceremony were magnificent and impressive spectacles, second only to the actual scenes themselves. The representation of the Sea-bathing was also wonderfully true to life. The audience witnessed the bathers jumping into the water and the spray caused by the plunge rose into the air and descended again in fleecy showers.

The Lumière films continued to prove a major source of entertainment. Their run of pictures at the Star of Erin in January 1897 'eclipsed' the accompanying music hall acts and crowded the house to 'suffocation'.[4] Six weeks of Professor Jolly's Cinématographe followed. These 'Animated Photographs' with titles such as People Walking in Sackville St, Traffic on Carlisle Bridge and the

13th Hussars marching through the City were amongst the first filmed scenes of Dublin. Prof. Jolly's Cinématographe also provided Cork's first film show at the opening of Dan Lowrey's Variety Theatre on Easter Monday, 1897. Lowrey also reopened the Star of Erin as the Empire Palace in Dublin on 13 November 1897 and once again it was the Lumière films which provided the finale. By then control of the theatre had begun to shift to the English Moss and Stoll variety theatre organisations.

Between 1896 and 1909 Irish exhibition began to grow. Films were included in music hall shows, screened in town and village halls, fairgrounds and any location where a building could accommodate an audience and where a travelling projectionist could set up his apparatus. It was not until 1909 that Ireland's first permanent cinema, the Volta, opened. The idea for the cinema originated in Trieste when James Joyce's sister, Eva, commented that Dublin, a city larger than Trieste, had no cinema. James Joyce took up the idea with four local businessmen including exhibitors with cinema interests in Trieste and Bucharest. They agreed to put up the necessary capital while Joyce would organise the venture in return for a 10 per cent share of the profits. Joyce arrived in Dublin on 21 October 1909 and set about acquiring premises. This he did a week later when he located 45 Mary St, near Dublin's main thoroughfare, Sackville St. He then proceeded to convert the premises into a cinema. Two of his Italian partners arrived a few weeks later and went with Joyce to both Belfast and Cork in search of further premises. Another partner and the cinema's manager, Novak, arrived from Italy in early December accompanied by an Italian projectionist.[5]

For the opening of the Volta Cinema on 20 December 1909 Joyce chose a varied programme. *Devilled Crab* was a comedy while *Bewitched Castle* was 'a magnificent fantastic picture' according to the *Dublin Evening Mail*.[6] Other films in the 35–40 minute programme were *The First Paris Orphanage*, *La Pourponnière* and a story of patricide, *The Tragic Story of Beatrice Cenci* (1908) which *The Freeman's Journal*[7] described as 'very excellent' but complained that it

> was hardly as exhilarating a subject as one would desire on the eve of the festive season. But it was very much appreciated and applauded.

The *Dublin Evening Mail* had also found the films 'very praiseworthy' and the Volta 'a fine hall'.

Despite the favourable notices for the new venture poor weather gave the cinema a slow start. Joyce did succeed in obtaining a permanent licence for the cinema from the Recorder but by this time his enthusiasm had begun to wane. He left Dublin for Trieste with his sister, Eileen, on 2 January leaving the management of the Volta in the hands of Novak. Richard Ellmann takes up the story:[8]

> . . . the Volta stumbled and fell. Under Novak's management the theatre failed to break even. Stanislaus suspected, perhaps rightly, that his brother's neglect of the enterprise had doomed it. Certainly James would have been able to sense the quirky turns of the Dublin public better than a Triestine bicycle shop proprietor. The heavy emphasis on Italian films probably did not help much. The partners decided they must cut the theatre adrift so as to avoid losing more than the 1600 pounds they had already invested, of which Novak had himself contributed the larger share. Joyce asked his father to offer the Volta to the Provincial Theatre Co., an English firm; but before John Joyce bestirred himself, Novak negotiated the sale to them for a thousand pounds, a loss of forty per cent.

The Volta was sold to the Provincial Theatre Co. in July 1910. Later, as Ellmann notes,[9] Joyce 'laboured briefly under the impression that he would receive £40 as his share, but his partners . . . undeceived him'. The Volta was to continue as a cinema until the later 1940s, by which time it had 420 seats.

The Volta provided the catalyst for a rapid expansion in the number of cinemas over the following few years. By 1916, 149 cinemas and halls were listed as showing motion pictures and, by the end of the silent period, 1930, there were 265 cinemas and halls throughout the island as a whole.[10]

With the exception of occasional images of landscape and scenes of people or events as photographic records, the films shown to Irish audiences during the early years of exhibition were almost exclusively foreign-produced. The first native company to exhibit and distribute films, Irish Animated Picture Company, was in business at the beginning of the century and its projectionist, Louis de Clerq, made the first Irish documentary, *Life on the Great Southern and Western Railway* (1904).[11] The pioneer English inventor and film-maker, Robert Paul, who screened films in Belfast and Cork at the very beginnings of film exhibition, later made two

Irish films. *A Cattle Drive in Galway* (1908) was an Irish Land War film and *Whaling Ashore and Afloat* (1908) recorded these activities off the Irish coast.[12] Another English film pioneer, Arthur Melbourne-Cooper, owner of the Alpha Picture Co., London, chose Ireland as the main location for the longest film made up to that time. Melbourne-Cooper set out with his brother from Paddington Station, London on 12 October 1907 in a 'specially constructed observation coach' on which his camera was fixed to make the 3,000 feet *London to Killarney* (1907). Distributed in four parts — Glimpses of Erin, Irish Life and Character, The Railway from Waterford to Wexford and Transferring Mails at Queenstown — its contents varied from film of Killarney and the Giant's Causeway (!) to an old couple dancing a jig. On this trip they also made a comedy, *Irish Wives and English Husbands* (1907), which starred a local Killarney girl, Kate O'Connor, who subsequently achieved fame as the girl on the posters issued by the Great Western Railway Co. advertising tours to Ireland.[13] While this film is probably the first fiction film made in Ireland it was not until three years later, in 1910, that there began the most active period of fiction film-making of the silent period.

During the 1910s and early 1920s indigenous film-makers and sympathetic foreigners produced a range of material — from historical dramas to comedies and love stories — based on both Irish novels and plays as well as original scripts. It was the historical films which were to prove of particular importance in their contribution towards advancing nationalist consciousness. The comedies and love stories provided general film fare. The most important fiction film companies were the American company, Kalem, and their ex-employees, 1910–14, and the Film Company of Ireland, 1916–20, while General Film Supply's *Irish Events* newsreel, 1917–20, regularly recorded contemporary events.

Kalem

The first of those to make an impact in Ireland was Sidney Olcott, director of the Kalem films. Born in Toronto, Canada, of Irish parents, Olcott was one of Kalem's top directors, having made a one reel version of *Ben Hur* in 1907. After a series of successes with location shoots, he was given the oportunity to film outside the US. He chose Ireland and in 1910 he arrived at Queenstown (now Cobh), Co. Cork. With him was Gene Gauntier, the scriptwriter from *Ben Hur* and the actress who was to play the lead in most of the Kalem films made in Ireland. Before her retirement from films in 1918 she was to write or act in 500 films. The third member of the crew was cameraman George Hollister. They made their way to Killarney where they shot one fiction film, *The Lad From Old Ireland*, which is regarded as the first American film made on location outside the US.[14] The three film-makers then proceeded to Dublin where they stayed before returning to the US.

Following the commercial success of *The Lad From Old Ireland* Kalem sent a much larger crew and stock company to Europe the following summer. Once again their first stop was Ireland and their base the small village of Beaufort, near Killarney. During an 18 week stay they made 17 films, a remarkable output considering the primitive, electricity-less environment. George Hollister, who once again acted as cameraman, set up a laboratory in which the films were processed.[15] The films made show a very wide interest in Irish subjects. They varied from a tale of gypsies, *Gypsies in Ireland*, to the historical films *Rory O'More* and *Ireland the Oppressed*; an adaption of a Tom Moore poem, *You'll Remember Ellen*; and the first of what was to become a series of adaptions of the plays of Dion Boucicault, including *The Colleen Bawn* (in which Olcott played Danny Mann) and *Arrah-na-Pogue*.

After their stay in Kerry the Kalem company travelled to Europe, touring 15 countries during the remainder of 1911 and in 1912 from where folk tales, dramas and travelogues were sent back to Kalem. The international success of their tour was *From the Manger to the Cross* (1912), the first major life of Christ, which was made in Egypt and Palestine with Gene Gauntier as the Virgin Mary. Later in 1912 the Kalem crew returned to Killarney where they made an adaption of Boucicault's *The Shaughraun* and the historical film, *For Ireland's Sake*. Two years later Olcott returned to Ireland to make a controversial historical film, *Bold Emmet, Ireland's Martyr*, for his own production company. While he made another Irish-theme film in the US, *The Irish in America* (1915), thereafter Olcott's career was orientated towards mainstream feature production, directing Mary Pickford in *Madame Butterfly* (1915), and Valentino in *Monsieur Beaucaire* (1924).

A wide range of themes are evident in Olcott's Irish-made films. Irish nationalism is sympathetically portrayed while English rule in Ireland is unfavourably contrasted with America which proves to be the escape route from both political oppression and poverty. Within Ireland a tension can also be identified in the representation of the relative leadership positions in the community of outlawed rebels and priests. The community itself, however, is seen as a repository of collective opposition to the English presence. Of equal interest in these characterisations is the depiction of the social ostracism of the informer or collaborator with the English authorities.

It is hardly surprising that the films Olcott made in Ireland for his American employers and orientated towards an (Irish) American audience should wish to characterise America as the land of bounty, freedom and opportunity. *The Lad From Old Ireland* (1910) opens with the harsh conditions on the land in Ireland but quickly transports its hero, Terry (played by Olcott), to the more lucrative work opportunities of New York. Ten years later, his fortune made, the hero returns home in the nick of time to save his sweetheart, Aileene (Gene Gauntier), from eviction.

Subsequent Kalem films put greater emphasis on America as a refuge for Irish political or military activists. Two of the most overtly political films in this respect were *Rory O'More* (1911) and *For Ireland's Sake* (1912). In *Rory O'More* the film's hero, Rory (Jack Clarke), is on the run from British soldiers but is captured after a chase. Jailed and sentenced to death he is rescued just as he is about to be hanged. A waiting ship then takes him to America with his girlfriend Kathleen (Gene Gauntier) and his mother (Mrs Clarke). In *For Ireland's Sake* the rebel, Marty (Jack Clarke), is on the run but is captured with his girlfriend, Eileen (Gene Gauntier). Once again free, this time from jail, they head, as the inter-title has it, 'To the West/ To the West/ The Land of the Free'.

Both these films, and the provocatively titled *Ireland the Oppressed*, made the following year, brought Olcott to the attention of the British authorities. Following representations made to Kalem's head office Olcott was threatened with recall to the US unless he steered clear of controversial subjects. This forced Olcott temporarily to abandon historical subjects in favour of adaptions of Boucicault plays.[16] However, *Arrah-na-Pogue* (1911) was a drama of the 1798 Rebellion. Olcott was to find himself in further controversy with his film about the leader of the 1803 Rebellion, Robert Emmet, made in 1914. When shown at Dublin's Rotunda in 1915 it had to be withdrawn when the authorities claimed it was interfering with their recruitment drive in Ireland. Indeed, Olcott's movements must have been monitored during the shooting of the Robert Emmet film, especially after he provided the film's props-guns for a parade by the nationalist Irish Volunteers in Killarney. Olcott himself was not slow in expressing his Irish nationalist views. He 'left no doubt as to where his sympathies lay', as Proinsias Ó Conluain reported.[17]

It was not just the British authorities that Olcott had to be wary of. From his arrival in Killarney his movements were also monitored by one of the most powerful figures in the community, the priest. While filming *The Colleen Bawn*, the third film made in 1911, the Catholic members of the Kalem unit were given an unpleasant surprise by the local priest:

At Mass one Sunday, the local priest substituted for his usual sermon a verbal assault on the 'tramp photographers' who had invaded the peace and quiet of Beaufort. These intruders, he said, were posturing as Irishmen, portraying the Irish as gypsies and ne'er-do-wells — worse, they were even donning the priestly garb and were making a mockery of all that Irish people held most sacred. He had himself seen two members of the film company with painted faces making love before the camera in a churchyard, thus desecrating the bones of his parishoners' ancestors, and he was perturbed to know that some local lads and lasses were, for a few paltry shillings, selling their souls to the devil by taking part in these vile activities. There was much more in a similar vein, culminating in an appeal to the sturdy men from the Gap of Dunloe to drive out this menace to faith and morals. Catholic members of the Kalem Company, who were present at the Mass and who had listened with an almost superhuman restraint to this tirade against them, remonstrated with the priest afterwards, attempting to explain their work to him — but without success. Olcott finally set out to see the Bishop of the diocese and the American Consul in Cork, and eventually obtained an apology from the priest, who was also transferred to another parish. He was now able to proceed with his work, with the full collaboration of all the people — a collaboration which extended from a loan of silver candlesticks or complete kitchen furnishings, to a willingness to swim rivers or jump from castle parapets.[18]

It is tempting to examine Olcott's films in terms of his attitude to the Catholic Church. In *The Lad From Old Ireland* the priest is seen as an ineffectual bystander in the cottage as the eviction is about to proceed. It is only the returned emigrant with his American money who can retrieve the situation. A more complex exploration of the role of the priest is seen in the historical films. In both *Rory O'More* and *For Ireland's Sake* priests are characterised ambiguously. In *Rory O'More*, made before the priest's attack on the Kalem unit, a priest, Fr O'Brien (Arthur Donaldson), 'sacrifices' himself as the inter-title has it, on the scaffold to free Rory. In *For Ireland's Sake*, made the following year, a priest, Fr Flanagan (Sidney Olcott), provides the file which Marty and Eileen use to escape from jail. In both instances the priest facilitates the escape of the rebel to America but in so doing robs Ireland of the alternative leader of the community. Indeed, in *For Ireland's Sake* the priest is shown throwing a gun which Marty has taken from one of his captors into a river. The obvious implication here is that in American democracy, such guns will not be needed, but the priest's act nevertheless has the effect of maintaining the *status quo* in Ireland.

The character and leadership of the community by priests and rebels turns on collective as well as individual action. In *Rory O'More* it is an informer, Black William (J. P. McGowan), who leads the British soldiers to Rory's hideout and then demands his arrest following an incident when Rory saves a pursuing soldier from drowning. The officer in charge wishes to release Rory but Black William wants his reward. In court the whole community are united as one behind Rory and even the officer pleads for leniency. In *For Ireland's Sake* communal solidarity is strengthened when, under the cover of a pub brawl, the community allow Marty to escape by taking on the soldiers and divesting them of their guns. Later, the community are seen as victims of repressive British Army retaliation. Marty's eventual capture is now shown to be the result of a British Army 'spy', not an informer, observing Eileen on her visit to Marty's hideout. If an informer is involved in an Irish historical film his depiction mainly serves as a means of showing communal cohesiveness and unity. His (for it is never her) difference defines the community's solidarity in opposition to the British presence.

This communal cohesion, nevertheless, serves to disguise important social distinctions among the Irish themselves, especially in relation to land ownership. With the exception of the depiction of the land agent, the establishment's equivalent of the informer, in *The Lad From Old Ireland*, the first film of the period to address itself, if somewhat obliquely, to social relations on the land was Olcott's *You'll Remember Ellen* (1911). In this film a young aristocrat (Jack Clarke), who is dressed as a peasant, comes across a young peasant woman, Ellen (Gene Gauntier). They fall in love and with her parents' blessing they marry. But times are hard and they go on the road in search of work. Eventually they come to Rosna Hall, a huge mansion, at which point it emerges that he is Lord and now she is, of course, Lady of Rosna Hall. Such collapsing of social relations on the land into young love was an extreme example of the suppression of social difference common to all land-theme films of the period. It is, perhaps, not surprising that Olcott, in common with many contemporary observers, should orientate his films away from the often complex social and economic structure on the land towards a radical nationalist anti-Englishness. Concentration on historical military struggle was also a key feature of another nationalist film, *Ireland a Nation*.

Ireland a Nation

Walter MacNamara, an Irishman who had been living in the US for a few years, spent five months in Britain and Ireland in 1914 making this historical drama. The film is mainly centred around Grattan's Parliament, the 1798 Rebellion, the Act of Union and the 1803 Rebellion, despite MacNamara's claim that it was an 'elaborate review of the history of Old Erin from 1798 to 1914'.[19] The interiors were shot at Kew Bridge Studios, Twickenham, London, and the exteriors in Ireland.

One of the interiors was of Robert Emmet's trial when a segment of his famous speech from the dock is depicted. With one eye on his American audience MacNamara chose a part of the speech when Emmet (Barry O'Brien) defends himself on the grounds that he tried to achieve for Ireland what Washington did for America. By basing itself on the 1798 and 1803 Rebellions *Ireland a Nation* cast doubt on constitutional nationalism. Daniel O'Connell occupies only a minor place in the total film and Henry Grattan is depicted as ageing and ineffectual. He is seen as entirely unable to cope with Lord Castlereagh's manoeuvrings prior to the dissolution of the Irish Houses of Parliament and the passage of the Act of Union.

Two quite distinct sets of newsreel footage were later added as an epilogue: first in the early years of the film's distribution and subsequently during the War of Independence. Claiming that the 'Nationalist party gave us unofficial sanction',[20] MacNamara added, however incongruously, footage of John Redmond, leader of the (constitutional) Parliamentary Party at Westminster and of a Home Rule meeting. Later prints of the film contained footage of Eamon de Valera's long tour of America in 1919–20, British Army brutalities, the deaths on hunger strike of Terence MacSwiney and Michael Fitzgerald in 1920 and Lloyd George reviewing Black and Tans on their way to Ireland. The emphasis of this latter material more clearly corresponds with the radical nationalism highlighted in the film and was hardly surprising as it was chiefly directed at an Irish-American audience.

By the second decade of the twentieth century huge numbers of Irish had emigrated to the United States and more than one million, or one in four of all Irish-born people then alive, were living in America in 1920. Irish-American support for the nationalist struggle in Ireland had been an important feature of the nationalist movement since the Fenian campaign of the 1860s. As if to emphasise the importance of America to Irish nationalism, the dramatised film ending, set during the Famine, involves an emigration sequence followed by the title 'The Land of Golden Hopes — America'. This message reinforces the newsreel ending which includes an inter-title 'Ireland Today' followed by shots of the Statue of Liberty and the American flag. In view of this homage to 'the land of the free' it is not surprising that *Ireland a Nation* had 'a remarkable run in Chicago, where it was shown for 20 consecutive weeks to huge crowds'. It also proved popular in other American cities.[21]

Irish audiences were not given the opportunity to display such enthusiasm. *Ireland a Nation* was submitted to the Press Censor for viewing on 10 November 1916 and given a certificate three weeks later with the proviso that six scenes and their titles be removed. The scenes to be excised were a raid by soldiers on a hillside mass; Sarah Curran being 'roughly handled by soldiers'; the execution of Emmet; an inter-title, 'A Price of £100 dead or alive on the head of every priest'; and the Irish flag's display at the end of the performance. In the newsreel section, footage of a 1914 Home Rule meeting, and an unspecified telegram from John Redmond had also to be removed.[22] The decision to cut out the newsreel footage gives an interesting insight into British military and political thinking in the post-Rising period. Within six months of the Rising even constitutional nationalists were being treated with the same suspicion as the nationalist movement's military wing.

The rights to *Ireland a Nation* for Britain and Ireland had been acquired in 1916 by Mr T. A. Sparling of the Bohemian Picture Palace, Phibsborough, Dublin, nearly two years after the film was completed. This delay was occasioned by the loss of the first print of the film bound for Ireland which sunk with the *Lusitania* on 7 May 1915. Sparling booked Ireland's largest cinema, Dublin's Rotunda, to show the film in January 1917. On 5 January, however, unknown to Sparling, a letter was written on the notepaper of the Dublin Express and Mail, publishers of the *Dublin Evening Mail*, drawing the attention of the police to an advertisement in the newspaper for *Ireland a Nation*. This film, the writer declared, was 'of a bad type, indeed, the man in charge of it [Sparling?] expresses astonishment that it has passed the British Censor!'

Inspector George Love was dispatched to report on the film's first screening on 8 January. He reported that none of the items objected to by the Press Censor were shown. But, he added, the one hundred persons present received the film 'with applause throughout, except some slight hissing, when Lord Castlereagh and Major Sirr were exhibited'. Love added that the film 'has a tendency to revive and perpetuate, incidents of a character, which I think at the present time are most undesirable and should not be permitted'.

That night an officer from Military Headquarters attended the screening and on the basis of his report it was decided that the film was

> likely to cause disaffection, owing to the cheering of the crowd, at portions of the film, the hissing of soldiers who appeared in the film, and the cries made by the audience.

The General Officer Commanding in Chief, Sir Bryan Mahon, decided to ban the film forthwith but found that Sparling had a Censor's certificate. The military then asked the Press Censor to withdraw the film and this was done. However, Mr Sparling went to see Sir Bryan Mahon on 9 January and it was agreed that Sparling would himself re-censor the film and 'cut out parts which seemed to be objectionable'. Sparling was then allowed to show the film that night with Military Headquarters staff present. It had been agreed with Sparling that if there was a repetition of the first night's demonstrations then Mahon would issue an order prohibiting subsequent performances. But the military reports on the second night were even more adverse than those of the first night:

The murder of a British soldier by a rebel was greeted with
prolonged and enthusiastic applause . . . [The] appearance of
[a] British soldier [was] greeted with boos, groans and hisses
. . . [There were] continuous seditious and traitorous cries.

As a result Mahon issued an order prohibiting the screening of the
film throughout Ireland. His order referred to the 'seditious and
disloyal conduct' of the audience. Further exhibition of the film in
Ireland, it stated 'is likely to cause disaffection to His Majesty, and
to prejudice the recruiting of His Majesty's forces'. The order was
served on Sparling on the afternoon of the third day of the film's
run. As it arrived during a screening of the film, the film was
immediately stopped and the admission price returned to the
audience.

Sir W. P. Byrne, the Under-Secretary for Ireland, who liaised
with the Censor and the military on the matter agreed with these
measures but took a realistic view of the film's contents:

A romantic version of the sordid story is so widely current in
Ireland and [available] in pictures and Reading Books and in
the Press and on the Stage so often that it would be difficult to
exclude it from the Cinemas.

Whatever his political affiliations Sparling had been deprived of
a lucrative income from the film. He had invested heavily in
renting the Rotunda and paying for the rights to the film. In consequence he complained bitterly through his solicitor to Dublin
Castle. He sought financial compensation since 'the financial
aspect has placed me in an exceedingly crippled condition'. Despite the evidence to the contrary, including newspaper reports,[23]
Sparling stated that 'there was no disturbance of any kind during
the screening of the film'. The Under-Secretary agreed to meet
Sparling and a friend, W. P. Nash. At the meeting on 3 February
Sparling stated that the film 'was one of the best and most valuable
ever exhibited and was worth at least £8,000 or £10,000'. Sharing
an unusually high regard for the aesthetic taste of Irish audiences
he stated that the applause in the theatre 'was largely due to
admiration for the excellence of the picture'. Sparling and Nash
added that

there was no more excitement than about any ordinary film.
The few cries which may have been heard of 'Up the Rebels'

and so forth, gave rise to no particular notice, and soon stopped. They added that there were no more than can be heard any night in any one of the half dozen London cinemas where current events shown by *Pathé Gazette* are exhibited.

While they felt entitled to heavy compensation they sought permission to continue showing the film since it 'would prove a gold mine', and many offers had been made to purchase the rights for provincial distribution. Their request was turned down though Sparling retained the rights for the film in Britain. All they received from Dublin Castle was a letter stating the refusal to show the film in Ireland. Sparling thought that this would help in his demand for compensation from the Defence of the Realm Losses Commission.

In February 1918 *Irish Limelight* reported that the War Losses Commission had adjourned a decision on Sparling's claim. Commission Chairman Lord Terrington is recorded as giving Sparling a sympathetic reception and blaming, unsurprisingly, the response to the film on the audience. He added that 'Irish people might make similar remarks even in church as far as he knew'!

Irish audiences had to wait until 1922 before they had another opportunity to see *Ireland a Nation*. By then the Irish political and constitutional framework had undergone fundamental change. The Anglo-Irish Treaty had been approved three weeks earlier by Dáil Éireann. Huge crowds attended 'this truly remarkable film' according to the *Dublin Evening Mail*.[24] It was, the *Mail* continued, 'a picture of unusual and, incidently, topical interest . . .' This was an appropriately ironic conclusion to the *Ireland a Nation* saga. It was, of course, the unionist publishers of the *Mail* who had started the controversy which led to the film's banning in 1917. Now that an Irish State seemingly committed to constitutional politics had become a *fait accompli*, even they could join in the welcome to a representation of Ireland's 'advanced nationalist' history.

Film Company of Ireland

It was, perhaps, not surprising that 1916 saw the registration of the most important Irish film production company of the silent era. The Film Company of Ireland was registered by Henry M. Fitzgibbon and James Mark Sullivan in March 1916, only a month before the Easter Rising. Sullivan had emigrated to the US with his family from Killarney when he was a boy and had become a successful lawyer there. On his return to Ireland he decided to introduce a fully professional approach to indigenous film production.

The first films produced in 1916 by the Film Company of Ireland (FCOI), however, were destroyed during the Easter Rising, or 'lost in the Dublin fire' as the first issue of Ireland's first film magazine, *Irish Limelight*,[25] described the Rising. The FCOI offices, located as they were near the headquarters of the Rising in Sackville St, were also destroyed in the fighting. Despite losing an expert producer and cameraman who had been hired by the company and who left as a result of the Rising,[26] production was resumed that summer and by October nine short films had been made. All except one were directed by J. M. Kerrigan, a well established leading actor at the Abbey Theatre, who later became a Hollywood character actor playing in such films as John Ford's *The Informer* (1935). Kerrigan made his debut as a cinema actor in the first of the productions to be released, *O'Neil of the Glen*. The cast also included Abbey actor Fred O'Donovan, already famous for his portrayal of Christy Mahon in J. M. Synge's *The Playboy of the Western World*. Other actors in this film were J. M. Carre, Nora Clancy, Brian Magowan,[27] who was to become the leading actor of the company, R. V. Justine and J. Smith.

O'Neil of the Glen was an adaption by W. J. Lysaght of Mrs M. T. Pender's story of the same name. Set in Ulster, it concerned an incident whereby Don O'Neil (Kerrigan), the son of a landed proprietor, saves the life of Nola (Clancy), daughter of Tremaine (Magowan), a solicitor, who had defrauded Don's father. Meanwhile, Nola is being blackmailed by her suitor, Graves (O'Donovan), but Dan and Nola fall in love and Graves is overcome. *O'Neil of the Glen*, a three reeler, was premièred at the Bohemian Picture Theatre, Dublin, on 7 August 1916. It ran for one week, twice the length of the normal exhibition pattern. The *Dublin Evening Mail*, reporting considerable provincial interest in the film, commented[28] that

the people of . . . Ireland will have the privilege of witnessing one of the finest cinematographic productions shown for quite some time . . . a really first-class picture-play, and one that is sure to bring the work and the players of the Film Company of Ireland right into the forefront of popularity with audiences and trade alike.[29]

While this first film dealt with a 'realistic' subject, most of the other films released in 1916 and early 1917 were comedies. These also proved very popular with Dublin audiences, many of them being given three or four cinema runs during their first six months on release. *A Girl of Glenbeigh*, 'a powerfully dramatic story of Irish life . . . taken amidst some superb Irish scenery',[30] was screened five times in Dublin in 1917. Many of these films starred J. M. Kerrigan, Fred O'Donovan and Kathleen Murphy including *A Woman's Wit*, 'a big attraction',[31] which was shown on three occasions in January 1917 alone. *The Food of Love*, another comedy, was set in Glendalough and was 'full of real Irish humour' and 'magnificent' scenery.[32] *The Widow Malone* was a one-reel comedy about a rich widow who feigns poverty in order to thwart a councillor and a schoolteacher. According to the *Dublin Evening Mail*[33] it was 'an agreeable change from the usual knock-about comedies so abundantly supplied'. *The Miser's Gift* was a comedy about a girl and her lover who get a mean father dreaming of leprechaun's gold after they make him drunk! *An Unfair Love Affair* with Kerrigan, O'Donovan and another of the FCOI (and Abbey) actresses, Nora Clancy, was about a man who wins a girl by foiling his rival's plot with a tinker. *The Eleventh Hour*, a three-reel drama with Magowan and Murphy, was directed by O'Donovan. *A Puck Fair Romance* was a one-reeler.

In its second year of production the FCOI began to shift away from comedies. This was a reflection, perhaps, of the increasingly intense political, and later military, events in Ireland from 1917 onwards. While *A Passing Shower* and *Rafferty's Rise* were both 1917 comedies, the two major productions were a six-reel rural drama, *When Love Came to Gavin Burke*, and an eight-reel adaption of Charles Kickham's novel, *Knocknagow*, directed by Fred O'Donovan.

In adapting *Knocknagow* as their first major production the FCOI opted for one of the best-known books and authors of the nineteenth century. Kickham was the son of a prosperous drapery shop owner and was associated with the brief 1848 Rising, one of the main events of which took place not far from his home. Later, when a writer for the Fenian movement's newspaper, *The Irish People*, he was arrested and sentenced to 14 years in prison. He was released within four years mainly due to his ill-health. The year after his release, 1870, saw the publication of the first parts of *Knocknagow* in serial form. This highly derivative[34] novel, 600 pages long, very quickly became established as the most widely read Irish rural novel of the nineteenth and perhaps the twentieth centuries[35] after its first complete publication in 1873. The immediate catalyst for the making of the film was probably the screening in Dublin in September 1916 of D. W. Griffith's *The Birth of a Nation*. *Knocknagow* had the kind of epic sweep which made it an obvious choice for the theme of Ireland's first major film. Notwithstanding its suitability for cinematic adaption, the novel and film diverge at a number of points including its precise dating.

It is generally accepted that the novel is set in the 1850s or even the 1860s while the film, according to the opening title, 'depicts the joys and sorrows of the simple kindly folk who lived in the homes of Tipperary seventy years ago'. Thus the film is set in 1848, at the height of the Famine, as the FCOI's publicity booklet makes clear. The vast bulk of the novel is taken up with a series of often convoluted love stories which eventually lead to a number of marriages. With the exception of the last hundred pages where various loose ends are rather crudely tied up, the book is dominated by long rambling interludes of conversation and often anxious internal dialogue about personal relationships. In the film, however, much more emphasis is placed on relationships to the land. In this respect two characters are central: the land agent Pender (J. M. Carre), 'the one black cloud', who is seeking to clear the land of tenants to make way for more profitable cattle grazing, and the sturdy labourer with a small patch of land, Mat the Thrasher/Mat Donovan (Brian Magowan).

The most numerous inhabitants of the land, small farmers and cottiers (the characters precise economic relationship to the land is not identified either in book or film), are dispirited and down-trodden by the actions of the land agent. One of those small farmers is Mick Brian. In Kickham's book the Brians are already evicted and living in a shelter in a ditch whereas in the film the eviction scene is shown. This cinematic decision has two particular resonances. Many members of a contemporary cinema audience could recall the emotionally charged mass evictions less than 40 years before during the Land War while also associating such evictions with the Famine years of the 1840s. As Pender prepares for the evictions, Mat tells him that 'there will be stern reckoning for this day, if not in our time, then when other men will know how to deal with the oppression'. The eviction of the Brians follows. Neighbours are held at bay while Pender and the bailiffs burn the cottage. Later, another family, the Hogans, are evicted.

The Hogans, hard working small farmers, have considerably improved the land and have a son in the English army.

The result of evictions is either starvation at home or emigration. When Mat also declares that he'll go to America the anti-emigration cry is made explicit: 'What curse is on this land of ours, when men like Mat Donovan are forced from its shores'. This form of direct address is absent from the book and no doubt had powerful resonances amongst Irish audiences in America. As Mat leaves Ireland he cries, 'Good-bye, dear Ireland, you are a rich and rare land although poverty is forced upon you'. Mat's absence is brief as Pender schemes to frame him for his own theft of the landlord's rents. After being arrested in Liverpool, he is brought back to jail in Ireland. When he is eventually cleared of the crime a title declares that like Mat 'We must cultivate under every dire circumstance, patience and fortitude, to outlive every slander and to rise above every adversity. We are a moral people above crime, and a clean-hearted race must eventually come into its own.' It is not hard to imagine how that call to national pride and unity affected Irish nationalist audiences on the threshold of the War of Independence.

Pivotal to the book was the relative oppression perpetuated by both the largely absentee landlord, Sir Garrett Butler (Charles Power), and the well-off, if indebted, large tenant farmer, Maurice Kearney (Dermot O'Dowd), towards their tenants and subtenants. In the film, by contrast, the landlord is seen as a benign, if somewhat simple-minded man who, when made aware of the eviction tactics of his land agent, immediately returns to Knocknagow and restores harmony. Kearney, who is depicted as an exploiter of both his subtenants and his servants and labourers in the book, is now sanatised and promoted to a position of positive leadership in the community such that labourers and small farmers led by Mat the Thrasher cheer his outfoxing of the land agent. In fact, Mat goes so far as to state that Kearney 'is never too prosperous not to stand by his country and his people'. Kearney responds by rebuking the landlord and declaring to Sir Garrett that 'the men of your class, Sir, are guilty of starving a people in the midst of plenty'. Bearing in mind that Kickham refers to the eviction by Kearney of a family of his 'under-tenants', such a speech re-directs the film towards an accommodation with the big farmers, then perceived as opponents of Sinn Féin. Indeed, one of Kearney's visitors is recorded by Kickham as describing the living conditions of Kearney's workmen as 'disgraceful' with seven or eight men huddled together in one outhouse, lying on rotten straw and covered with old blankets and quilts. There is an indication, however, that Kearney's defence of the marginal classes is a late conversion, since at the beginning of the film Sir Garrett and his nephew, Henry, have breakfast on Christmas morning at the Kearneys. This serves to emphasise the close class affinities of the two families. Indeed the first quarter of the book has Henry in residence as a house guest of the Kearneys and he spends much of his time trying to convince Kearney's daughter to marry him.

This subtle realignment of the major themes in *Knocknagow* needs to be placed more firmly in the context of the events of 1917 and early 1918, the period during which it was made and released. Throughout the summer and autumn of 1917 when filming and post-production work was carried out, the shifts in public perception of the events of Easter 1916 became more pronounced. In June the remaining Sinn Féin prisoners, including de Valera and Countess Markievicz were released. They were greeted by enthusiastic crowds on their return to Dublin. In July de Valera won a by-election to Westminster on an absentee platform; the following month William Cosgrave took another parliamentary seat. In September, a hunger striker, Thomas Ashe, died after forcible-feeding; 30,000 marched in the funeral procession while countless thousands lined the streets. In October, de Valera took over the leadership of Sinn Féin and in November he became President of the nationalist movement's military wing. Throughout the country that winter thousands drilled, using hurleys as substitute guns, for the coming fight. In February 1918, 28 prisoners went on hunger-strike in Mountjoy Jail, Dublin. By then the prospect of conscription being extended to Ireland was becoming a reality.

In this increasingly charged environment, the release of a film such as *Knocknagow* was certain to be interpreted in the light of current events. It received its first showing to an invited audience on 6 February 1918. Its first public showing in Dublin was on 22 April when it commenced a one-week run at the Empire Theatre. The first day of the Empire Theatre run was hardly chosen by accident. It was exactly two years to the day since Easter Monday, 1916, the date of the Rising. But this première was also sandwiched between momentous events for the future of the nationalist movement. The previous day, a Sunday, saw hundreds of thousands of people signing an anti-conscription pledge after mass. For the first time all segments of nationalist Ireland, the Irish Parliamentary Party, Sinn Féin, the Labour Movement and others had joined in a conference to co-ordinate this united response to the passing of the Conscription Bill on 16 April. They also sought and received the support of the Catholic hierarchy for the pledge which was, in effect, a plebiscite of Catholic nationalist Ireland. Fifteen hundred delegates to a Trades Union Congress decreed a 24 hour general strike against conscription. This strike, held on 23 April, the second day of *Knocknagow*'s run, was totally successful. These events had served, as Dorothy Macardle[36] put it, 'to unite in a common effort men who had contended mightily against one another for a decade'.

Echoing the contemporary view that the anti-conscription campaign had served as a unifier of Irish Catholic nationalist consciousness, the *Dublin Evening Mail* observed,[37] on the day before the pledge was due to be signed, that the film *Knocknagow*, itself concerned with such unity, 'should make a very strong appeal to all classes of playgoers'. *Irish Limelight*[38] also promoted this view: 'It visualises the genius of its famous author in a manner that cannot fail to appeal to all classes and creeds'.

That *Knocknagow* should find common cause amongst the Irish and deal sympathetically with the landlord as well is hardly surprising in the context of contemporary events. The suppression of internal contradiction within and between the Irish was after all crucial to the form of nationalist unity envisaged by nationalist leaders, especially de Valera. It was not just a 'Labour Must Wait' view which was to the fore at the 1918 General Election when Sinn Féin won an overwhelming victory over the Parliamentary Party. The difference between the various rural classes needed to be suppressed also. In view of how Irish rural classes became reorganised as a result of the Famine and the Land War this is to be expected. In *Knocknagow* some threads of the future changes may be seen. The Brians and the Hogans, whether small farmers or cottiers, were part of the huge marginal classes who either were evicted through inability to pay for their holdings, were decimated through emigration or died through starvation or disease in the Famine. These were the 'losers' during the 1840s and 1850s. Other 'losers' were the landless labourers who had little or no security but, who in both book and film, are mobilised to underpin the worth of the larger tenant-farmers. For the Kearneys, however, the Famine, if anything, would have been a period of opportunity. With the marginal classes reduced to a fraction of their pre-Famine numbers, and many landlords made bankrupt, the more prosperous tenant-farmers (and others, often nonfarmers) were able to expand their holdings. Those such as the Kearneys would also have gained from the Land War of the early 1880s when they could consolidate their holdings through gaining fixity of tenure, fair rent and freedom of sale. For those outside these arrangements such as the remaining landless labourers and marginal land holders, and those promoting more radical solutions including nationalisation of land, little opportunity for improving their position was possible.[39]

Knocknagow's displacement of social relations on the land away from inter-class and internal Irish conflict accorded with contemporary nationalist politics. Sinn Féin, for example, while adhering to a policy of land redistribution, did not envisage a radical transformation of social relations on the land, as indeed the history of the Irish state since Independence confirms. That a tenant-farmer, urban middle class-led nationalist movement should seek to bury economic differences was hardly surprising. What is perhaps unique about *Knocknagow* in this regard, at least as a film made in 1917, is that it chooses not to displace all Ireland's wrongs on to an absentee (read English) landlord. Instead the odium is directed at the land agent who, as he is characterised in the film, has close affinities to the callous agent in *The Lad From Old Ireland* and the slinking informer of *Rory O'More*. Thus in *Knocknagow* we find landlord, small and large tenant-farmers and labourers all united against the reprehensible agent.

With its narrative resolving both economic and personal conflict, *Knocknagow* proved a 'triumphant' commercial success in Ireland and was distributed in the US and Britain.[40] In Boston it showed for three weeks and 'took more money than the much "boosted" [*The*] *Birth of a Nation*'.[41] However, when shown in Britain in 1919 *The Bioscope*[42] complained about 'its vehemently Irish point of view' and thought it had 'more than a soupçon of underlying propaganda'. It was 'dangerously tinged with political feeling'. While finding the narrative at times difficult to follow and suggesting the attention of an expert editor, *The Bioscope* nevertheless conceded that this film was 'by no means without charm and interest'.

The land question was given a new inflection in the FCOI's second major feature, *Willy Reilly and his Colleen Bawn* (1920). The choice of subject and director, John MacDonagh, also signalled an even closer affinity than hitherto between the FCOI and the accelerating struggle for independence. By the time of the production of *Willy Reilly and his Colleen Bawn* in 1919 the war was intensifying and many FCOI personnel were overtly sympathetic to or involved in the nationalist movement. They included George Nesbit, who plays Squire Folliard, and Jim Plant (Sir Robert Whitecraft), both of whom used false names in the credits to avoid detection. John MacDonagh had the greatest cause for concern. He was the brother of the executed 1916 leader, Thomas MacDonagh, and was possibly a member of the IRA. Thomas MacDonagh was also one of the founders of the breakaway group from the Abbey Theatre, the Irish Theatre Company, which had a much more radical nationalist programme than the Abbey. The FCOI, and John MacDonagh in particular, became more closely identified with the Irish Theatre Company from 1918 onwards. MacDonagh also used a pseudonym, Richard Sheridan, possibly after the eighteenth-century playwright and politician, Richard Brinsley Sheridan, in the credits to protect himself in the role of Tom the Fool. The film was shot at St Enda's, Rathfarnham, to further emphasise the film's nationalist reference points. This was the school founded by Padraig Pearse, the executed 1916 leader, and Thomas MacDonagh as a response to British education in Ireland which Pearse characterised as 'the murder machine'. The school's stress on Irish language, culture and history made it an important symbol for Irish nationalists. These references were not lost on the authorities either and production was interrupted when 'some of the cast were arrested and carried off to spend time in British prisons'.[43]

During the filming of *Willy Reilly and his Colleen Bawn* John MacDonagh displayed quite openly his sympathy for the nationalist movement. He made a short film for the Republican Loan Bonds campaign which featured Michael Collins, Arthur Griffith and other prominent nationalists. In Ireland the film had unorthodox exhibition when Volunteers entered cinema projection rooms, ordered the projectionist at gun point to remove the film being shown and to put on the Republican Loan film instead. By the time the authorities had been alerted, the Volunteers and the film had disappeared.[44]

While *Willy Reilly and his Colleen Bawn* had a much less direct message than the one contained in the Republican Loan film it had an equally forceful impact on contemporary audiences. Just as *Knocknagow* displaced tensions between landlords, tenant-farmers and other classes, *Willy Reilly* . . . sought to dissolve tensions between Protestant and Catholic landowners. The film is based on William Carleton's 1855 novel, *Willy Reilly and his Dear Colleen*

Bawn, subtitled 'A Tale Founded on Fact'. By the time Carleton wrote the book, the tale of the young couple had been immortalised in often rude ballads and verse. Carleton's 450 page novel weaves the story of the young Catholic man and the young Protestant woman against a background of contemporary events. It is set between the mid-1740s, when the bigoted anti-Catholic Lord Chesterfield was Governor-General of Ireland, and the 1750s, when the anti-Catholic penal laws became increasingly ignored or liberalised.

MacDonagh ignores the broader international perspective of the book with its references to the attempts by the Scottish 'Pretender' to secure the English Crown. He confines himself to the effect that the further anti-Catholic restrictions on inter-marriage, introduced by Lord Chesterfield, have on the young couple. While necessarily compressing the material and cutting out various sub-plots and minor characters, MacDonagh does not essentially alter the book's narrative in its exposition of contemporary religious attitudes.

Both film and book open with the kind but bigoted Protestant Squire Folliard being rescued from highwaymen Red Raparee and his men by a young Catholic gentleman and landowner, Willy Reilly (Brian Magowan). Willy announces that he is one of The O'Reillys, thus emphasising his Gaelic aristocratic ancestry. He is also, as the inter-title puts it, the 'instrument of God's will' in rescuing the Squire. Willy has a group of his own men, a sort of private army of his tenants and servants. At one stage they defend the Squire's house against Red Raparee's plan to kidnap the Colleen Bawn, the Squire's daughter Helen (Frances Alexander). The Squire declares himself helpless except for the presence of Willy and his men.

The affinity between O'Reilly and the Folliards and indeed most of the Protestant clergy is quickly established through their dress and demeanour. Thus, as the relationship between Helen and Willy develops, the narrative revolves around three main issues: the attempt by the Squire to convince Willy that he should change his religion in order to marry Helen; the response to Willy by another of Helen's suitors, Whitecraft, a bigoted Protestant; and the support Willy receives from sympathetic Protestants.

Central to Willy's dilemma is how he can protect his substantial property against Whitecraft's resort to the sections of the anti-Catholic penal laws which restricted land ownership by Catholics. However, a solution emerges through the close social affinity, except for religion, between Reilly and the Protestant gentry. As the novel records, Reilly has one thousand acres, a big house, tenants and servants and a fluency in three Continental languages. He is also leader of the Catholics in the area and has close personal relations with the 'liberal and fair-minded' Protestants including Rev. Brown and a friendly landlord, Hastings. It is Hastings who secures his property through a not uncommon device used during the penal era for Catholics of substantial means, for, as T. A. Jackson observes,[45]

> The [Penal] Code had a different effect upon different classes of the subjected Irish population. For the Catholic land-owners there were ways of escape. They could make a formal submission to Protestantism. They could convey their estates in trust to sympathising Protestants who could as the nominal owners shelter them from the law while leaving them in con-tinued possession in fact. With Protestant connivance they could provide education for their children in England or on the Continent. A sense of class-solidarity made the bulk of the Protestant landowners collaborate with them in evading all the more offensive personal restrictions of the Code.

However, 'the great mass of the Irish people were debarred by their poverty . . . from any such easy way out', adds Jackson.

To underpin Willy's affinity with the Squire, his house is almost identical to that of the Squire's, the result perhaps of using the two sides of St Enda's for both houses. In order to subordinate religion to class the discussion between the Squire and Helen and the Squire and Willy is presented less in terms of fixed theological beliefs than in terms of integrity and being true to oneself. If Willy did change to Protestantism, Helen tells her father, he would not be himself. The Squire eventually accepts Willy as his son-in-law, but, as is demonstrated in the book, it is not a late conversion to religious pluralism, but because he is concerned about Helen's melancholia following Willy's exile for allegedly abducting her.

Not only is Reilly a good landowner, giving a rent-free cottage and garden to one of his tenants, Widow Buckley, who harbours him while on the run, but his character is as pure as that of the Colleen Bawn. His attachment to his religion is sufficiently devout to make him a potential martyr. By contrast his rival for Helen's hand, Whitecraft, is not only unpleasant and uncouth but has a bitter, blood-thirsty attitude to Catholics in general and priests in particular. In addition, as Carleton sketches him, he has a very dubious personal morality, having at least one illegitimate child and a relationship with at least two other women. His interest in Helen, as Carleton puts it, is both sensual and avaricious. This issue of a reprobate sexual morality is absent from the film, perhaps in deference to conservative Irish reaction to even hints of aberrant sexuality following the response to J. M. Synge's *The Playboy of the Western World* in 1907.

The stumbling block to the marriage was the penal restriction on Catholic/Protestant inter-marriage which also limited the rights of inheritance of Catholics. But by the end of Willy's seven-year exile, about the mid-1750s, these restrictions had become modified or increasingly ignored. In 1757 the Duke of Bedford promised to abridge the laws. But by then, according to Carleton's narrative, the Reillys and their children have left Ireland and settled on the Continent. Their children, it is said, would distinguish themselves in European armies. For MacDonagh, the narrative ends earlier with the Squire still alive and an image of religious and familial harmony for the audience to take away.

At one level the film appears to display a naiveté often seen when Irish nationalists approached Protestant difference. This is especially true in the humanistic resolution of the sectarian divide in the form of young love. On the other hand, the choice of Carleton's novel, set as it is in the mid-eighteenth century when even the Protestant Ascendancy were not equated with unionism, indicates a desire to find common pre-Union ground between the religions. Nevertheless, that difference was unlikely to be overcome by kindly Protestant gentlemen allowing their daughters to associate with (gentlemen) Catholics. The wishful thinking of the film which shows the bigoted Protestant, Whitecraft, being charged after the intervention of his fellow Protestants was further underscored by a line (not incidently in the book) given to the Protestant clergyman, Rev. Brown: 'Rising above every consideration is the fact that we are fellow Irishmen'.

The première of *Willy Reilly and his Colleen Bawn* at the Bohemian Cinema, Dublin, on 19 April 1920 left no one in any doubt about the particularity of these contemporary resonances. It was, of course, the fourth anniversary of the Easter Rising. By this date the war situation in Ireland had been intensifying for many months. At the end of March General Macready had been appointed Commander-in-chief of British Forces in Ireland with a free hand to crush the Rebellion. To this end, the dreaded Black and Tans began arriving in Ireland from the end of March. By this stage the Volunteers may have numbered as many as 15,000 (though the British thought as many as 100,000 were under arms) and they were already quite successful in pushing the police out of rural Ireland. On 5 April 60 Volunteers went on hunger-strike at Mountjoy Jail. A week later the Irish Labour Party and the Trades Union Congress called an indefinite general strike in support of the hunger-strike. After three days the prisoners were unconditionally released. In this environment of relative success, and with the severest repression yet to come, nationalists almost ignored the crucial 'Partition Bill' then going through Parliament.

For *Irish Limelight* the optimism of *Willy Reilly and his Colleen Bawn* was very welcome. While it deemed it 'remarkable' that the film was beating the commercial success of *Knocknagow* it declared[46]

it is not so remarkable when one considers the temper of the public mind at the present time and when one realises that in the hearts of most of the Irish people is a yearning to have buried forever the mean wicked head of bigotry wherever it rises.

More recently Liam O'Leary[47] expressed the same view:

The story is of particular interest today in its plea for tolerance and friendship between Catholic and Protestant . . .

There was a more serious intent in the depiction of the economic relationships between Whitecraft as a Protestant land grabber and Willy which had a critical and ironic contemporary resonance. Since 1918 land grabbing from Anglo-Irish landlords and later Catholic big farmers was leading to serious divisions within the nationalist movement. These actions had led to intense anxiety amongst southern unionists about their role, if any, in a future Ireland. Eventually, in a resolution proposed by Austin Stack, and accepted by Dáil Éireann on 29 June 1920, two months after the release of *Willy Reilly and his Colleen Bawn*, it was decreed that for the most part land claims made in land cases were 'of old date, and while many of them may be well-founded others seem to be of a frivolous nature and are put forward in the hope of intimidating the present occupiers'. Furthermore, and reflecting the broad coalition of social forces Sinn Féin wished to mobilise, it decreed that 'the present time, when the Irish people are locked in a life and death struggle with their traditional enemy, is ill-chosen for the stirring up of strife among our fellow countrymen; and that all our energies must be directed towards the clearing out — not the occupiers of this or that piece of land — but the foreign invader of our Country'.[48] Stack, who was in charge of the Republican courts which enforced the Dáil decrees, was given the military backing of the Republican forces. The fact that 299 land cases were dealt with in 23 counties between May 1920 and June 1921 is an indication of the success of this policy.[49] It may not be ironic, therefore, to view the intervention of the Protestant, Hastings, in protecting Willy's ancestral lands as a signal to Catholic nationalists that Anglo-Irish landlords were not all of the Whitecraft variety.

Stylistically *Willy Reilly and his Colleen Bawn* has been compared favourably with the best of contemporary Swedish productions[50] and its undoubted sophistication made it popular with foreign audiences when distributed in the United States, Britain and Spain.[51] Indeed, John MacDonagh was no newcomer to film-making. While acting on the New York stage in 1910 MacDonagh provided the script of a D. W. Griffith film, *The Fugitive*.[52] But *Willy Reilly and his Colleen Bawn* was to be the Film Company of Ireland's swansong. With war conditions in Ireland worsening, it is even surprising that *Willy Reilly . . .* got made. Such an avowedly nationalist group of people would have been particularly exposed in the increasingly open military confrontations. John MacDonagh himself was on a list for arrest and he went to Scotland both to avoid detention and to exploit *Willy Reilly and his Colleen Bawn*.[53] And, since James Mark Sullivan himself was a friend of Michael Collins, he, too, would have been under surveillance by the authorities. But an unforeseen event hastened the demise of the Film Company of Ireland. In an influenza epidemic, Sullivan's wife and child died. Afterwards Sullivan returned to the United States, thus depriving any would-be film-makers of the most important Irish film producer of the period.

The FCOI films, themselves, continued to be viewed favourably at another crucial moment of the independence struggle. *Willy Reilly and his Colleen Bawn*, *Knocknagow* and another FCOI film, *Paying the Rent*, were shown in two different Dublin cinemas for a week from 19 December 1921, while the Dáil debate on the Anglo-Irish Peace Treaty was in progress. However, the humanistic pleading of *Willy Reilly . . .* must later have seemed quite irrelevant once the outcome of the Treaty debate became evident and resulted in splits in Sinn Féin and the IRA which led ultimately to

Civil War. Indeed, the political and military events from 1918 had left no one in any doubt about the limits of Cupid replacing politics. The optimistic hopes displayed in *Willy Reilly . . .* of co-joining Catholics and Protestants without religion being related to broader social and historical questions was quickly shattered in the early 1920s. During the period from the conclusion of the Anglo-Irish Treaty in December 1921 to March 1923 192 Protestant-owned big houses and clubs were burned down by anti-Treaty forces.[54] And in May 1922 five months after the Treaty had been approved by Dáil Éireann, a deputation, including the Church of Ireland Archbishop of Dublin, asked, rather pathetically, of Michael Collins 'to be informed if they were to be permitted to live in Ireland or if it was desired that they should leave the country'.[55]

If there had been any doubt about the suppression of the most awkward features of Irish reality in *Knocknagow* and *Willy Reilly and his Colleen Bawn*, three other FCOI films, two of them comedies, provided additional evidence of the approach to Irish themes adopted by the FCOI. *Rafferty's Rise* (1917) deals with a Royal Irish Constabulary constable who is a favourite with women but is only interested in becoming a sergeant. The depiction of the bumbling, ineffective policeman made *Rafferty's Rise* popular[56] and in the climate of 1917 even the RIC could be seen in a non-contradictory light. However, during the War of Independence the RIC were a principal target of the IRA. In 1920 alone 176 RIC men were killed while only 54 soldiers died.

When the issue of rent, the mediating exchange in social relations on the land, was brought to the foreground in another FCOI comedy, *Paying the Rent* (1920), the problem was displaced into the winds of fate at the races. A tenant, Paddy Dunne (Arthur Sinclair), who is on his way to pay the rent with borrowed money is waylaid by two friends, one a suitor to his daughter Molly. They convince Paddy to go to the Curragh races where the Irish Derby is being run. The horse he backs wins and Paddy has the rent money and he is also able to repay the borrowed money. While Paddy is away at the races the family are under threat of eviction for non-payment of rent. Mrs Dunne borrows more money from another of Molly's suitors, Thady, but she has to agree to allow Molly to marry him. All ends happily when Paddy turns up at the church as Molly and Thady are due to marry. Molly switches partners as the bewildered priest agrees to the change. The film was produced by John MacDonagh, and photographed, surprisingly, by Brian Magowan.

By contrast, the FCOI's *When Love Came to Gavin Burke* (1917) anticipated the conservative ethos which was to be a feature of the new Irish state. A young woman, Kate, is engaged to a poor farmer, Gavin Burke. However, she rejects him for the easier life as the wife of a hotelier. But Kate's husband lapses into alcoholism and he ruins the business. Meanwhile, Gavin is becoming prosperous but bitter and introspective. While out riding, the increasingly impoverished hotelier falls from his horse and subsequently dies. Kate's daughter, who is with her father, turns up at Gavin's nearby door seeking help. Later, when she cheers up Gavin's dour disposition, he offers her a home but he rejects Kate. Years pass, and in a replay of Kate's youth, her daughter is being pursued by two suitors, one rich and one poor. Unlike her mother, she chooses the one she loves, the poor one. Only then, when Gavin has given away his wealth to Kate's daughter, thus returning to his original frugality, does he accept Kate in marriage.

Though unique amongst Irish films of the period in its exploration of the nature of the family, it was clearly intended to reinforce a traditional morality. Punishment is the reward for the woman who chooses pleasure instead of poverty and happiness, a theme not uncommon in Hollywood films of the period. The representation of a conservative morality is further underlined through the contrast between the hard-working small farmer, Gavin, and the alcoholic hotelier, and by extension, town resident and businessman. Such unfavourable rural/urban oppositions were to become a feature of the ideology of the new state.

Whatever the limitations of the two major fiction film production companies, Kalem and the Film Company of Ireland, working in Ireland during 1910–20, they did produce the first positive fictional images of Ireland on film. Lewis Jacobs assessed Kalem:[57]

The traditional (Irish) trade-marks of shiftlessness, clay-pipe smoking and the kettle of beer were . . . discarded. *You'll Remember Ellen, Kerry Gow* (from Irish 'Gabha' or blacksmith) and *The Colleen Bawn* metamorphosed the 'Begorrah and b'gosh' comedian into an authentic social being moved by real emotions. Irish pride of heritage and the injustices of Ireland's past were explained in such films as *The Mayor of Ireland, The O'Neil* (from *Erin's Isle*), *Rory O'More* and *Ireland the Oppressed.*

It is unlikely that present-day critics would agree with Jacobs but as Proinsias Ó Conluain observes[58]

> Olcott made a sincere effort to portray Ireland and the Irish as he found them, and to deal sympathetically with their history.

Irish Limelight[59] had also found that even the Film Company of Ireland's first films presented Ireland

> to the rest of the world as she had never been known before; to let outside people realise that we have in Ireland other things than the dudeen, buffoon, knee breeches and brass knuckles.

The magazine added that the press and people of Ireland had given 'generous and unanimous approval' to the films. *Irish Limelight* also stated that with the films already distributed to America, England, Australia, Italy and France, 'a substantial industry has taken root . . .'.

General Film Supply

In addition to fiction film-making, foreign companies provided Irish audiences with most newsreel or actuality images during the first 25 years of film in Ireland. The main companies were *Pathé Gazette*, the *Gaumont Graphic* and during World War I, the *War Office Gazette*. The foreign source of actuality material was only one aspect of what was sometimes seen as overtly propagandist films shown in Irish cinemas.

In late 1913 or early 1914, for example, a British Army recruitment film being screened at Dublin's Grafton Cinema led to the first organised resistance to this type of film. Two of the radical nationalist movement's constituent organisations, Inghinidhe na h-Éireann (Daughters of Erin) and Na Fianna (The Fianna), a sort of nationalist 'Boy Scout' movement, met in Countess Markievicz's Leinster Rd house to make plans to disrupt the opening night's showings. They 'entered into this work with gusto', though as one of the participants recalled later,[60]

> there were a large number of 'respectable' people, who thought we were dragging the Cause in the gutter by breaking up an objectionable meeting or raiding a theatre.

The Grafton's provocative external advertisements had depicted in 'glowing colour' life in the British Army. Writing in 1934 one participant observed that

> in those days we were not so experienced in the work of making a demonstration in a picture house as we would be to-day. We paid our money and walked into different parts of the theatre. The picture, a very obvious recruiting one, was divided into two parts, the first of which was to run the first three days, and the second for the latter part of the week.

While they hesitantly interrupted the first night's showing they returned a few days later with reinforcements.

The propaganda value of newsreels had already been recognised by nationalists. The 1913 Wolfe Tone commemoration ceremony at Bodenstown, Co. Kildare was filmed by a newsreel cameraman and exhibitor, J. T. Jameson. This footage was shown two or three times nightly from 22 June at the Rotunda and Rathmines. In a letter to John Devoy in New York, Thomas J. Clarke, one of the 16 to be executed after the Easter Rising, wrote that[61]

> No pictures he has ever shown (and he has been fourteen years in the business) ever received such tremendous applause. The old round room [the Rotunda] appeared to shake. The pictures are grand. He is to show them next week in Galway, then in Tralee. Afterwards Queenstown, then Cork, then the Curragh, then back to Rathmines and the Rotunda . . . He and I are now good friends and I'm glad. He with his ring of picture houses showing our pictures will do good business and the Dublin newspapers may go to hell or to the Empire.

Jameson's company, Irish Animated Picture Co., operated three of the nine cinemas in Dublin in 1913: the Rotunda, Theatre de Luxe and Volta Picture Theatre.[62] In his letter to Devoy, Clarke also suggested that he write about the film in America. With Jameson already doing some business with America, he anticipated the positive benefit of American showings for the nationalist cause.[63]

It was not until four years later that production of a regular Irish newsreel began. In 1917 Norman Whitten's General Film Supply company established the *Irish Events* newreel. By the end of the year 24 editions had been produced. *Irish Events* quickly became a regular feature of Irish cinema programmes due to the ease in producing newsreels and the continued availability of topical subjects. While one of the first efforts was a record of the Irish pilgrimage to Lourdes, another was of the return in June 1917 of the Sinn Féin prisoners. Since Bonar Law had announced the imminent release of the prisoners on 15 June Whitten had been on the alert for their arrival in Dublin. When the first contingent arrived at Westland Row station on the eighteenth he was there with his camera. Whitten was given every facility to film the proceedings, shooting 350 feet of film. He rushed back to his laboratory in Great Brunswick St to process and print the films. By 3 p.m. that day three copies had been printed, fully titled and rushed by taxis to the picture houses.[64]

> Some of the ex-prisoners and their friends could not resist the temptation to see themselves 'in the pictures', and a contingent marched up to the Rotunda in the afternoon. They cheerfully acceded to the genial manager's request that they should leave their flags in the porch, and, when inside, gave every indication of enjoying not only 'their own film' but the rest of the programme.

Demand for the newsreel came from all over the country and when supplies ran out other footage of the Irish Volunteers and National Volunteers and the funeral of O'Donovan Rossa was sent. When these were exhausted Irish-theme films such as Kalem's *The Shaughraun* and *The Colleen Bawn* were taken. By filming these events and others that followed over the next few months, such as the opening of the Irish Convention, the funeral of Mrs MacDonagh (mother of Thomas and John), the Phoenix Park demonstrations, and the Twelfth of July celebrations in Belfast, *Irish Events* quickly established itself as part of most cinema programmes. Not only was it an Irish company making profits in Ireland which were kept in Ireland, *Irish Limelight* declared,[65] but they were made with an Irish audience in mind. This, the magazine pointed out, was not the case with the *Pathé Gazette* and the *Gaumont Graphic* which are 'English for the English'.

While much of the *Irish Events* series was taken up with sporting events, social occasions and other uncontroversial material it ran into direct confrontation with the military authorities when it produced, in 1919, a compilation newsreel connected with the nationalist struggle. This half hour compilation, *The Sinn Féin Review*, showing 'the picturised story of the Sinn Féin Movement from 1916 to the Present Day', included the only film of de Valera taken in Dublin since his escape from prison two months earlier. A chief superintendent investigated when he saw this provocative statement on a large poster in the window of General Film Supply. He immediately established that the Phibsboro Picture House was negotiating to show it. After a report[66] was sent to Dublin Castle, W. P. Byrne, the Under-Secretary for Ireland, referred the matter to the Press Censor. An intelligence officer was ordered to investigate and steps were taken to prohibit its exhibition. That it was referred to the GOC-in-chief is indicative of the sensitivity with which the issue was perceived. He offered army support if necessary but suggested that intervention was a question for the civilian and not the military authorities. Following the precedent of *Ireland a Nation* in 1917 it was decreed a matter for the police. On 8 April General Film Supply was told that *The Sinn Féin Review* must be submitted for police inspection. Whitten arranged this viewing for the police four days later. The investigating police report, which was sent to the Chief Secretary's Office, was co-authored by George Love who had written the original police report on *Ireland a Nation* two years before.

This report detailed the contents of the half hour film and described it as[67]

> a glorification of Sinn Féin and wherever exhibited would, no doubt, be good Sinn Féin Propaganda and might in that way be objectionable to members of an audience holding different views.

The detectives reported that Whitten wished to screen it in Drogheda the following week. A police superintendent, Oliver Brien, who had taken charge of the *Ireland a Nation* investigation, appended his view. 'This would appear to be Sinn Féin propaganda pure and simple', he declared. The Chief Secretary's Office concurred and ordered the film to be seized. By then the film was being screened at the Boyne Cinema, Drogheda (managed, it was claimed, by a Sinn Féin suspect), where it was seized by a contingent of police.[68]

Whitten immediately complained to the Chief Secretary about the police methods used in seizing the film. The police had threatened to break down the door with a hatchet if entry was resisted. He pointed out that many items in the *Review* had been included in *Pathé Gazette* and the *War Office Gazette*, though, no doubt, with different inter-titles. He even enquired of the Chief Secretary whether he could fulfil his contracts for film bookings.[69] It was, after all, the third anniversary of the Easter Rising. Despite further complaints to Dublin Castle, Whitten was not given permission to screen the *Review* again.[70]

By 1919 the life of a newsreel cameraman in Ireland must have become increasingly precarious. With the change in tactics by Irish nationalists from political action in 1917 and 1918 to overt military struggle in 1919 filming of such events became more difficult and dangerous. Had the newsreel company been able to film any military engagements from the nationalist perspective it is certain that they, too, would have been suppressed. The company seems to have ceased making the *Irish Events* series in 1920.

Such experiences had an important addendum early in the legislative life of the new Irish state. During the debate on the 1923 Censorship of Films Bill the leader of the Labour Party, Thomas Johnson, requested of the Minister for Home Affairs, Kevin O'Higgins, that the words 'social order' be replaced because it could restrict educative or propagandist films:[71]

> If this or any such scheme had been in operation, say, in 1914 or 1915, 'social order' would have meant one thing. Today it would mean another. 'Social order' to some minds has a very narrow meaning, and pictures designed to subvert social order may simply mean pictures with a message which do not seem to fit in with the particular Censor's view of certain property relations.

Johnson's amendment that 'contrary to public morality', a phrase from the Constitution, be substituted for 'social order' was accepted by O'Higgins.[72]

As things turned out few overtly political films were produced within Ireland after Independence. But this did not restrain the Film Censor from bluntly declaring in relation to imported films in an interview in 1947 that 'anything advocating Communism or presenting it in an unduly favourable light gets the knife',[73] notwithstanding the existence of Johnson's amendment to the Censorship of Films Act.

Whitten did not abandon film-making but made an entry into the drama terrain of the Film Company of Ireland. In 1919 he established a film studio at Killester, Dublin, where he made a feature-length life of St Patrick. Six years earlier *The Life of St Patrick* had been made by J. Theobald Walsh of the Photo Historic Film Company, an American organisation. It had been well received:[74]

> Highly endorsed by the Clergy . . . Every scene taken on the exact spot made memorable by Ireland's Apostle and enacted by Irish peasants [*sic*] in ancient historical costumes.

In the Days of St Patrick (1920), which was produced and directed by Whitten, and photographed by General Film Supply's *Irish Events* cameraman J. Gordon Lewis, was a far more elaborate affair. Dealing sympathetically with the life of St Patrick, it was set at three different periods of the saint's life: at ten, sixteen and as an adult (Ira Allen). It contained an epilogue of contemporary news-reel footage including Irish memorials to the saint and the Arch-bishop of Armagh, Cardinal Logue. It was, as the publicity hand-out described it, 'a pleasing, edifying and instructive treat'. It also 'ambitiously employed chariots, pirate galleys and all the accoutre-ments of epic cinema'.[75]

In the Days of St Patrick opened in three Dublin cinemas on 15 March 1920, St Patrick's Day week. With Irish and English language inter-titles, the film was variously described as 'remark-able',[76] 'magnificent'[77] and 'outstanding'. The *Evening Herald* continued:[78]

> The film is all that has been claimed for it, and is one of trans-cendent beauty . . . each and all the participants in the mag-nificent presentation show a carefulness regarding histrionic [*sic*!] detail that invests each scene unfolded with charm . . .

The Irish Times[79] endorsed this view:

> None will miss the opportunity of seeing this remarkable his-torical picture. It is the outcome of Irish minds, hands and hearts, and presents the life of our patron saint with studied truth. It is a wonder picture for children . . .

St Patrick's simple pre-Norman christianity, common as it was to all 'Irish' people from the fifth to the fifteenth centuries, was obviously comforting in the context of contemporary anxieties.

Not only did the film's events pre-date the Reformation but it did not have to deal at all with the English presence in Ireland. As with *Willy Reilly and His Colleen Bawn*, which was released a few weeks later, the more awkward features of Irish history of the previous 150 years could be safely ignored.

Irish Free State, 1922–30

The very month the Treaty was approved, January 1922, a columnist in *The Irish Times*,[80] in the course of a summary of the work of indigenous film-makers, reported on the need to

> build up our own school of cinema interpretation, and absolutely adhering to our own technique as we evolve it. By doing this we will, in time, as we become more thoroughly masters of this new art, establish a standard of interpretation that will bring to the markets of the world a product peculiarly our own which will receive a reasonable share of the world's patronage.

'Experience gained by previous efforts', the writer continues to quote an unidentified authority on Irish film production,

> has taught the lesson that we must produce features in which the country and the people can take national pride. We must start by being Irish in our point of view, and when our work is finished it must be of such a character that there will be no doubt in anyone's mind that the result attained is all the time Irish. This does not necessarily preconceive narrowness of treatment; it merely means that the only picture worth making in Ireland is an Irish picture.
> Perhaps eventually a distinctive school of Irish film production will be evolved somewhat on the lines of the native dramatic movement, so that just as the Abbey Theatre play has a peculiar charm of its own, an Irish film will make a distinctive appeal wherever it may be shown. The subject is one which deserves the thoughtful attention of all who are desirous of seeing native production placed on a proper basis.

This enlightened viewpoint was also evident in an earlier article in *The Irish Times*[81] when the writer had noted that it is gratifying to know that despite numerous handicaps, every picture, with one exception, made in Ireland has *easily paid its original cost from receipts in this country alone.* The prospect here is exceedingly rosy, and it only needs a man of enterprise, experience, and capital to put the Irish film producing industry on a sound basis. (my italics)

Why then did the new state and native capital fail so miserably to foster an indigenous film industry given the film activity of the previous decade? The answers lie in the nature of the international film industry after World War I, the insularity of the nationalist movement in its perception of (popular) culture and the enormous economic and logistical problems facing the new State.

By the time the Irish Free State was established the world economic order had taken a further major shift across the Atlantic. This was as true of the film industry as it was of industrial production in general. World War I had given the American film industry the opportunity to expand production, consolidate its position, evolve new production techniques and create new markets. These developments were aided considerably by the condition of European film industries in the aftermath of World War I. European production had been decimated either physically through the war itself or decapitalised through the allocation of resources to more urgent needs. By 1922 Hollywood had become such a dominant force in world cinema that it has never since been seriously challenged. Nevertheless, some European film industries were making hesitant steps to resist the American challenge. Even so it was not until 1928 that Britain introduced its Cinematograph Act with its cultural protectionist policy of establishing a quota of British films. By then the Irish situation was similar to that in Britain: about 90 per cent of the films on release were American.

Irish political and military events in the early years of the Irish Free State, especially two years of intermittent Civil War, were hardly conducive to film production. And if, as has often been stated, the post-colonial experience is subject to a range of difficulties all contributing to a feeling of disillusionment, then Ireland conformed to that pattern. The intense period of change in Irish society since the 1880s, but especially since 1916, was now coming to an end. The acceptance of the Treaty ensured a more homogeneous Irish state where the type of complex accommodation which an island-nation would have required was now no longer needed or encouraged. In view of the serious economic problems in its early years, especially in agriculture where the majority of people worked, little interest in film production could be expected. Indeed, film was more likely to have been associated with radical Sinn Féin and the IRA. Thus, for a Free State government with its support amongst big farmers, the professions, business and the institutionalised Catholic Church such experimentation would have been seen as detrimental to the social stability which was the main priority in the post-Treaty years.

Another dimension to the problem was the manner in which education and culture were represented in the new state. The collapse in support for the Irish language and culture organisation, the Gaelic League, following the establishment of the Free State indicates two conclusions. One is that the Gaelic League had served primarily as the ideological cement of the nationalist movement and now could be dispensed with. This decline in the radical role of the Gaelic League was augmented by a second factor, the institutionalisation of Irish culture. This was reflected in the appointment of a senior Gaelic League figure, Professor Eoin MacNeill, as Minister for Education. Another Gaelic League ideologue and vigorous opponent of the anti-Treaty forces, Ernest Blythe, was Minister for Finance, 1923–32. In short, the direct struggle was now seen to be over and the Gaelic League's activities, always of more concern to the middle classes than others, could now be incorporated within the structure of the new middle class state.

Thus what hope there was of an Irish film industry was unlikely to originate from the Free State government. Indeed, many in the Government would have been opposed to film *per se* or judged it in purely Catholic-moral terms, as was demonstrated by the speedy passage of the Censorship of Films Act, 1923, one of the first pieces of legislation to be passed by the Free State Parliament.

Private capital, as hoped for by *The Irish Times*, did not show much more enthusiasm for native film production than the government. The first films to be made in the new Irish state were modest comedies produced by Norman Whitten and directed by John MacDonagh in 1922. They were unlikely to serve as a challenge to the increasingly sophisticated American films which already dominated Irish screens, and were far removed from the overt nationalist themes which figured so prominently in the previous decade.

The Casey Millions was a four-part comedy-drama set in the village of Killcasey where two down at heel actors (Barrett

MacDonnell, Chris Sylvester), attempt to defraud the Caseys whom they claim are heirs to an American estate. They proceed to measure the Caseys' skulls for a fee to determine which of the skulls corresponds to that of the late American. The defrauders are forced to flee when they develop designs on their host's daughter, the lover of the farm hand, who turns out to be the real beneficiary of the estate. *The Irish Times*[82] regarded it as 'far and away the best Irish-made film, [showing] real comedy and restraint', while *The Irish Independent*[83] found 'a vein of genuine humour in the picture'.

By 1922 John MacDonagh had established a considerable stage presence with the straight play *The Irish Jew*. Between 1922 and 1924 he also produced a series of revues and sketches, often with Jimmy O'Dea in the shows, which proved very popular. For O'Dea, who acted in all three of the 1922 films, this was one step towards making him this century's most popular and versatile Irish comedian. One of these shows, a libretto by MacDonagh, was adapted as *Wicklow Gold*, the second film to be released. Jimmy O'Dea's role in this film, as in all eleven films he was to play in, was far removed from the Dublinese he was so successful in popularising.[84]

Wicklow Gold concerned an old Wicklow farmer, Ned O'Toole (Chris Sylvester), who believes that the rivers of Wicklow are filled with gold. He attempts to arrange a match for his son Larry (Jimmy O'Dea), to a 'strong' farmer's daughter but he is thwarted when Larry's lover Kitty (Ria Mooney), and her mother, Widow O'Byrne (Kathleen Carr), trick Ned into believing that there is a gold deposit in the river that runs through Kitty's mother's land. *The Irish Independent* described the film as 'a series of excellent and highly amusing pictures'[85] while *The Irish Times* thought that 'the humour is the more enjoyable because it is native, and the acting is certainly clever'.[85] When *Wicklow Gold* was revived at the La Scala in 1925 *The Irish Times* complained about some excessive gesturing and an overabundance of close-ups. The writer thought the story 'cleverly conceived and [it] swings along from one humorous position to another'.[87]

The third film produced was *Cruiskeen Lawn*. This was a convoluted story about an ageing racehorse, Cruiskeen Lawn, the property of poverty stricken Boyle Roche (Tom Moran), who shares his name with the legendary master of the Irish Bull, and who is also the owner of a dilapidated mansion. Roche is in love with Nora Blake (Kathleen Armstrong), whose father, Dick Blake (Fred Jeffs), is heavily in debt to one of the 'new rich', Samuel

Silke (Jimmy O'Dea). Darby (Chris Sylvester), the Roches' rheumatic ex-jockey, meets Dublin Dan (Barrett MacDonnell), a quack medicine man, who sells him an 'Elixir of Life'. By accident, Cruiskeen Lawn drinks this medicine and becomes rejuvenated. When Boyle sees the horse's transformation, Cruiskeen Lawn is entered to run in the Callaghan Cup. He then arranges a bet with Silke of £10,000 to £500 that Cruiskeen Lawn will win. But the elixir begins to wear off and a frantic effort is made to find Dublin Dan to secure more medicine. Needless to say all turns out well in the end: the Roches and the Blakes are restored to financial security, and Boyle and Nora plan to marry.

After a trade show in London attended by the Irish High Commissioner, James MacNeill, *The Irish Times* described it as the first Irish film to bear the Free State Trade Mark. The writer also pronounced the film 'a great success'. The story was 'clearly told, with considerable humour . . .'[88] It is somewhat ironic to find Whitten and MacDonagh engaged in the production of comedies at the moment when the hopes of Irish nationalists were about to be shattered in the gloom and despondency that permeated the country after the outbreak of Civil War in the late spring and summer of 1922. For two men who had been so involved (albeit in very different ways) in the events after 1916, the retreat to comedy was one reflection of their disillusionment. As the decade progressed, however, few film-makers did attempt to look back on the events of the 1916–22 period. It is noticeable that the general tendency was to concentrate on the military events of the War of Independence and to ignore the more painful political differences of the Treaty and its bloody aftermath. The first of these films to be produced and the only indigenous War of Independence film made during the 1920s was *Irish Destiny* made in 1925 about the events in Dublin and environs four years earlier.

Irish Destiny was written and produced by Dr Isaac Eppel, owner of the Palace Cinema, Dublin. It was directed by George Dewhurst and photographed by Joe Rosenthal, a veteran Boer War cameraman. The film had a love story set against the background of the struggle between the IRA and the Black and Tans. It included a reconstruction of the burning of the Customs House and contained hold-ups in the city, raids and arrests in a country village, the plotting of an ambush and the running fight which follows an attack on the military and the auxiliary RIC, the Black and Tans.

The exteriors were filmed in Wicklow and Dublin while

Shepherd's Bush Film Studios were used for the interiors. Amongst the actors in the film were Frances MacNamara (née Alexander) and her partner from *Willy Reilly and his Colleen Bawn*, Brian Magowan, Patrick Cullinane, Cathal McGarvey, Una Shiels and Daisy Campbell. Men who had participated in the War of Independence provided expert advice including ex-Col. 'Kit' O'Malley, who had been Adjutant of the Dublin Brigade, IRA and who played the Commandant of an IRA Battalion.

The release of *Irish Destiny* was timed to coincide with the tenth anniversary of the Easter Rising, opening on Easter Saturday, 3 April 1926. Booked for one week at the Corinthian it proved so popular that it was retained a second week, breaking the house box office records in the process. This success was helped by extremely favourable reviews. 'The acting and photography . . . are above reproach', declared the *Dublin Evening Mail*.[89] In other reports the *Mail* added that

> it will bring back to the minds of many the exciting times which have passed in Ireland. Raids and arrests by the Auxiliaries, reprisals and ambushes, are all realistically depicted.[90] *Irish Destiny* contains the highest elements of art, action, scenery and photography. It is a triumph for Irish enterprise.[91]

It was, no doubt, this desire to develop Irish film enterprise that led to the organisation of a public forum on the future of film production in Ireland during *Irish Destiny*'s cinema run. At this 'luncheon party' in Clery's Restaurant Dr Eppel remarked that Ireland had numerous advantages for film production

> chief amongst them being incomparable scenery, light of an artistic nature, small cost of production, and the ready market for Irish productions in foreign countries.[92]

The Minister for Posts and Telegraphs, J. J. Walsh, who had been a director of the Film Company of Ireland, reviewed the film work of the previous decade. An Irish-American, Robert Emmett O'Malley, emphasised the importance of countering anti-Irish propaganda in America. To this end the chairman of the Forum, Alderman J. Stanley, said there would be little difficulty in convincing their fellow-countrymen in America that the Ireland of today and the Black and Tan period was the Ireland portrayed by

Dr Eppel in *Irish Destiny* and not the Ireland envisaged by Sean O'Casey. What was fresh in Mr Stanley's mind was the controversy which had erupted the previous February over the production of *The Plough and the Stars*, O'Casey's play set during the Easter Rising. Another speaker at the forum was James Dolan, Parliamentary Secretary to President Cosgrave and Government Chief Whip, who declared that film was important in developing tourism. It was this policy which was set in train by the Minister for Industry and Commerce, Patrick McGilligan, a few months later when, on 31 July 1926, a memorandum was circulated to the government.[93]

The memo revealed that the government had been receiving numerous requests from Irish embassies and legations, especially from Washington and London, urging the production of a government information film. London High Commissioner, James MacNeill, sought the production of a film by autumn 1926 when the film activities of the Empire Marketing Board were due to expand to coincide with the Imperial Conference. The memo recognised the value of *Irish Destiny* and a recent film about Ford's Cork factory. Nevertheless, it sought the production of one film of a 'propagandist' type, such as has been made by other countries. Though the Government approved the proposal in principle on 17 August 1926, the contract for the film was not placed until 1928. McConnell-Hartley, the country's largest advertising agency, produced the film, *Ireland*, which was completed and shown to government on 16 July 1929. Later in the year it received its première at the opening of Dublin's Savoy Cinema, on 29 November 1929.

Ireland contained the images that were to become the stock representations of Ireland in its bid to attract tourists: Government Buildings, Bank of Ireland, Trinity College, O'Connell St, Leinster House and the wealthy Dublin coastal areas of Howth, Dun Laoghaire, Dalkey and Killiney. A selection of sites to promote Ireland as 'a seat of ancient culture', included Glendalough and Clonmacnoise, while Cork, Parknasilla, Kenmare, Donegal, Horne Head fishing, Galway and Lough Corrib indicated the variety of Irish tourist locations. (Killarney, interestingly, seems to have been omitted from the film.) The working of Connemara marble and the Royal Dublin Society's Horse Show with its Inter-Military Jumping Competition reflected the twin poles of later tourist films: the Western idyll and the world of the Anglo-Irish aristocracy. Unlike later tourist but occasional informational films the Irish Army and Air Force were shown in training, on manoeuvres and in exhibition work.

An alternative direction for Irish film production was indicated by the establishment of the Irish Amateur Film Society in 1930. An hour-long film, *By Accident*, written and directed by J. N. G. (Norris) Davidson, a Dublin-born Cambridge University student at the time, was a psychological study about a morbid and introspective young man (C. Clarke-Clifford), who is mesmerised by a young woman (Olive Purcell), with whom he finds it impossible to communicate adequately. The young man's mental state is conveyed using double photography, flash-backs and a non-linear narrative. Scenes include terror-stricken vertigo on top of Nelson's Pillar and the young man driving a motor car through O'Connell St at a busy time and running down a pedestrian. On getting out of the car he finds that the man he has killed is himself.

Under the headline 'Dublin May Rival Hollywood' *The People* reported that *By Accident* 'may lead the way to a flourishing new industry for the Free State'.[94] This type of exaggeration was to become all too typical in the debates about Irish film production as they developed from the 1930s onwards. The *Dublin Evening Mail*[95] was equally forthright but was concerned to place a different emphasis on the film. Choosing to ignore the young man's obsession with the young woman, the writer rather bizarrely contrasted the film with Hollywood product:

There will not be any suggestion of either night-clubs or the underworld, nor any nigger minstrel show. Not even one cocktail will be mixed. On the contrary, the story, such as it is, has a strong didactic tendency. It might have been suggested by Adam Smith's *Theory of Moral Sentiments*.

By Accident was screened at the Peacock Theatre during the last week of August 1930 with two shorts, *Bank Holiday*, a documentary by Mary Manning, and *Pathetic Gazette*, which was a skit based on an incident in the legend of Cuchulain and Deirdre. Abbey Theatre director and playwright, Lennox Robinson, introduced the films as ones which 'may prove to be the beginning of a real Irish art of the cinema'. He complained that the cinema had fallen into the hands of capitalists in its early days and the nascent artistry was buried under millions of dollars.[96]

Thus, at the end of the silent period, and nearly a decade after Independence, a one-hour amateur silent film is hailed as Ireland's challenge to Hollywood. The body of films which had been produced in pre-Independence Ireland, with a content more radical than anything produced in the early years of the new state, had been almost completely forgotten. Additionally, commentators from the 1930s onwards were frequently to remark as each new indigenous film was produced that it was unique, the first of its kind, and so on. This form of amnesia, as we shall see, had probably less to do with the absence of a written history of film and Ireland and more to do with the ideological suppressions of independent Ireland. But the silent period represented an initial important phase in indigenous fiction film-making that in volume, quality and relevance to contemporary and historical events in Ireland, was not to be emulated until the 1970s.

Notes

1. Eugene Watters and Matthew Murtagh, *Infinite Varieties: Dan Lowrey's Music Hall 1879 – 97*, Dublin: Gill and Macmillan, 1975, p. 165. Much of the information on film shows at Lowrey's theatres is taken from this book, pp. 165 – 70.

2. Michael Chanan, *The Dream That Kicks: The Prehistory and Early Years of Cinema in Britain*, London: Routledge and Kegan Paul, 1980, p. 130. In the original *Freeman's Journal* advertisement Lowrey declared that the April shows were to cost £200 per week.

3. Quoted Watters and Muragh, *Infinite Varieties*, pp. 166 – 7.

4. Ibid., p. 168.

5. Richard Ellmann, *James Joyce*, New York: Oxford University Press, 1959, pp. 310 – 12.

6. *Dublin Evening Mail*, 20 December 1909, p. 2.

7. *Freeman's Journal*, 21 December 1909, p. 10. Made by Albert Capellani in 1908, it was based on Shelly's drama *The Cenci* (1819), which in turn had been derived from a well-known Italian fable. At least three other versions were subsequently made: in 1926, 1956 and 1969. The story concerns Beatrice's revenge on her tyrannical father whom she kills (or arranges to kill) following his rape of her. See Julian Petley's review of the 1969 version in *Monthly Film Bulletin*, Vol. 53, No. 626, March 1986, pp. 91 – 2.

8. Ellmann, *James Joyce*, pp. 321 – 2.

9. Ibid.

10. *Kinematograph Year Book*, 1916 and 1930.

11. George Morrison, cinema entry, in Brian de Breffni (ed.), *Ireland: A Cultural Encyclopaedia*, London: Thames and Hudson, 1983, p. 64.

12. Liam O'Leary Film Archives Newsletter, 1 December 1982.

13. Anthony Slide, 'A British Film Pioneer in Ireland', *Vision*, Vol. 3, No. 1, Winter 1967, pp. 5 – 6.

14. Proinsias Ó Conluain, 'Ireland's First Films', *Sight and Sound*, Vol. 23, No. 2, October–December 1953. p. 96.

15. Ibid., p. 98.

16. Ibid., p. 97.

17. Ibid.

18. Ibid.

19. George Blaisdell, 'Irish History on the Screen', *The Moving Picture World*, 29 August 1914, p. 1245. This article gives a colourful and no doubt exaggerated account of MacNamara's adventures while making *Ireland a Nation*. However, MacNamara was the scriptwriter for a huge 1913 hit, *Traffic in Souls*, a white slave trade story, which was the first major sexploitation film.

20. Ibid.

21. *Irish Independent*, 11 January 1917, p. 3.

22. This and subsequent memos and letters on the censoring of *Ireland a Nation* may be found in File 11025, State Paper Office, Dublin Castle.

23. *Irish Times*, 11 January, p. 5, reported that the reasons for the banning were that 'it treats the rebel cause in sympathetic manner' and the accompaniment of 'tunes in keeping with nature of the film . . . have added to the fervour of the demonstrations of approval'.

24. *Dublin Evening Mail*, 31 January 1922, p. 5.

25. *Irish Limelight*, Vol. 1, No. 1, January 1917.

26. *Irish Times*, 14 January 1922, p. 9.

27. I have standardised this spelling since, in addition to this version, McGowan and MacGowan are used in film credits and the press.

28. *Dublin Evening Mail*, 5 August 1916, p. 5.

29. Ibid., 26 August 1916, p. 5. The *Mail* added that when *O'Neil of the Glen* was showing at the Bohemian it had 'created a perfect furore' but unfortunately no details of the disruption caused are included in the report.

30. Ibid., 27 January 1917, p. 6.

31. Ibid., 20 January 1917, p. 6.

32. Ibid., 4 November 1916, p. 6.

33. Ibid., 9 November 1916, p. 6.

34. R. V. Comerford in his *Charles J. Kickham: A Study in Irish Nationalism and Literature*, Dublin: Wolfhound Press, 1979, identifies Goldsmith's *The Deserted Village* and Charles Dickens, Kickham's favourite author, amongst *Knocknagow*'s influences: 'The most glaring case of an idea borrowed from Dickens is Norah Lahy, the doomed consumptive girl, too good for this life — a disastrous imitation of Little Nell in *The Old Curiosity Shop*' (pp. 200–1). From George Eliot's *Adam Bede* (1859) Commerford asserts (p. 201) that there 'can be no coincidence about the resemblances between the upright village carpenter Adam Bede' and Mat the Thrasher. Comerford continues: 'Putting it all together to create his greatest character would be beyond his powers of composition without a model to guide him and, without a doubt, Adam Bede is that model'.

35. According to E. R. R. Green, 'Charles J. Kickham and John O'Leary', in T. W. Mooney (ed.), *The Fenian Movement*, Dublin: Mercier Press, 1968.

36. Dorothy Macardle, *The Irish Republic*, London: Corgi, 1968, p. 232, orig. 1937.

37. *Dublin Evening Mail*, 20 April 1918, p. 4.

38. *Irish Limelight*, Vol. 2, No. 2, February 1918, p. 8.

39. These particular struggles during the Land War were the subject of a 4,000 feet film, *Rosaleen Dhu* (Dark Rosaleen) which had been made by the Celtic Cinema Co. This company had been established by William Power, a Bray, Co. Wicklow, barber, and other locals. Its first production was a one-reel comedy written, produced and directed by Power, *Willie Scouts While Jessie Pouts* (1919). *Rosaleen Dhu* (1920) was the first film shown at the re-opened Rotunda. According to a writer in the *Dublin Evening Mail* (1 May 1920, p. 2) it was a 'well acted drama, dealing with the early days and most exciting incidents of the Land League'. The narrative included an eviction scene as a result of which a Fenian has to leave Ireland: 'He joins the Foreign Legion and marries an Algerian girl, who, when he returns to Ireland, turns out to be an heiress to an Irish estate'! (as reported by Padraig Ó Fearail, 'When Films Were Made at Bray', *Irish Times*, 16 August 1977, p. 8). Later in 1920 production began on *An Irish Vendetta* but while filming one of the sequences at a racecourse, Power was thrown from a horse. When he died a fortnight later, the Celtic Cinema Co. died with him.

40. *Irish Limelight*, Vol. 2, No. 6, June 1918.

41. *Evening Telegraph*, 13 December 1919, p. 4.

42. *The Bioscope*, 16 October 1919, p. 58.

43. Taylor Downing, 'The Film Company of Ireland', *Sight and Sound*, Vol. 49, No. 1, Winter 1979/80, p. 44.

44. John MacDonagh's unpublished memoirs quoted, Liam O'Leary, *Cinema Ireland 1895–1976*, Dublin Arts Festival, 1976, p. 11. This 42-page booklet was published to coincide with an exhibition held in Trinity College, Dublin. This exhibition led to a further ten years of private research on Irish film history by Liam O'Leary. The resulting collection was deposited at the National Library of Ireland in 1986. An affectionate documentary on his life, *At the Cinema Palace: Liam O'Leary*, was made by Donald Taylor Black (Poolbeg Productions, 1983). Liam O'Leary's involvement in film in Ireland will feature in the period from the 1930s to 1950s. At that time he used the Irish version of his name, Liam O'Laoghaire, and references are cited accordingly.

45. T. A. Jackson, *Ireland Her Own*, New York: International Publishers, 1947, p. 69.

46. *Irish Limelight*, Vol. 4, No. 1, 1920.

47. Liam O'Leary Film Archives, programme note, 1980.

48. J. Anthony Gaughan, *Austin Stack: Portrait of a Separatist*, Dublin: Kingdom Books, 1977, pp. 136–7.

49. Ibid., p. 138.

50. George Morrison, *Hibernia*, 7 May 1976, p. 32.

51. *Irish Limelight*, quoted Liam O'Leary Film Archives programme note.

52. O'Leary, 1976, *Cinema Ireland*, p. 10.

53. Ibid., pp. 11–12.

54. Patrick Buckland, *Irish Unionism 1: The Anglo-Irish and the New Ireland 1885–1922*, Dublin: Gill and Macmillan, 1972, p. 279.

55. Quoted, ibid., p. 288.

56. *Irish Limelight*, Vol. 1, No. 11, November 1917, p. 6.

57. Quoted, Ó Conluain, 1953, op. cit., p. 98.

58. Ibid.

59. *Irish Limelight*, Vol. 1, No. 1, January 1917, p. 3.

60. 'John', 'When the Fianna Raided a British Propaganda Film', *An Phoblacht*, Vol. 9, No. 47, 22 December 1934, p. 8.

61. Thomas J. Clarke, 'The Bodenstown Film' to John Devoy, 25 June 1913, in *Devoy's Post Bag: 1871–1928, Vol. 2, 1880–1928*, William O'Brien and Desmond Ryan (eds), Dublin: C. J. Fallon, 1948, pp. 410–11.

62. *Kinematograph Year Book*, 1913, p. 322.

63. In his biography, *Tom Clarke and the Irish Freedom Movement* (Dublin: Talbot Press, 1936, p. 127), Louis N. Le Roux quotes a letter from Clarke to Devoy (5 January 1914) in which Clarke reveals his hope that a benefit film show for the Wolfe Tone Fund will be held under Jamieson's (*sic*) auspices at the Rotunda on 4 March. Clarke hoped that the Bodenstown film and that of the previous November's Manchester Martyrs (of 1867) procession would be included in the benefit programme.

64. *Irish Limelight*, Vol. 1, No. 7, July 1917, pp. 16–17.

65. Ibid., Vol. 1, No. 8, pp. 18–19.

66. This and other reports, memos and letters referring to *The Sinn Féin Review*, may be found in File 11025, State Paper Office.

67. This report was dated 12 April 1919 and addressed to the Chief Secretary's Office.

68. District Inspector, Westgate Barracks, Drogheda to RIC, Dublin Castle, 17 April 1919.

69. Michael J. Bowers, Whitten's solicitor, to Chief Secretary, 17 April.

70. Bowers to Chief Secretary, 28 April.

71. *Dáil Debates*, Vol. 3, Col. 753, 10 May 1923.

72. Ibid., col. 1001.

73. Richard Hayes, quoted, John Gerrard, 'Irish Censorship or Fighting for Cleaner Cinema', *Sight and Sound*, Vol. 18, No. 70, Summer 1949, p. 82.

74. Quoted, Anthony Slide, 'The Silent Cinema and Ireland', *Vision*, Vol. 3, No. 4, Autumn 1967, p. 20.

75. O'Leary, 1976, *Cinema Ireland*, p. 23.

76. *Dublin Evening Mail*, 16 March 1920, p. 7.

77. *Evening Herald*, 13 March 1920, p. 5.

78. Ibid., 16 March 1920, p. 3.

79. *Irish Times*, 16 March 1920, p. 9.

80. Ibid., 28 January 1922, p. 9.

81. Ibid., 7 January 1922, p. 9.

82. Quoted, Martin Dolan, *The Irish National Cinema and its Relationship to Irish Nationalism*, University of Wisconsin-Madison, Ph.D. thesis, 1979, p. 90. Published, Ann Arbor, Michigan: Xerox University Microfilms. This thesis should be treated with critical caution as it contains numerous Irish historical and filmic inaccuracies.

83. *Irish Independent*, 31 October 1922, p. 6.

84. For reminiscences of his stage career and an account of the films he

acted in see Donald Taylor Black's film documentary, *Remembering Jimmy O'Dea* (Poolbeg Productions, 1985).

85. *Irish Independent*, 21 November 1922, p. 6.

86. *Irish Times*, 21 November 1922, p. 3.

87. Ibid., 15 December 1925, p. 6.

88. Ibid., 27 November 1924, p. 6.

89. *Dublin Evening Mail*, 3 April 1926, p. 2.

90. Ibid., 6 April, p. 5.

91. Ibid., 10 April, p. 2. Such a reconstruction of recent events proved too controversial for the British Film Censor. Thomas C. Robertson reports in his *The British Board of Film Censors* (London: Croom Helm, 1985, p. 186) that *Irish Destiny* was one of only six films banned by the BBFC in 1926. Another was Eisenstein's *The Battleship Potemkin*. (The first British Film censor was Irish-born T. P. O'Connor, who had been elected Parnellite MP for Galway in 1880, but from 1885 to his death in 1929 was MP for the Liverpool district of Scotland. He became the first paid film censor in 1917.)

92. 'Irish Film Production; Bright Future for Industry', *Irish Independent*, 10 April 1926, p. 6.

93. The memo may be found in File S 5105, Department of the Taoiseach.

94. *People*, 24 August 1930.

95. *Dublin Evening Mail*, 10 July 1930, p. 3.

96. *Irish Independent*, 26 August 1930, p. 10.

2

1930s Fictions

Kevin Rockett

It was, perhaps, appropriate, given the type of Free State which was evolving, that Ireland's first sound film should be a record of the Catholic Emancipation Centenary celebrations. Screened for the first time on 1 July 1929 at Dublin's Capitol Cinema, this historic footage shared a cine-variety programme with two Hollywood comedies and the twelve Capitol Tiller Girls. Such an unusual combination must have bewildered the priests and nuns who would have flocked to see the Emancipation celebrations on film, especially in light of the increasingly virulent anti-cinema (and anti-dancing) campaign being mounted by the Catholic hierarchy during the 1920s. As American and English sound films became the norm in Ireland's cinemas in the early 1930s, the Church intensified its anti-cinema campaign, a development which mirrored the experience of other countries.

The introduction of Anglo-American sound films into Ireland was accompanied by the elimination of the few remaining European films from Irish screens. This loss of European cinema, regretted as it was by literati and intellectuals, led to the formation of the Dublin Amateur Film Society in 1930 and the Irish Film Society in 1936. At a political level support for an alternative supply of films to the British and American film industries was given by Fianna Fáil's Sean MacEntee eight months before becoming Minister for Finance after that party's victory in the 1932 general election. He called for a redirection of the policies of film distributors from dependency on Anglo-American product. He instanced Soviet cinema and in particular Pudovkin's *Storm Over Asia* (1928), which had been shown in a small Dublin cinema after the major exhibitors refused to screen it, as an example of the type of film which should be distributed.[1]

Apart from these objections to Anglo-American cinema, attention was focused more intently on the brash new world of sound cinema itself with its cacophony of sounds hitherto only available on the small numbers of gramophones and radios. American and British accents in the cinema provided a rude shock to those who had been engaged in an ideological struggle to establish a distinctive Irish cultural identity. The Irish language lobby in the person of Cu Uladh, President of the Gaelic League, complained about the volume of English being spoken in Irish cinemas. He regarded sound cinema as bestowing unfair advantage on English over Irish!

Others merely focused on the quality of English spoken in films. Writer and Senator, Oliver St. John Gogarty, denounced[2] commercial sound cinema in 1930 during the Senate debate amending the 1923 Censorship of Films Act to allow for the censoring of sound films because

> They never use the English language, as it is used by the English. They use a cosmopolitan lingo which is always degrading, and which is distracting the English speaking nations from the source of the language and from its own centre. It is a form of making national sentiment eccentric, and I think that without drawing on that vision of our self-righteousness we ought to abolish talkies utterly.

A lengthy article in *The Irish Statesman*[3] by 'Tin, Tin, Tin' trenchantly attacked sound cinema and declared that

> a war is raging — a great wordy war — that will tear the English language to tatters, and affect the clean speech of the nations who are not sheltered behind a barrage of native tongues.

Since the restoration of the Irish language as the vernacular was official state policy and one of the aims of Fianna Fáil, the volume of English spoken in sound films might have become a political or cultural issue. But, after the initial hostile reaction, this aspect of the effect of sound cinema in Ireland was largely disregarded. A more potent source of conflict was to be found in the content of Anglo-American cinema. To assess that issue it is necessary in the Irish context to separate the term into its constituent parts.

American cinema was perceived mainly as an 'immoral' influence, bringing into Catholic Ireland alien images and ideas such as triangular relationships leading to the destruction of the nuclear family, the temptations of jazz dancing and the like. The vigilant Film Censor ensured that what passed the self-censoring filtering process of the London and Dublin offices of the distributors (since after all the Censor had to be paid even for the viewing of banned films) would be further refined. The severity of Irish film censorship is demonstrated by the statistics of about 3,000 films banned and about 8,000 cut since 1924.[4]

With the temporary resurgence of British cinema in the early and mid-1930s there was a partial break with the dominance of American films on Irish screens. The international success of *The Private Life of Henry VIII* (1932) was evidence of this recovery. British-theme historical films, however, also carried with them jingoistic baggage, especially for an Irish audience. In December 1934 a direct attack by radical republicans on the Savoy, Dublin, and provincial cinemas led to the withdrawal of newsreel of a royal wedding. In the light of this response it was deemed prudent, for example, to cut the American-produced Indian Raj film, *The Lives of a Bengal Lancer* (1935). When shown in Dublin in April 1935, Rupert Brooke's provocative poem, 'England, My England' was removed while 'Land of Hope and Glory' was substituted for 'God Save the Queen'. Indeed, it was also deemed wise not to screen the George V celebration film, *Royal Cavalcade* (1935).[5] The fate of a print of Alfred Hitchcock's version of Sean O'Casey's *Juno and the Paycock* (1930), a play in disfavour amongst Catholics and nationalists alike, illustrates the ease with which the twin concerns of morality and nationality co-joined. When shown in Limerick, a print of the film was seized and publicly burned.

It was another 'Irish' feature which provoked the first direct attack by an Irish group against an offending film. *Smiling Irish Eyes* (1929) was an extreme example of the American stage-Irish films which were common in the silent and early sound periods. Set in Ireland and America, it concerned a musician, Rory O'More (James Hall), who works in a peat bog. After he emigrates to America, his sweetheart, Kathleen (Colleen Moore), follows but she wants to bring him back to Ireland. She returns home in a huff after seeing him kiss a woman in a theatrical production in which he plays the violin. They are reconciled when Rory unexpectedly returns to Ireland. Then the whole family emigrates to the United States.

It began its run at the Savoy, Dublin, on 7 February 1930, just over two months after President Cosgrave had officiated at the opening of the new cinema. The response to the film may be gauged from the headline to the review in the normally restrained and conservative *Irish Independent*:[6] 'Grotesque Scene/An "Irish" Film in Dublin'. The *Dublin Evening Mail's* article,[7] 'Stage Irishman Prominent in Savoy Presentation', declared that

> the people are all preposterous. The Kerrymen are shown as a truculent, stupid lot, and there are two brothers obviously lineal descendants of the stage Irishman who was so much in vogue in other countries a hundred years ago, who spend every moment of their time hammering each other.

At a fair near Killarney the two are joined by another who 'rushes up to them with the eager query: "Is this a private row or can anyone join in?" '. Colleen Moore (who, despite her Irish-sounding name, was the American-born Kathleen Morrison) plays 'a stupid, sentimental, unreasonable girl, and her superstitious belief in [a] "wishing well" is certainly objectionable'. Writing in *The Irish Statesman*[8] Mary Manning declared that

> If an international prize was offered for the worst film ever made *Smiling Irish Eyes* would undoubtedly win it. I even defy Mr. Frank O'Connor to show me a worse play, and I understand this is going pretty far. Boucicault stands as a stern and uncompromising realist beside the makers of this picture of Irish life.
>
> At times waves of nausea swept over me and the screen became a blur. Mercifully the dialogue was almost completely inaudible except for the occasional 'arrah' from the aristocratic Sir Timothy Tyrone.
>
> Rory O'More [is] complete with side-whiskers and knee-breeches, scratching interminably on his fiddle. There was a prolonged interval during which I wished passionately Tom Moore had never lived. Enter Colleen herself; she plays with the pigs. O, yes, she plays with the pigs for quite a long time . . . Evidently the producers have run out of real Irish costumes, for there are Breton fisherfolk and Tyrolese peasants mingling in the crowd.
>
> The only hope for the suffering Irish public is that Colleen will 'go' Russian; otherwise I see no help for it, unless

Mr. Montgomery [the Film Censor] comes to our rescue.

Mr Montgomery, however, had no power under the Censorship of Films legislation to restrict the showing of such sentimental and stage-Irish films. But the Savoy management themselves later claimed that they had cut out some of the most objectionable parts of the film. This was insufficient for those who decided to take direct action against the offending picture. On the first night a group of National University students and others, including a future President of Ireland, Cearbhall Ó Dálaigh, actor Cyril Cusack and Liam O'Leary rushed into the cinema. They drowned out the sound of the film with cries of 'Take it off' and 'It's an insult'. The film was stopped and the Savoy's general manager, an Englishman, F. Knott, came on the stage. He complained that the demonstrators had broken into the cinema but they retorted that he had broken into the country. When they began to sing Irish songs and continue to argue, Knott agreed to meet a deputation to discuss the film's withdrawal. He sought to continue that evening's performance and to take a vote in the cinema afterwards to determine what his patrons thought of the film. Even this approach was abandoned when he was told firmly that 'It was an insult to ask Irish people to vote on whether they were Irish or not . . . In other words we are to vote whether we are stage-Irishmen or not'.[9]

Six months later the first film of the sound era to challenge such images of Ireland was screened in Dublin. Frank Borzage's *Song O' My Heart* (1930), with John McCormack and Maureen O'Sullivan in her first film, was produced as a conscious rejection of stage-Irishism. McCormack, the greatest lyric tenor of his time and an extraordinarily popular concert singer, had been signed to sing in *Song O' My Heart* for £100,000. When the Fox Film Production Unit arrived in Dublin Mary Manning wrote[10]

In the first place, it means a certain amount of the Hollywood gold will be spent in this country. Secondly, the film, when made, will be exhibited all over the world, which will mean free international publicity and, furthermore, as there is to be a background of mountains and sea, the tourist propaganda ought to be considerable. Thirdly, it is a picture of modern Ireland. An accurate picture. There are to be no colleens, shillelaghs, squireens or begorras . . . An Irish super-talkie of modern Irish life, for the first time accurately and intelligently portrayed on the screen, is a chance for the Free State to show the world.

On its release all newspaper writers were agreed that *Song O' My Heart* was an artistic and commercial success. A six-week record breaking run at the Metropole was followed by three weeks at the Corinthian and two weeks at the Theatre de Luxe. A 'masterpiece' declared the *Dublin Evening Mail*.[11] McCormack's singing of eleven songs was regarded as the highlight of the film but the conscious attempt to break with stage-Irishism was also favourably recorded. This view was articulated by McCormack and J. M. Kerrigan, who helped cast the film and who acted in the role of a jarvey. McCormack's great idea in producing the film, the *Saturday Herald*[12] reported,

> was to offset some of the ridiculous pictures of Ireland that were given. He and Mr. Kerrigan had done everything to eliminate all the stage Irish atmosphere from the film, and if he had succeeded in his object of killing these stage Irish performances he would be the proudest man alive.

The *Dublin Evening Mail*[13] added:

> the scenes of Irish life in this picture are true representations, and the Irish characters are typically Irish. This alone would make the piece worthy of notice, for no race has suffered more at the hands of American and English film and stage productions than has ours.

Irish musical dramas and musical comedies remained popular with foreign and native film-makers during the 1930s. The first indigenous sound 'feature' (actually 49 minutes) was a musical, *The Voice of Ireland* (1932), directed by Col. Victor Haddick. Songs interspersed a narrative about a traveller who returns home and meets old friends. This 'rather scrappy musical scenic'[14] was, in large part, a vehicle for Northern Ireland singer and actor Richard Hayward. Hayward and Haddick collaborated with Donovan Pedelty on another of the enduring Irish-theme genres of the 1930s, the comedy. *The Luck of the Irish* (1935) was an adaption of a novel by Haddick. This horse racing comedy concerned an Irish country gentleman (Jimmy Mageean) who pawns his castle in hope of victory for his horse in the Grand National. Another

Pedelty/Hayward film was *The Early Bird* (1936) in which villagers rebel against a puritanical woman. *Devil's Rock* (1938), a romantic adventure, was produced by Hayward and Germain Burger, and starred himself and Geraldine Mitchel.[15] Like many other inexpensive productions of the period they probably were made under the wing of the British Cinematograph Act's 'quota quickie' provisions, which allowed for the inclusion of Irish-produced films as 'British'.

Another Hayward/Pedelty production, *Irish and Proud of It* (1936), was a story about a food tablet manufacturer who becomes entangled with a Chicago gangster's moonshiners. This was a story by Dorothea Donn Byrne, who had provided the story for one of the few features made in Ireland in the 1920s, *Land of Her Fathers* (1925), by John Hurley. The impressive cast of that film included Micheál MacLiammóir, Phyllis O'Hara, playwright Frank Hugh O'Donnell, Tom Moran, Michael Dolan, Eileen Crowe, F. J. McCormick, Barry Fitzgerald and Maureen Delaney. Her husband, Donn Byrne, had his novel *Hangman's House* filmed in America by John Ford in 1928 and his *Destiny Bay* was adapted by Tom Geraghty, John Meehan and Brinsley MacNamara to provide the script for Britain's first Technicolor feature, *Wings of the Morning* (Harold Schuster, 1937). This story of two generations concerns the marriage of an Irish nobleman to a gypsy in 1889 and romance amongst their descendants in 1936. John McCormack provided the songs.

Another writer who provided material for foreign productions about Ireland was L. A. G. Strong who scripted *Irish For Luck* (Arthur Woods, 1936, Britain), and who had a novel produced as *Dr. O'Dowd* (Herbert Mason, 1940, Britain). Incidently, one of Strong's novels, *The Director* (1944), set in rural Ireland during the making of a film there, has parallels with Sidney Olcott's experience at the hands of a local priest in Kerry in 1911. Lennox Robinson also worked on British films. He co-scripted *The Blarney Stone* (Tom Walls, 1933, Britain), and adapted George Birmingham's popular work, *General John Regan* (Henry Edwards, 1933, Britain), a story of how Irish villagers invent a mythical hero to fool a rich American. An M. J. Farrell (Molly Keane) and John Perry play was adapted as *Spring Meeting* (Walter C. Mycroft, 1941, Britain). This comedy concerns a widow's attempt to marry her son to the daughter of her ex-fiancé, who is mean but wealthy.

The most popular Irish-made comedy of the 1930s was Jimmy O'Dea's triumph in *Blarney* (1938). Since he had acted in the

MacDonagh comedies in 1922, O'Dea had only played in one film, the British-produced, *Jimmy Boy* (John Baxter, 1935), which was co-scripted by his writer and business partner Harry O'Donovan. *Blarney* was the only film the partners made for their own production company, O'D Productions. They also co-wrote the script. *Blarney* centres on a jewel robbery which is observed by a tramp (Jimmy O'Dea) selling cough mixtures possessing magical qualities. The jewel thieves (Ken Warrington, Julie Suedo), are pursued to the border by the tramp turned detective. There, the rural policemen, the Southern Civic Guard (Noel Purcell), and the Northern RUC Sergeant (Rodney Malcolmson), vie with each other to catch the thieves and win the innkeeper's daughter (Hazel Hughes). At the end of *Blarney* the border barrier is symbolically knocked over as Jimmy attempts to kiss the barmaid (Myrette Morven) across the physical divide.

Blarney opened for a two-week run at Dublin's Savoy Cinema on 7 January 1938. O'Dea in the role of the tramp was 'a pathetic little figure with a bowler hat reminiscent of Chaplin'.[16] O'Dea's humour was of the Chaplin kind, 'helplessly wistful, yet cannily clever'.[17] In general, *Blarney* was regarded as 'an entertaining production'.[18] *Blarney* is unusual in the repertoire of indigenous film-making with its 'debunking' of the Border as *The Irish Press* characterised the ending.[19] Other commentators and film-makers, however, were to take a much more serious view of the Border in a number of realist dramas of the War of Independence. Indeed, films of the Anglo-Irish War and its legacy of the border were to become very popular with Irish cinema audiences in the 1930s.

Interest in films about the War of Independence needs to be placed in the context of contemporary Ireland. If film-makers were concerned to explore 1930s Ireland they had to look no further than the increasing number of realist novelists and short story writers. If not formally innovative, they were at least challenging consensual images of the country and the vision Eamon de Valera was increasingly casting over it. As Terence Brown notes,[20] the Irish short story of the 1930s and 1940s

> registered a social reality that flew in the face of nationalistic self-congratulation. Instead of de Valera's Gaelic Eden and the uncomplicated satisfactions of Ireland free, the writers revealed a mediocre, dishevelled, often neurotic and depressed petit-bourgeois society that atrophied for want of a liberating idea.

With the notable exception of Michael Farrell's *Some Say Chance* (1934), a story linked to the moral decay of the city about how a mother turns to prostitution when a father emigrates to Australia, film-makers in the 1930s turned their back on an exploration of contemporary Ireland. Had Irish film-makers explored contemporary Ireland in a realist manner it is debatable, anyway, as to how long they would have been tolerated or given financial assistance. One of the most successful new Irish writers of this period was Liam O'Flaherty, whose banned contemporary novel, *The Puritan*, was very effectively adapted in French by Jeff Musso in 1938. This story concerns a young journalist and religious fanatic who murders a woman whom he deems immoral. His guilt at her murder leads him to the depraved haunts he previously despised until in the end he confesses his crime to a prostitute. If the film had been submitted to the Film Censor, like the book it too would certainly have been banned. Instead of the production of such incisive contemporary films a selective 'realism' required a revisiting of the War of Independence and an exploration of the military and personal response but not the social and political struggles in that conflict.

This approach had been established as early as 1929 when a silent version of another O'Flaherty book, *The Informer*, was made in Britain by American-born director of German films, Arthur Robison. Six years later John Ford chose O'Flaherty's book as the basis of the first of his Irish-theme sound films. Ford's film proved very popular when released in Ireland, though Irish audiences were lucky even to see it. Banned by the Film Censor, it was one of only 17 films during 1930–39 where the Censor's banning decision was reversed by the Censorship of Films Appeal Board. The success of *The Informer* (1935) led to Ford's second Irish project, Sean O'Casey's Easter Rising play, *The Plough and the Stars* (1936).

A protégé of Ford's was Irish-born, Brian Desmond Hurst, who had worked with Ford in Hollywood and made an Irish-theme film, *Irish Hearts* (1934), from the novel *The Night Nurse*, by Dr J. Johnston Abraham. This was a story about a young surgeon whose love for two women is bound up with his struggle against an outbreak of typhus. In 1935 Hurst made a 40-minute version of J. M. Synge's *Riders to the Sea* which was funded by English star Gracie Fields, and included Sara Allgood, Denis Johnston, Kevin Guthrie, Ria Mooney and Shelah Richards. It played to mixed reviews when Gracie Fields was performing at the cine-variety

Theatre Royal in July 1936.[21] Hurst also made the first British film on the War of Independence, *Ourselves Alone* (1936).

Set in 1921, *Ourselves Alone* concerns how RIC Inspector Hannay (John Lodge) and English intelligence officer Captain Wiltshire (John Loder), are both in love with the same girl, Maureen Elliott (Antoinette Cellier). When Wiltshire unwittingly kills Maureen's brother Terence (Niall McGinnis), a secret IRA leader, Hannay claims responsibility recognising that it is Wiltshire whom Maureen really loves. *Ourselves Alone* proved to be a popular if limited rendition of the military struggle an *Irish Press* writer declared[22]

> This is probably the sweetest piece of excitingly unhistoric history that has come our way. Will it be the 'lie agreed upon' when they print the sagas?

In another review of the film the writer added[23] that *Ourselves Alone* 'proves conclusively that we like IRA pictures no matter how inaccurately they are done'. He concluded that while the film was 'a long lie . . . perhaps the truth wouldn't make a film — that Elstree could produce'.

The first indigenous attempt to counter this 'lie' in the 1930s was made the previous year, 1935, when a silent version of the title story of Frank O'Connor's first book of short stories, *Guests of the Nation*, was screened. Somewhat exceptional in the O'Connor canon, this War of Independence story was adapted by playwright and director, Denis Johnston, during the summers of 1933 and 1934, into a 50-minute film. O'Connor's story is narrated by Bonaparte, one of two young IRA men guarding two English prisoners, Belcher and Hawkins, in an isolated cottage during the War of Independence. The short story opens with friendly repartee between the Irish and English soldiers and a clear indication of a close bond between the four. But unknown to Bonaparte and his friend, Noble, the two soldiers are being held as hostages. When the English authorities refuse to exchange IRA prisoners for the soldiers, and execute four IRA men, Donovan and Feeney, an IRA leader and Intelligence Officer, respectively, arrive at night to carry out the retribution. Bonaparte and Noble are shocked but co-operate as Donovan carries out the executions. Hawkins, a pro-pounder of Communist and Anarchist ideas, offers to change sides but he is shot first. Belcher, dour and quiet, nonetheless speaks at length at his own graveside in the bog. When the IRA men return to the cottage the old woman who lives there suspects what has happened and falls to her knees to pray; Noble does the same. The story ends with Bonaparte stating that he never felt the same about anything that happened afterwards.

Johnston's film follows the outline of the original story but there are a number of additional scenes in the film. While O'Connor's story focuses exclusively on events at or near the cottage, the film shows a marching column of IRA men, an ambush of an English convoy at which two IRA men are captured, tense developments outside Kilmainham Jail while people pray for the IRA prisoners, a woman courier who passes on the news of the executions, a dance which is alluded to in the story and a playing down of the execution scene. While the story details the individual response to the executions, the film uses the simple device of showing four pairs of footprints in the mud going out and only two returning. In addition, the tempo of the editing, in particular at the ambush, contrasts with the slow pace of the story. In fact this section is clearly influenced by Eisenstein's montage: extreme close-ups of 'typed' faces intercut in rapid succession provides a strong sense of IRA camaraderie, unity and determination.

While the bathos and concluding isolation of the narrator are absent from the film, there is ultimately little difference between short story and film. Despite occasional representations of collective action, motivation and conflict are collapsed into emotion as individual actions dominate the conflict. Little indication is given as to why the people were fighting, merely that they were pawns in a system outside their control.

The film was produced on a minimal budget: interior sets were built outdoors in a Dublin backgarden,[24] while the inexperience and lack of resources can be seen most obviously in scenes where sun reflectors were used to focus light on actors. But the film did include a wide range of people who were already well known or were about to become famous. Mary Manning worked on the script while her brother John was one of the camera-people. The actors included Barry Fitzgerald, Shelah Richards, Denis O'Dea, Hilton Edwards, Fred Johnson and Cyril Cusack.

The film was premièred at the Gate Theatre on 20 January 1935. Amongst the audience was the Fianna Fáil Minister for Defence, Frank Aiken, who had supplied armaments for the film, and Frank O'Connor who had played a minor part in the film as a member of the Flying Column. O'Connor said afterwards[25] that he was surprised at the result of the work of this enterprising company. In its own way it is as fine as anything produced by the Russian producers, and I think that the Government would be well advised to provide the necessary money to have the picture re-filmed. It would add to the prestige of the Irish abroad, as showing the great spirit of the War of Independence, and the spirit of comradeship that existed between the opposing forces, as well as the devotion to duty of the men who fought . . . [The film] tells the story better than literature could ever draw it. It is a piece of film work that Ireland can really be proud of.

The press response was generally favourable, forgiving the film's technical crudities, while concentrating on the film's tragic resolution and exhorting all involved with the production to continue making films. *The Irish Independent*'s J. A. P.[26] (Joseph A. Power) regarded it as the best picture yet made in Ireland despite not having the experience and aids of Hollywood or Elstree. He added that Johnston had raised the story 'to the heights of tragedy'. *The Irish Press*[27] agreed when describing it as 'an epic'.

If *Guests of the Nation* presented the War of Independence in terms of tragedy, *The Dawn* released the following year had no such inhibitions and as a result set off a lively controversy. By any account *The Dawn* is one of the most remarkable films made in Ireland. The circumstances of its making are as surprising as the finished film. Tom Cooper, a Killarney garage and cinema owner, set out with a group of friends in 1934/5 to make the first full-length indigenous Irish sound feature. The film, set during the struggle between the IRA and Black and Tans, was made 15 years after this most bitter phase of the War of Independence had ended. Donal O'Cahill, who played a central role as planner, co-writer and actor, wrote an account of the making of *The Dawn* in 1937. He reported that the catalyst for the film came from Joseph Power's repeated suggestions in *The Irish Independent* about the possibilities of film production in Ireland. These prompted Tom Cooper to make a film in Killarney. Cooper assembled his friends and acquaintances who began to construct a sound-proof studio and make improvised film equipment, including processing facilities and editing tables. 'Only the barest essentials were imported', according to O'Cahill.[28] Cooper involved the Kerry Electric Company whose manager became Chief Technician. A large building with electricity supply nearby was adapted as a studio; 50

yards away rushes were viewed at the 'Picturedrome'. Without even discussing the topic of the film, an unstated assumption led to 'an obvious theme'. The subject of the War of Independence had a particular poignancy for some of the actors in that they participated in events similar to those depicted in the film. Production began in May 1935 and involved a total of 250 people who worked on every available Sunday and holiday with night work often continuing until 5 a.m. throughout the summer.

When *The Dawn* was released in Dublin in August 1936 it 'electrified' the city, according to *Irish Press* film critic Liam MacGabhann.[29] It had a three-week run at the 2,057-seat Capitol which, taken in conjunction with *Ourselves Alone*'s five-week record breaking-run at the 620-seat Grafton shortly before, indicated the popularity of Irish War of Independence films. Its receipts compared favourably with those for 'other outstanding pictures' and thus probably proved to be the only Irish-produced sound fiction feature to recoup all its production costs and more in Ireland.[30] *The Dawn*'s popularity may be linked to the radical nationalist polemic it articulated: 'the fight must go on', a direct statement to the audience declares towards the end. Such a view was espoused by Fianna Fáil with its anti-Treaty origins and, indeed, that party was ideologically mobilised to underpin *The Dawn*'s message. The motto of the Fianna Fáil newspaper, *The Irish Press*, Do-chum glóire Dé agus onóra na h-Éireann (For the glory of God and the honour of Ireland), was the prominent caption on *The Dawn*'s publicity poster.[31] Thus Fianna Fáil, with its radical republican, anti-Treaty background, would have been in agreement with *The Dawn*'s conclusion and its clear reference to the continuing existence of the border in the 1930s. Of course, Fianna Fáil's rhetoric about the border did not inhibit it from suppressing any nationalist military adventures against the Northern Ireland state from the mid-1930s onwards.

Reviews of *The Dawn* reflected the moral and political preoccupations of the period. The film's absence of sex was favourably commented on though a surviving British print of the film includes a drunken Black and Tan molesting a woman serving in a bar, a scene which appears to have been deleted from surviving Irish prints. Liam MacGabhann[32] declared that the 'kiss close-up' was 'despised' by *The Dawn*. A writer to *The Connacht Tribune* recorded a more generalised disaffection amongst Irish-Irelanders with the content of Anglo-American cinema and its influence in Ireland. The writer also criticised the sexual mores and class preoccupations of film actors on and off the screen:[33]

> There are, of course, those who, taking as their criterion the honky-tonk, Tin Pan Alley dope served up to a patient film-going public by Hollywood's much married 'stars' and the wooden snobs of Elstree will go to an Irish film prepared to find fault.

By contrast, the writer declared, *The Dawn*

> is very fine in every way, but especially in the fair, impartial light it throws on the historical aspect of the fight for freedom in the Anglo-Irish war. This film should really have been officially sponsored by the Old I.R.A. Association, since it gives a better idea of their struggle than all the literature that has piled up around those stirring days and the heroes who faced the might of the mightiest empire of all time.

An English priest, Fr Valentine, Director of London's Catholic Film Society, wrote a somewhat hysterical piece after *The Dawn* was shown in London. He complained that the film did not deal with de Valera's 'experiment in the corporate State' and he enquired why the film was seeking 'to fan the flames of dying hate'. Quoting a programme note that stated that the film ends in a somewhat 'Pudovkin manner', Fr Valentine declared that not only was the film in the Pudovkin manner but was also in the 'Soviet tradition'. Overall, the interpretation of the film could lead to the view that 'Ireland today is a fit breeding ground for anti-clericalism and Communism'.[34]

This is a misleading and, indeed, ironically inaccurate reading of the film. *The Dawn*, in fact, supresses any social tensions which might appear between the Irish themselves. The film's main nationalist catalysts, the Malones and the O'Donovans, clearly belong to a different social stratum than the rest, as is indicated by their houses and accents. Indeed, the men under IRA leader Dan O'Donovan's (Tom Cooper) command are most likely property-less workers. The film does not pursue this issue, concentrating instead on military struggle with humorous and romantic inter-ludes. In passing it is worth noting that what work (other than military work) is represented concerns a brief cleaning up of O'Donovan's front lawn. This work is performed by one of his workers (who is also an IRA man) to indicate normality to a raiding military force. The work in the garden (with its arcadian overtones) is the nearest any of the characters get to agricultural production. Another indication of the suppression of social difference in the film is the manner in which the taint of traitor since Fenian times is treated in a 'respectable' family, the Malones. The origins of this taint are displayed in a pre-credits silent sequence. Set in the 1860s, it is shown to be wrongly ascribed when an informer, ill-kempt and stooped, reminiscent of Black William in *Rory O'More*, is seen slinking into a wood as the Fenians are captured. When it transpires during the film's surprising denouement that the English-accented Billy Malone (Donal O'Cahill), a grandson of the Fenian, is in fact the IRA's key intelligence officer the family are reintegrated into the community.

Irish unity is further reinforced through the representation of the Royal Irish Constabulary. Brian Malone (Brian O'Sullivan), Billy's brother, is expelled from the IRA because of his grandfather's tainted memory. Out of pique he joins the RIC, but on witnessing Black and Tan brutality and hearing of an impending attack on the IRA, he deserts to warn them. With his father (James Gleeson) and his younger brother, he eventually joins in the IRA's ambush of the Black and Tans. At another point in the film, an RIC man is seen passing intelligence information to the IRA. Interestingly, this sympathetic representation of the RIC may have aided its censorship passage in Northern Ireland where it was cut in three places while *Ourselves Alone* was banned.[35] Of course, Northern Ireland's unionists would have regarded such RIC behaviour as 'traitorous'.

While there were no contemporary critical comments regarding the naturalising of social difference in the film, there was concern about the use of nature in the military sequences:[36]

> It perhaps gives too pleasant a picture of the guerilla war in Ireland . . . They loll in beautiful wooded glades or on rocky crags overlooking a picturesque winding road. The sun is beating down on them as they sing and joke with each other, while waiting for the lorries of the Tans to come round the bend to death.

March of Time's originator and European representative, Louis de Rochemont, encapsulated the production's diverse elements when he described Tom Cooper as 'a sort of Rousseau of filmdom, preaching the return to the elements of his craft . . .'[37]

The Dawn also came to be used as a metaphor for a nascent film industry:

> *The Dawn* may well herald the dawn for which most Irish cinemagoers have been anxiously awaiting, when we shall be released from the bondage of Hollywood. The title, therefore, may be symbolical.[38]

Liam MacGabhann commented[39] that

> The Killarney men have shown the way. Support and not surprise should be the outcome. Killarney must be made the Hollywood of Ireland, if Irish history and Irish culture are to be presented fairly and preserved intact in celluloid record. We want another Killarney film, and the subject must be the concentrated beauty of Irish ideals.

Writing a review of *The Dawn* for *An Phoblacht* (The Republic), Maud Gonne MacBride declared that the film was 'a triumphant justification of that [two years] work both from an artistic and national standard'. She observed that[40]

> there are thrills, breathless enough to satisfy the taste and craving of many to forget the monotony of dull and uneventful lives, which have been the success of so many Wild West and of the gangster films.
> It establishes not the possibility but the certainty that Ireland will be able to compete in film production with Hollywood or any of the great film industries of the world, and that while we shall always enjoy the artistic work of other nations, the work of our own artists is equally great. We owe a debt of gratitude for this to [Tom Cooper].

Even Donal O'Cahill said that[41]

> When all is said, if we have achieved nothing else we have blazed the trail and proved beyond all doubt that Irishmen can make films in Ireland.

But it was not to be. Hibernia Films, Cooper's company, made only one more film, *Uncle Nick* (1938), and Donal O'Cahill, who established a breakaway group, made only one film, *The Islandman*

(1939). *Uncle Nick* was produced and directed by Cooper. It concerns a rich but miserly returned 'Yank', Nicholas Skinner (Jerry O'Mahony), who is beset by all except one of his relatives who try to get their hands on his hidden gold. When he is kidnapped, and the gold stolen, the police are called. Perhaps, it was comforting in economically stringent Ireland to be moralising about how money only brings greed. Nevertheless, *The Irish Times*,[42] somewhat in awe of Cooper's achievements, declared that Cooper 'has performed feats bordering on the miraculous'. The *Saturday Herald* cautioned[43] that there was 'still a long hard road to travel before they can hope to fight in the market abreast with foreign competitors'.

Following the international success of *Man of Aran* (1934) it was hardly surprising that O'Cahill's choice of location, if not theme, was similar to Robert Flaherty. *The Islandman* (which is also known as *West of Kerry*), promoted a similar set of values, though unlike *Man of Aran*, it included an explicit depiction of the rural/urban divide. In *The Islandman* a Dublin medical student, Neil, goes on holiday to the Blasket Islands. While there he falls in love with Eileen, but she is already 'promised' to a local fisherman, Liam. Back in Dublin Neil hears Eileen singing on the radio and decides to return to the Blaskets and settle there. Eileen's and Neil's love cannot be hidden but before there is a resolution of the triangular relationship Liam falls overboard during a fishing expedition. Neil rescues him but he is badly hurt. Before he dies at home he joins Eileen's and Neil's hands together, thus accepting their relationship. The cast included Cecil Ford, Eileen Curran, Brian O'Sullivan and Gabriel Fallon.

The Islandman was screened for a week at the Carlton, Dublin from 31 March 1939. Both *The Irish Times* and *Saturday Herald* regarded it as marking another milestone towards an Irish film industry. There is the inevitable comparison with *Man of Aran*.[44] Indeed, the *Saturday Herald* went so far as to declare that Robert Flaherty's seascapes had been taken as models for the Blaskets' film. The *Dublin Evening Mail*[45] prescribed more use of 'God's gifts of ocean and rock to build up a background for the story, which would have conveyed the eternal struggles and triumphs of the islanders against nature'. Liam MacGabhann[46] thought an opportunity had been available to bring out 'the fineness of the old Gaelic life against the sordidness of the city half-life'. He also complained about bringing what he termed the 'red triangle' to the Blaskets. The triangular relationship between Neil, Liam and

Eileen, 'the belle of the Blaskets', as the *Mail* described her, also brought out the disapproval of the *Herald* and *Mail*.

This is both ironic and instructive. In 1937 O'Cahill[47] had recalled how he had told Cooper in the early discussions on *The Dawn*, in 1934, that he 'hadn't seen three films in as many years and, unless Hollywood and Elstree gave up playing on the eternal triangle, I should feel no inclination to improve'. Whether they may have wished it or not the Kerry film-makers had had their agenda set for them by Hollywood in their unconscious adoption of its traditional narrative forms. To have followed the logic of that form of film-making would have required a serious engagement with commercial cinema. But for most of them film was a temporary interlude to other activities, which was one reason why there was no continuity of film production in Ireland.

Tom Cooper, for example, was expanding his exhibition interests having owned one cinema, the Casino, Killarney, when making *The Dawn*. By 1947 he had four Casinos (Tramore, Rathmore, Doneraile and Killarney). For others, such as Denis Johnston and Jimmy O'Dea, film was merely a temporary interlude to their widely different interests in drama and variety. Only the Irish Film Society provided a serious and sustained commitment to film-making and the person who was central to its emergence was Liam O'Leary. O'Leary had been a member of a fringe theatre company, the Dublin Little Theatre Guild, an active founder member of the Irish Film Society and a writer on cinema in the monthly publication, *Ireland To-Day* (1936–8) and other publications. The Film Society's one notable drama success as war approached was a 20-minute film, *Foolsmate* (1940), based on an incident during the Black and Tan war. It was directed and photographed by Brendan Stafford from a script by Geoffrey Dalton. Stafford was later to become an experienced director and cameraman working in Britain and Ireland, sometimes with Liam O'Leary.

Thus by the end of the 1930s Irish fiction film production by private individuals remained periodic and intermittent. The absence of any organised means of learning about film-making in Ireland was a crucial hindrance to the development of a native industry. The example of *The Dawn*, as one writer[48] noted, provided one solid fact with which to counter the querying of indigenous film-making ability. However, potential private investment in Ireland was very small despite the rapid expansion in industrial development under the wing of economic protectionism in the 1930s. No private concern showed any serious willingness to invest the sums required for an indigenous film industry which could produce films for distribution abroad. The uncertainty about distribution and the absence of experienced technicians and production facilities in Ireland made it unlikely that native private investment would enter this economically hazardous business. Thus lay and religious commentators interested in promoting a native film industry, looked to the state to establish one. However much the state may have desired an Irish film industry it showed a marked reluctance to enter this unpredictable business and was more concerned in the first instance with satisfying its own informational needs.

Notes

1. *Dáil Debates*, Vol. 39, Cols. 1464–66, 2 July 1931. It is worthwhile recalling the content of *Storm Over Asia* as it helps place MacEntee's comments in their anti-colonial context. 'During the British occupation of Mongolia a young Mongolian partisan is seriously wounded and captured. He is discovered to be a descendant of Genghis Khan and the various representatives of international capitalism decide to try to set him up as a puppet king. However, he escapes, and leads the people in their liberation' (quoted from *BFI Distribution Library Catalogue*, 1978, p. 36). The writer adds that some critics tried to make out that the soldiers were White Russians, but 'the imperialist forces are quite obviously British, and are quite openly protecting capitalism in the shape of American trading interests' (ibid.).
2. *Senate Debates*, Vol. 13, Col. 1010, 7 May 1930.
3. 'The Talkies', *Irish Statesman*, Vol. 13, No. 14, p. 268, 7 December 1929.
4. Kevin Rockett, 'Film Censorship and the State', *Film Directions* Special Censorship Issue, Vol. 3, No. 9, 1980, p. 13.
5. *Irish Times*, 30 April 1935, p. 4; 7 May 1935, p. 6; and 14 May 1935, p. 4.
6. *Irish Independent*, 8 February 1930, p. 10.
7. *Dublin Evening Mail*, 8 February 1930, p. 6.
8. *Irish Statesman*, Vol. 13, No. 25, p. 497, 22 February 1930.
9. The account of the events at the Savoy is taken principally from 'Scene in a Dublin Cinema', *Irish Independent*, 12 February 1930, p. 11. See also *Irish Times*, 12 February. p. 7.
10. 'Hollywood in Dublin', *Irish Statesman*, Vol. 13, No. 2, p. 34, 14 September 1929. Frank Borzage's interest in an Irish-theme film may have been partly motivated by his Dublin-born wife.
11. *Dublin Evening Mail*, 13 August 1930, p. 2.
12. *Saturday Herald*, 2 August 1930, p. 2.
13. *Dublin Evening Mail*, 12 August 1930, p. 7.

14. Liam O'Laoghaire, *Invitation to the Film*, Tralee: The Kerryman, 1945, p. 157.

15. *Monthly Film Bulletin* complained about the film's 'halting and uncertain' production, the 'conventional acting' and the 'tiresome dragging in of "local colour"' which all lead to an ' "amateurish" film', Vol. 5, No. 51, 31 March 1938, p. 69.

16. *Dublin Evening Mail*, 8 January 1938, p. 9.

17. 'Border Blarney Held', *Irish Press*, 18 January 1938, p. 5.

18. *Saturday Herald*, 8 January 1938, p. 7.

19. Op. cit.

20. Terence Brown, *Ireland: A Social and Cultural History, 1922–79*, London: Fontana, 1981, p. 159.

21. The enthusiasm of the *Dublin Evening Mail*, 11 July 1936, p. 9, and 14 July, p. 7, was not shared by *Irish Times*, 14 July, p. 4: '. . . seldom . . . has any work of art been transferred from its own medium into another with such lamentable insensitiveness'.

22. *Irish Press*, 14 July 1936, p. 5.

23. Ibid., 21 July 1936, p. 5.

24. See stills supplied by Denis Johnston in Kevin Rockett, *Film and Ireland: A Chronicle*, Dublin: A Sense of Ireland, 1980 (booklet).

25. 'First Wholly-Irish Film Shown', *Irish Press*, 21 January 1935, p. 7.

26. 'Fine All-Irish Amateur Film', *Irish Independent*, 21 January 1935, p. 7.

27. *Irish Press*, 21 January 1935, p. 7.

28. Donal O'Cahill, 'And so we made *The Dawn*', *Father Matthew Record*, Vol. 30, No. 4, April 1937, pp. 215–18.

29. '*The Dawn* Declared a Triumph', *Irish Press*, 25 August 1936, p. 5.

30. 'Enthusiasm for Kerry Film', *Irish Independent*, 22 August 1936, p. 12.

31. O'Cahill, 'And so we made *The Dawn*', p. 218.

32. *Irish Press*, 25 August 1936.

33. An Cathach, quoted, *Irish Press*, 26 January 1937, p. 5.

34. *Catholic Herald*, 25 March 1937, p. 10.

35. O'Leary, 1976, p. 23.

36. 'N.', *Leader*, Vol. 72, No. 19, 6 June 1936, p. 443.

37. Quoted, Alfred Dennis, *Father Matthew Record*, Vol. 29, No. 10, October 1936, p. 557.

38. *Evening Herald*, 22 August 1936, p. 7.

39. *Irish Press*, 26 January 1937, p. 5.

40. M. G. McB., 'Studio in East Avenue', *An Phoblacht*, Vol. 11, No. 13, 6 June 1936, p. 1.

41. O'Cahill, 'And so we made *The Dawn*', p. 218.

42. *Irish Times*, 4 April 1938, p. 4.

43. *Saturday Herald*, 2 April 1938, p. 9.

44. *Irish Times*, 3 April 1939, p. 4; *Saturday Herald*. 1 April 1939, p. 9.

45. *Dublin Evening Mail*, 1 April 1939, p. 4.

46. '*The Islandman* — What World's Away', *Irish Press*, 4 April 1939, p. 5.

47. O'Cahill, 'And so we made *The Dawn*', p. 215.

48. J. D. S. (John D. Sheridan), *Father Matthew Record*, Vol. 29, No. 9, September 1936, p. 482.

3

Documentaries

Kevin Rockett

Ethnicity and landscape

It is a bitter testimony to the history of film production in Ireland that even in the relatively inexpensive category of documentaries the best-known film, *Man of Aran* (1934), should be foreign-produced. Superficially, at least, Irish economies of scale explain why this should be. In the stringent economic reality of 1930s Ireland, Robert Flaherty's British-produced *Man of Aran* had a budget, as an originally conceived *silent* film, far greater than any indigenous *fiction sound* film until the late 1950s. With £30,000 to £40,000, Flaherty had the luxury of shooting 37 hours of film over two years on the Aran Islands to make the 74-minute film.[1] Not only did he have a flexible time schedule and an indulgent budget but his lifestyle on Aran contrasted rather severely with the island primitivism depicted in this 'poetic documentary'.[2]

Nevertheless, it would be an understatement to suggest that the production and subsequent screening of *Man of Aran* was anything less than an Irish national event. Throughout its production not only was its progress treated as news but many visited the islands to observe the making of the film. (Denis Johnston's play *Storm Song* is a direct result of his experiences while visiting the *Man of Aran* set.) When *Man of Aran* was premièred in Dublin on 6 May 1934 President de Valera, members of the Executive Council, the diplomatic Corps, and many others including W. B. Yeats and Eoin MacNeill, were amongst the audience. The overwhelmingly positive endorsement of the film as a realistic representation of the Aran Islands belied its careful, even painstaking, construction.[3] Its critical reception, especially by Dorothy Macardle,[4] a writer

71

closely associated with President de Valera, also reinforced the retreat from 1930s social and economic reality which was also to be seen in the fiction films of the period. In this instance the displacement was not towards a limited assessment of the War of Independence but on to the mythic humanism of *Man of Aran*.

With such a depoliticised notion of documentary being endorsed by a radical nationalist, it is hardly surprising that Irish documentary production did not follow the British route in the 1930s. There, an active group of film-makers presented an oppositional cinema through documentary production with their focus on the working class and social problems. Irish film-makers made little or no attempt to explore such a reality in the 1930s and chose to reproduce in the main both the ahistorical ethnicity represented in *Man of Aran* and its economic off-shoots, the tourist-landscape film.

One of the first of these films was made by J. N. G. Davidson. He knew the Aran Islands well and accompanied Flaherty on his first visit there in late 1931 as an employee of the Empire Marketing Board's Film Unit. Abandoning the experimentation indicated in *By Accident*, he made an ethnic short, *Dancers of Aran* (1934): 'A rather slight exercise in the methods of our more advanced school of documentary', according to the *Monthly Film Bulletin*.[5]

Man of Aran spurred the government to its single documentary project of the 1930s. Taking advantage of the *Man of Aran* production, the government proposed that an Irish-language short should be made to accompany the main film in cinemas. To this end the Dáil voted a grant of £200[6] to a Flaherty-produced short intended to present on film the Irish story-telling tradition. *The Irish Press*[7] was so impressed it published an editorial, 'The Irish Talkie Comes'. This called for a short, professional production which Ireland could be proud of. The film, *Oidhche Sheanchais* (Storyteller's Night), was, surprisingly, filmed at Gaumont Studios, probably during the time the *Man of Aran* cast were dubbing the soundtrack for *Man of Aran*. The storyteller was the well known *seanchaí*, Tomás Ó Díorain. He related a sea fishing story at the hearth of a rural cottage. His audience consisted of the principal members of the *Man of Aran* cast: Maggie Dirrane, 'Tiger' King, Patch Ruadh and Michaeleen.

Though not shown as a support to *Man of Aran* when screened in Dublin in March 1935, nearly a year after its projected release, it nevertheless received a reasonably polite reception.[8] The limitations of the film identified by reviewers may in part be explained by the film's small budget. Another reason may have been

Flaherty's lack of Irish which no doubt contributed to the film's static form. Writing a decade after the film's release, Liam O'Leary gave the most accurate and blunt explanation for the film's shortcomings:[9]

> The script which was foisted on [Flaherty] by our enlightened Department of Education was utterly devoid of any filmic content . . .

A more complete view of the West of Ireland was to be found in Michael Eldridge's study of a small farmer and his community in *The Life of Michael Flaherty*. He was seen drawing seaweed for manure, cultivating a potato patch, co-operating with his neighbours and fishing. Cottage family life and a pilgrimage to Croagh Patrick were also shown. The depiction of this harsher realism of the countryside is rare in the 1930s and 1940s as uninhabited landscape began to be used to promote the developing Irish tourist industry. These tourist-landscape films were produced mainly by the Irish Tourist Association under the auspices of its secretary, David Barry. J. N. G. Davidson, Brendan Stafford and Richard Hayward were amongst the directors of these films. As the retreat from contemporary social issues continued, more general political and national questions took hold as film subjects.

Fianna Fáil and political documentary

March of Time can be credited with making the first filmed documentary overviews of Ireland when in 1936 and 1943 they made editions in Ireland. Sensitive to the depiction of Ireland on film, the Fianna Fáil government ensured that the Irish Legation in Washington was satisfied that both photography and commentary would be entirely objective before the crew of the 1944 edition came to Ireland. It was also revealed in the Dáil that staged shots of a social function in Dublin which had been objected to would not be used in the film.[10]

March of Time's *The Irish Question* (1944) contrasted 'vigorous and aggressive' Belfast with the rural life of the South. The film mainly focused on the South's agriculture and educational, religious and political institutions. Some of the images, such as barefoot children entering a rural school, could hardly have pleased the government. Despite March of Time's reputation for realism, when it came to explaining the crucial contemporary issue, Irish neutrality during World War II, it retreated into the stereotype of Irish irrationality or illogic:

> Ireland's unhappy history under British rule was an important factor in Eire's decision to remain neutral, a decision which the freedom-loving nations of the world found difficult to comprehend. But those who would understand this proud and sensitive people today and in the future should look, not to logic, but to the poetry of the Irish.[11]

Towards the end of the war the government turned its attention to a film which was not simply intended to fulfil a news function. However, not everyone was happy with the possibility of government-produced films, especially if they deviated from solely informational needs. In 1946, Liam O'Leary wrote[12] that 'one can see the easy primrose path to ballyhoo propaganda, chauvinistic and false but geared to the machinery of Party'. There is no doubt but that the reference was to the government's sponsorship of a film to commemorate the one hundredth anniversary of the death of Thomas Davis, *A Nation Once Again* (1946), which had been first shown three months earlier. Ironically, Liam O'Leary appears in the film as a member of a concert's audience.

Mixing narrated documentary and dramatised historical sequences, *A Nation Once Again* presents Davis's ideas in the context of contemporary Ireland. Davis, who was 'a prophet of a cultural revival', anticipated government publications policy; Davis, who was 'realist as well as visionary', foresaw turf production, which was expanded on a large scale during World War II to replace the drop in fuel imports; Dublin Airport is 'a symbol of the New Ireland'. An Irish language class echoes Davis's denunciation of industrial Britain by highlighting rural values in its discussion of farmers' work.

As in *The Irish Question*, *A Nation Once Again* focuses on the presentation of the past, since, as the narrator puts it, for Davis 'Ireland's past was his textbook'. In nationalist ideology, the past was usually mobilised to establish the nature of the island-nation, at least for those of a nationalist persuasion. In a relevant sequence which begins with a shot of a cloudy sky, a voice-over declares: 'There it is, a cross in the sky, a portent for the future, the hope that the men of the South and the men of the North may yet meet on the Banks of the Boyne to witness a treaty of mutual concession, oblivion [*sic!*] and eternal friendship. There is a cross in the sky and Ireland must not swerve for its flashing'. This apocalyptic description and imagery is followed by a resonance of pre-Union conciliation: a shot of Dublin port looking towards the sea and a shot of the magnificent eighteenth-century Customs House.

There is, however, a sharper, less conciliatory sequence later in the film. Using images of Irish dancing and of Gaelic football, activities closely identified with modern Irish nationalism, it is asserted that Davis's teaching is

> the sure basis on which to plan a united nation free from shore to shore and the hope of all true Irishmen is that in this as in most things else this man was prophet as well as leader.

An Irish audience did not need to be reminded that 'all true Irish-men' had its inclusions and its exclusions despite the film's earlier, more conciliatory, tone. Nevertheless, the film's lack of reference to religion is striking and, perhaps, it is this unstated secularism, a view espoused by Davis, which might ultimately lead to a resolution of the North-South divide. These issues were generally ignored by reviewers though Liam MacGabhann[13] hoped for a more direct statement on the North:

> the Border problem and our partition wrong was under emphasised. World distribution of this film would have been a good medium of stressing the evil of the crooked lie.

Another writer[14] observed that it was the best argument yet for the establishment of an Irish film studio. A writer in *The Irish Independent*[15] commented that

> We have seen ourselves and our country on the screen often enough. Englishmen, Scotsmen and Americans have come here with their cameras and sent us back their celluloid impressions. Sometimes these impressions made us angry, sometimes we just laughed. Seldom if ever were we satisfied. Admittedly it is not a very big effort — our resources do not lend themselves to big efforts — but it is a step in the right direction. In the cinema, as elsewhere, it is possible to be effective without being spectacular and I venture to say that this is our most effective and most competent essay in film-making to date.

An alternative to this form of State-sponsored propaganda film (which only cost £3,000) had been indicated through the Irish Film Society and its even more modest productions. Though its first film, *Foolsmate*, was a War of Independence drama, awareness of the British documentary movement, and the socially committed documentaries produced in Britain and America, was generated by Liam O'Leary in the 1940s. In his *Invitation to the Film*, published in 1945, he placed himself firmly in the Grierson context of seeing documentary as a social tool showing people how the democratic system and its institutions operate. At a School of Film Techniques organised by O'Leary in 1943, Irish Film Society members showed some of their films which along with *Foolsmate* included *Tibradden* (John White), *Fishing Village* (Peter Sherry), *Campa* (Kevin O'Kelly) on boy scouts, *Dance School* and *Aiséirghe* (1941), both by Liam O'Leary. This last film 'set out to show that true national consciousness goes skin-deep and that the lesson of 1916 has yet to be learned'.[16] The opening showed a sequence of English-language headlines followed by a rapid montage of cinema posters with ironic titles introducing the notion that 47 years after the foundation of the Gaelic League the Irish language was no nearer its restoration than in 1893.

In the 1946 article[17] in which he criticised the production of government propaganda films, O'Leary had asked rhetorically whether the Irish would accept films on social problems:

> Would we stomach the making of films which reveal our less attractive characteristics — our unemployed, our slums, our emigration, our escapism, our trusted educational system?

Eighteen months later O'Leary was to find the ideal outlet for these ideas of socially-committed documentary when he was asked to produce a short election campaign film for Clann na Poblachta (People of the Republic or Republican Family), a new political party. With its policies of radical republicanism and social commitment, the party attracted younger and urban voters. By making this film, O'Leary was to give Fianna Fáil a rude filmic shock only two years after the obfuscation of *A Nation Once Again*. Liam O'Leary was assisted on the making of the film by the cameraman/director from *A Nation Once Again*, Brendan Stafford, and writer Maura Laverty.

To check the mobilisation of the new party, de Valera called an election for February 1948 against a background of serious economic problems and a recent unpopular Supplementary Budget which included big increases in entertainments tax. Though Clann na Poblachta won only ten seats in the general election it was sufficient to help form an inter-party government without Fianna Fáil. The fear of a major breakthrough into Fianna Fáil's electoral support led to bitter attacks on the Clann during the election campaign. One of the targets of that attack was *Our Country*.

The film was made under the banner of Irish Civic Films in a fortnight during December 1947. Irish scenes were intercut by direct camera statements by three of the Clann's principal members, Sean MacBride, Noel Hartnett and Noel Browne. The synchronised sound statements were shot at Elstree after the three flew to England in secret to film them. Our Country, it is declared at the film's opening, it your country. But the short, astringent film lists the failures of Fianna Fáil's 16 years in office: emigration continues (this 'slow bleeding to death of the nation') as queues at Dublin's UK permit office are shown; an unused plough high-lights the failure to increase agricultural production; a shoeless working-class boy is contrasted with images of imported luxury goods; a shop's empty shelves and signs of 'No Eggs', 'No Bacon' emphasise the shortages of even essential foodstuffs. This situa-tion, the narrator tells his listeners, is 'contrary to religion and civilisation'. The narrator asks rhetorically: 'What is wrong with Ireland? Must the population decrease until we are extinct?' The replies come from the three spokespeople and the narrator who demand an afforestation programme and point to the need for well-equipped sanatoria. In conclusion Sean MacBride warned of the dangers of communism, made sure he was seen as explicitly Christian and attacked the lack of policies for the future:

> You the people cannot stand the decadence which is under-mining the spirit of our people. The evils of communism and of State control are the results of public indifference. What we need above all is enthusiasm and an independent public opinion based on Christian social principles. Instead of flag waving, instead of national records and self glorification what is needed is a policy based on reality. Instead of recrimina-tions and self glorification based on past events the need is vision, enthusiasm and a plan for the future.

The film was launched on an unsuspecting public and it was

regarded by *The Irish Times*[18] as a 'departure from the usual run of political propaganda'. This article, entitled 'Film Show in Streets', related how, in Longford, a screen was set up on one side of the main street and the film projector opposite. Later in the evening it was shown in a cinema in the town. *The Irish Times*[19] reported two days later that the film was being seen by thousands in Irish towns and villages which had no cinema. It was being shown in main streets, at fairs and in markets, 'an innovation which has attracted widespread attention . . . [where] . . . the screen has been a wall, the side of a house or a large doorway'. Fifty copies were in distribution throughout the country to 300 cinemas. The film, *The Irish Times* observed, was in the style of an American newsreel.

With Fianna Fáil under serious electoral threat for the first time since taking office in 1932, the anti-Fianna Fáil response being generated by the film could not be ignored. In an editorial, 'Their Secret Weapon', the Fianna Fáil newspaper, *The Irish Press*,[20] sought to defuse the film's impact. It attacked the film's lack of reference to Clann na Poblachta: 'They are not very proud of it, however, for neither in the publicity nor in the commentary is there mention of the film's authorship'. (Or that the three speakers were Clann candidates in the election.) Indeed, there is no reference to Fianna Fáil in the film either, though the implication is clear. The editorial concluded with the most basic of all nationalist taints, association with England:

> When documentary films are made at Elstree about social conditions in England the work of municipal authorities is always acknowledged and public men and officials are usually represented as chief actors. But this film, which was also made there, was about 'our country' — Ireland. Why the difference, and why the secrecy? Unless, of course, the Clann had good reason to be ashamed of their propaganda film even before they put it on the road.

These hints at complicity with outside forces were picked up by Fianna Fáil's Minister for Health, Sean MacEntee, in a speech the next day. MacEntee[21] sought to link MacBride and the Clann with the IRA, communists and the English. He hinted that the IRA may have been the source of the Clann's funds and specifically for the making of *Our Country*. (MacBride had been Chief of Staff of the IRA in 1936 but he accepted constitutional politics with the 1937 Constitution.) If it were true, MacEntee asked, that the

Clann 'had no money', how could the Clann

> pay for the film which the Elstree Studios had made for them?
> This film was a bogus film, in so far as it purported to give a
> fair and average presentation of the conditions of our people.
> It was a lie from beginning to end.

MacEntee continued with the claim that MacBride's speeches
gave succour to anti-nationalists. He also suggested that the Clann
'had been financed by an international organisation with its Irish
headquarters in Belfast'. This was probably a reference to the Irish
Workers League which was reconstituted as the Communist Party
of Ireland in 1948 and is somewhat ironic in light of MacBride's
anti-communism. MacEntee then proceeded to attack Liam
O'Leary who 'was not a grocer's assistant', as he appears in the
film

> but a civil servant or ex-civil servant who had been given
> special facilities to act as producer to the Abbey Theatre. In
> this film he was acting as a bogus grocer's assistant, pleading
> a bogus scarcity to a bogus customer, who certainly did not
> look as if she were suffering from malnutrition, notwith-
> standing the placard 'No Eggs', 'No Bacon', no this and no
> that, so prominently displayed in the film. The one essential
> element missing from that statement was 'No Truth'.

MacEntee then tried to link the Irish Film Society to the production of the film. In doing so he sought to paint the Society as pro-
communist by declaring that he 'had been struck by the very large
proportion of pictures of Russian origin which the Society had
been showing over the past few years'. Coming from a politician
who had praised Pudovkin less than 20 years earlier, MacEntee's
turn about may in part be explained by political expediency or
simply be part of the general wave of anti-Communism in the post-
war Western world. Nevertheless, the Secretary of the IFS, L. G.
Carr Lett, felt it necessary to write to *The Irish Times*[22] pointing out
that only six of the thirty-two films shown in the previous four
years were of Russian origin. He also denied that the IFS' 'slender
resources' had been placed at the disposal of the film-makers.

MacEntee made two further points in his speech. He wondered
whether footage had been provided by the Irish (*sic*) Film Institute
since the Institute received state funds.

These subventions were not intended to facilitate the dissemination of lying propagandist films about this country,
whether that dissemination took place here or abroad.

This is an odd allegation since the National Film Institute of
Ireland was a very conservative lay Catholic body, and included
two friends of de Valera's amongst its twelve-person list of sub-
scribers when it was registered as a company in 1945: Professor
Alfred O'Rahilly of University College Cork and Padraig Ó
Caoimh, Secretary of the Gaelic Athletic Association. MacEntee's
other point was that he was sure that

the managers of reputable [picture] houses . . . would refuse
to show it because it was one brazen lie from beginning to
end. If they did show it, the public would know that they were
showing it not as the proprietor of picture houses, but as
political propagandists.

The cinema owners, however, had an excellent reason for showing
the film: their self interest in ousting Fianna Fáil from office. Two
weeks earlier, on 16 January, the October Supplementary Budget
increases in entertainments tax came into force. Within six months
of taking office the coalition government rescinded the entertainments tax increases. It was not until 20 years later with the release
of *The Rocky Road to Dublin* that another independently-produced
documentary provoked such public interest and controversy.

Post-war modernisation and government films

Despite the production of a small number of information films by
an Army film unit and independent companies during World War
II as part of war preparations,[23] it was not until the late 1940s that
film came to be used regularly in information campaigns. The
Department of Local Government (for whom Liam O'Leary made
road safety films) took the initiative. It was not, however, until
Noel Browne became Minister for Health during the 1948-51
coalition government's period of office that professionally-made
drama-documentaries were made. Some of these were directed by
playwright and actor Gerard Healy, and featured many well-
known actors. Tuberculosis, diptheria and hygiene featured in
these accomplished films.[24]

The drama-documentary film initiative of the Department of Health was only one aspect of the promotion of film-making by the coalition government. This was to be expected since Clann na Poblachta had promised to establish an Irish film industry in its 1948 general election manifesto. To this end, in 1950, the Minister for Industry and Commerce, Liam Cosgrave, reported in the Dáil that the Industrial Development Authority had been instructed to explore the feasibility of establishing a film industry in Ireland.[25] And, as Minister for External Affairs, Sean MacBride set up a Cultural Relations Committee within his Department.

Liam O'Leary, who was invited to join the committee, wrote an Advisory Report in 1949 in which he set out the case for funding of films. The first film project of the Cultural Relations Committee, *W. B. Yeats — A Tribute* (1950), concerned the life and work of Yeats. It was produced by the National Film Institute of Ireland, the main producer of government-sponsored films in the 1940s and 1950s. Scripted by John D. Sheridan, it was photographed and directed by George Fleischmann and the sound was recorded by Peter Hunt, These two latter names recur on documentary film credits throughout the post-war period. Peter Hunt and his wife Iris had come to Ireland from England and set up a sound recording studio in Dublin's St Stephen's Green. George Fleischmann had a much less conventional introduction to Ireland. During the war, while working as a Luftwaffe cameraman, the reconaissance aeroplane in which he was travelling crash-landed in Co. Waterford. On his release from internment he was reunited with his 35mm Arriflex and he began to work on Irish short films. It is indicative of the primitive state of film production in Ireland in the immediate post-war period that Fleischmann was the only person who possessed such equipment.

Following the choice of a record of President O'Kelly's pilgrimage to the Vatican, *Ireland-Rome* (1950), the Cultural Relations Committee's third film was Liam O'Leary's *Portrait of Dublin* (1952). It concentrated in the main on eighteenth-century Dublin. By the time the film was completed the coalition government had been defeated in the 1951 general election. The new Fianna Fáil Minister for External Affairs, Frank Aiken, took the opportunity to exact revenge on Liam O'Leary's Clann na Poblachta activities and refused to release the film. This action effectively ended O'Leary's film directing career as he has not made a film since.

Nevertheless, film-making remained of considerable interest to Frank Aiken. In 1954 an External Affairs-sponsored film, *Fintona*

— *A Study of Housing Discrimination*, was shown after it had been shot, in part with a hidden camera, in Co. Tyrone. It alleged anti-Catholic discrimination in the allocation of housing by the unionist councils of that county. The film was distributed by the Anti-Partition League in London and was shown to British audiences. The Northern Ireland government objected to it and asked the Westminster government to protest to the Irish government. The Northern Ireland government complained that this 'overt inter-ference by a "friendly" government in the internal affairs of another country was intolerable'.[26] In due course the British Ambassador to Dublin lodged a protest about the film with the Secretary of the Department of External Affairs. What was also of concern to the Northern Ireland Cabinet was that this film was the first in a proposed series of documentaries. The next one was due to deal with the gerrymandering of elections by unionists in Northern Ireland. This film was never made. Fianna Fáil was once again replaced by a coalition government following the 1954 general election.

This film initiative is exceptional in choosing Northern Ireland as its subject as most of the government films of the period were concerned with the social and economic modernisation being initiated in the Republic. These changes were not confined to Ireland but were part of a pattern existing throughout Europe in the post-war social democratic transformation of European societies. The complexity of the Irish modernising process can be seen at its most intricate in a film made to advertise the Rural Electrification Scheme, a government project to bring electricity to rural areas. Part of the scheme was funded by the Marshall Aid Programme's Economic Co-Operation Administration (ECA) which, in Ireland, amongst other supports, aided the training of engineers and other technicians.

The Promise of Barty O'Brien (1951) is a 49-minute drama-documentary written by Seán Ó Faoláin[27] and funded by the ECA. The film positively locates the ECA in the Irish modernising process through its advocacy of, and support for, training to aid the expansion of the electricity grid to rural Ireland. Most of the film is told in flashback at Dublin Airport when Barty O'Brien (Eric Doyle) returns from the United States after training for two years as an electrical engineer. Barty relates to an American traveller in transit the story of his struggle to convince his father (Harry Brogan) to allow him to train as an engineer. In this flash-back, a peat-fired power station is seen being built near his family's small farm and cottage. Barty's fascination with it leads him secretly to learn about electricity by attending nightschool and getting a job in the plant. Knowing of his father's disapproval of innovation he colludes with his mother (Eileen Crowe) and sister (Doreen Madden) to install electricity in their cottage. This action, taking place significantly on Easter Sunday, leads to the film's central conflict between father and son.

During this argument, Mr O'Brien, a 1916 fighter, is depicted as restraining the modernising and industrialising dynamism of youth. Eventually a form of compromise is achieved which allows Barty to study in America, courtesy of the ECA. On his return, Barty remains uncertain whether his 'promise' to his father to work on the family farm will have to be honoured. But resolution has been realised while he was away. His sister has married a progressive young farmer who has merged his adjoining farm to the O'Briens' land, thus making a more efficient economic unit. Barty's 'promise' is not now confined to his family but to Ireland and its future economic prosperity.

To reach this point of progress a series of narrative transformations have taken place. The urban environment where progress and modernity is located is not in Ireland but in America. Dublin is seen as an alien, inhospitable place, filmed mainly at night with Barty alone and friendless. America, by contrast, is presented as a place of speed and light in a brief collage of skyscrapers, hydro-electric plants and consumer domestic appliances. In this way, rural Ireland is seen to gain the benefits of progress without confronting its own urban and thus industrial centres. Indeed, the village/town beside which the O'Briens live is almost all of thatched cottages and thus merely a minor extension of the countryside. Additional evidence of the film's ambiguous attitude to urban Ireland is to be found in the Easter Sunday exchange between Barty and his father. When Barty declares that he'll go to Dublin his father retorts: 'Are you mad. Out into the hungry city . . . We'd have to pay for every bite that went into your belly'. This, of course, reinforces the view that the produce of the land does not require work (or is not part of commodity exchange) and that somehow urban dwellers get handouts and do not work. There is even an indication that the film glosses over the nature of electricity generation itself when Barty tells his family that every time they turn on the electricity they will think of him. This indicates to say the least a mystical rather than a functional relationship to electricity.

The Promise of Barty O'Brien had a very unusual crew. While a number of Irish people worked on the film (including Brendan Stafford, who photographed it) it was directed by a Russian, George Freedland, who was a friend of Pudovkin and had translated his writings into German. The production manager, Ulli Picard, had also worked in that capacity on Max Ophuls' *Lola Montes*! It was well received in Ireland:[28]

> It demonstrates conclusively that good motion pictures can be made by Irish technicians. *Promise . . .* is the first all-Irish propaganda movie worth serious consideration *as* a movie. The Government-sponsored films made till now have merely been highly expensive lantern lectures. They were a series of pretty pictures hooked up with a mechanised lecturer on the sound track.

Despite the production of such professional drama-documentary information films in the 1950s it would be a great mistake to assume that the government had a major commitment to these smaller scale indigenous projects. By the mid-1950s the government was already turning its attention to television, which was later largely to satisfy its information needs. 1962 saw the first full year of the national television service, Telefís Éireann (now RTE). With the advent of television the production of government-sponsored information films correspondingly declined. The exceptions in the 1960s were tourist and industrial promotion films for foreign distribution. However, in this area, Irish State bodies and the Department of Foreign Affairs had to succumb to the demands of the British distribution duopoly, Rank and ABC. To have Ireland presented on either Rank's weekly *Look at Life* series or ABC's *Pathé Pictorial* it proved necessary to employ these companies to make films about Ireland. Thus Irish film-makers were deprived of some of the already limited state sponsorship for documentaries. Nevertheless, the Department of Foreign Affairs Cultural Relations Committee funded one of Ireland's best-known 'quality' documentaries at this time. Patrick Carey's *Yeats Country* (1965) was made for the one hundredth anniversary of the birth of W. B. Yeats. It used images of landscape and skyscape in the Sligo region to evoke Yeats' poetry. It is probably the most widely seen Irish documentary ever produced. It has also won many major awards. The film was universally acclaimed with Quidnunc's observations in *The Irish Times*[29] quite typical

If the Department of Foreign Affairs had never done anything else in the field of cultural propaganda, they would have earned every laurel wreath at my bestowal for their latest venture in the medium.

By contrast the major independent documentary of the 1960s, *The Rocky Road to Dublin*, dealt directly and angrily with the legacy of the past. Written and directed by Irish-born Peter Lennon, Paris correspondent of *The Guardian*, it was photographed by Raoul Coutard, who is best known for his collaborations with Jean-Luc Godard. Those interviewed in the film included writer Séan Ó Faoláin, diplomat and writer Conor Cruise O'Brien, film director John Huston, *Irish Times* editor Douglas Gageby, theatre producer Jim Fitzgerald, and Fr Michael Cleary. They responded to the issues in a fresh, even direct way. History and sexuality were two key themes in Lennon's 'personal description of a community which survived nearly seven hundred years of English occupation and then nearly sank under the weight of its own heroes and clergy'.[30] First shown at the Cannes Film Festival in 1968, it developed a degree of notoriety when it was adopted as an example of a challenging new cinema by students at Cannes and later at Paris during the May events. The question posed by an article about the film in *Life*,[31] 'Was the Irish Rebellion Really Fought in Vain?', was the one most apposite to the film and the one which helped involve it in controversy in Ireland. While defending the film in *The Irish Times* Fergus Linehan wrote that[32]

[it] introduces a breath of fresh air into an area too often concerned with the glossy Bord Fáilte [Irish Tourist Board] advertisement image of Ireland. This, one would hope, is one of the kinds of picture which would emerge from a native film industry . . . owing nothing to any establishment ideas about how this country should be projected.

But, unfortunately, such critical independent documentaries have been rare though RTE has often taken up many of the issues raised in the film. The most numerically productive independent documentarists in the 1970s and 1980s have been nature film-makers, Eamon de Buitléar and Gerrit Van Geldern, and crafts-orientated film-maker, David Shaw-Smith. All three work closely with RTE.

Versions of historical revision

It was another state-aided but independent body, the Irish language and cultural organisation, Gael Linn, which was the most important source of Irish language films from the mid-1950s until the early 1970s. With the exception of two editions of a government newsreel, *Irish Pictorial Review* (1950), Gael Linn's *Amharc Éireann* (A View of Ireland), was the first regular indigenous cinema newsreel since the demise of *Irish Events* in 1920. Most of the 267 editions produced between 1956 and 1964 were made by Colm O'Laoghaire, who was also a producer of sponsored documentaries. During the 1960s and early 1970s Gael Linn also produced a series of documentaries most of which were directed by Louis Marcus. These films used a relatively accessible Irish language narration with humorous or visually interesting contents. The topics included an Irish music festival, *Fleá Ceoil* (1967), horses, *Capallology* (1968), and children learning through play, *Pásti Ag Obair* (1973). It is, however, for two major actuality films that Gael Linn as a film production company is mostly remembered.

Mise Éire (I Am Ireland, 1959) and *Saoirse?* (Freedom?, 1961) were the first feature-length films made in the Irish language. These two 90-minute films present with available graphic, photographic, newspaper, and most importantly, filmic material, events leading to Independence and its immediate aftermath. In 1952 George Morrison began work on a catalogue of Irish film material and had indexed 300,000 feet of Irish actualities by the time *Mise Éire* was first shown. Only about 20 per cent of the material was found in Ireland.[33] Made on 35mm, they were distributed widely in Irish cinemas, though their international distribution has been limited as only Irish language versions exist.

Mise Éire dealt with the nationalist struggle up to the victory of Sinn Féin in the 1918 general election while *Saoirse?* brought the events up to the outbreak of Civil War in 1922. The première of *Mise Éire* as the final film of the Fourth Cork Film Festival on 30 September 1959 was attended by Tánaiste (Deputy Prime Minister) Sean MacEntee. Irish reviewers were unanimous in their praise, only questioning the film's exclusively Irish language soundtrack. At the time of the film's release Louis Marcus, an assistant on the film, described[34] it as 'truly an event of the most shattering consequence, not only for Irish cinema but in the general life of the country'. He added that 'the material has been treated with the greatest of respect; it has not been slanted politically or in any other way, and Morrison has indeed sometimes left himself with an inadequate coverage of certain events rather than falsely utilise material from other sections'.

This attention to film detail is a hallmark of the films. The technical achievement in collecting and preserving this crucial historical footage makes both films of inestimable value. Hitherto only minor attempts had been made to preserve Irish actuality material. Nevertheless, the assemblage of such material amounts to more than the act of preservation. From the beginning the narrator alerts us to an historical view that film technology and film stock are passive recorders of the world. Photography, the film informs us, opens 'a new window . . . on to the past by which we can look at it through twentieth century eyes'. However, these twentieth-century eyes do not simply look through the window but also reorganise and select historical material. As a result the organic development of history which the film then promotes is much more than simple reproduction but a carefully selected view of the past.

Indeed, both *Mise Éire* and *Saoirse?* employ images of nature to underpin or naturalise a particular nationalist vision of the past. What George Morrison describes as 'poetic imagery'[35] is, in part, the use at a number of points in both films of waves and sea hitting a rocky shore to evoke the continuous past of the Irish nation and the eternality of nature and of Ireland. Morrison has suggested[36] that *Mise Éire* was in fact designed as a deliberate critique of romantic nationalism. This is hard to square with the general lack of critical distance in the film from the events portrayed. In contrast to the emotional narration and music which underpins the images of the rise of Irish nationalism, the depiction of Belfast (and, thus, opposition to Irish nationalism) is confined to the grim description of religious sectarianism:

> The city of Belfast is tense — racked with fear and hate — the seeds of evil were sown here long ago and now are come to fruit. A city fighting against itself and rent with many wounds — Christian fleeing from Christian in fear.

Such a limited representation of this period of Irish history accorded quite closely to 1950s and early 1960s attitudes in the South.

Mise Éire and *Saoirse?* are in effect official histories of the struggle for independence produced at a particular time of transition in Irish society. This remains so in spite of a question mark being added to *Saoirse*. (A planned third part, on the inter-war period, unsurprisingly, was never made.) Thus the contrasting reception of the two films is instructive. The enthusiastic response to *Mise Éire* when shown at Cork was to be expected but the negative reception given to *Saoirse?* at Cork two years later is somewhat misleading. While recognising that the period covered in *Saoirse?* could not continue the optimistic triumph of *Mise Éire*, reviewers also wished to look forwards to the international world of the future and not to re-investigate the past. In *The Evening Herald* Desmond Rushe observed that[37]

> It is of necessity a depressing, jarring film with the seed of national disunity growing inexorably until [it] erupt[s] in Civil War. There is none of the romantic heroism of *Mise Éire* here and the ending is one of stark tragedy as against defiant and triumphant resurgence.

Fergus Linehan's *Irish Times* article was titled 'Not for Export'[38] while David Nowlan became entangled in a controversy in the same newspaper following his disparaging article on the film. After his article was published a reader wrote to defend the film but Nowlan asked[39] in his reply that his adversary should not

> drive us back to the narrow, nationalistic and parochial extreme of having to praise all native products simply because they are Irish; let us develop some sense of proportion in the essentially international world into which we are moving.

Despite this response from the younger journalists a clearer view of the importance of *Saoirse?* for the older generation was evident at the Dublin opening of the film in 1961. In attendance were Fianna Fáil Tánaiste Sean MacEntee and two other Fianna Fáil ministers, Frank Aiken and Michael Hilliard. All three had fought on the anti-Treaty side in the Civil War. Also in attendance was General Richard Mulcahy, who had been Chief of Staff of the Republican Army during the War of Independence. Unlike the others he had supported the Treaty and later succeeded W. T. Cosgrave as leader of Fine Gael. To publicly signal this Civil War ecumenism a party of Old IRA who had fought against one another in the Civil War paraded from the stage of the cinema to the street after the screening.[40]

By the end of the decade the perspective on such military events had noticeably altered. With the renewal of the Northern Ireland conflict in 1969/70, serious reconsideration, not just of political positions but of filmic images and narration, began. One such film-maker working in this context is Louis Marcus who has made more than 30 documentaries since 1960. He was the director of a 1966 50th Anniversary of the Easter Rising commemoration film for Gael Linn, *An Tine Bheo* (The Bright Flame), the producer/director of a Clarke-of-Civilisation-type series, *The Heritage of Ireland* (1978), and the one hundredth anniversary film on the birth of Padraig Pearse, *Revival: Pearse's Concept of Ireland* (1979), which was commissioned directly by the Department of the Taoiseach under Jack Lynch.

The Heritage of Ireland, according to Louis Marcus in a 1980 interview,[41] presented 'successive invasions of this island as contributions rather than persecutions . . .' Commenting on the changes between the 1966 and the 1979 films, he said that

> Ireland is, of course, obsessed not so much with history which I don't think it wants to know about but with various mythologies which change from time to time. The difference between *An Tine Bheo* . . . and the Pearse film . . . is a fair example of how mythologies shift . . . Neither hagiographers nor his detractors have seriously treated this part of his writing which is by far the largest part of it [in the Gaelic League newspaper] and wish to shy away from it because the Pearse who emerges is a liberal intellectual of an intensity that I don't think this country is yet mature enough to take on. [But] the Pearse film is not an attempt to undermine the traditional mythology.

Rather than being a 'revisionist' he states that

> our interpretation of this history has been utterly simplistic and naive. Even though the shadow of the North during the past ten years has soured the enthusiasm of a great many people for Irish nationalism, what we had been taught for the last fifty years is not Irish nationalism as its practitioners of 1916 understood it but a very sentimentalised version. I don't see the value of trying to destroy Irish nationalism which I don't think can be done in the long run anyway. The value I see is in trying to give it the maturity and the unprovincialism with which Pearse invested it.

Even this 'revised nationalist' position which promoted a more complex view of the island of Ireland as a nation is an issue now ignored by government-sponsored films.

In the 1960s, an additional impetus to the exploration of Irish historiography was provided by the advent of Telefís Éireann. New television techniques were employed to reconstruct the past, placing, for example, a modern current affairs reporter into a reconstructed Easter Week in *Insurrection* (1966), RTE's main drama for the fiftieth anniversary celebrations of the 1916 Rising. A government-sponsored documentary, *Irish Rising 1916* (George Morrison, 1966), on the events of the Rising was followed by film of 1966 Dublin with the emphasis on modernity and technology. Even Bord Fáilte's simple presentation of history as an interesting backdrop to Ireland changed. In this respect *Green For Ireland* (1967) marks the end of an era. In this film, which opens at the Abbey Tavern, the narrator announces that 'English tourists [sit] applauding the rebel songs of 1916 while delighted Americans croon sad emigrant choruses'. The visitors enjoy the 'green shoots of Irish paradox' because 'Ireland is rich in magic and decorated with bright contradictions'. This sequence is followed by images of night-time Dublin where statues, including one of Parnell, are shown. The narrator continues:

Outside in the night stand the statues of the worthies just as they might in any other city, only in Dublin a lot of the worthies were rebels, not rulers, and the pious inscriptions are lively with insurrection.

In the 1970s and 1980s Irish history on television became more extensively covered with two British television series, Robert Kee's *Ireland: A Television History* (BBC, 1982) and Thames Television's *The Troubles* (Thames, 1982) being widely shown.[42] RTE, however, has been more probing in its exploration of Irish history with *The Making of the Land League* and *The Legacy of the Land League* in 1979 and *The Age of de Valera* (1982) written by historians Joseph Lee and Gearóid Ó Tuathaigh. For the first time there was an attempt to relate social and economic differences within Ireland to political and ideological constructions of Irish nationality. RTE's entry into the terrain of historical drama, such as the 1798 drama series *The Year of the French* (1982) or its series on German spies in Ireland during World War II, *Caught in a Free State* (1983), has been less critical or interpretative.

RTE, however, has chosen, in the main, to ignore Northern Ireland except for immediate news stories. A weariness in the South about the possibility of establishing a long-term viable solution to the conflict there is reinforced by the Irish government's ban from RTE radio and television of representatives of nationalist and unionist para-military organisations and their political fronts. This policy has led to the downgrading of Northern Ireland as a subject of documentaries and dramas since the mid-1970s. In contrast, extensive assessments of the South's society and economy on RTE current affairs programmes have contributed significantly to these areas of debate and these programmes have maintained consistently high audience ratings. The cultural expression for many of those brought up with these social and economic changes following the internationalisation of the Irish economy from the late 1950s onwards has been through British and American popular culture, and music in particular. A hallmark of these developments since the 1960s has been a positive interaction between indigenous cultural forms and international cultures. In earlier decades, especially from the 1930s to the 1950s, it was the desire to challenge, if not emulate, by far the most popular mass cultural experience of that time, the Cinema, which saw the attempt to build an Irish-Hollywood, if not an Irish-Elstree.[43]

Notes

1. J. A. P., '*Man of Aran* in Dublin', *Irish Independent*, 7 May 1934, p. 7.

2. Harry Watt, who worked as an assistant on the film for a year, was recorded as saying: 'The extraordinary thing was that Flaherty lived like a king in these primitive places . . . I never lived so well in my life'. They had brought a *cordon bleu* cook to Aran and 'we had two grown men just to put peat on the fire'. Quoted in Elizabeth Sellers, *The Rise and Fall of the British Documentary: The Story of the Film Movement Founded by John Grierson*, Berkeley: University of California Press, 1975, p. 29. Grierson had convinced Michael Balcom to finance the film through Gainsborough Pictures, a subsidiary of Gaumont-British.

3. As Flaherty himself put it: 'We select a group of the most attractive and appealing characters we can find, to represent a family, and through them, tell our story. It is always a long and difficult process, this type finding, for it is surprising how few faces stand the test of the camera' (typescript, *Account of the Making of the film — Man of Aran*, 'Flaherty Papers', Box 31, p. 3, Columbia University, New York).

4. 'The Man of Aran — and of Ireland', *Irish Press*, 7 May 1934, p. 6.

5. D. F. R., *Monthly Film Bulletin*, 1934, p. 97.

6. *Irish Press*, 14 June 1933, p. 1.

7. *Irish Press*, 14 June 1933, p. 6.

8. *Sunday Independent*, 17 March 1935, p. 4; *Dublin Evening Mail*, 19 March, p. 2; *Irish Times*, 19 March, p. 4.

9. Liam O'Laoghaire, 1945, p. 159.

10. Frank Aiken, Minister for the Co-ordination of Defensive Measures, *Dáil Debates*, Vol. 92, Cols. 402–403, 1 December 1943.

11. *Monthly Film Bulletin* commented that the Irish people 'are in no mood for worrying about the rest of the world and are not conscious of any unfairness in their attitude towards the Allies', Vol. 11, No. 126, 30 June 1944, p. 77. *The Irish Question* was March of Time 9th Year, No. 11.

12. Liam O'Laoghaire, 'What Price Irish Films?', *Leader*, Vol. 92, No. 20, 15 June 1946, p. 16.

13. L.MacG., 'The Davis Film', *Irish Press*, 25 March 1946, p. 4.

14. Cinema correspondent, 'Proof That It Can Be Done', *Irish Times*, 25 March 1946, p. 2.

15. Film Critic, 'Davis Story May Give a Lead', *Irish Independent*, 13 May 1946, p. 3.

16. O'Laoghaire, 1945, p. 95.

17. *Leader*, 15 June 1946, p. 16.

18. *Irish Times*, 22 January 1948, p. 3.

19. Ibid., 24 January 1948, p. 5.

20. *Irish Press*, 26 January 1948.

21. Ibid., 28 January 1948, p. 5.

22. *Irish Times*, 30 January 1948, p. 3.

23. Amongst the films made was the Department of Agriculture's sponsorship of the Irish National Film Unit production of *Our Daily Bread* (1943) on the wheat-growing campaign. This unit had been formed by Richard Hayward, Michael Scott and Roger Greene. Another film made during the war was *Ireland's Call to Arms*. It was produced by Gordon Lewis, the cameraman from the 1920 film *In the Days of St Patrick*.

24. Healy's drama-documentaries included *Voyage to Recovery*, on tuberculosis; *Stop Thief!* was an anti-diphtheria film; and *The Art of Reception* was a tourism-business film. Healy also made documentaries on savings and the electricity supply system.

25. *Dáil Debates*, Vol. 123, Cols. 1573–74, 30 November 1950.

26. Ed Maloney, 'Film on housing discrimination leads to protest', *Irish Times*, 1 and 2 January 1985, p. 14.

27. The ambiguity displayed by Seán Ó Faoláin towards modernisation and the Irish urban/rural divide (p. 166) and his attitude to commercial cinema was forcefully stated in a book published two years before *The Promise of Barty O'Brien* was released: 'Their triviality, their debasing cheapness of thought, their tinsel dreams infect the most remote villages'. From *The Irish: A Character Study*, Old Greenwich, Connecticut: Devin-Adair Co., fourth edition 1979, p. 151.

28. Kevin O'Kelly, *Sunday Press*, 19 August 1951, p. 9. By way of historical addendum to this film it should be noted that by the time *The Promise of Barty O'Brien* was released the Marshall Aid Programme had shifted from direct economic aid to being linked to defence agreements.

Since Ireland refused to join NATO this was the beginning of the end of the ECA programme in Ireland (See *Irish Times*, 30 December 1982).

29. *Irish Times*, 9 April 1965, p. 11.

30. Contemporary publicity handout, 1968.

31. *Life Atlantic*, 22 July 1968.

32. 'An Eye on Ourselves', *Irish Times*, 13 May 1968, p. 10.

33. Tom Hennigan '*Mise Éire* Festival Highlight', *Sunday Press*, 4 October 1959, p. 19.

34. *Irish Times*, 3 October 1959, p. 12.

35. 'The Making of *Mise Éire*', *Irish Times*, 28 December 1979, p. 8.

36. As Morrison put it in 1981: '*Saoirse?* illustrates how the bourgeois revolution of 1916 (hence the lace curtain in the main title background of *Mise Éire*) could not sustain itself and deteriorated, ultimately, into civil war and neo-colonialism. This is also a reason why *Saoirse?* has never been as popular a film, in Ireland, as its predecessor. *Saoirse?* makes no concessions to romantic nationalism'. 'Film-making', in *The Achievement of Sean O'Riada*, p. 69, Bernard Harris and Grattan Freyer (eds), Irish Humanities Centre, Ballina, and Keohanes, Ballina and Sligo, and Dufour Editions Inc., Chester Springs, Pennsylvania, 1981.

Sean O'Riada's blending of traditional Irish and classical musical forms popularised a renewed interest in Irish music through his band, Ceolteoiri Cualann, and his music scores for *Mise Éire*, *Saoirse?* and *An Tine Bheo*. These soundtracks were reissued in 1979 by Gael Linn. O'Riada also wrote the music score for the film version of *The Playboy of the Western World*. He died in 1971.

37. *Evening Herald*, 28 September 1961, p. 18.

38. *Irish Times*, 23 October 1961, p. 8.

39. Ibid., 16 October 1961, p. 7; see also, 'Gloomy Sermon at Cork', ibid., 11 October, p. 8, and 14 October, p. 9.

40. 'An Epic Occasion', *Irish Independent*, 21 October 1961, p. 15.

41. Interview with Kevin Rockett, *IFT News*, Vol. 3, No. 12, p. 11, December 1980.

42. See Bob Ferguson, *Television on History: Representations of Ireland*, Media Analysis Paper 5, London: University of London Institute of Education, 1985 (booklet).

43. A fairly comprehensive collection of the government-sponsored and state-aided documentaries and drama-documentaries discussed here are held at the Irish Film Institute and are included in my unpublished *Irish Film Catalogue* (Irish Film Institute, 1982), which lists more than 300 Irish films. In his *Short Story: Irish Cinema 1945–1958* (BAC Films, 1986), Kieran Hickey makes considerable use of the IFI collection. This film presents the social concerns of the information films, the few indigenous fiction films of the period, the acting, writing and directorial talent displayed in the films (with, perhaps, an overstatement of the role of Gerard Healy) and the limited but encouraging initiatives made by the 1948–51 coalition government. The film seeks to distil the events of the period in its search for modernising and internationalising developments. In doing so the film displays impatience with Ireland's passion for the past rather than the present.

One omission in the film is worth noting. In 1956, during the period which the film covers, Gael Linn began making the Amharc Éireann newsreel. This was the beginning of Gael Linn's long involvement in film but there is no reference to the organisation in the film. In light of this oversight (or attitude to Irish-language film-making?) it is of interest to note that *Short Story* begins with film of Orson Wells on the set of *Othello* and in the opening sequence of the short *Return to Glennascaul*, which was directed by Wells' friend Hilton Edwards, and who acted in *Othello*. Wells' scenes were shot in Italy and in themselves can hardly be said to have contributed much to Irish film production. While the film displays antagonism towards the establishment of a film studio in Ireland in 1958, this privileging of Wells, the international star, in the film undermines its thesis in support of indigenous film production.

4

An Irish Film Studio

Kevin Rockett

Early proposals

As we have already seen, the production of even modestly budgeted documentaries and fiction films in the 1920s and 1930s was always economically difficult. While a once-off sound feature such as *The Dawn* might recoup its production costs in Ireland, such an experience was unlikely to be repeated if fully professional commercial films were produced. In the mid-1930s, the period in which the most vocal demands for an Irish film studio emerged, Irish cinema box office accounted for less than 5 per cent of that of the United Kingdom, or £1.75 million in 1936.[1] As the sound era progressed, Ireland came to be seen as a minor province in the English language territories dominated by American cinema: a branch plant of a branch plant as later economists would characterise Ireland's peripheral economic relationship to Britain and America.

Such native economic realities discouraged Irish film investors, who could see little prospect of generating any significant return on their capital in the home market. Additionally, any would-be Irish film entrepreneurs would have lacked the expertise and contacts essential in securing foreign distribution contracts. In this environment, it is hardly surprisingly that assertive advice often replaced analysis, especially of the difficulties facing the distribution of Irish films. Some of the most revealing and conflicting commentaries and advice for the potential Irish film producer can be found in the section 'What Kind of Films Should We Make?' in the 1943 publication, *Irish Cinema Handbook*.[2] A wide variety of writers proposed the making of Irish costumed historical dramas (similar in style to those made in Britain in the 1930s and 1940s), the production of Irish plays and novels, including Kickham's *Knocknagow*, and films about contemporary social issues.

Such proposals would have required the facilities of a fully-equipped film studio and, predictably, the book's preface called for such an initiative. This preface was written by the book's uncredited editor, Fr Richard Devane, SJ, the most vociferous advocate of a comprehensive Irish film policy during the 1930s and 1940s. Following a long campaign, Devane had a major success in 1938 when he convinced Taoiseach Eamon de Valera to set up an enquiry into the cinema in Ireland. Completed in 1943 (though never published) this report, *The Film in National Life*, was the product of an Inter-Departmental Committee headed by the Department of Industry and Commerce. Amongst its recommendations was the establishment of a modest National Film Studio.[3]

The proposal contained in *The Film in National Life* proved too limited for the film ambitions of the Minister for Industry and Commerce, Sean Lemass. He considerably expanded the report's recommendations in two submissions to the Cabinet, in December 1946 and September 1947. Lemass had become frustrated with the inadequacy of a series of private studio proposals which had been submitted to his Department during the previous decade. The first of these plans had been an American/Abbey Theatre project in 1937 which sought to build on the success of the Abbey Players in the two John Ford-Irish films, *The Informer* (1935) and *The Plough and the Stars* (1936). Like many other proposals submitted to Industry and Commerce and the Taoiseach's Department,[4] especially in the immediate post-war period, the initial enthusiasm was not followed up with capital investment either in studios or feature film production. The most comprehensive and sustained sets of proposals came rather surprisingly from Gabriel Pascal, a Hungarian-born film producer and director, and his mentor, Bernard Shaw.[5] The Shaw/Pascal proposals are of interest in that they parallel Lemass' own proposals and received the support of both de Valera and Lemass.

The original Shaw/Pascal submission to government concerned the building and equipping of an Irish film studio.[6] Later, this goal was abandoned in the search for production finance for the film versions of Shaw's *St Joan* and *Androcles and the Lion*. A number of well-known Irish people were attracted to the projects: solicitor Arthur Cox, who became Pascal's Irish representative; Dan Breen,

Fianna Fáil T.D. and legendary War of Independence fighter; Fr Cormac, OFM, who became involved on the recommendation of Archbishop McQuaid of Dublin; Irish language theatre director and actor Frank Dermody, who had submitted proposals in 1944 for the training of Irish language actors; and businessman Joseph McGrath. With the exception of McGrath, boss of Irish Hospitals Sweepstakes and one of Ireland's wealthiest men, none of the others had access to large amounts of capital. It was revealed at the company's final meeting that even with McGrath involved, only £41,000 had been committed to the company.[7] (This sum included £10,000 from McGrath and £1,000 from Breen.) Shaw, who reacted impetuously to this state of affairs, severed his contract with the company. In a bitter and recriminatory letter to Cox, Shaw declared[8] that £1½ million was needed by the company if it was to succeed. This amount was, of course, well outside the means of those involved in the company and, as de Valera[9] put it in a letter to Shaw, Irish investors regarded the project as 'highly speculative'.

A similar attitude was adopted by Cabinet to Lemass's proposals. In their most comprehensive form Lemass's proposals advocated the building and equipping of a two-studio block and administrative offices at a cost of half a million pounds.[10] He also sought a system of guarantees on the capital invested in films and the interest charges on that capital. In a memo on an earlier version of the proposals for a studio the Minister for Finance, Frank Aiken, argued against them on social, economic and cultural grounds.[11] Lemass had envisaged that the studios would be made available primarily for the use of foreign producers. It was this proposal in particular which led to Aiken's contemptuous dismissal of Lemass's memo. Such foreign producers were fickle and domestic producers would be unable to afford the rents at the studios. Furthermore, Aiken argued, while supporting the more modest studio proposals contained in the Inter-Departmental Committee report,

> If this country is going to spend money on the film business, it should be spent on the production of Irish films by Irish organisations and not in the provision of facilities which at present suit foreigners but which might well be far too elaborate for the requirements of domestic producers.

While Lemass lost this particular battle in the 1940s he was to win

97

the war a decade later when he was once again Minister for Industry and Commerce. Needless to say, in the international nirvana that Lemass was mapping out for Ireland, Aiken's strictures on serving the needs of indigenous film-makers were ignored.

Ardmore Studios

In the mid-1950s three incongruously different strands came together and with financial aid from the Department of Industry and Commerce built Ireland's first (and only) permanent film studio. One of the key figures was Emmet Dalton, whose distinguished military career during World War I, the War of Independence and the Civil War had been left behind to become a film producer and distributor in Britain. He entered discussions with Ernest Blythe, chairman of the Abbey Theatre. Dalton sought Blythe's support in adapting a series of Abbey plays for television as their first project. The third strand was represented by Louis Elliman, whose family had sold much of their exhibition interests to Rank in 1946 and who was now Rank's managing director in Ireland. Elliman had also helped in producing two short fiction films with the Gate Theatre in the early 1950s: *Return to Glennascaul* and *From Time to Time*. Dalton, Blythe and Elliman were joined by Abbey Theatre director Lennox Robinson, to form Dublin Theatre and Television Productions. Their only joint project was an adaption of George Shiels's 1925 play *Professor Tim* at a cost of £30,000.[12]

During the course of the film's shooting in January 1957 Louis Elliman revealed that a quarter of a million pounds was going to be spent on a film studio in Ireland by an associate company, Dublin Film Productions Management.[13] Negotiations had been going on for two years and they envisaged a big market for Irish-produced films in American television. Joining Dalton and Elliman as directors of the new company were Abe Elliman, Louis's brother, and Cornelius P. McGrath, a barrister and bookmaker. The success of a second project, an adaption of St. John Ervine's play *Boyd's Shop*, convinced Dalton that the establishment of an Irish studio for the production of Abbey play adaptions, not big budget features, was a viable proposition. Dalton's involvement had also been encouraged by the new boss of RKO, the distributors of *Professor Tim*, who offered him a twelve pictures in one year deal. The agreement, which was never realised, would have involved fifty-fifty financing by Dalton and RKO, provided RKO could choose the star and director. While visiting Hollywood, Elliman had also become convinced of the potential of an Irish film studio. Dalton and Elliman then bought Ardmore, a 35 acre estate with a large house near Bray, Co. Wicklow, about twelve miles south-east of Dublin, for £5,000. Its location, one mile from the sea and a wide range of mountainous and flat terrain nearby, made it an attractive base for both studio and location shooting.[14]

Dalton and Elliman were probably also encouraged by the return of Sean Lemass to the Department of Industry and Commerce in 1957 following that year's general election. Lemass was now Tánaiste and heir apparent to de Valera. He had also been a colleague of Dalton's in the Dublin Brigade of the IRA though they had taken opposing sides in the Civil War. In the more open and expansionist economic climate which was evolving in the late 1950s Lemass saw fit to fund the studios with a grant of £45,000 from the Industrial Development Authority and a debenture loan of £217,750 from the State Development Bank, the Industrial Credit Company, both semi-state bodies within the responsibility of the Department of Industry and Commerce. Lemass did not reveal this investment at the time and it only came to public notice in 1963 when a Dáil question elicited the information from the Minister for Finance, James Ryan.[15] By that stage Lemass had been Taoiseach for four years.

Ardmore Studios was largely planned and staffed in technical grades by English personnel. Some minor technical and craft positions were filled by Irish people. The studios comprised three sound stages (two 100 × 80 ft and one 60 × 50 ft) and a recording theatre (60 × 30 ft) with full dubbing and mixing facilities. There was no processing laboratory. It was regarded by the trade press as being well equipped and professionally run.[16]

In his opening address on 12 May 1958 Lemass emphasised the employment and export, rather than cultural, value of the studios.[17] He said that it was marking an important development in the economic history of Ireland and as such the occasion was of great national importance. Lemass reported that when the promoters of the studios had come to him he promised the greatest possible help his Department could give them. This statement was endorsed by Louis Elliman, Ardmore's managing director, when he declared that the assistance received from Industry and

Commerce 'had been absolutely invaluable'.

Writing in a special feature on Ardmore in *The Daily Cinema* in December 1959, the executive producers of the first international production made at the studios, *Shake Hands With the Devil*, declared,[18] as their article was titled, 'Enthusiasm — all the Way'. Despite some severe weather the film was brought in on schedule, 60 days, and within budget, £600,000. They added that there had been 742 set-ups and access to London to process film and receive rushes had not been a problem.

In order to attract further foreign productions to Ardmore, Dalton persuaded the Industrial Credit Company to establish a subsidiary, the Irish Film Finance Corporation (IFFC), in January 1960. The IFFC, however, made no specific provision for the production of Irish films or the encouragement and employment of Irish film personnel. It was 'designed as an inducement to foreign film producers to use Ardmore Studios'.[19] This almost inevitably led to a restrictive agreement between Ardmore management and the English film technicians union, ACTT, whereby Ardmore would be regarded as a UK studio for purposes of Eady finance, if only ACTT members were employed on these productions. Any lingering hope of Irish people gaining experience on visiting productions vanished. Even electricians, a traditional film technician category, were excluded from productions. This caused a series of bitter labour/management/producers disputes between 1962 and 1964.

During this dispute, which resulted in the Irish electricians union, ETU(I), placing pickets on Ardmore during the shooting of *Of Human Bondage*, Ardmore management never displayed any sympathy for the position of the Irish technicians. Indeed, when in receivership for the first time in 1964 the Receiver was granted a High Court injunction preventing ETU pickets on the film *Ballad in Blue*. Louis Marcus[20] has succinctly described the behaviour of Ardmore management during this period. Not only did they fail to intervene on the electricians' behalf but the studio 'clearly demonstrat[ed] its nature as a hireable facility to which Irish film employment was quite irrelevant'. He added that

One can see, too, the extent to which Ardmore had become part of the British Film Industry in the determination — and the power — of the British unions to close production there if it threatened to leave their orbit. But most significant and most ironic of all is that the dispute at no stage involved Irish cameramen, sound recordists or other film technicians. It could not possibly do so; for — apart from the electricians — no other body of Irish film technicians could get a foothold in Ardmore from which to challenge the British monopoly.

Prospective Irish film producers were likewise at a serious disadvantage. With the English exhibition circuit dominated by the Rank and ABC duopoly there was little hope of unknown Irish people getting the distribution guarantee demanded by the IFFC. The result was that English producers who were already receiving Eady finance now also had access to IFFC money. While the IFFC-supported films needed a distribution guarantee the IFFC got little of its money back. It lost heavily in the first half of the 1960s and finally withdrew from film financing. The irony was that Irish state money was helping finance British films made in Ireland from which Irish people were excluded by the ACTT agreement.

Between 1963 and 1967 the Industrial Credit Company wrote off IFFC debts, waived interest due on Ardmore's debenture loan and still recorded losses. Marcus estimated[21] in 1967 that £506,317 had been advanced by way of loans, of which only £39,000 had been returned, leaving a total of £467,317 outstanding. Marcus concluded[22] that the three quarters of a million pounds invested at Ardmore (£¼ million in buildings; £½ million through the IFFC) 'were of negligible benefit to an Irish Film Industry'. He had, in fact, titled one of his articles, 'The Irrelevance of Ardmore'. In this regard he contrasted the studio-based productions being encouraged at Ardmore with seven short Irish films which won or had been nominated for international awards and concluded that their total production cost was £30,000.[23]

Even as a commercially operated company Ardmore was an abject failure. The Industrial Credit Company placed it in receivership in 1963. It was then run as a hireable facility by the Receiver, William Sands, until he sold it in 1966. It was bought by a consortium which included television producer Richard Afton, Hubert and Patrick McNally, and a London banker, Judah Binstock. A company chaired by Binstock, New Brighton Towers, took full control of Ardmore the following year. New Brighton's business experience as a proprietor of gambling casinos may or may not have been the most suitable background for running the studios. The flamboyant Lee Davis was appointed managing director but he was ousted by New Brighton in 1970 following allegations of mismanagement, an unexplained loss of £25,000 and the employment of Isle of Man consultants without board approval. After the studios were placed in receivership by National Westminster Bank they were bought by a new company, Ardmore Studios International (1972). This was run by George O'Reilly, a former actor and artists' manager, and its board members included Bing Crosby, 'an old friend', and then Irish resident John Huston.[24] O'Reilly had been attracted by that year's government decision to allow films to be included with manufacturing as an industry whose exports would be tax free. The bulk of the money invested, £260,000, came from a Scottish motor tyre and car accessories businessman, Thomas Farmer, who sought a quick return on his capital. The company was undercapitalised and after four months O'Reilly was dismissed and Ardmore's third receiver appointed. By this stage 55 films had been made at Ardmore since 1958, 27 having been made in the first five years.

On this occasion Ardmore entered a new phase of ownership when the state, in the form of RTE, bought the studios on behalf of the Minister for Industry and Commerce, Justin Keating, for a total, including fees, of £450,000 in 1973.[25] RTE ran a profitable business servicing filmed advertisements and documentaries until 1975 when Keating renamed Ardmore the National Film Studios of Ireland (NFSI). He appointed a board with English film director, but Irish resident, John Boorman as chairman. An RTE producer, Sheamus Smith, who had worked in current affairs, including a 1960s farming programme for which Keating was reporter, was made managing director. (In 1986 Smith became Irish Film Censor.) The other members of the NFSI board during this period included cameraman Vincent Corcoran, the head of RTE's Film Purchasing Department, Bill Harpur, the ICC's Louis Heelan, who had been involved with the IFFC, trade unionists Michael McEvoy, who organised the expanding group of Irish film workers in the Irish Transport and General Workers Union, and Ruaidhri Roberts of the Irish Congress of Trade Unions, and one of the NFSI solicitors, Martin Marren.

Until the studios were placed in receivership seven years later, the NFSI spent considerable sums on new equipment, dressing rooms, entertainments and travel. Despite these inducements to foreign producers the NFSI failed to maintain any consistent production at the studios. As a result it went through a series of increasingly desperate financial crises while still receiving substantial sums from the Exchequer. In 1980 the Minister for

Industry and Commerce, Desmond O'Malley, revealed[26] in the Dáil that to the end of 1979, £1.3 million had been given to the NFSI by way of grants. In addition, the studios company had an overdraft of £850,000. In 1978 the Oireachtas Committee on Public Accounts noted[27] that 'the Department was seriously concerned about the losses . . . about which there had been a considerable amount of inter-departmental debate and agonising'. The agonising and losses continued for another four years. With accumulated debt and losses at the NFSI approaching unacceptable levels (a loss of £¾ million was expected in 1982) the company was put into receivership by the Minister for Industry and Commerce, Albert Reynolds, in April 1982. Two years before, in 1980, Louis Marcus had estimated that state losses at Ardmore since 1958 had amounted to £10 million or more at 1980 prices.[28] In August 1984 the studio company was returned to private hands when the facility was bought by Pakistani-born businessman and recent recruit to film production, Mahmud Sipra. Before any film project was even begun at the Sipra Studios the collapse of some of his other business ventures, including a major link in the Johnson-Matthey Bank crisis, also brought the downfall of his studios company. In January 1985 some of the studios' creditors asked for a Receiver to be put in to take charge of the studios again. During 1985 and 1986 a number of applicants sought to purchase the studios from the Receiver. The most persistent interest came from the American-based company headed by Mary Tyler Moore, MTM Enterprises, for whom Morgan O'Sullivan's Tara Productions acted as Irish agents. Eventually, in September 1986, the High Court approved the sale of the studios to an Irish/American consortium which was made up of MTM, Tara and the Irish state's 'enterprise' agency, National Development Corporation, for a total of £1.5 million. Immediately, plans were put into effect for the refurbishment of the studios at a cost of one million dollars. The studios, which will serve, in effect, as a European production base for MTM television projects, will also be marketed by MTM in North America and Tara in the rest of the world as a film-making centre available for hire.

Ardmore Studios and the Abbey Theatre

In 1978 Tom Hayes summed up the initial policy of the Ardmore Studios company when he noted that [29]

Their basic idea was to build an Irish film industry powered by the Abbey Theatre. Perhaps they saw themselves as in the line of development of Yeats and Lady Gregory. Abbey actors were placed under contract and Abbey plays were given a screen treatment by professional screen writers.

In retrospect it can be seen that the influence of the Abbey Theatre on Ardmore was hardly surprising. Emmet Dalton's decision to adapt Abbey plays in the mid-1950s was merely a continuation of an association between the Abbey and film-making going back 40 years.

In its very first issue in January 1917, *Irish Limelight* saw the Abbey Theatre as being inseparable from film production in Ireland:

> The [Film] Company [of Ireland] did not make the mistake that anyone would do to tell an Irish story on the pictures . . . [There] was quick acknowledgement by the people of Ireland that they appreciated the presentation of actors who had brought Irish drama into a high place in the theatrical world. . . . Any Film Company starting in Ireland without representation from the group of actors who have developed Irish drama would have lacked an essential element in striving for high artistic and general acceptable success.

In *Irish Limelight* the following month the Film Company of Ireland and Abbey actress Nora Clancy commented on the success of the Abbey personnel:

> the initial success of the Abbey Players as cinema artists was due to the fact that the Abbey school always insisted upon striving after natural characterisation. Consequently they were more adapted for cinema acting than most artistes.

And forty years later a critic was to comment on Paul Rotha's *No Resting Place* (1951), a story about Irish travellers from the novel by Ian Niall, in which there were many Abbey actors, as follows:[30]

> It is still regarded by many judges as the best effort to establish what might be called the Abbey school of filming — filming which would display the real-life integrity of the best Continental models.

One could take issue with the notion of 'an Abbey school of filming' even if only by noting that Abbey actors were rarely given 'lead' or 'star' roles. Nevertheless, they seem to have had little difficulty in gaining screen work. In 1947, for example, the year in which Abbey actors received their most notable praise for their performances in Carol Reed's *Odd Man Out*, one writer could observe[31]

> It is an old joke in Dublin that the only members of the Abbey Theatre's staff who have never been offered film contracts are the Irish wolfhound and his mistress who have appeared for over forty years on the programme.

One reason for the surge of interest in Abbey personnel as film actors in the 1940s may have been a recognition of the depth of talent at the Abbey. Another reason may have been the desire of the actors themselves to abandon the increasingly parochial, Irish-Irelander policy being pursued by Ernest Blythe since he succeeded Yeats in the early 1940s.

The success of Abbey actors in international commercial cinema was not matched by the frequency or quality of Abbey play adaptions, as the mixed reception given to *Riders to the Sea* (1936) indicated. Indeed, few Abbey plays had been adapted for the screen until Emmet Dalton made it a central plank of Ardmore policy. Louis D'Alton's record-breaking 1947 comedy, *They Got What They Wanted*, was one of the few Abbey plays made as a film in the immediate post-war years. Retitled *Talk of a Million* (1951) when made as a British film, the story concerns the Monaghans and their five children. Though poverty-stricken, they are given extensive credit when it is thought they are the heirs to an American estate. By the time it is established that another family are the real beneficiaries of the estate, they have succeeded in setting up business enterprises and skilfully outfoxing a local gombeen.

The successful outwitting of a gombeen was also central to the first of the six plays Emmet Dalton was primarily responsible for adapting as films. In *Professor Tim*, 'professor' of zoology, Tim (Seamus Kavanagh) returns to an Irish village after 20 years of seafaring. Apparently poor himself, he succeeds in purchasing the estate of his niece's (Marie O'Donnell) once wealthy fiancé, Hugh (Ray McAnally), to stop it falling into the hands of a local landlord (Geoffrey Golden). After Tim has secured the estate he gives it to his niece and her fiancé as a wedding present.

Another George Shiels play, *The New Gosoon*, which was retitled *Sally's Irish Rogue*, was the first of the Ardmore Studios' adaptions to be released. Set in Wicklow, it concerned the relationship between Sally (Julie Harris) and Luke Casey (Tim Seely) who has irresponsible characteristics similar to those displayed by Hugh in *Professor Tim*. Seeking to assert his independence from his mother (Marie Kean), Luke sells his sheep to buy a motorcycle. Simultaneously, he breaks his promise to marry Sally, daughter of village poacher, Rabit Hamil (Harry Brogan). During his spell of freedom, Luke develops a relationship with Biddy Henly (Finola O'Shannon), daughter of a local horse dealer, John Henly (Phillip O'Flynn). After a series of mishaps, including his fierce pursual by Biddy's father, Luke returns to Sally. It was a slight, if occasionally amusing, film. One reviewer's complaint was that it upgraded the economic status of the participants from that depicted in the play.[32] It also raised an issue which was to recur in Irish assessments of Ardmore films. While Julie Harris was praised for her exuberance, Tim Seely was badly miscast as Luke.[33] The commercial cinema's demand for even a minor foreign 'name' actor in Irish films was to become a source of complaint in Irish reviews and amongst Irish actors themselves.

The second of the Abbey plays adapted at Ardmore was Walter Macken's *Home is the Hero*, which was in production at the studios when they were opened by Lemass. The film concerns Paddo (played by Walter Macken), the 'Goliath of Galway', who, in a drunken rage, accidently kills the father of Maura (Marie O'Donnell), childhood sweetheart of his son Willie (Arthur Kennedy). During his five years in prison Paddo's place as head of the family is taken by Willie. On Paddo's return he resumes his former role as dictatorial head of the family. Emotional conflict with his family leads inevitably to physical conflict with his son and daughter Josie (Joan O'Hara). He tries to stop both Willie from marrying Maura, and Josie from carrying on a relationship with the village playboy. Paddo almost kills another man before Willie subdues him into accepting a more responsible role as husband and father.

When *Home is the Hero* opened in Dublin in April 1959 Walter Macken was widely praised for his performance. 'One of the greatest characterisations the screen has ever given us', Tom Hennigan wrote in *The Sunday Press*.[34] Writing in *The Sunday Review*, Liam MacGabhann[35] agreed and added that 'the film shows more truly than any yet how great a team are those Abbeyites'. He also observed that 'the value of Ardmore to the nation is evident in this well-produced and sincerely acted picture'. *Home is the Hero* also brought the first indications of doubt concerning the Abbey play adaptions. In *The Sunday Independent* Ken Shaw observed[36] that the film could not get away from its stage origins.

Another play adapted by Emmet Dalton Productions in 1959 was Hugh Leonard's *The Big Birthday*. Retitled *Broth of a Boy* in Britain, it concerned Tony Randall (Tony Wright), who is touring Ireland collecting material for a television company. On his arrival at the village of Ballymorrisey, the people are due to celebrate the one hundredth and tenth birthday of Patrick Farrell (Barry Fitzgerald), who is believed to be the oldest man in the world. Tony is anxious to televise the event and he manages to persuade Patrick's grand-daughter, Sílín (June Thornburn), to help. Patrick himself and his eighty-year-old son, Willie (Harry Brogan), are less keen on the idea as Patrick had falsified his age years before in order to get a pension. They disappear on a poaching expedition and when they are caught red-handed by Desmond Phillips (Godfrey Quigley), a landlord who covets Sílín, Patrick assaults him and the vindictive Phillips has him arrested. In the end Patrick is let off with a caution, his birthday is televised and Tony and Sílín decide to marry. Irish reviews regarded it as the weakest of the Ardmore play adaptions but the Abbey actors and Barry Fitzgerald in particular were praised for their performances.[37] George Pollock was criticised for his poor direction which was not up to the standard of his *Rooney* (1958),[38] a comedy about a Dublin dustman adapted from the London-location novel by Catherine Cookson.

St John Ervine's 1936 play *Boyd's Shop* was another Emmet Dalton production but despite predating the establishment of the studios was not released in Britain until 1960. In this film John Haslett (Vincent Dowling) arrives in the village of Donagreah determined to start a modern grocery. He finds himself up against the long-established Boyd's shop and the indifference to innovation of the local people. In the end he joins forces with Boyd (Geoffrey Golden) and becomes engaged to Boyd's daughter Agnes (Aideen O'Kelly). *Boyd's Shop*, the *Monthly Film Bulletin* reported,[39] largely wasted 'the professionalism of Dublin's Abbey Theatre Players . . . on a naive and self-consciously charming story . . .' These four films pale in comparison with the most complex of the theatrical adaptions made at Ardmore, the 1959 Emmet

Dalton production of Louis D'Alton's 1953 play *This Other Eden*.

This Other Eden was adapted for the screen by Patrick Kirwan and Blanaid Irvine, was produced by Alec C. Snowden and directed by Muriel Box, the only feature made at Ardmore which was directed by a woman. A prologue to the main action of the film is set during the War of Independence. It shows an important IRA man, Commandant Jack Carberry, driving to a rendezvous with his friend Devereux (Niall McGinnis) to discuss an end to the war with a British officer. Carberry, however, is shot by Black and Tans and ever since it is thought that the officer betrayed him. After the film's titles the action moves forward about 20 years to the village of Ballymorgan, Carberry's birthplace, where the villagers are preparing to erect a statue to Carberry. His memory pervades the film but, as is demonstrated at the beginning of the film, that memory is now literally being spat on. The village post-man, Pat (Phillip O'Flynn), stops at the memorial cross erected at the spot where Carberry was shot and uncaringly spits at it.

This Other Eden is a thematically complex satire which, through its interrogation of the legacy of the past, touches on a range of contemporary issues including emigration, the wealth of nuns, political hypocrisy, gombeenism, mob violence, illegitimacy, modern art, and cultural and linguistic difference. The conduit through which these themes are explored is Englishman Crispin Brown (Leslie Phillips). On his arrival in the village he meets four of the film's central characters: Devereux, now the editor of the local newspaper; Clannery (Harry Brogan), an anti-English nationalist; McNeely T. D. (Paul Farrell), the local politician; and McRoarty (Geoffrey Golden), hotelier, garage owner and auctioneer.

Brown, however, does not conform to the stereotype Englishman. He bewilders Clannery, for example, by offering sympathetic understanding of Ireland's colonial past. Indeed, at one point he declares, while reversing a well-known adage, that it is for the English to remember and for the Irish to forget the past. Brown's characterisation echoes that of Broadbent in Bernard Shaw's *John Bull's Other Island* (1907), though unlike Broadbent, Brown is not cynically manipulating the Irish. In *This Other Eden* that opportunity is reserved for the Irish themselves, in particular the gombeen McRoarty, and the politician McNeely. The focus of that manipulation is the legacy of the past. Devereux, who is the most direct link in the community to the War of Independence, maintains an ambiguous attitude to Carberry's memory. He complains to McNeely that that memory has been 'embalmed in words'. Nevertheless, it is McNeely who makes the speech before the statue is unveiled, ironically enough, by Devereux himself.

The statue is a crude modern art sculpture which becomes an object of ridicule to the villagers and the target of virulent denunciation by the 'more Irish than the Irish themselves' Brown. When the statue is blown up the villagers suspect Brown and in a perverse reversal of their earlier attitude turn their ire on him as an interfering outsider. They besiege his hotel and in another ironic narrative twist the mob is calmed by Clannery. Eventually it is revealed that the statue was destroyed by prospective cleric Conor Heapy (Norman Rodway), who turns out to be Carberry's illegitimate son. But, lest it be thought that the Irish hero, Carberry, was immoral it is also revealed that Conor was conceived while Carberry was on the run. There was no opportunity to marry and Conor's mother, who was also Devereux's sister, died in childbirth.

Brown, too, turns out to have a connection to the War of Independence. He is the illegitimate son of the officer Carberry and Devereux were due to meet on the fateful night in 1920. He explains that his father resigned his commission in protest at the Black and Tan ambush, thus indicating a degree of honour amongst the soldiers of the opposing sides. This honour is seen to be absent amidst the pettiness of much of the generation which survived the War of Independence, especially that represented by McRoarty and McNeely. By contrast, the younger generation, Irish and English, have much in common. Besides their illegitimacy, Crispin and Conor are both attached to Maire, McRoarty's daughter (Audrey Dalton). Indeed, the film closes with Crispin and Maire planning to marry, much to the surprise and irritation of McRoarty, who finds that he has to provide the local mansion, which he sought to sell to the nuns in his capacity as auctioneer, as Maire's dowry.[40]

It is interesting to speculate on the relationship of the characters in *This Other Eden* to Emmet Dalton's own life. Dalton was a hero of the War of Independence, a very successful Irish army general and was with Michael Collins when he was shot at Béalnabláth. After being an enigmatic leader he drifted into relative obscurity from the mid-1920s until his involvement with Ardmore Studios. Was, therefore, *This Other Eden* a signal from his past, an attempt to redress, if not rewrite, history?

Devereux, a confidant of Carberry, as Dalton was of Collins, had been suspected even by the villagers of responsibility for Carberry's death. Because Dalton accompanied Michael Collins on his fateful journey in 1922, Dalton, too, lived under a cloud of suspicion about what happened there. While it may only be hinted at in print,[41] speculation about those events have included allegations similar to those ascribed to Devereux. Of course, in the film's prologue we see that it is the Black and Tans who shoot Carberry, though he remains alive when the film cuts to the later sequences. Devereux then sacrifices himself to a small village newspaper, cynically dealing with the 'truth' of past and present, in order to raise Carberry's son, his nephew. Similarly, Dalton had to emigrate after being forced to resign as first Clerk of the Irish Senate and work as an insurance salesman and other obscure jobs before becoming a film producer. There is also a parallel with Brown's father. Dalton resigned as one of the Chiefs of Staff of the Free State Army in protest at the treatment of anti-Treaty republicans during the Civil War when he refused to support the increasingly repressive measures of the Free State government.

This Other Eden was made during an important period of transition within the dominant Irish political and government party, Fianna Fáil. After being head of government for 21 of the previous 27 years, Taoiseach Eamon de Valera was elected to the largely ceremonial post of President in June 1959. He was immediately succeeded as Taoiseach by Sean Lemass. The new outward-looking world represented by the persona of Lemass now developed apace. Thus the world première of *This Other Eden* at the Cork Film Festival on 25 September 1959 might have been the occasion for an assessment of the film's critical look at the past and at the present. But it is an interesting commentary on the sensitivity of the issues explored in the film that it is not possible to find any comment of note in Irish newspapers after it was shown at Cork. Perhaps *This Other Eden* was made too early and, indeed, may have been seen as too cynical even for the new Lemass era. It was, of course, the same Cork Film Festival which eulogised over *Mise Éire*, the celebratory film of the period of the struggle for Independence up to 1918.

The Abbey play adaptations made at Ardmore did not provide the resurgence of Irish Cinema first seen during the Abbey's early vibrant years. By the 1950s the Abbey itself was a shallow imitation of its past and as with the Abbey itself reviewers were to tire quickly of the Abbey films. In a review of *Saoirse?* in 1961 Fergus Linehan observed[42] in *The Irish Times* that any film which transcends 'the Ardmore rehash of yesterday's Abbey hit' was deserving of close attention. Indeed, the influence of the Abbey Theatre has tended to be an inhibiting influence on Irish Cinema such that one critic[43] in 1980 could declare that the 'Abbey led movies down [a] cul-de-sac'.

Ardmore and international productions

Before the establishment of Ardmore Studios only a small number of Irish-theme features had been made in Ireland since the war. The best-known were the British-produced *I See A Dark Stranger* (Dir: Frank Launder, 1945), *Hungry Hill* (Brian Desmond Hurst, 1946), *Captain Boycott* (Frank Launder, 1947), *Odd Man Out* (Carol Reed, 1947), *Another Shore* (Charles Crichton, 1948), *No Resting Place* (Paul Rotha, 1951) and *Stranger at My Door* (which is also known as *At A Dublin Inn*, 1950). The outstanding American-produced film was John Ford's *The Quiet Man* (1952). Ford also made *The Rising of the Moon* (which is alternatively known as *Three Leaves of a Shamrock*) in 1957. Irish exteriors were joined to studio interiors which were filmed in Britain or America. With the establishment of Ardmore Studios, interiors could now be shot in Ireland and Emmet Dalton recognised that if the studios were to become commercially viable then international productions had to be attracted to the studios.

Following the success of *Shake Hands With the Devil* (Michael Anderson, 1959), the next year another IRA story, this time set in Northern Ireland during World War II, was made. This was an adaption of Arthur J. Roth's 1958 novel, *A Terrible Beauty* (Tay Garnett, 1960). Of central economic importance to these films was the inclusion of a 'star'. Following James Cagney in *Shake Hands With the Devil*, Robert Mitchum was cast in *A Terrible Beauty*. This policy of casting foreign leads in Irish-theme films could have disastrous consequences. The most glaring and crude miscasting was in the role of Christy Mahon in J. M. Synge's *The Playboy of the Western World* (Brian Desmond Hurst, 1962). A minor English star, Gary Raymond, was patently incapable of interpreting the rhythm and nuance of Synge's words. Another odd choice was Rod Taylor in the role of Sean O'Casey in the film of his autobiographies, the John Ford/Jack Cardiff film, *Young Cassidy* (1964).

Other Irish-theme films made in the 1960s were *The Quare Fellow*

(Arthur Dreifuss, 1962), an adaption of Brendan Behan's play; Edna O'Brien's novel *The Lonely Girl* was adapted as *Girl With Green Eyes* (Desmond Davis, 1963) and one of her short stories was made into *I Was Happy Here* (Desmond Davis, 1965); Joseph Strick made a controversial version of James Joyce's *Ulysses* (1967); *The Violent Enemy* (Don Sharp, 1968), was an IRA story set in modern Ireland; and *Paddy* (Daniel Haller, 1969), was an adaption of Lee Dunne's novel, *Goodbye to the Hill*. This latter film concerns the amorous adventures of a Dublin working class lad who, as *Monthly Film Bulletin* described him, was a 'cross between *Alfie* and *The Ginger Man*'.[44] *Paddy* has the invidious distinction along with *Ulysses* and *Of Human Bondage* (Ken Hughes/Henry Hathaway, 1964) of being three films made in Ireland in the 1960s which were banned by the Film Censor.

Nigel Patrick's *Johnny Nobody* (1960) was probably the most peculiar Irish-theme film made in the 1960s. In this film a best selling author Mulcahy (William Bendix) is shot dead outside a church by a mysterious stranger who becomes dubbed Johnny Nobody (Aldo Ray). In a plot which 'goes from improbability to improbability to a finale which is downright unbelievable'[45] the local priest (Nigel Patrick) is framed as a sex maniac, as he investigates the murder, by a woman (Yvonne Mitchell) who turns out to be Nobody's wife. Meanwhile Nobody is cleared of the murder but dies of a heart attack afterwards in a courtroom argument with Fr Carey. It transpires that Nobody was a religious fanatic and explorer from whom Mulcahy had stolen the theme of Nobody's forthcoming book.

The 1970s and 1980s also saw a number of Irish-theme films being made in Ireland by foreigners. Brian Friel's well-known play, *Philadelphia Here I Come* (John Quested, 1970) was set during the last night of an American-bound Irish emigrant; *Quackser Fortune Has a Cousin in the Bronx* (Warris Hussein, 1970) was an excellent Dublin comedy; Walter Macken's children's story, *Flight of the Doves* (Ralph Nelson, 1971) followed runaway children from Britain to Ireland; John Huston's *The Mackintosh Man* (1973), a spy thriller, contained a section shot in Connemara; and *Un Taxi Mauve* (Purple Taxi, 1979) concerns a Frenchman who comes to Ireland and develops a wide range of relationships. *Purple Taxi* was the only film with a cash investment from the National Film Studios of Ireland. For about £260,000 the NFSI received a 7 per cent stake for English language territories except North America. The NFSI had no artistic control over the production and it received a poor critical and box-office response in Ireland. This was not the case with the Irish-theme blockbuster film of the post-war period. *Ryan's Daughter* (David Lean, 1971) ran for nearly a year in a first-run Dublin cinema.

Another aspect of international productions was the use of Ireland as a non-Irish location. Before the establishment of Ardmore only a few films had used the country in this way. Due to wartime restrictions in Britain, the Irish army provided the troops for the Agincourt sequence in Laurence Olivier's *Henry V* (1944), which was shot in Wicklow. In the 1950s *Knights of the Round Table* (1953) and Irish-American John Huston's *Moby Dick* (1956), for which Youghal, Co. Cork, was used as a base, were the first major features which used Ireland merely as a location and not for a specifically Irish subject film.

The first Ardmore-based film to so use Ireland was also the first Irish Film Finance Corporation-financed production, *The Siege of Sidney Street* (1960). It is, perhaps, no coincidence that this film about the 1912 London anarchist siege should have been produced, directed and photographed by Robert S. Baker and Monty Berman. As close collaborators with Emmet Dalton they produced four of the six Abbey plays made by Dalton's companies. Emmet Dalton produced another of the IFFC-funded films when he made *The Devil's Agent* (1961), a story concerning a wine salesman, George Drost (Peter Van Eyck), who is involved with Soviet and US Intelligence in Austria, Germany and Hungary. It was directed by John Paddy Carstairs, who had directed two Irish-theme films, *Talk of a Million* (1951) and *Treasure Hunt* (1952) from the play by M. J. Farrell (Molly Keane) and John Perry. Dalton also made *Middle of Nowhere* (1960) and *Lies My Father Told Me* (1960).[46] This latter film was a transposition of a book by Ted Allen, originally about a poor Jewish boy and his grandfather in Montreal in the 1920s, into Ireland and the Irish. Both these films were directed by Don Chaffey and part-funded by the IFFC.

Most of the features made in whole or in part in Ireland in the 1960s and based at Ardmore were, however, shot using Ireland as a foreign location. Medieval England can be seen in *Sword of Sherwood Forest* (Terence Fisher, 1960); Berlin in *The Spy Who Came in From the Cold* (Martin Ritt, 1966); World War I in *The Blue Max* (John Guillerman, 1966) and even Tibet and China in *The Face of Fu Manchu* (Don Sharp, 1965) and *The Vengeance of Fu Manchu* (Jeremy Summers, 1967). Others came seeking access to the Irish Film Finance Corporation moneys which supported films mainly during 1960–62. Of the 15 so funded, five were second features produced by Bill and Michael Luckwell. Four of these were directed by Max Varnell in 1962: *Enter Inspector Duvall*, *A Guy Named Caesar*, *A Question of Suspense* and *Murder in Eden*. The fifth Luckwell-produced film was *Ambush in Leopard Street* (J. H. Piperno, 1962). This pattern was to continue in the 1970s and 1980s with films as various as John Boorman's *Zardoz* (1973) and *Excalibur* (1981), Robert Altman's *Images* (1972), *The First Great Train Robbery* (1979) and Alain Tanner's *Light Years Away* (Les Années Lumières, 1981).

Despite the intermittent film-making activity in Ireland (much of which did not need to utilise Ardmore's facilities) and the availability of considerable government funding, there was a recognition within a decade of its opening that Ardmore was not going to lead to the establishment of an Irish film industry. Long before state investment became defined in terms of financial losses it was also accepted that Ardmore was not going to serve as the panacea for indigenous film production. Even government departments and state agencies recognised that reality.

Irish Film Board

Ardmore's failure to respond to the needs of Irish film-makers was comprehensively analysed, as we have seen, by Louis Marcus. The mixture of disillusionment, disappointment and anger which pervades Marcus's articles helped focus the government's attention on Ardmore's failure to respond to Irish needs. The visit of Taoiseach Jack Lynch to the set of John Huston's *Sinful Davey* (1968)[47] was followed by the establishment of the Film Industry Committee with Huston as chairman. The result of this committee's deliberations, *The Report of the Film Industry Committee* (1968), is the only published government investigation into Irish film production. This committee was broadly based and amongst its members were film-makers Louis Marcus, Patrick Carey and Tom Hayes. The other members included Lord Killanin, who had co-produced *The Rising of the Moon* and *The Playboy of the Western World*; Louis Heelan of the Industrial Credit Company; the manager of Ardmore Studios, W. Eades; independent exhibitor Michael Collins; and representatives of Rank's and ABC's Irish subsidiaries.

The Report recommended that pre-production finance of up to

£10,000 be made available to international commercial features with budgets up to £200,000. As the Report noted, 'the possibility that genuinely Irish feature films costing more than £200,000 would be made is remote but is not ruled out'.[48] Drawing a parallel with film production in France, Denmark, Sweden, Poland, Czechoslovakia and Hungary, 'none of whom have established themselves in the mass-US market',[49] the Report suggested a more modest scale of feature production with budgets up to £50,000. These films would be produced for the 'art' house market and should be supported up to the full cost of production with repayable loans. Their makers would be those Irish people who were graduating from documentary production, television and commercials. Shorts film production, the area where Irish film-makers had the greatest experience, should also receive an annual subvention of £55,000 to £75,000. Steps should also be taken, the Report adds, to encourage the production in Ireland of television commercials. This policy was achieved in 1973 when the Irish Film Workers Association and the ITGWU blocked the use of imported crews to shoot Irish commercials.

Unlike previous attempts to enact legislation for an Irish film industry, *The Report of the Film Industry Committee* was acted upon with relative speed. The credit for ensuring the publication of the Film Industry Bill (1970) must lie in the main with the Society of Film-Makers of Ireland who maintained the pressure on the government for film legislation. The society welcomed the Bill (indeed they had a direct input in its formulation) which followed closely the recommendations of the Film Industry Committee Report. They declared that they had reservations about some of the definitions of what constitutes an 'Irish' film but, nevertheless, they accepted that the Department of Industry and Commerce were faithful to the Report's recommendations.[50]

The Bill envisaged the establishment of a seven-person Film Board to administer its provisions. In addition to the pre-production costs of up to £10,000 for features with budgets of up to £200,000 and full production investment in features costing up to £50,000, the Board could also support prestige and experimental shorts costing up to £15,000. Despite the positive intentions contained in the Bill it did not get a second reading in the Dáil. Like many things that year it was a victim of the arms crisis, a change of Minister and a shelving of the proposals. It was a decade before another Film Bill was published. In the meantime Irish commercials makers and the Irish film-making sectors expanded.

When the struggle for an Irish Film Bill was revived a broader grouping of support was identifiable. The threat to indigenous film production this time was not so much from foreign producers *per se* but their surrogates, the National Film Studios of Ireland's management and board and their allies in the film industry. These latter were more concerned with high wages on foreign productions than the more modest income then available from the budgets of indigenous films. But from the mid-1970s onwards independent film-makers became grouped around the ITGWU, the Irish Film Workers Association, established in 1972 and renamed in 1977 the Irish Film and Television Guild, and later the Association of Independent Producers of Ireland, now known as the Association of Independent Film-makers. With important institutional support from the Arts Council they were able to contrast the vibrancy and commitment of independent film-makers with the failure of the NFSI to make any worthwhile contribution to indigenous film-making. An extreme example of the limited support given by the NFSI to indigenous production was revealed in the letters page of *The Irish Times* in 1977. Joe Comerford's *Down the Corner*, a film about Dublin working-class teenagers, received a concession of £10 per week off the renting of an editing bench at the studios.[51]

On coming to office in 1977 the Minister for Industry and Commerce, Desmond O'Malley, decided to obtain an independent analysis of the NFSI. This was submitted to him by London consultants Arthur D. Little & Co. in May 1978. Two of their recommendations were that an independent Film Board should be set up and that it should be allocated a fund of £4.1 million. In the meantime O'Malley met representatives of all sections of the film industry. During this period the central struggle was between those independent film-makers who sought to have any film production finance administered independently and made available to Irish film-makers, and the NFSI which sought to gain control of a £2½ to £3 million revolving production fund.[52] To this end it sought and failed to incorporate the independent film-makers into an NFSI-led united front. One public instance of the intentions behind this strategy had been revealed at the 1978 Cork Film Festival. What was ostensibly a forum on the future of an Irish film industry organised by the NFSI excluded the most vocal critics of an NFSI-led film industry.[53]

Eventually on 25 November 1979 the government published two Bills. One was to regularise the film studios as a semi-state company and the other was the Irish Film Board Bill. It was another eleven months before the debate proper, the second reading, began in the Dáil. The debate was opened by O'Malley as the Minister responsible for film production. He revealed that the NFSI had sought to ensure that the legislation should provide for a film financing and distribution subsidiary company of the NFSI. This proposal had been rejected following the analysis of the consultants' report.[54]

After the publication of the Bill a joint submission was made to the Minister by the Association of Independent Producers of Ireland, the Irish Film and Television Guild and the Film Section of the Irish Transport and General Workers Union. This submission, popularly referred to as the 'Yellow Book', clearly demonstrated a different approach to that pursued by the NFSI. They sought, for instance, an amendment to the Bill which would have required the Film Board to allocate at least 80 per cent of all Film Board moneys to Irish film-makers, in effect, incorporating a statutory 'Irish-dimension' into the Bill. Their demand was a response to the policies pursued at Ardmore where the encouragement of foreign companies had taken precedence over support for indigenous production. O'Malley, however, rejected this proposal while confirming Fianna Fáil's long-standing policy of encouraging foreign capital to invest in Ireland. He stated[55] that he was

> very often surprised at the apparent criticism against international projects as if they were almost a discouragement to the Irish film-makers. Surely two or three of this type of project a year, if carefully selected in order to ensure viability, are to be welcomed and could flourish in conjunction with the activities of Irish film-makers.

It was clear that the government had no intention of acceding to a specific indigenous film production policy. The independents' attitude to the studios was that they should continue in existence, now that they were built, but they should operate as an unsubsidised hireable facility and not as a production company. Furthermore, the independents argued, international commercial cinema projects originating outside Ireland should not be given production finance. O'Malley was obviously unwilling to support this view which collided with the general thrust of government economic policy.

One of the significant characteristics of the Dáil debate on the

Film Bill was the insistent demands made that the Film Board be given a statutory distribution function and that a film archive be established. O'Malley rejected the statutory requirement for an archive on the grounds that the Board's broad brief included that possibility and it was essential that film production should be given priority in the Board's early years. He also rejected the demands on distribution with the speculation that on completion of a film a producer might simply dump a film on the Board's doorstep and expect that it be distributed. While this was an unlikely scenario it has been the case in the early years of the Board's existence that distribution remains a difficult problem to solve. When O'Malley introduced the bill in the Senate he conceded the fundamental point made in the 'Yellow Book' that the bill did not give specific recognition to an 'Irish-dimension' in the Board's activities. A phrase from the Broadcasting Authority Act (1960) was then introduced into the bill: 'In so far as it considers it appropriate, the Board shall have regard to the need for the expression of national culture through the medium of film-making'. While the term 'national culture' lacks the precision contained in the phrase 'Irish film culture' which had been proposed by the Labour Party in the Dáil, at least it recognised that Irish projects should be given priority 'in so far as it considers it appropriate' by the Board. However, no particular proportion of the total moneys to be allocated to Irish film-makers was suggested. Another amendment agreed to was to identify as one of the Board's activities the need to establish a national film archive.

The Senate debate, in common with that in the Dáil, offered few original or controversial contributions. One of the few critical speeches came from Independent Senator, John A. Murphy. He called for films which addressed themselves to Irish audiences in the first instance. He declared that the bulk of the money should go to Irish film-makers and that 'public money had been thrown away on film studios'.[56] When the limited amendments were returned to the Dáil they were passed with a minimum of discussion.

Although the Irish Film Board Act (1980) was passed in December, it was a considerable time before a Board was appointed. The eventual appointment of the Industrial Credit Company's Louis Heelan as chairman and John Boorman and Cork Film Festival Director Robin O'Sullivan as members caused apprehension amongst independent film-makers. With only three of the seven places filled, a quorum under the terms of the Act, the Board went

ahead with an investment decision which was to prove highly provocative from the independent film-makers' point of view. The
Board had been allocated £200,000 for the part of 1981 which
remained after their appointment and £100,000 of this money was
invested in Neil Jordan's first feature, *Angel*. This amount consti-
tuted less than 20 per cent of the film's budget while the remainder
was provided by the new British television channel, Channel Four.
The controversy arose from the fact that Film Board member,
John Boorman, was the film's executive producer, a director of the
film's production company, The Motion Picture Company of
Ireland, and while Neil Jordan was already established as a short
story writer and novelist his only previous film was a documentary
about the making of Boorman's *Excalibur*. Additional resentment
was felt by independent film-makers when it became clear that
Angel was the only project to be allocated funds in 1981. (Money
was actually returned to the Exchequer at the end of the year).
Following widespread criticism from independent film-makers,
including a threat to boycott the Board's proceedings, Heelan
resigned in December 1981.

The attitude of the independents to the Film Board's investment
in *Angel*, and the response by both Jordan and Boorman to the
criticism of the Board's decision, was to have a long-term negative
effect on Irish film production. The issue forcefully entered the
public domain at the Third International Festival of Film and
Television in the Celtic Countries, which was held in Wexford
from 28 March to 2 April 1982, when the attending delegates,
press and film-makers were invited to a screening of *Angel*. A
meeting of the Association of Independent Producers was called to
coincide with the screening as a means of registering the AIP's disapproval of the manner of its Irish financing. This act, which in
retrospect some would concede was politically inappropriate, left
deep scars which have resurfaced on numerous occasions since.
The matter was fuelled by some injudicious comments at the time
and since then by both Jordan and Boorman. The personalised
manner of the controversy has tended to obscure more fundamental questions which the issue raised, especially the relationship
between smaller scale indigenous productions over which Irish
artistic control would be retained and larger budget co-productions
or exclusively foreign-financed Irish-theme films.

Following Heelan's resignation, RTE's then Head of Features
(and now an independent film-maker) Muiris MacConghail was
appointed chairman of the Film Board for a four-year term in

January 1982. There was relief amongst film-makers at this appointment. MacConghail's career in RTE had shown him to be an advocate of Irish film production and informed on the difficulties of indigenous culture in a 'peripheral' society such as Ireland. The other members appointed to the Board for a four-year term were theatre impresario Noel Pearson and writer Carolyn Swift.

It is indicative of the perceived lack of importance of the independent film-makers by the Department of Industry and Commerce that when AIP Chairman Tiernan MacBride, one of the prime motivators of the independents' campaign, and Irish Film and Television Guild Chairman Michael Algar were appointed to the Board's two remaining places, their terms were only for one year.

Until he himself resigned in April 1982, the month the National Film Studios of Ireland were put into receivership, John Boorman did not attend a meeting of the expanded Board. Boorman's resignation was, perhaps, confirmation of his view that he would not now be able to allocate the amounts of money he would have wished to international productions. In an insensitive and entirely unreflective comment on his own involvement in Irish film policy and, indeed, on Ireland in general, Boorman was later to declare[57] that 'There is a narrowness of approach, there's a lack of ambition in this country. There's a sense of being in love with failure . . .' Boorman's place on the Film Board was allocated in December 1982 to casting director Nuala Moiselle.

The following March when his one-year term was complete Tiernan MacBride was reappointed for a further year, and Michael Algar, now the Board's Chief Executive, was replaced by independent film-maker Louis Marcus. Sixteen months later MacBride and Marcus were reappointed for a further year. Unexpectedly, in March 1985 the Minister for Industry and Commerce, John Bruton, decided to rescind the appointments of all the Board's members. However, two months later this decision was reversed when the Board was given a three months period of office and this was then extended by a further two months. This uncertainty did little to allay fears about the perceived lack of commitment by Industry and Commerce to Irish film production. Eventually in October 1985 a new Board was appointed with Muiris MacConghail continuing as chairman and Tiernan MacBride as a member. The other members were all new to the Board: playwright Hugh Leonard (who resigned due to pressure of work three months later), exhibitor Kevin Anderson, film producers John Kelleher and Morgan O'Sullivan, and Industry and Commerce Principal Officer Paul Bates. All were appointed for a two-year period. Writer Jennifer Johnston (whose father directed and mother Shelah Richards acted in *Guests of the Nation*, 1935) replaced Leonard on the Board.

The uncertainties of the future were further fuelled in August 1986 when responsibility for the Irish Film Board was transferred from the Department of Industry and Commerce to the Department of the Taoiseach's junior Minister of Arts and Culture. While the ending of Industry and Commerce's 50 year reign in Irish film is to be welcomed, the reasons for which I think are demonstrated above, the role of the Arts and Culture Minister during the coalition government's term of office leaves very little hope that it will fare any better in its new home. However, in January 1987, towards the end of the coalition government's term of office, the Minister published the first Government White Paper on cultural policy in Ireland, 'Access and Opportunity'. In this document two film institutions were identified as deserving support: the Irish Film Board and its search in particular for a liberal tax regime for film production and the Irish Film Institute's film cultural project, the Irish Film Centre.

It is too early yet to assess the success or otherwise of the Board's policies.[58] It has funded a wide selection of fiction and documentary films, given development money to film-makers, funded the researching and writing of a report on an Irish Film Archive, and aided Irish film festivals. The first 13 completed projects in which the Board invested cost a total of approximately £2,785,000. The Board invested approximately £780,000 or 28 per cent of this sum.[59] With a policy objective of not investing more than 50 per cent in any one project it has been essential for all film-makers to make co-production arrangements with Irish and British television stations, and raise Irish private investment. This latter development has been aided by the availability of various tax arrangements which has encouraged Irish private investment in film production.[60] £246,000, or 48 per cent of the budget of the 1984 film *Anne Devlin*, was raised in this way, while £60,000, or 37 per cent of the budget of *Pigs* (1984) was Irish private investment.

David Collins, producer of *Pigs* and initiator of the Arts Council Film Script Award in the 1970s, and ex-RTE Controller of Programmes John Kelleher, made the most dramatic use of tax arrangements for private investment in films through a new company, Strongbow. In 1984 Strongbow raised more than one million pounds from shareholders through a Business Development Scheme. With investments from the Film Board (£100,000) and Channel Four (£600,000) Strongbow produced the £1.7 million feature film *Eat the Peach* (dir: Peter Ormrod, 1986). *Eat the Peach* is a wryly amusing tale about two unemployed men who build a Wall of Death in the backyard of one of their houses in the middle of a flat-landscaped peat bog. *Eat the Peach* attempted to negotiate the difficult terrain of established Irish stereotypes in the cinema and the need for a so-called 'international' Irish film. Its success may be judged from its three-month-long run in a first-run Dublin cinema and a gross box office of nearly £400,000 nationwide during its first six months. Shortly after the release of *Eat the Peach* Strongbow invited further shareholders investment and raised another £300,000. In summer 1986 Strongbow produced a largely Channel Four/RTE financed £2.2 million television series, *When Reason Sleeps*, directed by Robert Wynne-Simmons and RTE's Tony Barry.

The establishment of the Irish Film Board has encouraged new developments in Irish film culture as well as providing a focus for the gradual evolution of an indigenous film industry. Its future success will as likely be determined by the availability of a sympathetic tax regime for private investment as by the cash allocations from the state. Its future will ultimately be measured by the commitment and quality of indigenous film production. On the evidence of the last decade, as we will see in the next chapter, there is every reason to be optimistic for the future.

Notes

1. Simon Rowson, 'The Value of Remittances Abroad for Cinematograph Films', *Journal of the Royal Statistical Society*, Vol. XCVII, Part IV, 1934, pp. 638–9. Rowson put the number of Irish cinemas at 5 per cent of the number in Britain while the distributors estimated that the average earning power for films in Ireland was 3 per cent of the total for Britain and Ireland.

2. Dublin: The Parkside Press, 1943.

3. I have been unable to unearth a copy of this report. Its recommendations are taken from references made in government memos and correspondence.

4. The summary of the proposals contained here is based on files released to me by the Department of the Taoiseach. A more detailed account than is contained here concerning the 1930s and 1940s will be

published at a later date.

5. The correspondence and memos relating to the Shaw-Pascal proposals may be found in File S 13914 A, Department of the Taoiseach.

6. De Valera was in correspondence with Shaw on the proposals from 29 August 1946.

7. The meeting was held in November 1947.

8. Shaw to Cox, 30 November 1947. Cox replied on 5 December.

9. De Valera to Shaw, 30 December 1947. Shaw had written to de Valera on 2 December.

10. File S 13838, Department of the Taoiseach, contains this and other Department of Industry and Commerce proposals on a film studio in the 1940s.

11. The memo was dated 30 November 1946.

12. John Healy, 'All-Irish film studio ''by May'' ', *Irish Press*, 15 January 1957, p. 5.

13. Ibid.

14. See two RTE Television documentaries: *The Rise and Many Falls of Ardmore Studios*, 1973, Producer: Peter Kennerley; Reporter: Cathal O'Shannon. *Emmet Dalton Remembers*, 1978, Producer: Niall McCarty; Reporter: Cathal O'Shannon.

15. Louis Marcus, *The Irish Film Industry*, Dublin: Irish Film Society, 1967, p. 7. This booklet contains a series of articles reprinted from *Irish Times*.

16. *Daily Cinema*, 17 December 1958, p. 11, declared that Ardmore 'stands favourable comparison with the most modern studios of today'.

17. 'Minister Opens First Irish Film Studio', *Irish Times*, 13 May 1958, p. 4; 'Minister Opens Film Studios; Aimed at Export Market', *Irish Independent*, 13 May 1958, p. 2.

18. *Daily Cinema*, 17 December 1958.

19. Marcus, *Irish Film Industry*, 1967, pp. 12–13. The IFFC invested in a total of 15 films, 8 first features (*The Devil's Agent*, *Johnny Nobody*, *The Siege of Sidney Street*, *The Quare Fellow*, *The Playboy of the Western World*, *Stork Talk*, *Middle of Nowhere* and *The Very Edge*) and 7 second features (*Ambush in Leopard Street*, *Enter Inspector Duvall*, *Freedom to Die*, *A Guy Called Caesar*, *A Question of Suspense*, *Murder in Eden* and *Lies My Father Told Me*). These are listed as Appendix E, *The Report of the Film Industry Committee*, Dublin: Government Stationary Office, 1968.

20. Marcus, *Irish Film Industry*, 1967, pp. 9–10.

21. Ibid., p. 15.

22. Ibid.

23. Ibid., p. 16.

24. Business Diary, 'O'Reilly seeks an Irish films Revival', *Times*, 26 May 1972, p. 27.

25. Desmond O'Malley, *Dáil Debates*, Vol. 323, Col. 42, 15 October 1980.

26. Ibid., col. 44.

27. P. 57.

28. This statement was made at a seminar at the Institute of Contemporary Arts, London, to coincide with an Irish Cinema season at the ICA and the National Film Theatre, London, February 1980.

29. Tom Hayes, *Irish Times*, 13 June 1978, p. 8.

30. *Manchester Guardian*, 8 January 1959. This comment was made during the course of a review of a film about the history of the Abbey Theatre, *Cradle of Genius*, by Paul Rotha, Tom Hayes and Jim O'Connor.

31. Ibid., 7 February 1947.

32. 'Sally's Irish Rogue Gets Great Ovation', *Cork Examiner*, 29 September 1958, p. 6.

33. 'Irish Film Made in Month', *Irish Times*, 30 September 1958, p. 6; Nina Hibben, *Daily Worker*, 22 November 1958.

34. 'Walter Macken Triumphs', *Sunday Press*, 26 April 1959, p. 19.

35. L.MacG., 'Great Acting in Macken Movie', *Sunday Review*, 26 April 1959, p. 22.

36. 'Seeing is not Believing', *Sunday Independent*, 26 April 1959, p. 23.

37. Ken Shaw, *Sunday Independent*, 15 March 1959, p. 21; *Irish Times*, 16 March 1959, p. 8.

38. L.MacG., 'No Disgrace to our Touchy Temperaments', *Sunday Review*, 15 March 1959, p. 16.

39. *Monthly Film Bulletin*, Vol. 27, No. 318, July 1960, p. 97.

40. It is worth noting some of the differences between the film and play. In the play, Brown (who is known as Roger Crispin) is the actual officer Carberry was due to meet, not his son as in the film. Devereux is a more committed, if still cynical and provocative, commentator. His quirky view of Irish history sees some Irish who would be regarded as 'villains' by Irish nationalists as aiding internationalism. Dermot McMurrough who 'invites' the Normans into Ireland, 'was a typical Irishman with an international outlook, and the prosperity of his country at heart'. On his relationship with Carberry he states to Clannery at one point that 'there are plenty in Ballymorgan, to this day who'll tell you that I murdered Carberry — out of jealousy of his fame or because of a secret grudge'. Devereux does not unveil the statue as in the film and the ceremony takes place off-stage.

The play is set in September 1947 when the Labour government was in office in Britain. There are references to the 'Red Bolshevik' government at Westminster and Brown declares himself a socialist at heart but not in practice. Brown's mother was Irish while Clannery's was English! (*This Other Eden*, Dublin: P. J. Bourke, 1954 and 1970).

41. This controversy was reopened with the publication of John M. Feehan's *The Shooting of Michael Collins*, Dublin/Cork: The Mercier Press, 1981.

42. Fergus Linehan, 'Not for Export', *Irish Times*, 23 October 1961, p. 8.

43. Ciaran Carty, *Sunday Independent*, 13 January 1980.

44. *Monthly Film Bulletin*, Vol. 37, No. 434, March 1970, p. 58.

45. Fergus Linehan, *Irish Times*, 19 February 1962, p. 10.

46. *Lies My Father Told Me* was made in its original setting by Jan Kadar in 1975.

47. This particular production and supportive comments by John Huston on Irish film production serve as an American illustration of what had occurred with ACTT in Britain. John Lehners, head of the Hollywood AFL Film Council, accused Huston of 'attempting to establish a

sanctuary for runaway production in Ireland'. In characteristic fashion and a headline in the same issue of *Variety* (3 April 1968, pp. 1 and 11) to match, 'Irish John Huston Blasts John Lehners', Huston retorted that he was attacked unfairly. He declared that 'there is no desire on my part to bring pictures from the U.S. to Ireland. My aim is to start a native film industry in Ireland. Ireland is full of talent and places to shoot in — other than studios'.

Huston added that he wished 'to foster Irish pictures made by the Irish. The question of making foreign pictures there was settled long before I put my oar in. I'm interested in nourishing and developing an Irish film industry, independent of the rest of the world in order to air the talent of Eire. This attack was on ill-considered, or unconsidered grounds. It was absurd'.

48. *The Report*, op. cit., p. 40.

49. Ibid., p. 18.

50. *Showcase*, October/December 1970, p. 48.

51. 'The Irish Film Industry', *Irish Times* letters page, 7, 9 and 15 December 1977.

52. See interview with Sheamus Smith, managing director NFSI, *Business and Finance*, 27 July 1978.

53. See Kevin Rockett, 'Cork Film Festival and Irish (Film) Culture', *In Dublin*, No. 55, 30 June – 13 July 1978.

54. *Dáil Debates*, Vol. 323, Col. 44, 15 October 1980.

55. Ibid., Col. 50.

56. *Senate Debates*, Vol. 95, Cols. 517 – 18, 10 December 1980.

57. Interviewed in programme six, 'New Directions', part of Ulster Television's series, *A Seat Among the Stars: The Cinema and Ireland*, screened on Channel Four, 1984. See Kevin Rockett, 'Stars Get in your Eyes', *Framework*, No. 25, 1984, pp. 28 – 41. Similar generalised comments were made by David Puttnam, producer of *Cal*, in *Sunday Press*, 15 September 1985, p. 2.

58. The Board's policies may be viewed through the prism of what was stated by all sectors of the film industry, film organisations and interested persons at a one day public hearing held on 4 April 1982. These presentations were later published as the *Proceedings of the Public Hearing of Bord Scannán na hÉireann/Irish Film Board*, Dublin: Irish Film Board, 1982.

59. In the Annual Reports of Bord Scannán na hÉireann/Irish Film Board for 1981 – 2 and 1983 the 13 films in which the Board invested £780,000 are listed. They are: the feature films, *Angel* (1982), *The Outcasts* (1982), *The Country Girls* (1983), *Anne Devlin* (1984), *Pigs* (1984); short fiction films: *Our Boys* (1981), *The Schooner* (1983), *Attracta* (which, exceptionally, received almost 75 per cent of its £139,393 budget from the Board; 1983), *John, Love* (1983); documentaries: *At the Cinema Palace: Liam O'Leary* (1983), *Atlantean* (1984), *The Algonquin Trilogy* (1984), and *Wild Ireland* (1985). (The prefix of 'approximately' used with the investment and budget figures is to indicate that a small number of the figures have been converted from sterling to Irish pounds in the calculations). The Board published a booklet, *Irish Films* (1984), which lists these and other films to which it has advanced money.

60. See Paddy Woodworth, 'Reeling in the Money', *Magill*, May 1986,

for the role of tax money in Irish films. See also Paddy Woodworth, 'The Price of Freedom', *Magill*, 7 March 1985, for the use of tax money by RTE and its importance in co-production deals.

5

Breakthroughs

Kevin Rockett

There have been extensive social, economic and cultural changes in Ireland since the beginning of cinema in 1896. Those 90 years can be divided into three broad periods: the last 25 years of the struggle towards an independent state; the first 35 years of inward-looking, cultural and economic policies by governments dominated by the two complementary sides of Sinn Féin and the IRA which divided over the Anglo-Irish Treaty; and the period since the late 1950s during which most protectionist measures have been abandoned and the Irish economy and Irish culture have become 'international'. The advent of Sean Lemass as Taoiseach in 1959 gave political expression to the new policies, which helped lead to nearly 400 foreign companies being set up in Ireland in the 1960s alone. These developments were accelerated by Ireland's overwhelming support for EEC membership in a 1972 referendum. An indicator of these changes is the demographic evidence which had identified two crucial shifts in Irish society by the late 1970s. During the previous three decades there had been a major migration from rural to urban areas and there had been a significant alteration in the relationship to work. This had led to a dwindling away of the viability of self-employment and a corresponding shift towards large-scale employers and well-qualified employees.[1]

These changes resulted in a greater interest in and awareness of economic issues as was indicated by the massive but politically unfocused demonstrations in 1979 and 1980 calling for a progressive shift in taxation away from Pay As You Earn workers towards business, farmers and professionals. In contrast it could be argued that the failure of the South to mobilise behind the H-Block campaign during 1980 and 1981 was an important contributory factor

127

in its defeat. These events are further evidence of a shift in emphasis within the South in relation to Northern Ireland, over which a historic compromise is being sought by the Irish and British governments. The general public support in the South given to the 1985 Anglo-Irish Agreement indicates how far the South has shifted since the last mass expression of Southern nationalism, the 1972 burning of Dublin's British Embassy following Derry's Bloody Sunday.

The economic and ideological changes in the South helped lead to a shift towards political fragmentation and class politics. The instability of traditional political allegiances from the 1973 general election onwards is one indicator of these internal changes. Closer scrutiny of the South itself began to replace the traditional displacement of all Ireland's wrongs on to the old enemy. The socio-economic changes which have become manifest since the 1960s have brought in their wake significant diversity and originality to Irish artistic production as well as critical and interpretative assessments of Ireland's past and present.

That diversity was aided by legislative liberalisation and institutional initiatives. The relaxing of the state's book and film censorship from the mid-1960s onwards was an indication of changing attitudes. The 1973 Arts Act which increased the Arts Council's power and funds was to prove an important institutional stimulus to artistic change. This Act also allowed the Arts Council for the first time since its establishment in 1951 to make funds available for film purposes. In parallel with the institutional changes, by the mid-1970s a number of different and unco-ordinated strands were leading hesitantly towards greater fiction film production. In particular, an increasing number of Irish students from art colleges both in Dublin and London began making films; documentarists of an older generation began working with actors and narrative; isolated individuals learned about film-making through amateur cine clubs or worked by themselves before progressing to professional work; RTE personnel who had gained training while working in television left to make their own films; people who worked on advertising commercials branched out to other film activities . . . Some of these received institutional support through the Arts Council's commitment to independent 16mm productions. In this regard the initiation by the Arts Council of the Film Script Award in 1977 was to prove of major significance in encouraging indigenous film production. RTE contributed significantly to this scheme and film clubs (Dublin's Project Cinema

Club and the Irish Film Theatre) and film societies helped give a broad film cultural background to film-making.

While there was a general commitment amongst 'independent' film-makers to indigenous productions not all strands coincided. Differences existed between those committed to a more critical indigenous film culture and those concerned with 'international' commercial films with or without Irish themes. The concerns, however, of this chapter are with the group of film-makers who have sought to inflect their films with a critical engagement with both social and filmic discourses in Ireland. In this regard, from the mid-1970s onwards Irish fiction films began exploring a more secular and historically reflective society. A more complex notion of the past was examined; the family became a location of instability and fragmentation; sexuality was examined if albeit obliquely and hesitantly; repressive Catholic education was relived on the screen; the use of landscape as an idealised backdrop for Irish arcadian beauty was partly discarded; working-class experience made its appearance for the first time; experiments in film form challenged narrative's traditional supremacy.

The Arts Council's first Film Script Award was made to Bob Quinn's *Poitín* (Poteen, 1978) from a script by Colm Bairéad. *Poitín* was the first consciously sustained questioning of the romantic view of the countryside through the presentation of another form of realist view of the West of Ireland than that hitherto available on film. As film critic Ciaran Carty put it in an article titled 'A West With Warts':[2] Quinn

> implicitly de-romanticises the Robert Flaherty image of the rugged West as a place of primal dignity where man does noble battle with the elements and frail currachs brave the relentless Atlantic surf while women stoically tend the stewpots at turf fires, centuries of endurance and waiting etched on their windswept faces.

Quinn sought to present the lives of the Connemara people as being as harsh and severe as that of an urban experience but in a landscape which is just 'a fact of the environment'. As Carty adds, 'significantly the entire story is shot inland, in stoney valleys and shapeless villages, away from the prima donna sea, deliberately avoiding the standard postcard splendour'.

The narrative centres around a poteen-maker (Cyril Cusack) and his two selling agents (Niall Toibín, Donal McCann) from whom the police seize poteen. They subsequently steal the poteen back from the police and then sell it, keeping the proceeds of the sale for themselves. After a long drinking session they seek more drink at the lakeside cottage where the poteen-maker lives with his adult daughter (Mairéad Ní Conghaile). In this climactic scene they in turn threaten the poteen-maker, destroy the kitchen, knocking a religious icon from the wall in the process, and terrorise the poteen-maker's daughter. One of the agents even impotently attempts to molest her. By then, the poteen-maker has provided the agents with a leaking boat which is to be used to recover the poteen from the lake bed but which leads to their deaths.

Although the poteen-maker is located outside the law he still remains within a set of social values and while the countryside is presented more harshly than before it nonetheless remains the repository for traditional values. Religion, economy and sexuality are intertwined so that the final revenge, ostensibly for stealing the poteen, is also for the transgression of social and sexual codes by these social outcasts, the selling agents.

In Neville Presho's *Desecration* (1981), another Film Script Award winner, the countryside is also seen as a site of conflict between old values and new economic imperatives. In this film the friction between a restorer of an ancient monument (Eamonn Keane) and a gombeen hotelier (Tom Hickey) is mediated by a city geologist (Johnny Murphy) who comes to an island in search of mineral deposits. The geologist's sympathy towards the preservation of the past is overwhelmed by the monument-smashing mob incited by the greedy and ambitious hotelier who realises the potential economic benefit to his business of the tungsten deposits located on the monument's site.

The countryside is also seen as a locus of repression and violence in contemporary society in Kieran Hickey's *Exposure* (1978) while in Tommy McArdle's *The Kinkisha* (1978) rural life is explored in the framework of inherited superstition. Robert Wynne-Simmons' *The Outcasts* (1982), while set in pre-Famine times, also represents the countryside as a locale of conflict and instability. In Cathal Black's first film, *Wheels* (1976) from the short story by John McGahern, the only son (Brendan Ellis) of a midlands small farmer returns to the family farm he has abandoned for the city. He is met with hostility by his father but with sympathy by his stepmother. The slow pace of the rural environment reinforces the enclosed nature of country life and it is with relief that the son returns to the city and his friends.

However, it is an indication of the power of the pastoral tradition in Ireland that the central section of the first film to represent the lives of working-class Dubliners is set in an orchard. In Joe Comerford's *Down the Corner* (1978), based on the short book by Noel McFarlane, a group of teenage boys climb a high orchard wall to get into a veritable Garden of Eden in concrete Ballyfermot. While this may appear on the surface to be a return to the rural simplicity which is absent from their city lives this particular Garden of Eden proves to have its own snake bite when one of the boys cuts his foot on a broken bottle and has to be taken to hospital.

This film foregrounded work for the first time as a central activity in the lives of working-class people. But the steel mills' work depicted at the beginning is short lived as the worker is made redundant. His subsequent deterioration into drunkenness and isolation parallels the boys' own idleness. However, the lives of the boys allows for a naturalistic and sympathetic portrayal of the community and its institutions: school, hospital and homes, where pressures of space and money confine the inhabitants.

Confinement of a more particular order was to be seen in an earlier film by Joe Comerford, *Withdrawal* (1974), which was based on the book by David Chapman. It concerned the relationship of a junkie and his girlfriend, who is confined to a mental hospital, and the mental patients who live self-preoccupied lives. This theme was underpinned by the film's formal coolness and dark, sombre style. This was an early and ignored representation of such forgotten people. It was another decade before such images began to impinge on Irish national consciousness.

Cathal Black also looked at Dublin's marginal class sub-cultures when he examined a group of disparate individuals in a Dublin squat in *Pigs* (1984). *Pigs* was written by Jimmy Brennan who also wrote and delivered *Withdrawal*'s voice-over narration. In *Pigs* Brennan plays the central character, Jimmy, in a group of outcasts and marginalised people who squat in a disused tenement house. There is a drug dealer, Ronnie (Liam Halligan), a black pimp, Orwell (Kwesi Kay), and his prostitute girlfriend Mary (Joan Harpur), a paranoid schizophrenic, Tom (Maurice O'Donoghue), and a middle aged ex-businessman, George (George Shane), who wishes to maintain a façade of respectability. As they settle in uneasily to their newly-acquired decrepit living quarters the group provide a series of witty encounters during the film's first half while during the second the reality of their social circumstances intrudes on their relationships. In the end they disperse: Ronnie to his parents' home; Orwell and Mary to a new flat; Tom for a new treatment without ECT; and George, acquiring a council flat in a Ballymun tower block, seeks to encourage Jimmy to join him. Jimmy, wary both of the intrusion by the others on the squat and of George's capacity for self-deception and lies, refuses. By then, Jimmy, too, has had a painful reminder of his own alienation, which is represented almost ironically by his wearing a towel/skirt instead of trousers in many scenes in the house. The incessant enquiring about his absent wife, now living in Scotland, and his homosexuality lead four tough teenage clients of the drug dealer to beat him up in his own bedroom. With the house empty and he, too, preparing to move on, two policemen (Pat Laffan, Johnny Murphy) come to arrest him on a charge of claiming social security for himself and his absent wife.

Another marginal class group is that of the itinerants, the subject of Joe Comerford's *Traveller* (1982), a Film Script Award winner written by Neil Jordan. In this film, a match-made traveller couple, Angela (Judy Donovan) and Michael (Davy Spillane) go from Limerick in the Republic to Northern Ireland to acquire radios and television sets to smuggle south of the border. On their journey north they stop in a small town where one of the manifestations of the new Ireland is to be seen: a café with its juke box and teenage sub-culture. Shortly afterwards they pick up a renegade republican, Clicky (Alan Devlin), whose life becomes interwoven with theirs. The journey leads them into the complexity of the Northern divide (itself a rare journey for Southern film-makers) and through an abandoned big house on their return trip. On this journey the couple also pause temporarily at the western coast but here too there is no peace or security. The restless Angela, who has come through a process of socialisation on this journey, decides to leave her husband, her background and the country of her birth if not national allegiance, to emigrate with Clicky.

Traveller, however, has a deeper social importance through its depiction of the nature of the family and the potential for liberation of women. Angela evolves towards a degree of independence not only from her match-made husband but through her husband's killing of her father. In this regard, her father's incestuous attack on her when she was thirteen had lead to *her* confinement for a year after she hit him with a bottle. Formally, this aspect of the relationship is alluded to during the film's opening sequence when a viewer could misread the images as indicating that father and daughter are lovers. While Joe Comerford would see the breakdown of the family as a metaphor for the continuing conflict in Northern Ireland,[3] at a more conventional level the family in *Traveller* has a closer affinity to other depictions of the family and sexuality in independent Irish films of the last decade. This is most often seen in the complete absence of a mother, as in *Traveller*, a substitute mother such as a stepmother in *Wheels*, or an overbearing mother as in *The Kinkisha*.

In Tommy McArdle's *The Kinkisha* (1978) the relationship of the young couple, Margaret (Barbara MacNamara) and Gerry (the film's scriptwriter, John McArdle), is imposed upon by Gerry's mother Gran (Catherine Gibson) in whose house they live. The kinkisha of the film's title is a baby born at Pentecost or Whit. According to a superstition in some parts of Ireland such a child will either kill or be killed unless a robin is crushed to death in the baby's hand during the first few weeks of its life. In the film Margaret is seduced (or raped?) by Gerry in a barn after leaving a community dance. She becomes pregnant, they marry and go to live on Gran's farm. The baby is born at Whit and Gerry and Gran send Margaret to catch the robin whose death will not only alter the child's destiny but will be a sacrifice which will expiate the sin of his conception.

While the ritual is intended as a means of expelling the guilt of pre-marital sexuality it also serves as a liberation for Margaret but not for Gerry. Indeed, the bearers of myth, Gran, Gerry and a mumbling, incoherent priest (Eamonn Keane) who visits Margaret in hospital after the birth, are seen as the most confined. In contrast to these three are the unattached and singing Tojo (David Byrne), a friend of Gerry's, and sensual Margaret, who transcends the social restrictions, despite her confinement as a wife/economic dependent.

This orientation towards myth as an indirect way of exploring the nature of the family was also to be found in *The Outcasts* (1982), a Film Script Award winner, written and directed by Robert Wynne-Simmons. In this mystical, even horror, film the family is motherless. Set in an undifferentiated but pre-Famine time the film is not overtly concerned with social and economic relations on the land, a central preoccupation of recent Irish historiography, but does nonetheless focus on conflicts which originate on the land through family, inheritance and community.

The outcasts of the film are a fragmented family: Maura

O'Donnell (Mary Ryan), the introspective, partly deformed daughter of a small farmer, Hugh O'Donnell (Don Foley); Maura's sister, Janey (Báirbre Ní Chaoimh), unmarried but pregnant and living with Eamonn Farrell (Máirtín Ó Flathearta), a member of a rival farming family; and another sister, Breda (Brenda Scallon), who is widowed and cannot remarry. The other outcast and the film's catalyst is the strange violin-playing Scarf Michael (Mick Lally), the fear of whose supernatural powers pervades the film.

Maura's physical (and social) handicap and a suspected relationship with Scarf Michael, who had been expelled from the community and had survived an attempted killing, emphasises Maura's difference from the community. An accumulation of adverse events which have happened since the night her pregnant sister got married are blamed on Maura by the community, But when his child dies Maura's brother-in-law, Eamonn, also turns against her. For Eamonn, though, it is the marriage alliance which is being disturbed. He, as the Heir-to-Two-Farms, is primarily interested in increasing his economic power. Like Scarf Michael, Maura, too, becomes an outsider as the myths of the past give way to new economic imperatives in the countryside.

This oppressive family environment is shown to permeate any historical period, class position or geographical location in the work of recent Irish film-makers. In Thaddeus O'Sullivan's adaption of a short story by Seán Ó Faoláin, *The Woman Who Married Clark Gable* (1985), there is a stylish and witty representation of an Englishman (Bob Hoskins) and his Irish wife (Brenda Fricker). Set in Dublin in the late 1930s the childless couple's unstated oppression is displaced on to the woman's fantasy of her husband as Clark Gable in *San Francisco*. But fantasy is what it remains until the husband shaves off his newly-acquired moustache and they return to their humdrum artisanal class existence. By then her guilt at her inability to have children has been painfully exposed.

In Bill Miskelly's version of Michael McLaverty's short story, *The Schooner* (1983), an elderly brother and sister are assumed to be husband and wife for much of the film. In this film an eight-year-old Belfast boy, Terry (Johnny Morley), comes to stay for the summer with his elderly aunt Annie (Lucie Jamieson), and her brother Paddy (Michael Gormley). Annie's life is dominated by memories of her husband Joe (Barry Lynch) who left her (Ann Hasson as Young Annie) to go back to sea as a ship's carpenter. Promising to return within three months he is now presumed drowned but Annie continues to hope for his return. Terry serves as a catalyst in easing Annie's melancholia but he is more interested in machines and television until he is given a model schooner with which to play. It is similar to the one Joe had departed in and when Terry fails to return one evening from the seashore where he is playing with it Annie presumes history is repeating itself. However, Paddy returns with Terry and thus, perhaps, gives continuing hope to Annie for Joe's own return.

That sense of loss and oppression was also to be found amongst those who remained together within the traditional nuclear family as well as those of a younger, more modern, generation. In Kieran Hickey's *Exposure* (1978), the Arts Council's second Film Script Award winner, these conflicts are transposed to a small isolated West of Ireland hotel. Three surveyors (two married, one single) and a French woman photographer are the only guests. The elderly manageress/owner and a servant girl are the only other characters. The married men, one middle-aged with a grown-up family, Dan (T. P. McKenna), the other Eugene (Niall O'Brien), newly-married with a young baby, feel confined by the demands of family life. This sense of oppression is reinforced through telephone calls to their wives. The young single surveyor, Oliver (Bosco Hogan), unaffected by these particular restraints, develops an attraction for the woman, Caroline (Catherine Schell), which becomes an open, carefree sexual relationship.

The older men increasingly withdraw into self-pity and drunkenness. In a climactic scene they swagger drunkenly upstairs and enter Caroline's bedroom. They rummage through her belongings and play fetishistically with her underwear. When Caroline and Oliver return to find the two older men in her room, Oliver's liberation is shown to be decidedly shallow. While he is shocked and attempts to console Caroline he quickly flees to his room as she exclaims 'Why?, Why?' A full circle is achieved in the penultimate scene when the three men are drinking together once more in the hotel bar. Male cameraderie has been restored and the threat of female sexuality expelled. A triumphant manageress looks on benignly. The last sequence counterpoints this ending. In the darkroom Caroline leaves the print she has taken of the three men in the developer without transferring it to the fixer when she puts on the light. Although a male equilibrium has been restored Caroline still retains an independent control. As the exposure fades away it is she who remains.

Both surveyors and photographer mediate the landscape but

Caroline's mediation is creative, her freedom continually reinforced by her ability to choose her subject-matter. By contrast the surveyors are subject to the technical needs of the Chief Engineer, their job and their job location. Additionally, Caroline, the catalyst for the action, is young, attractive, economically independent, sexually liberated and divorced. However, the limitation of her representation in an Irish context is that she is French, from outside rather than from within. The result is that the threat to the men can only be dealt with from afar and the native Irish women in the film, the manageress and the almost silent servant girl, become reduced to stereotypes.

Kieran Hickey's second film in a projected trilogy (all co-written by himself and Philip Davison), *Criminal Conversation* (1980), brought the exploration of sexuality away from landscape into Dublin's middle-class suburbs. The sexual cheating and hypocrisy of the *nouveau riche* middle-class businessmen (Peter Caffrey, Emmet Bergin) and their wives (Deirdre Donnelly, Leslie Lalor) is contrasted with the possibly more open relationship of a student (Garret Keogh) and his babysitter girlfriend (Kate Thompson). The film's final image of a wife's call for emotional help, switching on and off a bathroom's lightswitch, reflects the repressed acceptance of the *status quo*.

Oppression of a more general kind permeates Cathal Black's *Our Boys* (1981), which evokes Christian Brothers education in the 1950s, its religious pre-history and its subsequent effect on adult life. This mixture of drama and documentary used a complex structure with dramatised classroom sequences of pupils in the 1950s, *cinema vérité* interviews of ex-Christian Brothers' students, who were on the receiving end of the Brothers' tough corporal punishment approach to education, and newsreel from the triumphalist 1932 Catholic Eucharistic Congress in Dublin. *Our Boys* has a rarity value in that it is the only independent film to focus on an educational institution as such and indeed no recent independent film has dealt directly with the Catholic Church itself. Perhaps the nature and structures of institutions of power have yet to be fully recognised as subjects for Irish films. But while personal relationships, even the family, can be dissected in Irish films, *Our Boys*, the one film to deal with institutional power, is treated with such caution that six years after its completion it has yet to be shown on RTE, one of the film's backers.

The use of newsreel in *Our Boys* is paralleled in a black and white flash-back sequence recalling the Easter Rising in *Down the Corner*.

There, an elderly woman remembers how, when young, she and her boyfriend on the run killed a British soldier. However, this memory is a strange amalgam of the Easter Rising and the War of Independence. Indeed, the heroic memories of 1916–22 are far removed from the stark economic reality of the contemporary working-class environment. This is underscored in the following scene where there is an ironic visual display of the Irish flag. The two boys who were listening to the old woman's story walk across a bleak wasteland at the rear of the houses. Behind them on the backyard door entrances to the houses are painted the green, white and orange of the Irish flag. The past and national glory may lie behind them but the reality is in the foreground, the young working-class boys.

History itself as a site of struggle in contemporary Ireland and the first filmic steps towards a more critical assessment of Ireland's past were taken rather surprisingly by one of the inheritors of the radical nationalist past, Official Sinn Féin, now The Workers' Party. The film they sponsored, *Caoineadh Airt Uí Laoire* (Lament for Art O'Leary, 1975), was described by one national film critic as a 'breakthrough'.[4] It was also the first independently-produced film in the Irish language and, indeed, was the first major critical indigenous production of the 1970s. The film was a collaborative effort led by Bob Quinn, who had established a small film studio in an Irish-speaking area of Connemara. Quinn had quit his job at RTE to devote himself to making films in an area 'isolated by its language . . . from the American-English world'.[5] An important collaborator was English playwright, John Arden. A resident of Connemara, he plays the key role opposite O'Leary.

Lament for Art O'Leary is the name of the last great lament in the Irish language, written after the death of Art O'Leary by his wife Eileen. It is an intensely emotional expression of Eileen's grief at the loss of her husband. Art O'Leary was a descendant of Gaelic aristocrats who were dispossessed after the final defeat of the Gaelic chieftains by the English at the end of the seventeenth century. As a consequence tens of thousands left Ireland to join European armies throughout the eighteenth century and as mercenaries became known as The Wild Geese. Art O'Leary followed the European trail where he joined the Austrian Hussars, rising to the rank of captain, but unlike most of the other exiles he returned to Ireland. The film concerns the remaining six years of his life, 1767–73.

The film is structured around an amateur drama group in an

Irish-speaking area of Connemara rehearsing a stage production of the story of Art O'Leary under the direction of an Englishman (John Arden). During rehearsals of the 'play' filmed sequences of the eighteenth century are shown as part of the mixed-media production. Gradually more complete eighteenth century sequences are intercut with the modern-day rehearsal, as are 'documentary' interviews on the current political situation. In chronicling the last six years of Art's life, it presents his relationship with Eileen, his conflict with the English owner of his family's ancestral land, being made an outlaw and his death.

The events are woven together in a complex mosaic which mixes past and present and thus problematises the relationship of the eighteenth century to the present. As the film progresses the events in the present become fused with those of the past. The same actors play the eighteenth- and twentieth-century Art and Eileen while the play's director doubles as the eighteenth-century landlord. By choosing a boisterous actor with a loud and crude demeanour to play Art (and who has since become a well-known Irish language television personality), Séan Bán Breathnach, the character's actions are actually undermined rather than promoted. Art's foolish bravado in engaging in a personal fight with the English landlord is seen to be for reasons of personal pique and not part of concerted mass action. The film, as Workers' Party President Tomás MacGiolla noted[6]

> Is not another exercise in futile probing of myths, but essentially a comment upon reality in the present Ireland of 1975 . . . Defiance and resistance are not enough in themselves to liberate a people. Courageous campaigns of resistance, however noble their inspiration, will fail like the gesture of Art O'Leary if they try to ignore realities . . . Romantic acts of heroism or defiance may inspire people but will never organise them.

Despite this design the film ends up endorsing this viewpoint both by the way it employs emotional effect and in the way it suppresses Art and Eileen's class difference from the peasantry.

Nevertheless, *Lament for Art O'Leary* is significant not just for its content but in the way it raises issues of formal innovation, the first Irish film to do so. Its self-reflective and multi-layered unfolding of the narrative outline draws attention to the film's construction and thereby invites the audience to participate in uncovering its meaning. Film is used in the theatrical space, actors in the present comment on their eighteenth-century costumed appearance and the interchangeability of actors between the present and the past all lead to a questioning of the reality of historical truth.

An investigation of the past and its relationship to narrative is also to be found in Tommy McArdle's feature *It's Handy When People Don't Die* (1982). Set in the winter of 1797 and during the 1798 Rising *It's Handy* . . . concerns Art (Garret Keogh), through whom the audience experiences the events set in an isolated valley in Wexford. Art overhears fragments: about France, the militia, yeomen, war and Gorey, a town about which he knows nothing. He is tempted to join the Rebellion but quickly returns home and goes into hiding, afraid of the women's reaction to his decision. From his hideout in the hills he watches the dead return, observes the events of the community and listens to the stories which the villagers tell. Searching for meaning and explanation he tries to assemble these into a coherent narrative. Overhearing of a supposed victory at Vinegar Hill he sets off for battle. Before leaving he makes a speech to the assembled women which consists of jumbled pieces of information, half truths and stories he has heard while in hiding. The women observe him silently as he circles them on the white horse of which he had formerly dreamed.

The central issue for the film is not so much the psychological motivation for Art's decision to act as his socialisation into the pattern of narrative and myth which allows him to act. Thus what the film rejects is the possibility of any simple reflection of the past. Through Art it highlights instead the process of selection and reconstruction from which the events of the past are explained. This discrepancy between historical events and mythic construction is emphasised through the film's treatment of the *seanchaí* (or storyteller). Art attempts to gain the *seanchaí*'s (Brendan Cauldwell) help in making sense of the events but the *seanchaí* maintains his distance and locks himself in a windowless cabin to construct the storytelling myth.

The narrativisation of personal and social history was of central concern to Pat Murphy, writer and co-director with John Davies, of *Maeve* (1981). Returning to her native Belfast Maeve (Mary Jackson) attempts to engage with her father's (John Keegan) stories and the more explicit political 'narratives' of republicanism and feminism. This questioning of narrative at a thematic level is paralleled by an enquiring and self-reflective approach at a formal level. Camera movements displace the centrality of characters while the very process of film production is continuously drawn attention to. Pat Murphy returned to history with a more conventional narrative about *Anne Devlin* (1984), which is mainly set around the events of the 1803 Rebellion and its aftermath. Although the film does not break as decisively with narrative conventions as did *Maeve*, it still employs moments of narrative rupture which pose questions about the representation of women in history. *Maeve*'s co-director, John Davies, also returned to a more conventional narrative form in the Frontroom production *Acceptable Levels* (1983), but this maintains an interest in the mediation of events through film and television in its treatment of a television documentary on the effects of violence in Belfast.

The formal innovation displayed by *Maeve* and *Lament for Art O'Leary* was also to be seen in two of Thaddeus O'Sullivan's experimental films. Best known as a cameraman, he has photographed *Anne Devlin*, *Our Boys*, *Pigs*, *Traveller* and a short experimental film, *Waterbag* (1984) for Joe Comerford. He has also directed (and shot) a number of films, including *A Pint of Plain* (1975) and *On a Paving Stone Mounted* (1978), both of which deal with Irish emigrant experience in London and, as in the case of the latter, the emigrant's perception of Ireland is contrasted with the Irish experience. Both films also explore the conventions of narrative and documentary film-making. Writing about *A Pint of Plain* Marc Carlin noted[7] that

all things denoting 'British Realism' were being unusually mobile. Pub tables, phone boxes, tea cups; film objects ordinarily so imprisoned in the folds of the actors who use or touch them as to become indistinguishable, were eyes loosed from gravity. It was hallucinating to see the props of British Cinema drifting from their moorings as if a poltergeist had invaded the land. That the 'furniture' was at last flying was solely due to the fact that the characters central to the film were all exiles/immigrants. As such, everything they touched became separated from them losing that one-dimensionality which ownership renders to object and human alike. If this vicarious feeling against all things British was manifesting itself during the viewing, it was largely due to a reaction against the unchallenged realism of so many English films; a realism in which the demonstration of the 'accuracy' of the decor has become the *raison d'être* of a certain British cinema.

In *On a Paving Stone Mounted* (the title comes from a legend as to St Patrick's mode of transport to Ireland) emigrants' experience is examined through a continuous deconstruction of the process of film-making and audience expectations of character and narrative. The film is divided in two parts: the memories of Ireland seen through 'documentary' footage and as direct experience of the emigrant in London, shot as acted reconstruction. The typical memories of Ireland are presented through the annual religious pilgrimage on Croagh Patrick and the annual Puck Fair, a market/festival in Kerry. The emigrants' experience is seen in terms of the staircase of a boarding house where people meet and tell stories, a tourist's interaction with people and a club where traditional Irish music is heard. There is also a prosperous returned emigrant who is contrasted with his Dublin friends. The Dubliners' lives are seen through the stories they tell and exchange while the emigrant remains aloof and silent. As Thaddeus O'Sullivan puts it[8]

The film is about memories, a patchwork of spare, reduced, cynical memories. Not simply 'the past' but a production of remembrance by the emigrant, of an identity as emigrant of a place elsewhere where one is in place, at home . . . Memories as also part of understanding what is remembered. Thus the film returns to the story-teller who was introduced, but not yet seen in the opening shot, to memories of Ireland and Irishness and the construction of memories from remembrance, the job of the professional storyteller. The memories becoming fiction, and the fiction becoming the memory, the 'back home' in Ireland.

The film concludes with professional *seanchaí* Eamonn Kelly's stage show telling of the returned emigrant from America with his exaggerated tales of the grandeur of New York. But his storytelling is undermined by the repetition of a short segment of his story which distances the audience from the narrative flow. Nor does the film offer easy identification with 'characters'. Psychological identification with a character's point of view is not presented. Instead roving camera movements, unexpected, non-associative editing, mixing drama and documentary, alternating sound levels and occasional unexpected silences contribute to a shifting mosaic where the audience fights to make 'sense' and create meaning.

O'Sullivan concludes[9] that *On a Paving Stone Mounted*

can tell only half the story . . . for women, Irish women are absent, 'typically'. This poses a question to the film, not just of a flaw but to the very Irishness it presents.

Part of that 'flaw' of bringing to the surface women and sexuality is formally alluded to in the film through the role of the male Church. On top of Croagh Patrick the camera's point of view, fixed in the crowd of the windswept congregation, observes the priest in an enclosed glass cage saying mass, removed from the people, at a higher level. In another short sequence at Sandycove 'gentlemen only' bathing place, near where the Joyce Tower of the opening sequence of *Ulysses* is located, a pan follows a naked man as he tiptoes surreptitiously in the background as a priest comes into frame in the foreground. The priest sits in the visually dominant position, silent, unchallenged, facing the camera and the film's audience. This sequence contrasts with an English woman's memory of Ireland: her experience of swimming naked in the sea off the West coast is sensual, soft, unrepressed but equally imcomplete. This romanticism of the West is sharply contrasted with another of her memories of Ireland, a memory of Dublin, where, as she puts it, barefoot children live in poverty unlike elsewhere in Europe.

Conclusion

These twin poles of the romantic West of Ireland and urban Dublin serve to highlight the difficult path which Irish film-makers face. A tension exists between the dominant international view of Ireland with its stereotypes usually located in the rural idyll and the attempt by indigenous film-makers to bring to the fore alternative versions of Irish history and society, an interaction with contemporary issues and an interrogation of these stereotypes themselves.

In seeking to do this, indigenous film-makers have not always been aided by the institutions which should have been their allies. The state's often limited policy in perceiving of film as an industry in the manner of any manufacturing plant ignored the critical difference between the sets of images Irish people would produce and those made by international film interests. As has been demonstrated in the long saga of an Irish film studio, time was wasted and resources were allocated to a project which failed to take cognisance of the particular power and importance of film images of Ireland. The economic imperative behind this desire to compete at an international level abdicated the production of images of Ireland to foreigners. This area of debate is, however, far from resolved. While the studios may no longer be a state-subsidised facility, the impetus behind such a project remains. Ironically, the matter may now be largely determined by the way in which 'independent' film-makers and Irish film producers perceive their own future.

As indigenous film-makers increasingly gain international recognition the pendulum will begin to swing once more towards making international films but with a more 'authentic' Irish dimension. While Irish film-makers must fully engage with commercial cinema as they shift away from smaller scale 'independent' productions and make films for a mass audience, this does not necessarily entail the need for a cultural compromise. Such a compromise will, however, need to be made if the scale of budgets increases such that the international co-productions shift decisions of form and content from Ireland to England or America. If budgets increase above, say, half a million pounds, most of which could be raised in Ireland, towards one, two or three million pounds, then decisions on Irish films will not remain in Ireland. This issue presents a new challenge to Irish film-makers, film institutions and the Irish state. If the errors of the past are to be avoided then artistic control of Irish-theme films must remain in Ireland while Irish film-makers need to fully appreciate the necessary compromises of international co-productions.

Nevertheless, the notion of the false opposition, 'commercial'/ 'non-commercial', needs to be challenged also. As was demonstrated by the five-week Dublin run of the supposedly 'difficult' and 'non-commercial' *Anne Devlin* in 1984, there is an audience for films which are designated 'demanding' or simply 'different'. The public interest in *Anne Devlin* was precisely because of its specific Irishness. Indeed what has characterised the success of national cinemas since the 1950s, whether it was Italian neo-realism, French New Wave, New German Cinema or emerging cinemas in Cuba, Brazil or Australia has been the emphasis on their national difference in the first instance, not their 'international look'. The appeal of the myriad features of the Irish perspective is also the main strength of the emerging Irish Cinema.

Notes

1. See David B. Rottman and Philip J. O'Connell, 'The Changing Social Structure', in *Unequal Achievement: The Irish Experience 1957–1982*, Frank Litton (ed.), Dublin: Institute of Public Administration, 1982, pp. 68–72.

2. *Sunday Independent*, 26 February 1978, p. 31.

3. For an extended account of *Traveller* see Kevin Rockett, " 'Like an Expedition . . .' ", *IFT News*, Vol. 5, No. 2, pp. 4–6, February 1982.

4. Ciaran Carty, 'A Movie We can be Proud Of', *Sunday Independent*, 9 November 1975, p. 15.

5. Quoted, Ciaran Carty, 'Why I'll always be a foreigner in Connemara', ibid., 7 November 1976, p. 2.

6. Publicity booklet, Dublin: The Workers' Party, 1975.

7. *British Film Institute Productions Catalogue 1977–78*, London: BFI, 1978, p. 35.

8. Ibid., p. 38.

9. Ibid.

PART TWO:
Representations of Ireland

6

Images of Violence

John Hill

Introduction

There has never been any shortage of representations of Ireland and the Irish on the cinema screen. From the early days of silent cinema through to the present day, Irish characters, situations and settings have exercised a continuing attraction for both film-makers and audiences alike.[1] The source of these images, how-ever, has rarely been Ireland itself. In the absence of any sustained output from an indigenous Irish film industry, it has been the cinemas of Britain and the United States of America which have been responsible for the vast majority of films to have dealt with Ireland and the Irish.[2] What these cinemas have provided, of course, is not simply a vast quantity of films but also ways of looking at their subject. To take a broad, if somewhat schematic, overview, two main sets of images have predominated. On the one hand, Ireland has been conceived as a simple, and generally bliss-ful, rural idyll; on the other, as a primarily dark and strife-torn maelstrom.[3] Although apparently contradictory, these images do share a basic similarity. For, whether it be conceived as a vice or a virtue, both sets of images imply a contrast between the charac-teristics of Irish society and those of an apparently advanced and modern civilisation. In the former case, this usually assumes the form of a lament for the simple virtues of rural life which the advances of urban-industrial society have destroyed. In the latter, it is more typically a lament for the Irish themselves and their failure to accommodate to the standards of reason and order characteristic of a modern and 'civilised' society.

As would befit the differing histories of America and Britain in relation to Ireland, the responsibility for cultivating these ideas and images is not evenly shared. The massive Irish emigration to America, the contribution of Irish-Americans to Hollywood production and the sizeable constituency of Irish-Americans amongst American audiences have undoubtedly helped encourage a view of nostalgic pastoralism. Britain, on the other hand, with its more direct legacy of military and political involvement in Ireland, has undoubtedly preferred a darker and more brooding vision. This is, of course, a neat, if not altogether accurate, generalisation. The British cinema has fuelled more than one piece of bucolic fantasy in its time, while Hollywood has not entirely neglected the more turbulent events of Irish history. Nonetheless, it would still be appropriate to argue that it is the British cinema, rather than the American, which has most consistently chosen to paint its Irish characters black. Why this should be so may be explained in both historical and cinematic terms.

The images of the Irish constructed by the British cinema did not emerge newly-born but drew on a reservoir of ideas and images inherited from earlier historical periods. The associations of the Irish with violence had already enjoyed an extended career. Charles Townshend provides an appropriate summary:

> For centuries, English writers, both eyewitnesses and more distant observers, remarked with professions of shock and horror upon the peculiarly cruel and anarchic nature of Irish violence. From Giraldus Cambrensis's chilling vision of a nation 'cruel and bloodthirsty' and a country 'barren of good things, replenished with actions of blood, murder, and loathsome outrage', to Barnaby Rich's assertion that 'That which is hatefull to the World besides is only beloved and embraced by the Irish, I mean civill warres and domesticall discentions', the English perspective was clearly drawn.[4]

Such 'professions of shock and horror' did not simply represent the idiosyncratic attitudes of individual authors, of course, but were intimately connected to England's military and political domination of its neighbouring island. Cambrensis's notorious history of Ireland played an important political role in justifying Henry II's conquest of Ireland on the grounds of its civilising influence while Barnaby Rich's *A New Description of Ireland* (1610) was only one of a number of Elizabethan commentaries designed to bolster the reconquest and plantation of Ireland initiated during the Tudor period.[5] Moreover, the ideas and attitudes which such writings represented were destined to survive long after their initial purpose had been served. So successfully, in fact, that by the nineteenth century, 'the major characteristics attributed to the Irish — indolence, superstition, dishonesty and a propensity for violence' had, according to Ned Lebow, 'remained prominent in the British image for over six hundred years'.[6] But if derogatory images of the Irish succeeded in elevating military and economic exploitation to the status of a civilising mission they could also prompt the question of why the Irish should then prove so reluctant to accept the benefits of civilisation and resort to rebellion and uprising against their English benefactors. The answer, of course, was implicit in the designation of the Irish as violent. Violence, in this respect, was not to be accounted for in terms of a response to political and economic conditions but simply as a manifestation of the Irish 'national character'. By this token, the proclivity for violence was simply an inherent characteristic in the 'nature', if not the blood, of the Irish natives. Such racial conceptions, indeed, were to enjoy a spurious 'scientific' dignity in the nineteenth century when the new theories of social Darwinism combined with the political panic over the Fenians to create a view of the Irish as a species of anthropoid ape.[7]

The endurance of this particular image is testified to by the appearance of a portrait of Old Mother Riley's dead husband in *Old Mother Riley's Ghosts* (1940) — a picture of such a startlingly simian character that it might have been lifted directly from the pages of *Punch* some 60 years before. The influence on the British cinema more generally is not quite so crudely direct. It is, however, evident. For what British films about Ireland maintain is not simply the traditional inclination to portray the Irish as violent but also the inability to provide a rational explanation for the occurrence of violence. Two main attitudes towards violence predominate. In the first case, violence is attributed to fate or destiny; in the second, to the deficiencies of the Irish character. Both attitudes share an avoidance of social and political questions. It is only metaphysics or race, not history and politics, which offer an explanation of Irish violence.

It would be a mistake, however, to see the British cinema as simply submitting to an unbroken tradition of stereotyped representations. While there is an undoubted continuity, British films about Ireland also reworked and refashioned the old images according to changing political circumstances. Moreover, these films did not simply 'reflect' pre-existing ideologies of the Irish but also re-shaped them according to specifically cinematic conventions. Indeed, it could be quite plausibly argued that the dominant conventions of not only the British, but also American, cinema are by their nature inimical to social and political explanations of *any* human actions. The conventions of 'classic narrative', with their emphasis on individual characters as the agents of narrative causality, almost inevitably encourage the explanation of events and actions in terms of individual psychology rather than more general social, political and economic relations. The conventions of 'classic realism', with their dependence on observable realities, will similarly privilege inter-personal relationships at the expense of social and political structures.[8] What mainstream films are then able to say about social realities is necessarily constrained by the conventions which they employ. But while the British and American cinemas may share these basic conventions, there is also a sense in which they inhabit them differently. Each has evolved its own distinctive traditions of genre which, in turn, sponsor contrasting attitudes towards violence.

What this argument implies may be clarified by reference to Thomas Elsaesser's explanation of Hollywood in terms of an 'affirmative-consequential' model.[9] Elsaesser's argument is that if we wish to understand the 'affirmative' ideology of Hollywood we must also appreciate the aesthetic structure of 'consequence' in which it is embedded: that of narrativity sharpened and accentuated by generic dramaturgy. Narrative in itself is necessarily 'consequential' — not just linear (sequential) but also causal (consequential). However, this logic of 'consequence' is also heightened by the conventions of character (the central hero) and plot (the journey, the pursuit, the investigation) characteristic of the leading Hollywood genres. As Elsaesser explains:

> There is a central energy at the heart of any good Hollywood film which seeks to live itself out as completely as possible . . . the prevalent plot-mechanisms of the two major genres of the American cinema (the Western and the Gangster film) invariably conform to the same basic pattern. There is always a central dynamic drive — to get to the top, to get rich, to make it — always the same graph of maximum energetic investment.[10]

It is on this basis that Elsaesser goes on to argue that, irrespective of actual content, what remains consistent is 'a fundamentally affirmative attitude . . . a kind of *a priori* optimism located in the very structure of the narrative about the usefulness of positive action'. 'Contradictions', he continues, 'are resolved and obstacles overcome by having them played out in dramatic-dynamic terms or by personal initiative: whatever the problem, one can do something about it.'[11]

Integral to this structure, and one of the bases of its dynamism, is violence. For, by and large, the possibilities for positive action — what one can do — are dependent on an employment of force. As Andrew Tudor indicates in his survey of three predominantly American genres (the western, the thriller and the horror movie), one element is completely shared: 'the use of violence as the ultimate necessary solution to crucial problems . . . in terms of plot, in terms of emotion and in terms of morality, violence resolves all problems and tensions'.[12] This is, of course, an aesthetic rather than ethical argument. What is drawn attention to is not the external relationship between violence on the screen and the violence which may or may not occur elsewhere but, rather, the internal relationships between representations of violence and the conventions of narrative and genre. Violence, in this respect, is central to the positivism and dynamism characteristic of American cinema. As Tudor's conclusions suggest, it is violence which helps forward drives and ambitions, establishes character and identity, resolves problems and conflicts and ultimately affirms an ideology of advancement and development. The implications for the representation of Ireland may be suggested by reference to John Ford's 'Irish Western', *The Quiet Man* (1952). Sean Thornton (John Wayne) returns to Innisfree in pursuit of the peace and harmony which has eluded him in the United States. But, notwithstanding the film's title, both his reconciliation with Mary Kate (Maureen O'Hara) and his acceptance by the community more generally are dependent upon his participation in the donnybrook, or collective brawl. It is the resort to violence, in this respect, which holds the key to the narrative's resolution, uniting both wife and husband while bringing the community together. Violence, as Tudor suggests, resolves all problems and tensions.

This is not characteristically the case in the British cinema. For while the British cinema has been no less dependent upon narrative than its American counterpart, it has nonetheless lacked the genres which would match the dynamism and energy of the western or gangster film. Far more typical have been the light comedy or domestic drama in which the forward momentum of the American cinema is absent. As Charles Barr observes, British film plots are more usually circular than linear, more committed to renewing the *status quo* than engendering change and development (e.g. *Brief Encounter* or *The Blue Lamp*).[13] The expression of violence, in this respect, is not just less pronounced but also assumes a different complexion. Rather than providing a mechanism for problem-resolution, it is violence itself which so often represents the problem — or danger — which the narrative must resolve (especially if the *status quo* is to be confirmed). The meanings with which acts of violence are then invested are the reverse of those found in Hollywood. To take a slight, but pertinent, example. Made in 1954, *Happy Ever After* was no doubt intended to emulate the popular success of *The Quiet Man*. Like its predecessor, it shares the assumption that the inhabitants of a 'primitive' society like Ireland will be more 'naturally' disposed towards violence. But, whereas the violence in *The Quiet Man* allows John Wayne to fulfil his ambitions, its use in *Happy Ever After* is self-defeating. Intending to rid themselves of their new and unpopular squire, the villagers succeed only in damaging themselves. Violence, in this context, can only compound, not resolve, the difficulties with which the characters are presented. This is also true of British films with ambitions considerably more 'serious'. For be it comedy or problem drama, violence in the British cinema characteristically thwarts drives and ambitions, indicates character flaw or lack of self-identity, exacerbates problems and tensions and signifies either regression or fatalism.[14]

Odd Man Out: 'We're all dying'

It is the operations of fate, for example, which are the central preoccupation of one of the best-known of British fiction features about Ireland, *Odd Man Out* (1947), and its story of Johnny (James Mason), the IRA leader on the run. Stylistically, the film is heavily indebted to the examples of German expressionism and French poetic realism, as well as their American offspring the *film noir*, whose formal strategies conventionally carry meanings of preordained fate and determinism. Like its predecessors, the film's lighting is predominantly low-key with strong chiaroscuro contrasts and dark, ominous shadows. Compositions are claustrophobic and imprisoning with characters cramped into enclosed

interiors or dwarfed by their external environment (the consequence of the film's use of high angles and employment of wide-
angled lenses). The sense of doom and imprisonment suggested by
this style is underlined by the use of subjective sequences — now
buildings do literally bend over Johnny or turn into prisons — or is
made explicit by the screenplay. Thus Johnny is clearly identified
with a bird in a cage in the conversation between Father Tom
(W. G. Fay), Shell (F. J. McCormick) and Kathleen (Kathleen
Ryan). The implication is clear: Johnny may have escaped from
one prison but only to find himself in another — the dark and con-
fining spaces of the city.

The sense of Johnny as a victim, enclosed and entrapped by his
environment, is reinforced by the film's plot structure. Like
classical tragedy (cf. Sophocles' *King Oedipus*), the film relies less
on a dramaturgy of intrigue and suspense than the unfolding of the
consequences of an initial and irreversible error. Intimations of
doom are carefully marked from the beginning (e.g. the breaking
of Johnny's shoe lace just as he announces that things will 'go
fine') and then referred back to (e.g. Shell also breaks his lace),
while interest in Johnny's fate correspondingly shifts from whether
he will escape to the means by which he will be captured. Johnny,
in this respect, functions as a passive rather than active hero.
Unlike Elsaesser's model of classic American cinema, where there
is conventionally a central hero whose drives and motivations
structure the film's forward movement, Johnny less acts than is
acted upon, to the point, indeed, of requiring an actual physical
support. What is positive and affirmative in the American cinema
— the journey — thus becomes negative and regressive in *Odd
Man Out*. Pessimism, rather than optimism, is embedded in the
film's structure.

Johnny's inability to undertake positive action, or control his
own destiny, is underscored by the film's iconography. The Albert
Clock, for example, is used at both the beginning and end of the
film and appears throughout the course of the drama. The chimes
of the clock punctuate many of the film's most significant actions
(as in the shooting outside of Teresa's) while the clock itself is
apparently mobile, clearly in view not only from the gang's hide-
out but the homes of Teresa, Lukey and Father Tom as well.
While this may remind us that 'time is running out' for Johnny it
also confirms his passive and subordinate status. It is not so much
Johnny as time itself which is the real active force or dramatic
agent. This implication of forces outside and above Johnny,

controlling his destiny, is underlined by the film's employment of the elements. Like classic tragedy, it would appear that the significance of Johnny's actions is not confined to human relationships but extends to the world of nature as well. Johnny proceeds on his way through the city while external changes plot his progress: day gives way to night, sunlight to rain and then snow. As with the film's use of time, it is as if nature itself has ordained the journey he must make.

To this extent, the film finds a precursor in John Ford's version of *The Informer* (1935). Like *Odd Man Out*, this film also concentrates on the fatalistic consequences of an initial error and, also like *Odd Man Out*, draws upon the conventions of expressionism in doing so. This can be accounted for in terms of the problem which the film inherits from Liam O'Flaherty's original novel, i.e. the question of Gypo's motivation in informing on his erstwhile colleague. While Gypo's action may be connected to poverty, it has hardly been prompted by a rational decision. Indeed, the 'great, strong animal', as described by O'Flaherty, finds almost any thought difficult and is thus largely at the mercy of his 'prerational' physical impulses.[15] John Ford's film version attempts to add motivation by including Gypo's fantasy of an escape to America. But, as with Gypo's shortage of money in the novel, this information is more circumstantial than explanatory. The real solution to the problem of motivation which the film provides is found in its integration of character and environment, or its fusion of inner psychology and outer design. Abandoning the novel's quasi-naturalistic descriptions of Dublin slum-life, the film opts instead for a far more stylised, even abstract, portrait of the city.[16] The studio sets are kept spare and minimal and then enshrouded in a blanket of fog and shadow. The image of Dublin this creates is less 'realistic' than the external embodiment of Gypo's inner turmoil, as if the fog which clings to the buildings is also the 'fog' befuddling his brain. What then begins as a subjective, if instinctual, choice is now transformed into objective necessity, overtaking the hero as fate. Fatalism, in this respect, is implied not only by the film's dark doom-laden environment and its subordination of character to the elements but also by its use of symbols. The poster of Frankie McPhillip, the man on whom Gypo informs, clings to the characters' legs while the blind man, whom Gypo initially meets outside the barracks, returns to haunt him as if the agent of an abstract nemesis. Like Johnny in *Odd Man Out*, Gypo is thus less an active agent than an unwilling victim.

'I didn't know what I was doing', he explains pathetically to the IRA tribunal. It is only fate, or a metaphysical compulsion, which can finally render his actions intelligible.

But if it is Gypo's action in turning informer which signals his fatal flaw in the Ford film, it is Johnny's association with violence which appears to be responsible for his doom-laden trajectory in *Odd Man Out*. It is clearly established early on in the film that although Johnny has been serving a prison sentence for gun-running he no longer endorses his former means. As the men prepare for their robbery, Johnny assures Dennis (Robert Beatty) of his commitment to 'the cause' but airs his doubts with respect to the adoption of violence. 'If only we could throw our guns away', he laments (while ironically fitting his gun holster), 'and make our cause in the Parliaments instead.' It is a speech which is strategically important and a notable addition to F. L. Green's original novel which begins with the gang already embarked upon their raid on the mill. Its use in the film establishes an ethical and (parliamentary) political frame for Johnny which differentiates him from his more gun-happy colleagues and assists in underwriting the pathos of the film's tragedy, whereby it is he who, despite his renunciations of violence, becomes the one responsible for murder.

But, once so caught in the trap of violence, it is this which then ensures his downfall. It marks him as the 'odd man out' of the film's title, cutting him off from the community and abandoning him to the mercies of various 'outsiders' such as Gin Jimmy (Joseph Tomelty) and Shell. It also frustrates his relationship with Kathleen and, in this respect, the film goes much further than the novel in stressing a contrast between a commitment to violent activity, on the one hand, and conventional family life, on the other. This, in itself, is quite a typical characteristic of the British cinema. For if violence is generally seen to be negative and destructive, it is also contrasted with emotions and actions which are positive and constructive. For the British cinema, it is typically romantic love, the home and the family which fulfil this function. Once again, it is a characteristic of the dominant cinematic conventions that this should be the case. The individualising logic of both narrative and realism necessarily favours the private and the personal at the expense of the public and political. What is significant, then, is not simply that the personal and the political are assumed to be separate but that they are also set in opposition. It is romantic love and domestic stability which political violence inevitably damages; and only through an acceptance of love and domesticity that the divisions wrought by violence may be avoided or overcome.

Whether recognised or not, the British cinema's debt, in this respect, is to the plays of Sean O'Casey. For what is most firmly communicated in his Dublin trilogy, in particular, is not O'Casey's specific political criticisms of the subordination of working-class interests to nationalist ideals and leadership, but a much more general assault on, practically all, political ideals and violence for their corruption of the 'ordinary' 'human' values of love and domesticity.[17] If it is the women characters who emerge with most credit, it is because it is they who most clearly demonstrate the virtues of family life and most directly suffer the consequences of men's destructive commitment to political ideologies and actions. Ironically, the one film in which this should have been clearest — *The Plough and the Stars* (1936) — succeeds in inverting this basic message.

This was an American, rather than British, production and it is the American cinema's commitment to action, combined with director John Ford's own brand of Irish-American sentimentality, which was no doubt responsible for this major change. What the film is not content with is the restricted range of situations and settings provided by the play. Events and actions which are only reported in the play (the meeting, the occupation of the GPO) or not referred to at all (the execution of James Connolly) all now appear on the screen. Inevitably, these additions undermine the importance of the domestic sphere as the central site for action and with it the virtues that are to be found there. Moreover, by virtue of the manner in which they are presented (the studied tableaux of the procession and meeting, for example, or the low-angled shots of a silhouetted Connolly), the scenes of public and political action assume a dignity and nobility entirely at odds with the presentation in O'Casey's original. As a result, the film's ending is able to undercut the tragic pessimism of the play and replace it with political optimism. Jack Clitheroe (Preston Foster) survives to declare his continuing commitment to the fight for Irish freedom while the film proceeds to show documentary footage, narrating the achievement of Irish independence, as a vindication of the battle which has preceded. The family values and virtues which the original drama insist upon have by now been dealt a damaging blow. Family life is largely stripped of its attractions and is clearly no match for the heroism of political action. And, in a curious reversal, it is not the rebels who emerge as fanatics but rather Nora Clitheroe (Barbara Stanwyck) herself with her obsessive and monotonous demands that her husband should stay at home beside her.

But if the influence of O'Casey is not self-evident in an actual adaptation, it is more than apparent in the British films which follow. Returning to *Odd Man Out*, we can see how the contrast between family and violence has been adopted. An important scene, in this respect, is the one which takes place between Kathleen and Granny (Kitty Kirwan). Unlike her counterpart in the original novel, who takes an evident pleasure in the 'boyos' who are 'givin' the bloody peelers hell', Granny encourages Kathleen to heed the advice of the Head Constable and not to go in search of Johnny.[18] She tells her of Hughie Fitzpatrick, a gunman on the run like Johnny, whom she rejected in order to marry and have children. As De Felice sums up, 'Granny's allegiances are more with life than causes'.[19] 'Causes', on the other hand, imply a renunciation of love and marriage. 'As long as he lives', Dennis informs Kathleen, 'he [Johnny] belongs to the organisation.' That Johnny will never belong to Kathleen is borne out by the rest of the movie. Because of Johnny's involvement with violence, and his commitment to abstract causes, it is now too late: their romance must inevitably prove doomed. Kathleen rejects the old lady's advice and waits for her to fall asleep. Still hoping that she might be able to save him, she takes the gun which Granny has been concealing and goes off in search of Johnny. But, just as Johnny's fate had been sealed with the taking up of arms, so now is hers. Hitherto associated with the house (home) now she too becomes a wanderer of the city's night streets. A repetition of camera set-ups (of the steps and alley) immediately associate her with Johnny and Dennis, while her march into and then out of the lively and well-lit dance-hall indicates decisively her divorce from the life which Granny had wanted for her. All that now remains for the couple's love is one final embrace in death, shot down by the police, as their last remaining prospect of escape, the ship, embarks on its journey without them.

But how far is it then possible to interpret the film in political terms? The film's opening title, for example, disavows a close connection between the events of the drama and the political details of the North while the conventions employed certainly suggest a set of themes which are less specifically social than universal, applying less to any particular society than the 'human condition' as a whole. 'It's the truth about us all', as one piece of dialogue puts it, 'we're all dying'. This is certainly the case as put by Ernest Lindgren. 'The film . . . is concerned with something deeper and more fundamental in human experience than anything which happened in Ireland at a particular moment in history', he argues. 'One may feel that the director has realised his purpose well or ill, but that criticism is misguided which ignores a purpose so clearly defined, and tries instead to argue that the film should have concerned itself with something different.'[20] And, yet, the example is hardly so clear-cut. It is evident that the film strives to evacuate a number of concrete particulars — there is an imprecision about period and place, with neither Belfast nor the IRA explicitly named, compounded by an anti-naturalism of style and dialogue which by the end is openly allegorical. But, nonetheless, period and place are not removed altogether and there is still sufficient sense of particulars for the conflicts of the film to have a specific, and not merely general, content. The appropriate objection would be that the film does not so much omit political issues as displace them. As has been noted, a common complaint against the realist mode in film and television is that because of its necessary emphasis on the interaction of individuals it cannot adequately cope with broader socio-historical determinants (thus, in the case of Loach and Garnett's *Days of Hope*, the form inevitably pushes them towards conspiracy theory in their delineation of the General Strike);[21] by contrast, it might be argued that the universalising strategies of a film such as *Odd Man Out* likewise evacuates socio-historical determinants by pushing towards a level of abstraction where the explanation of human actions can only be in terms of the metaphysical operation of fate and destiny. *Odd Man Out*, in this respect, does not so much dispense with the political details of the North as rob them of their social and historical dimension. 'An individual does not act or will in the abstract', observes Parekh, 'but always within a specific social context.'[22] And it is by denying this 'specific social context' that the film not only obscures the conditions under which its characters' actions have taken place but the very reasons for which they have been undertaken in the first place. As the nationalist *Irish Press* was to comment at the time of the film's release, the film is devoid of any suggestion as to why 'this struggle goes on'.[23] Indeed, the British Anti-Partition of Ireland League apparently agreed and used the occasion of the film's release to issue a broadsheet. 'You have just seen, and no doubt you have been deeply moved by this British-

Irish masterpiece', it begins, 'but do you realise that the conditions prevailing in Northern Ireland have provided the background against which this terrible drama is worked out?' That it should still be felt necessary to have to ask such a question was no doubt a commentary on the film's own inability to raise it.[24]

But while the film may then be marked by a 'political reticence' it is not, as *The Irish Press* also suggests, without a 'political significance'. For by virtue of its attempt to construct a 'universal drama' from which the social and political specifics of Irish history have been removed, the film does not then avoid promoting a particular political viewpoint. Tom Nairn, for example, has noted the way in which the conflicts in the North are so often assumed to defy a rational explanation and how, as a result, a 'myth of atavism' is appealed to instead. Only 'a special historical curse', he writes, 'a luckless and predetermined fate can account for the war'.[25] And it is in effect precisely this myth which *Odd Man Out* endorses. For Johnny too is 'cursed', in this case, by the afflictions of violence and futile causes, and so, in turn, becomes the victim of an apparently 'luckless and predetermined fate'.

But while it may be Johnny's association with violence which then ensures his fate, the film's attitude towards violence is not straightforwardly one of opposition. For what the film also accepts, and, indeed, implicitly endorses, is violence at the hands of the state.[26] Thus while Johnny is responsible for a death at the mill, it is the police who are responsible for the killings of not only Johnny and Kathleen but also Johnny's fellow IRA men, Pat (Cyril Cusack) and Nolan (Dan O'Herlihy). Now, the legitimacy of police violence is, of course, a familiar ingredient of the crime film, and, in the British cinema, the characteristic mechanism for maintaining the *status quo*. It is precisely the violence of criminals, or juvenile delinquents, for example, which has to be contained in order for the social order to survive. In this context, however, the reliance on the police for a narrative resolution must inevitably obscure that it is the legitimacy of the state which is itself a political question. From this point of view, *The Irish Independent*'s conclusion that 'there is no question of taking sides' in the film is hardly self-evident.[27] For just as the political context and background of the activities of the 'Organisation' are rendered opaque so too are the context and background of the state itself. As befits the conventions employed by the film, the police are represented less as the functionaries of a state which has been created out of controversial and contested political circumstances than as the agents of an abstract fate or nemesis. The law which the police uphold, in this respect, is presented less as the work of human agency (and thus liable to challenge and change) than of divine will and it is striking how readily the language of the police ('this time he has shot and killed a man . . . he belongs to the law now') and church ('this is different . . . he's killed a man and he must pay the penalty') become interchangeable. The Northern Ireland state, in this respect, is not only exempt from political inquiry but, at least implicitly, legitimated as the repository of a divine and absolute justice.

The Gentle Gunman: 'Put away your guns'

'*Odd Man Out* displayed a very British reaction against political violence which was echoed in Ealing's *The Gentle Gunman*', writes Robin Cross.[28] Directed by Basil Dearden, from a play by Roger MacDougall, *The Gentle Gunman* (1952) took the IRA's English campaign of 1939 for its inspiration in its tale of IRA man Terence (John Mills), the 'gentle gunman' of the film's title, who turns his back on his former colleagues.[29] As Cross suggests, it also has much in common with *Odd Man Out*. Stylistically, it shares many of the former film's aspirations. Its interiors are similarly dark and cramped, frequently emphasising divisions between characters or subordinating them to décor or surrounding objects. Exterior action predominantly occurs at night. Unlike *Odd Man Out*, the film does employ rural locations but even here the atmosphere is dark and desolate: the IRA men's hide-out, for example, is an isolated roadside petrol station abandoned to the tracts of wilderness on the southern side of the border. Allegory is likewise not far from the surface with a prominent religious symbolism, and its intimations of martyrdom and sacrifice, culminating in young Johnny (James Kenney), again trapped into violence, meeting his death in the glare of car headlights, arms outstretched to form a cross.

Once again, the 'curse' of the Irish is their apparently perplexing proclivity for violence but, in this case, the explanation for this is less metaphysical, as in *Odd Man Out*, than an unfortunate flaw of the Irish character.[30] If not quite in the genes, politics and violence are, nonetheless, the 'game' which one generation passes on to the next. Thus Matt (Dirk Bogarde) steps into the shoes of his elder brother Terence once he decides to depart from the IRA, just as Johnny inherits his role from his father. The analogy of the game is both implicit and explicit. The film begins with the arguments of an Irish doctor, Branigan (Joseph Tomelty), and an irascible English visitor, Truethorne (Gilbert Harding). They are playing chess and the camera pulls back from a close-up of the chessboard to introduce the two characters. The shot is repeated shortly afterwards but only this time it is a bomb in a suitcase from which the camera pulls back in order to reveal the two IRA conspirators, Connolly (Liam Redmond) and Maguire (Jack MacGowran). What is a game of chess for Branigan and Truethorne is also a game played with bombs by the members of the IRA.

The theme becomes explicit in the film's use of dialogue. Molly (Barbara Mullen), like Granny in *Odd Man Out*, represents the voice of experience raised in protest against unnecessary suffering. She has previously lost her husband and, in the course of the film, also loses her son, Johnny. Like an O'Casey heroine, she speaks out against the violence in the name of the family and 'common-sense'. Indeed, such is the film's evident sympathy towards her character that she is allowed to make practically the same speech twice, first in relation to her husband and then in relation to her son:

> You killed his father, Shinto . . . leave Johnny alone.
> It was the English killed our father. (Maureen)
> No. It was Shinto. Joe was happy enough until you told him he was unhappy. And he was free until you told him he wasn't. And his fists were enough defence until you told him he needed a gun.

and later:

> Matt didn't kill Johnny, Molly. (Terence)
> No, it was the English. Like they killed our father. (Maureen)
> No, it was you [to Maureen] and you, Shinto. Johnny was only a lad. He'd still be playing hurley and football if you hadn't taught him the other game.

Little wonder then that an exasperated Raymond Durgnat was to complain that the film's treatment of the Irish question was 'presented exclusively in terms of the Irish struggling against their own tendency to violence'.[31] For the Irish alone have to accept

161

responsibility, in the words of Terence, for 'making trouble'. Freedom and happiness are quite possible if only the Irish could dispel their illusions and recognise it — a futility eloquently summed up for the film by an attack on an armed van in Belfast, at the cost of the lives of two men, in an attempt to rescue two prisoners who are in fact already 'f.. '.

But, as in the case of *Odd Man Out*, it's not so much that the film conveniently omits factors which might at least admit a small quotient of rationality to its characters' struggles (e.g. the legacy of English rule and partition) but that the film positively disputes their relevance by attempting to dissolve political problems into a de-contextualised humanism. As Durgnat puts it, 'whenever . . . complexity might threaten a generalisation, the team (Dearden and Relph) unhesitatingly sacrifice the former to the latter'.[32]

This is at its clearest in the film's representation of Terence. As the volunteer who turns his back on the IRA, it is he who joins Molly in denouncing the futility of violence as well as giving voice to an alternative set of values: in this case, a depressingly feeble appeal to little-man collectivism and the by now familiar virtues of domestic security and 'decency':

> I'm just as good an Irishman as ever I was . . . but there's no future for a man, woman or child in the whole of the world till we've learned that an Irishman is the same thing as an Englishman, a Frenchman, a Russian, a German, an Italian or an American. When it comes down to it, man for man, there's little bit of difference. It's the way we're all separated out into different countries that causes the trouble . . . I've lived over in England, I've lived with the people and worked with them. They've the same hopes as we have, the same fears. They pay too much rent and too many taxes, just like we do. They scrape and save for their kids in their old age just like we have to. It's not against people like that we should be working, it's with them. Can't you see it, man . . . it's peace we want, and security and a decent life. And we'll not get them shouting 'ourselves alone' at the top of our voices.[33]

As Sartre observes, albeit in a different context, 'his very declarations show the weakness of his position . . . he has no eyes for the concrete syntheses with which history presents him. He does not recognise the Jew, the Arab or the Negro, the bourgeois or the worker, but man alone at all times in all places the same as

The Priest as mediator: *Rory O'More* (1911) and *The Colleen Bawn* (1911)

Communal resistance: ruins in *Captain Lightfoot* (1955) and the big house in
Willy Reilly and His Colleen Bawn (1920). (Director John MacDonagh in centre
acting as the wise Fool)

James Cagney and Dana Wynter in the bleak landscape of *Shake Hands With the Devil* (1959)

Paradise regained: Maureen O'Hara in *The Quiet Man* (1952)

Beauty comes between the doubting (Richard Harris) and the committed (Robert Mitchum) in *A Terrible Beauty* (1960)

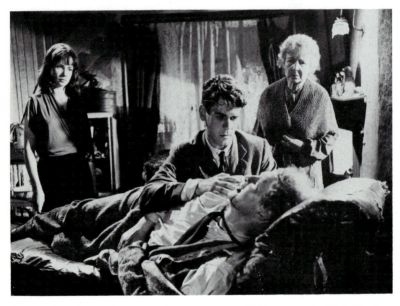

The outsider framed by contrasting stereotypes of Irish women in *Shake Hands With the Devil* (1959)

The burden of motherhood: Victor McLaglen and Una O'Connor in *The Informer* (1935) and Maggie Dirrane in *Man of Aran* (1934)

Figures in the landscape: male camaraderie in *Exposure* (1978) and female solidarity in *Maeve* (1981)

Constricting images: the IRA man as passive hero: *Odd Man Out* (1947); *Angel* (1982); *Cal* (1984)

Escape from modernity: Stephen Brennan and Eamon Morrissey in *Eat the Peach* (1986); Bob Hoskins and Brenda Fricker in *The Woman Who Married Clark Gable* (1985)

Stills appear by courtesy of the Stills Division of the National Film Archive, the British Film Institute Production Board, the Irish Film Board, the Irish Film Institute, B.A.C. Films, Brook Films/Set 2, Columbia-EMI-Warner, Rank, Strongbow, United Artists and Universal.

himself.'[34] It is thus a 'solution' to a problem which ends up evading the very social and political relationships, or historical 'syntheses', which have caused it to be a problem in the first place. As with *Odd Man Out*, the very conditions which would make the issues intelligible are, in effect, dispensed with.

But it is not only that the 'ideas' which the film presents appear so woefully inadequate to the problem at hand but that the film itself is also less than convincing in finding a format in which to express them. Part of this has to do with the film's approach towards violence. Although the film makes much of its espousal of pacifism, it still remains heavily dependent on the toughness of Terence (his ability to free the two prisoners, for example) for a successful execution of the plot. The superiority of Terence, in this respect, does not so much depend on the values which he articulates as the actions he undertakes to prove that he is really tougher than the 'tough guys'. But if the film convinces us that Terence remains 'masculine', despite the fact that he is 'gentle', it also succeeds in throwing this into doubt by virtue of its treatment of sexuality. In *Odd Man Out*, for example, it has been noted how the man's involvement with violence effectively obstructs the possibility of romantic and, by implication, sexual fulfilment. In *The Gentle Gunman*, however, this is not the case. Violence and sexual satisfaction are not opposed but interlinked. This is clearest in the film's representation of Molly's daughter, Maureen (Elizabeth Sellars). In contrast to her mother's traditional 'feminine' role of calling a halt to violence, Maureen employs her sexuality as a stimulus to further violent endeavour. She is initially involved with Terence but once he has abandoned the IRA she quickly withdraws her affections. She then proceeds to turn her attentions to his brother once he has proved his commitment to violence. Set within this context, the use of the gun now assumes unmistakeable phallic connotations: Matt takes aim with his revolver and Maureen looks on in delight and admiration.

The problem that the film now faces is that in order to rescue Matt from violence so it must also retrieve him from Maureen. The suppression of violence and sexuality, in this respect, go hand in hand. This is made evident at the film's close when Matt is forced to choose between his brother and Maureen and opts to take off without her. What the film then misses is any sense of the positive value which a more traditional romantic ending would have provided. Moreover, by virtue of the links which the film makes between sex and violence, it is inevitable that their abandonment of Maureen should be accompanied by implications of loss and repression (if not, in fact, 'castration').[35] For in turning their back on violence, so are they also rejecting the eroticism and excitement that goes with it. The 'decent', but anodyne, virtues, which the film has previously encouraged, offer, in this respect, a less than compelling compensation. The 'emptiness' of the men's decision would seem to be confirmed by the imagery which follows. The road along which they depart is seen to be bare and deserted. It is taking them away from the only community which they know and leads to an unidentified destination. It is also the same spot from which young Johnny had earlier left for Belfast and as such prompts associations with fatalism (with the roadside cross clearly visible as a reminder).

The film's inability to supply an adequate conclusion to the problems which it has let loose is confirmed by the ending overall. Just as the two brothers' destination is left open-ended so too is the outcome of the car chase between the police and the IRA. In absence of a satisfactory solution, the problem is allowed to 'go up in smoke' as the cars disappear behind dirt and exhaust fume. Moreover, true to the British cinema's pattern of circularity, the film returns to Branigan and Truethorne, still playing chess and still engaged in their apparently interminable argument. A rhetorical flourish is attempted — 'To England: where the situation may be always serious but never hopeless'. 'To Ireland: where the situation is always hopeless but never serious' — but succeeds only in casting doubt on the 'seriousness' of what has preceded. And, given that neither of these characters appear to have learnt or changed during the course of the film, it does rather put into question precisely those values of reason which the film has otherwise so loudly supported.

Shake Hands With the Devil and A Terrible Beauty: 'It's just killing'

Something of a similar pattern to *The Gentle Gunman* is also to be found in *Shake Hands With the Devil* (1959) and *A Terrible Beauty* (1960). In both the central hero is initially attracted to the IRA but, as with John Mills in *The Gentle Gunman*, ultimately opts for disengagement. Dermot O'Neill (Robert Mitchum) in *A Terrible Beauty* joins his local IRA Brigade as part of an anti-English campaign during World War II but once it is planned to raid a police barracks, where women and children will be at risk, he decides to desert, leave Ireland altogether and so enjoy the fruits of 'reason' which his friend and adviser, Jimmy Hannafin (Cyril Cusack), has been promoting. Kerry O'Shea (Don Murray) in *Shake Hands With the Devil* is initially opposed to violence but joins the IRA after his friend has been shot while attending a wounded IRA man in Dublin and he himself has suffered a beating at the hands of the Black and Tans (in one of the few, albeit individualised, examples in the British cinema of English, and not just simply Irish, malevolence).[36] By the end of the film, however, he has concluded that violence is no longer a means but an end in itself and decides to throw away his revolver.

The films avoid *The Gentle Gunman*'s pitfalls by insisting upon a much more rigid opposition between romance and violence. Thus, just as Jack Clitheroe must make a choice between his wife and Ireland in *The Plough and the Stars*, so Dermot O'Neill must decide between his sweetheart, Neeve (Anne Heywood), and membership of the IRA in *A Terrible Beauty*. Unlike Kathleen in *The Gentle Gunman*, Neeve opposes, rather than encourages, violence and will not marry Dermot until he agrees. Unlike the novel, where the two characters are only 19 and 20, their relationship has now dragged on for seven years. The romantic ending which eluded *The Gentle Gunman*, *A Terrible Beauty* is now in a position to supply. Dermot turns his back on the IRA and is rewarded with the hand of his sweetheart. Unable to find 'peace' in Ireland they now set off to enjoy the benefits of life in England. The ending of *Shake Hands With the Devil* is similar. Kerry falls in love with the IRA's English hostage, Jennifer Curtis (Dana Wynter). When she is threatened with execution, in retaliation for the death of an IRA prisoner, it is inevitable that Kerry will turn against his commandant in order to save her. Once again, it is love, rather than 'the cause', which must prove the more important.

It is not simply the virtues of romance, however, which clinch the films' case for non-violence. This also depends on the extent of the IRA's vices. The films, in this respect, expand upon the split in male characters already in evidence in *Odd Man Out* and *The Gentle Gunman*. Both these films had counterposed the cold and emotionless IRA killer (in both cases, Robert Beatty as Dennis and Shinto) to the fundamentally decent IRA member who has his doubts about their violent methods (Johnny and Terence). Both *Shake Hands With the Devil* and *A Terrible Beauty* retain this division but only now their two IRA commandants — Sean Lenihan (James

Cagney) in *Shake Hands With the Devil* and Don McGinnis (Dan O'Herlihy) in *A Terrible Beauty* — are not simply cold and emotion-less but positively pathological. In both cases, this pathology is closely connected to sexual abnormality. Sexual repression, rather than 'British oppression', would appear to be at the root of the two men's problems.[37]

McGinnis in *A Terrible Beauty*, for example, is a typical 'authoritarian': a firm supporter of the Nazis and an admirer of their discipline but also a sexual — as well as physical — cripple.[38] Rejected by Dermot's sister, Bella (Marianne Benet), his frustrations now find their outlet through violence. He attempts to detain Bella but is chided for his roughness. 'I love Ireland too,' he retorts, 'and watch the mark I leave on her.' The film's ending completes this logic. McGinnis does not, of course, 'free' Ireland but he does succeed in murdering Bella: an unintended, but symbolically fitting, conclusion for desire turned into violence.

This theme is developed in *Shake Hands With the Devil*. If McGinnis exemplifies the 'authoritarian', Sean Lenihan personifies the 'puritan'.[39] Dedicated to making Ireland 'a fit place to live in', his war is more on women, and the expression of their sexuality, than the traditional Irish enemy, the British. 'To all outward appearances he is the dedicated Irish patriot', observes Len Mosley. 'Underneath . . . he would like to see most women wiped out in the cause of purity.'[40] Violence against women had, of course, been a characteristic of the Cagney persona ever since Tom Powers had assaulted his mistress with a grapefruit in *The Public Enemy* in 1931. Hollywood's increasing preoccupation with psychological abnormality in the post-war period reinforced this early trend. In *White Heat* (1949), Cagney acquired an Oedipus complex; in *Kiss Tomorrow Goodbye* (1950), a sharpened sexual sadism. In casting him as an IRA leader in *Shake Hands With the Devil*, it was inevitable that many of these associations would follow. As Mosley suggests, it is, thus, women, rather than the British, who most unsettle the IRA man's composure and inspire his most vicious outbursts. This is signalled early on. Lenihan arrives at a 'safe house' to help the wounded Kerry but is distracted by the prostitute whom he finds there. Pulling out his gun, he grabs at her necklace and forces her on to her hands and knees. As she crawls on the ground before him, the action is observed through Cagney's open legs, with the camera placed low-angle behind him. A second prostitute, Kitty (Glynis Johns), suffers even more severely. Lenihan warns her to stay away from the IRA hideout in Wicklow and tries to strangle her when he catches her bathing. Like *A Terrible Beauty*, the violence then escalates into murder when Lenihan shoots Kitty at point-blank range, having falsely accused her of informing. Even this is not enough and Jennifer, now wearing the dead Kitty's clothes, is also threatened with execution. Unable to cope with his own sexual impulses, Lenihan, like McGinnis, can only release his desires through violence.

This emphasis, in the films, on sexual violence and psychopathology has three main effects: (1) it underlines the 'naturalness' of their romantic endings by highlighting not only the destructiveness of violence but also its sexual abnormality; (2) it confirms the 'pathology' not simply of the characters themselves but also of their political objectives; and (3) it undermines the possibility of a social and political explanation of violence. As Thomas Szasz suggests, the attribution of 'psychopathy' entails a 'falsification of value' whereby the actions of an agent are deprived of their legitimacy and rationality.[41] Violence, in this respect, can only be accounted for in terms of individual deviance and not in terms of its, quite possibly rational, social and political objectives. This attempt to refuse rationality is at its clearest in *Shake Hands With the Devil*. The film ends with Kerry shooting his erstwhile commander, Lenihan. 'You've forgotten what you're fighting for', he exclaims, 'It isn't Ireland or freedom . . . it's just killing.' What apparently justifies his remark is the signing of the peace treaty providing Dominion status for a partitioned Ireland. Lenihan's refusal to accept the Treaty, in striking contrast to the rest of his brigade, apparently provides the clinching evidence of his pathological blood-lust.[42] Now it is of course the privilege of fiction to rearrange the facts of history to suit its purpose, but the effect of this rearrangement should also be clear. As *The Irish Press* was quick to point out at the time: 'the suggestion that Lenihan, and consequently the men he typified, wished to continue the war merely for war's sake . . . is not true and does an injustice to those people who believed that a Treaty was not the object of their fight'.[43] However, it is only by denying the validity of the opposition to the Treaty, and, indeed, the reality of the Civil War which followed, that the film's condemnation of pathological violence can be sustained.

The Violent Enemy: 'The violence is deep'

Part of the stridency of the two films' repudiation of IRA violence may be accounted for in terms of the context in which they were produced. Both films were made at Ardmore at the time of a renewed IRA border campaign (1956–62) and although both films were dealing with events in the past they must also have been assumed to have a contemporary resonance. And, of course, by this time the IRA which fought against the Treaty had long since assumed government office and turned against their former organisation.[44] Moreover, the films' appearance coincided with the arrival of Sean Lemass as Taoiseach and the emergence of a new programme of economic modernisation which, at least by some, was perceived to hold out the prospect for a more peaceful means of resolution to the continuing problem of the North.[45] The link, in this respect, is probably no more than speculative; by the time of *The Violent Enemy* (1969), however, the relationship has become that much clearer. Made after a number of years of relative IRA inactivity and just before the beginnings of a new campaign in the North, it is less the issue of the border than the tension between the new-found 'affluence' of Irish society and traditional violent nationalism which the film adopts as its focus. Indeed, for Colum O'More (Ed Begley), the traditional IRA leader, it is affluence which is now the central enemy. Because of it, he claims, young Irishmen have sold 'freedom's birthright' in exchange for 'regular wages, mortgages and refrigerators, cars on the instalment plan' and, by way of 'an act of blood in defiance', he calls for the blowing up of an electronics factory as a 'gesture' and a reminder that 'a free and united Ireland is still the one cause worth blood'. His views, however, are not shared by the rest of the organisation. They are now devoted to constitutional political means — 'meetings and pamphlets' as O'More dismissively puts it — while Danny (Owen Sullivan), O'More's IRA colleague, not only works at the factory which O'More proposes to destroy but is also prepared to betray him in order to protect the 'thousand men on good wages' who work alongside him.[46] For Danny, times have now changed and O'More, like Lenihan in *Shake Hands With the Devil*, has simply 'shed blood for so long' that he can't 'lose his taste for it'.

Torn between these opposing ambitions is the film's central character, IRA member and border campaign veteran, Sean Rogan (Tom Bell) who has now returned to Ireland after his successful escape from an English prison. On the one hand, he is under pressure from O'More to participate in the destruction of the factory. On the other, he also shows sympathy for Danny. Danny, in fact, represents something of a *doppelganger* to Rogan. He was with Rogan the night he was captured and their subsequent careers might easily have been reversed. Danny is now 'looking prosperous' and apparently welcomes the 'peace and quiet'. As such he not only enjoys the conditions recommended to all Irishmen by John Mills but now also aspired to by Rogan. Like Johnny in *Odd Man Out*, Rogan's spell of imprisonment has stirred doubts about the value of violence while the benefits of 'affluence' clearly attract him. 'Neat Sunday clothes, a joint of meat waiting for them to go home to. It's good to see', he declares to a sceptical Hannah (Susan Hampshire). But, despite these ambitions, Rogan, like Johnny before him, finds himself unable to avoid the continuing lure of violence and it is his return to the 'old ways' which then ensures his subsequent downfall and denies him his seat at the Sunday dinner-table.

In this respect, the film also has parallels with *Odd Man Out*. For while Rogan may have escaped one prison, he still remains the captive of another. He stays at Leary's bar which he describes as 'a prison cell' and is effectively kept a prisoner by O'More and his colleagues who, at one point, lock him in his room (along with a portrait of Michael Collins!). Visually, this sense of imprisonment is reinforced by the style of the film with its tendency to shoot through fences and intermediary surfaces and so create a recurring sense of enclosure. It is also in evidence in the way in which the factory itself is represented. This is not immediately identified and, in absence of information to the contrary, could easily be mistaken — with its electrified fencing, tall perimeter lights, bare brick buildings and security barrier — for a prison. This feeling is reinforced when Rogan subsequently enters the building on the back of a swill cart and is repeatedly shot through a series of wires and fences. Although, at one level, this amounts to no more than a stylistic flourish it also hints at one of the film's central meanings. Rogan has broken out of one prison but only to find himself in another (a 'controlled environment', as Hannah puts it) and, as such, remains as unfree as he was before.

This is partly explained by Rogan's continuing association with out-of-date causes and methods. He stays with John Michael (Noel Purcell), a former IRA man crippled in an earlier mission — in a bar where time has stood still and the arms on the clock noticeably never alter. The place has become, in Rogan's word, a 'museum' with its poster of Countess Markievicz apparently no more than a historical exhibit. The film, in this respect, is at one with Danny in its rejection of traditional nationalism in the age of the 'affluent society'.[47] But, at another level, it is the character of Rogan himself which continues to make him a prisoner. 'Change, there is no change', explains O'More. 'The violence is deep in him and it never ends.' As if to prove his point, Rogan assaults a fellow prisoner in England and then brawls with O'More's fellow conspirator, Fletcher (Michael Standing), inside Leary's. He promises Hannah that there will be 'no more violence' but still ends up inflicting yet another merciless beating on Fletcher. 'We only pretend it's for something else', he comments to Hannah earlier on in the movie. 'It's for its own sake most of the time.' As if living through his own precepts, Rogan's explosions of excessive and unnecessary violence appear to confirm its basic lack of reason. As with *Odd Man Out*, it frustrates his romance with Hannah and denies him his peace and quiet.[48] But if, as O'More has put it, violence truly runs deep in him then once again he is more victim than willing agent — fated, once more, by the 'curse' of violence and its deep-seated grip on the Irish character.

But while it may be the film's intention to consign the characters of Rogan and O'More, along with their allegiances to violent nationalism, to the rubbish dump of history, the film is not without its points of ambivalence. Its approval of the affluent society, for example, is tempered not only by the manner in which it chooses to represent the factory (looking very much like 'the scab on the body of Ireland' which O'More proposes) but also its more general communication of the malevolence, and not just benevolence, of monetary values. This is, perhaps, clearest in the film's treatment of the explosion when Austin (Jon Laurimore) and Fletcher reveal their intention not simply to blow up the factory but to rob its vaults beforehand. Their subsequent use of the Irish tricolour to carry their takings, recorded in a striking series of no less than five close-ups, not only provides a motivation for Rogan's desire for revenge (it's 'the money' he subsequently explains to Danny) but also lends something of a credence to O'More's earlier warnings about the dangers of material corruption. Moreover, the fact that the two men are English suggests a connection with the factory itself. It is noticeable, for example, how, in contrast to the colours of the tricolour, the factory interiors are dominated by those of the Union Jack (blue, red and white). The implication, in this respect, may be less the redundancy of nationalism in an age of economic modernisation and affluence than the new forms of economic domination which such modernisation entails. O'More, for example, has already lamented the loss to Ireland of the factory's 'fat dividends' and, in a sense, the activities of the two Englishmen offer a concrete, and vivid, illustration. It is then, perhaps, something more than a coincidence that when Austin is first introduced he should have assumed the appearance of an English businessman, reading *The Times* and riding in a 'chauffeur-driven' Rolls. But the film's final irony lies with the nature of the factory's output. As O'More points out, the factory is, in fact, working on British Army contracts, producing 'arms' for the use of British 'soldiers'. It is not, after all, that violent methods have become obsolete. Rather, they have achieved a scale of organisation and rationalisation that makes Rogan's own brand of individualistic anarchism increasingly insignificant.

Hennessy and *The Long Good Friday*: 'Mad Micks' and Englishmen

Appearing when it did, *The Violent Enemy* was met by some bemusement. The Dublin *Evening Herald* was, in turns, amused and amazed by its 'highly . . . imaginative concept of the political climate', while the English *Monthly Film Bulletin* was concerned that it might be seen to be rubbing 'rather too much salt into old wounds'.[49] Indeed, it was a familiar experience for many of the films which had been made about Ireland to be chastised for their apparent 'irrelevance'. Writing on *The Gentle Gunman*, for example, Milton Schulman complained that the 'English no longer care' about 'the Irish question' and that the film's audience might just 'as well be listening to arguments about Schleswig-Holstein'.[50] By the time of the seventies, however, such cavalier indifference no longer appeared so appropriate. Indeed, now that films about Ireland could clearly be seen to be 'relevant' the complaints were reversed. Films were castigated for exploiting the 'troubles' for entertainment and film-makers who opted to deal with the issue became subject to political pressures. *Hennessy* (1975), for example, the first fiction feature to attempt to deal with the 'troubles', was practically banned in Britain. EMI Chairman, John Read, along with picture and theatre division head Bernard Delfont, viewed the film before deciding not to show it. The Rank organisation followed suit shortly after. 'Our decision is not a matter of commerce', declared a spokesman for EMI in an unfamiliar stance of civic virtue. 'It is a question of responsibility to the public and society in which we live.'[51] *The Long Good Friday* (1979) was exposed to similar difficulties. Made as part of a three-film deal with Lew Grade's Associated Communications Corporation it was originally intended for theatrical release. ACC, which included ATV, also wanted a television screening but demanded the film be cut by nearly ten minutes (removing some of the film's violence as well as references to the IRA and the British Army). These were rejected by the film's producer, Barry Hanson, and it was only after a protracted public controversy that the film was sold to Handmade Films who then secured its eventual cinema release.[52]

The grounds for anxiety in both cases are readily apparent. In *Hennessy*, British troops in Belfast are responsible for the deaths of innocent bystanders while, back in London, the police are as brutal and ruthless as their IRA counterparts (who on the evidence of the film are also more efficient). Moreover, sympathy is partly structured in favour of the modern Guy Fawkes, Hennessy (Rod Steiger), who only narrowly fails to blow up the Houses of Parliament. In *The Long Good Friday*, the IRA prove practically invincible (Lew Grade apparently found their representation too flattering) and, at least according to the dialogue, more than a match for the British Army. As this might indicate, both films also contain an element of political allegory. *Hennessy* suggests, albeit obliquely, the corruption of domestic British security, and erosion of civil liberties, which can follow the British state's continued involvement in Ireland while *The Long Good Friday* outlines the decline of an 'empire' when its rules are no longer accepted. But, despite these points of interest, the ability of both films to cope with the issues confronted still remains severely restricted.

On the face of it, *Hennessy* would seem to deviate from the normal British model. By adopting the revenge structure characteristic of the American cinema, it possesses the drive and momentum absent from many of the other British films. This is also matched by an energetic and aggressive choice of film style which relies on an elaborate and obtrusive use of zooms, acute angles, shock cuts, bright synthetic colours and loud, abrasive music. But, despite this allegiance to American norms of narrative and style, it still lacks the attitude of 'affirmation' which these conventions would normally supply. The reason is to be found in the film's resort to real 'characters' to validate its status as an 'authentic' political thriller. For, by organising its plot around the attempted assassination of an actual national figure — the Queen — it makes it impossible for the desire for revenge to be fulfilled. An audience will know, particularly when it sees actual newsreel footage of the Royal Family, that the assassination attempt must fail. The film's ending, in this respect, is a foregone conclusion. As a result, the interest of the audience depends less on suspense (will the assassination succeed?) than the fascination of the methods which the would-be killer employs. Thus for all of the film's dependence on drive and aggression, it is inevitable that the adoption of violence must, once again, prove futile and unproductive.

This does not mean, of course, that it is the film's failure to blow up the Queen which makes its treatment of the subject so inadequate. Rather, it is the absence of politics which accompanies it. For while the film may focus on a character who accepts, rather than rejects, the need for violence its interest in the choice is confined to the purely personal. This is clearly established by the film's opening. Hennessy refuses to supply his brother-in-law, Sean Tobin (Eric Porter), with explosives for the IRA. Although he is a former war hero, he no longer believes in violence. Unlike Tobin, it is his 'family', rather than 'Ireland', which he now puts first. What then motivates Hennessy's desire for revenge, and justifies his adoption of violence, is not any political cause but solely the loss of his wife and daughter at the hands of British troops. As with Dermot's brother Ned in *A Terrible Beauty*, the only compelling justification for violence is if it is undertaken in the name of the family.

The inevitable result is that the events in Northern Ireland are employed as no more than a coathanger for the film's tale of individual revenge. This is confirmed by the film's concentration on the loner. Like Flaherty in Tony Luraschi's *The Outsider* (1979), Hennessy now finds himself stranded between the British, on the one hand, and the Provisionals, on the other, just as his police counterpart, Hollis (Richard Johnson), is caught between the IRA and his superiors (in a sort of *Dirty Harry* sub-plot).[53] In both cases, the political context of the men's actions is rendered unimportant. The significance of the deaths of Hennessy's wife and child is purely psychological and no interest is shown in the causes or events leading up to them. Likewise, the IRA execution, shown in flashback, is evacuated of any meaning other than its relation to the largely personal tension between Hollis and Hennessy. Rather than attempt to explain it, the film merely uses the event to provide a 'dramatic balance' to its clash of individuals. The scene is thus 're-run' at the film's end: only now it is Hollis, rather than the IRA, who is wielding the gun and Hennessy, rather than Hollis, who is injured and limping. And, so, for all its novelty in focusing on the 'troubles', *Hennessy* is content to merely use them as a backdrop. The individual act of violence may be endowed with some sense of reason, but the larger political context, and the political violence it engenders, is left unexplained and, by implication, 'irrational'. The 'images of Belfast' with which the film begins, thus remain unused, neither establishing narrative, character or political pertinence. They remain just culturally familiar indices of the 'troubles' — 'a freak side-show', as Tom Nairn puts it, 'for *la societé du spectacle*'.[54]

Unlike *Hennessy*, *The Long Good Friday* does suggest that violent means may prove successful. But while the film may portray the IRA as apparent victors, it can only do so by invoking the ancient stereotype of the inexplicably violent and demonic Irish. The focus of the film is a sort of *Performance*-type confrontation between two counterposing ethics: rational, quasi-capitalist gangsterism on the one hand versus no-holds-barred political violence on the other. But in so far as narrative focus is almost exclusively confined to the activities of ganglord Harold Shand (Bob Hoskins), there is little room for exploring or explaining the ethic with which he is confronted. The film withholds the information necessary to identifying his attackers and their motivations for as long as possible, with the result that the audience is invited to share and identify with Shand's confusion and perplexity in uncovering who is 'having a go' at him, and why. Even when the IRA do finally make an appearance, they remain an obscure and shadowy presence, appearing as if from nowhere as they take off with Shand as their prisoner. It may be that this is the film's point. It is precisely Shand's inability to comprehend the nature of the political ethic confronting him which, allowing for the film's loose allegory, echoes the inability, or unwillingness, of the British state to come to terms with its Irish opposition. But, in so far as the film inscribes its own distance from the IRA characters, denying us any sense of interior relation with them, so it also confirms, rather than queries, the apparent inexplicability of their actions.[55] According to the film's director, John MacKenzie, the IRA's violence is being carried out 'with quite different motives and morality' from that which is employed by Shand. Indeed, he goes on to suggest that their motives may actually be 'purer' because not simply inspired by gain.[56] And, yet, this could hardly be justified on the basis of the film itself. Apart from the reference to extortion, the 'motives' and 'morality' of Shand's opponents remain a blank. It is not 'morality', simply a ruthless commitment to violence, which makes them 'superior' to their adversaries.

From here it is easy to see how many other British films, not so directly preoccupied with IRA violence, conform to an enduring pattern. Like *The Gentle Gunman*, *Shake Hands With the Devil* and *A Terrible Beauty*, Frank Launder and Sidney Gilliat's *Captain Boycott* (1947) is organised around the movement from violence to non-violence. Set in Co. Mayo in the 1880s, the villagers are divided over the best means to defeat their English landlord, Captain Boycott (Cecil Parker). Following a speech by Parnell, the advocates of physical force are converted to peaceful means of resistance and thus become the first to implement the 'boycott'. An avuncular Alastair Sim, as the village priest, benignly warns us 'to go home and leave violence be'. Pursuing a Labour victory allegory, Durgnat decides that the film is 'unequivocally on the side of the rabble'.[57] The evidence of the film suggests otherwise. A newcomer to the village, Mark Killain (Niall McGinnis), accepts the home of an evicted family. When he kills the former tenant in self-defence, the villagers are intent on vengeance. With the mob's descent into mindless violence (the abiding flaw of the Irish character) now imminent, it is up to Hugh Davin (Stewart Granger) to stand up for the virtues of non-violence. Whereas collective violence in *The Quiet Man* encourages social cohesion, it can only lead to social breakdown in *Captain Boycott*. Far from siding with the 'rabble', the film depends on the strength of an individual hero, backed by the moral authority of the Church, to re-establish order and 'reason'. Davin's motives, however, are not purely idealistic. He has fallen in love with Killain's daughter, Anne (Kathleen Ryan), and is concerned with her protection. As with so many other films, it is finally love, and the prospect of marriage, which most successfully combat the temptations of violence. The theme of Launder and Gilliat's other Irish feature, *I See A Dark Stranger* (1946), is similar. Here the young Bridie Quilty (Deborah Kerr) overcomes her inherited hatred of the English, such that she is prepared to spy for the Nazis, by falling in love with an English officer. As with *Shake Hands With the Devil*, the romance between political opponents undercuts the significance of

175

political relationships. Structural relations are collapsed into individual emotions and just because individual English men (and women) turn out to be personally quite pleasant so it is assumed, *à la* John Mills, that deep-seated political divisions may be forgotten.

Elements from both *Captain Boycott* and *I See A Dark Stranger* recur in David Lean's *Ryan's Daughter* (1970). Like *Captain Boycott*, the unity of purpose revealed in the rescue of arms from the storm degenerates into ugly mob violence when the villagers once again set upon an innocent victim. As with the former film, it is then up to the advocates of 'reason' — Robert Mitchum's schoolteacher and Trevor Howard's priest — to prevent the descent into chaos. Like *I See A Dark Stranger*, there is also a traversal of the Anglo-Irish divide via 'Romance'. But whereas love triumphs in *I See A Dark Stranger* it is destined to failure in *Ryan's Daughter*. The collapse of politics is, however, similar. Like *Hennessy*, the political conflicts are robbed of any substance and simply provide the backdrop against which the doomed passion must work itself out. If they have any meaning at all, it is only as a barrier to love and a common humanity.

Rejection of the mob and the de-contextualisation of Irish history are also a feature of *Young Cassidy* (1965). Very loosely based on the life of Sean O'Casey, the film is so committed to the myth of artistic isolation that the role of politics can only dwindle into insignificance. In order to develop as an artist, Johnny Cassidy/Sean O'Casey (Rod Taylor) must opt to abandon 'everything': his class, his political attachments, his family, his lover and, finally, Ireland itself. Far from existing in any dynamic or organic relationship with his native community, Cassidy's art can only thrive on separation.

In a film, at least in part the responsibility of John Ford, it may be tempting to cast Cassidy in the mould of the archetypal Fordian loner — like Ethan Edwards in *The Searchers* or Tom Doniphon in *The Man Who Shot Liberty Valance* — who acts on behalf of the community, even if he himself is unable to join it.[58] The comparison is revealing. For while we are made aware of the virtues of the community (marriage, family, school, law) in *The Man Who Shot Liberty Valance*, we are denied these in *Young Cassidy*. Cassidy's artistic development is solely an individual project, entirely at odds with collective values. The collectivity, in this respect, possesses only a negative value, degenerating into a howling mob as in the transport strike.

The transport strike represents the turning-point in Cassidy's development, marking not only the disdain for violence but also the beginning of his disengagement from politics. The importance of the strike is reduced to the personal significance of Cassidy's encounter with a young prostitute, Daisy (Julie Christie). He subsequently leaves the Irish Citizens Army (who were anyway 'under-rehearsed') and is a passive observer of the 1916 Rising, while enjoying a reunion with Daisy. The War of Independence intrudes when the Black and Tans show the bad grace to interrupt a bout of love-making with his neighbour, whilst the signing of the peace treaty provides no more than a prelude to Cassidy's production of *Shadow of a Gunman*. Thus in a dramatic, but nonetheless logical, reversal of his earlier attack on a policeman, Cassidy now relies on the police force to remove the mob from the theatre foyer.

It is, however, Basil Dearden's *The League of Gentlemen* (1960) which best sums up the British cinema's treatment of Ireland. During the course of this film, a group of disenchanted army veterans prepare for a daring bank robbery. As part of their plans, they raid an army camp in order to secure a supply of arms. The group's leader, Hyde (Jack Hawkins), warns his fellow conspirators of the precautions to be taken. 'When we leave our card we shall have to provide the authorities with a scapegoat', he informs them. 'In this case, I'm relying on the British character. We British will always give the Germans, the Russians, the Japanese and even the Egyptians the benefit of the doubt . . . but never the Irish.' And, sure enough, once the raid is completed, the newspapers dutifully perform their allocated role and blame it on 'Irish rebels'. It is an amusing, but also apt, commentary not only on the British 'character' but also the 'character', or characteristics, of the British cinema itself. For, as the survey suggests, it too has tended to blame the Irish as the source of conflict while ignoring, or even denying, the role of the British themselves. In particular, it has tended to blame the Irish for their violence while disregarding, or undermining, the relevance of the social and political context which might explain it.

It is a tradition, moreover, which is not simply confined to fiction film-making but which extends to media coverage of the 'troubles' more generally. Philip Schlesinger, for example, suggests how British television's coverage of Northern Ireland has relied on 'a series of de-contextualised reports of violence' which have failed 'to analyse and re-analyse the historical roots of the conflict'. And this, he continues, cannot but help to reinforce a dominant view of the 'troubles' as 'largely incomprehensible and irrational'.[59] Much the same verdict could apply to British films about Ireland. For they too have opted to focus on Irish violence while failing to place it in the social and political context which would permit its explanation. And, by doing so, they too have rendered the events with which they deal largely unintelligible.[60]

Angel: 'We know where the madness is'

It is all the more regrettable then that many of the same attitudes and assumptions are now appearing in the work of Irish film-makers. The representations of the Irish characteristically associated with sources outside of Ireland have now, apparently, become so 'natural' and 'normal' that they are providing a framework for certain sections of Irish film-making as well. Take, for example, *Angel* (1982), written and directed by Irish novelist turned film-maker, Neil Jordan, and financed, in part, by the then recently established Irish Film Board. Although one reviewer found it 'extraordinary' how the film appeared to emerge from 'no clear cinematic tradition', the evidence of the film suggests otherwise.[61] Indeed, as at least one critic spotted, the film has more than its share of similarities with *Odd Man Out*, not simply in its formal approach but also in the perspective on political violence which it then encourages.[62]

Like *Odd Man Out*, the film is concerned with the destructive power of violence. Danny (Stephen Rea) sets out on a trail of violent revenge, only to arrive at 'the heart of darkness'. In contrast to the affirmative logic of classic Hollywood — its faith in positive action and problem resolution — *Angel*'s use of the revenge structure is entirely negative in its implications. Danny's problems are only compounded, his actions achieve nothing save his own brutalisation. By the end of the film, he has come full circle, back where he began in the burnt-out shell of the dance-hall. Like Johnny before him, Danny too has been 'cursed'. He is, as Dee (Honor Heffernan) suggests, 'under a spell', the hapless victim of the very instrument of which he would be master. 'Pull out a gun', as Jordan explains, 'and things cease to be in your control.'[63]

This attitude would seem to be confirmed by the suggestions of homage to *Point Blank* (1967), a film directed by *Angel*'s executive producer, John Boorman. Both films end at the locations where they began and just as Walker in *Point Blank* discovers how he has been manipulated by the Organisation leader, Fairfax, so Danny in *Angel* now learns that he has been used by the police detective, Bloom (Ray McAnally) in order to uncover the assassins. While both men have assumed themselves to be in control of their actions, the endings reveal how they have also been turned into puppets. Indeed, to take the comparison further, it can be seen how Danny is, at least symbolically, already dead — like Walker in *Point Blank*, he only appears to have escaped death at the film's beginning. He reappears to join the band 'like a ghost', while Dee turns against him with the denunciation that he is 'dead'. Thus just as Walker 'considers the possibilities of revenge open to him if he had lived, and, at last, determines that they lead nowhere', so Danny sets off on his dream-like pursuit only to discover that his quest has been similarly futile.[64]

As with *Point Blank*, the theme of futility is approached through abstract means. Although set in Northern Ireland, the film deliberately eschews surface verisimilitude. In common with *Odd Man Out*, there is a similar imprecision about period and place, a similar reticence with respect to the political and religious identities of characters and organisations. Compositions are studiously mannered, the use of colour and lighting deliberately dreamlike. Dialogue is self-consciously 'poetic', avoiding naturalism and heavily dependent on allusion and reference (everything from Shakespeare to Monica Vitti). Like *Odd Man Out*, the ambition behind such an aesthetic strategy is also apparent, i.e. the pursuit of a 'message' about violence which is not just specific to Northern Ireland but also universal, or context-free, in its implications. 'My decision', as Jordan puts it 'was to make a film about the effects of violence . . . in a pure way.'[65]

Of necessity, this preoccupation with 'pure' violence requires a suppression of social and political specifics. Indeed, social and political questions are not simply by-passed, or, as in *Hennessy*, made subordinate to a tale of purely personal revenge, but are rendered irrelevant by virtue of the film's emphasis on the metaphysical origins of violence. Unlike *Odd Man Out*, however, this has less to do with the operations of fate (although there is a suggestion of this in Auntie Mae's reading of the cards) than the operations of the unconscious. As Richard Kearney suggests, the film is concerned primarily with an exploration of the 'psychic roots' of violence in terms of a 'metaphysics of the unconscious'. By emphasising 'the fundamental nexus between aesthetic creativity and violence' — Danny is a musician turned gunman — so the film is able to highlight 'the dark, hidden atavisms of the psyche' which, it implies, are the shared source of 'both poetic mystery and violent mystification'.[66] Stripped to this common psychic foundation, all violence, so the film would appear to be saying, is fundamentally the same. Once you take up the gun, observes police officer Bonner (Donal McCann), 'you only have the one tune'.

But while Kearney finds this both 'highly original and perceptive', its implications for an understanding of Northern Ireland are surely quite different. By attempting to show all violence as the same, irrespective of political context or motivation, the film defies the possibility of any political explanation, and, indeed, any political solution, to the conflicts which are occurring. Emptied of political content, violence simply becomes an 'evil' running deep in the collective unconscious. 'Everyone's guilty', as Bloom so unhelpfully puts it. Far from challenging the conventional view of the situation, the film merely ends up confirming the most commonplace perceptions of the 'troubles' as both futile and intractable. 'Seldom has the hopelessness of the Irish situation', as one reviewer put it, 'been so well captured on film'.[67] As with *Odd Man Out*, the attempt to create a 'universal' drama, while maintaining a recognisable Irish setting, only helps to confirm a view of the 'troubles' as unintelligible. 'We know where the madness is', one of the assassins tells Danny. So, too, will the film's audience. For by rendering political relations and motivations irrelevant, it is only the 'madness' of Nothern Ireland which *Angel* permits an audience to see.[68]

But, as with *Odd Man Out*, this avoidance of political specifics does not free the film from political implications. Donald Hounam, for example, argues that the film's view is consistent with that of Whitehall. By denying its political origins and motives, he suggests, paramilitary violence is simply represented as criminal.[69] By the same token, if the film's use of a decontextualising aesthetic strategy necessarily undermines the 'legitimacy' or rationale of political violence, so it also adds to the legitimacy of the state by de-politicising its activities as well. Like most crime films, *Angel* depends on the police for a narrative resolution and avoids the drawn-out rituals of the legal process by resorting to the more dramatically convenient device of an *ad hoc* execution.[70] While the film appears to be denouncing all violence, this turns out to be only partly true. Dee does refer to 'them' like Danny, but 'only in uniform'. However, there is no evidence that when Bloom himself 'takes up the gun' to shoot Bonner he suffers any of the same psychic consequences as befall Danny. Thus whilst all Danny's killings are shown in graphic and unpleasant detail, Bloom's own responsibility for murder is discreetly down-played by having him fire out of view of the audience. As would befit the crime film, Bloom's violence, unlike Danny's, is neither futile nor self-destructive because enacted in support of law and order. As with *Odd Man Out*, it is not the violence of the police, or state, which the film condemns, only the violence of their enemies.[71] Whatever the film-makers may claim, this amounts to more than simply a statement about 'pure' violence or 'violence in general'.

Cal: 'What a fucking country'

It is also the destructive power of violence which is central to *Cal* (1984), directed by Irish-born Pat O'Connor and scripted from his own novel by Northern Irish writer Bernard MacLaverty. As with *Angel*, it also has much in common with *Odd Man Out*. Like Johnny in *Odd Man Out*, Cal (John Lynch) is a luckless IRA volunteer who 'wants out' but is powerless to change his circumstances. As with Johnny, he is the victim of an initial and irreversible error — his involvement in the murder of a policeman — and so condemned to pay the penalty. 'Born under a bad sign', as the song he listens to would have it, Cal is evidently fated and his doom a foregone conclusion. He looks to Marcella (Helen Mirren), the policeman's widow, for salvation but their love, as the broken mirror dropped from Marcella's handbag warns, is necessarily destined to fail. They find temporary happiness in the disused cottage on the Morton farmstead but their past inevitably returns to haunt and destroy their relationship. With the sense of doom so all-pervasive, 'even Oedipus', suggests Richard Kearney, would have had 'more room for manoeuvre' than this story's unfortunate and tormented 'hero'.[72]

Inevitably, this has consequences for how the film is then able to deal with the 'troubles'. As with *Odd Man Out*, the adoption of the vocabulary of fatalism must work against a political explanation. Like Cal himself, the society which the film evokes is largely one of victims, passively enduring or futilely defying a world outside of their control. Derangement, disability or simply death are all that most of the characters can hope for.[73] In this way, the film lays great stress on the corrosive effects of the 'troubles' upon individual lives but is largely unilluminating on the political causes and relations which sustain them. 'The violence and the tragedy', as O'Connor puts it, is assumed rather than explained, accepted rather than analysed.[74]

This derives, in part, from the emphasis of the film on private lives and emotions. As with so many films before it, it is love, rather than political commitment, which the film values. Like *Shake Hands With the Devil* and *I See A Dark Stranger*, it sees the potential of love to triumph over political divisions; but, as with *Ryan's Daughter*, and in line with its mood of fatalism, it also laments the loss of private innocence when the world beyond impinges. The film, in this respect, amounts to something more than a 'love story' which 'just happens' to take place in Northern Ireland. For love is not simply in the foreground but also in opposition to the violent society around it. However, by centring on private emotions, and using them as the yardstick of political action, it is inevitable that the ability to deal with politics will suffer. The contest between love and politics is bound to be unfairly matched; its conclusion predictable. As Joe McMinn suggests, 'an intelligible and compassionate sense of History' lies beyond the reach of the story's romantic conventions.[75] So, while the film's central characters — the lovers — enjoy a degree of inner complexity, the characters who stand in for 'politics' are stripped of all except their malignance. The representation of the IRA leader, Skeffington (John Kavanagh), for example, is both archaic and all too familiar. He is puritanical (e.g. a teetotaller), sexually repressed (e.g. complaining of Crilly's use of the word 'fucking') and fanatical (e.g. given to quoting Pearse).[76] The conventionality of the type is only matched by the conventionality of cinematic treatment. Accompanied by an appropriately sinister soundtrack, he first appears out of the shadows, like Dracula, to force his 'prey', Cal, back into IRA action. Seen later in the back of the IRA's car, he is shot half in light and half in shadow in the conventional cinematic shorthand for dementia. Unable to represent the character with any degree of complexity, the film merely falls back on grotesquery. As Joe McMinn concludes, the choice between love and politics is collapsed into a struggle between 'the humane and the monstrous'.[77]

The film's inability to invest its view of the 'troubles' with any degree of political complexity is confirmed by the retreat into metaphysics. A metaphysical turn is, of course, implicit in the film's logic of fatalism. With the introduction of the Preacher

(Tom Hickey), however, it becomes quite explicit. The character is first seen, immediately following the initial killing and as the opening credits unfold, nailing a sign — 'the wages of sin is death' — to a roadside tree. He reappears later: first, when Cal is being driven to work and turns to watch him and, towards the film's end, when Cal, wandering through the town clutching his Christmas presents, comes across the Preacher declaiming the need for redemption. As with the blind man in *The Informer*, the Preacher is less a 'realistic' than symbolic character, personifying, as in the earlier film, the forces of fate and destiny. And, just as the events of the War of Independence are transformed into a mythic drama of sin and redemption by *The Informer*, so the underlying architecture of *Cal* is less social and political than theological. This is made evident by Marcella's story of the rape and murder of Maria Goretti and the subsequent reconciliation of the girl's mother and attacker in church. In fact, it is very reminiscent of *The Informer* when Gypo arrives in church to beg forgiveness from the mother of the man on whom he informed. In the same way, Cal returns to Marcella (despite the risk to his safety) in a final attempt to find redemption for his crime against her husband. It is this same pattern of sin and redemption which also explains the emphasis of the film on Cal's need for physical suffering.

Like Johnny in *Odd Man Out*, Cal, because of the film's fatalistic structure, is a passive, rather than active, hero. Unlike the hero in classic Hollywood, he can neither control events nor make things happen. But if, as Mulvey suggests, the demand for activity characteristic of Hollywood fits in well with sadism, Cal's inability to make things happen finds a clear expression in masochism.[78] He is beaten by Loyalist thugs on his way home, beaten by the army who raid the disused cottage and is apparently 'grateful' when the RUC officers who arrest him, prepare, as the novel puts it, 'to beat him to within an inch of his life'.[79] Pain is also self-inflicted when Cal stubs his hand with a lighted cigarette just prior to his second encounter with the Preacher. But while this may have a theological value, and ease Cal's path to redemption, it has little to offer to the world of politics. As Moynahan suggests, of the original novel, 'just how endurance of pain to the point of mortified flesh . . . can right wrongs in the real world of bombs, torture and power politics, as distinct from the mystic world of saints and martyrs, is left up in the air'.[80] Just as the story of Maria Goretti reinterprets sexual violence in religious terms, so *Cal* imposes a religious interpretation on the meaning of political violence ('sin') to which it then offers a religious, rather than political, solution ('redemption' through masochistic suffering).

Inevitably, this must obscure, as much as it illuminates, the social and political conflicts which are at the heart of the Northern Ireland 'troubles'. The imposition of religious meanings, in combination with the film's pattern of fatalism, can only confirm a view of the conflicts as the work of dark and atavistic forces. Cal's 'curse' is also the 'curse' of the Irish and 'Ulster's heritage', as Kearney suggests, emerges as 'some kind of congenitally inherited "original sin"'.[81] With the characters so condemned to the grip of primeval impulses, and unable to master their own destinies, it is only the authority and might of the RUC (who arrest Cal) and the British Army (who round up the IRA gang) which can restore a semblance of 'order'.[82] 'What a fucking country', observes the loyalist Dunlop (Ray McAnally). In the absence of any political perspectives on the situation in Northern Ireland, it would be hard for the audience of *Cal* to disagree.

Conclusion

It would be a mistake to see *Angel* and *Cal* as generally typical of recent Irish film-making but they are, nonetheless, two of the films to have enjoyed the most substantial commercial and critical success.[83] This is not, perhaps, surprising. For, as I have argued, they are also the two films which conform most closely to a long-standing tradition of representing Ireland on the screen and, as a result, have offered the images of Ireland most likely to correspond to the expectations of an international audience.[84] But, while the gain may have been a greater commercial appeal, the cost has been an image of the Northern Ireland conflicts which has done little to advance understanding. As with so many British films before them, both *Angel* and *Cal* have proved unequal to the challenge of their subject-matter and, as a result, have obscured, as much as they have illuminated, the issues with which they have dealt. This is not to suggest that there is then a 'correct' interpretation of the conflicts which films about Ireland should be supporting.[85] What it does imply, however, is that the ability to respond intelligently to history, and the willingness to engage with economic, political and cultural complexity, would need to be considerably greater than that which the cinema has so far demonstrated.

Notes

1. For a useful, if rather basic, survey of films about Ireland, especially during the silent period, see Roger B. Dooley, 'The Irish on the Screen', Parts 1 and 2, *Films in Review*, Volume VIII, No. 5, May 1957, and Volume VIII, No. 6, June 1957.

2. Other national cinemas have, of course, produced Irish-theme films but not in any significant number. The French provided a notable version of Liam O'Flaherty's *The Puritan* (1938) while the German cinema exploited Ireland's history of anti-English rebellion for wartime propaganda in such films as *The Fox of Glenarvon* (1940) and *My Life for Ireland* (1941). The latter film is discussed in Julian Petley, *Capital and Culture: German Cinema 1933–45*, London: British Film Institute, 1979.

3. This corresponds to Dennis Clark and William J. Lynch's distinction between the 'Old Country' and 'Irish Freedom' film. See 'Hollywood and Hibernia: The Irish in the Movies', in Randall M. Miller (ed.), *The Kaleidoscopic Lens: How Hollywood Views Ethnic Groups*, Englewood Cliffs, NJ: James S. Ozer, 1980.

4. Charles Townshend, *Political Violence in Ireland*, Oxford: Clarendon Press, 1983, p. 1.

5. For a useful historical survey of Anglo-Irish attitudes, see Liz Curtis, *Nothing But the Same Old Story: The Roots of Anti-Irish Racism*, London: Information on Ireland, 1984. See also, Ned Lebow, 'British Historians and Irish History', *Éire-Ireland*, Volume VIII, No. 4, Winter 1973.

6. Richard Ned Lebow, *White Britain and Black Ireland: The Influence of Stereotypes on Colonial Policy*, Philadelphia: Institute for the Study of Human Issues, 1976, p. 78.

7. See L. P. Curtis Jr., *Apes and Angels: The Irishman in Victorian Caricature*, Newton Abbot: David and Charles, 1971.

8. For a fuller discussion of the conventions of narrative and realism, see my *Sex, Class and Realism: British Cinema 1956–63*, London: British Film Institute, 1986, Chapter 3.

9. Thomas Elsaesser, 'The Pathos of Failure: American Films in the 70's', *Monogram*, No. 6, October 1975, p. 14.

10. Thomas Elsaesser, 'Vincente Minelli', *Brighton Film Review*, No. 15, December 1969, p. 12.

11. Elsaesser, 'The Pathos of Failure', p. 14. This is not to suggest that 'classic' American genre cinema is always necessarily 'affirmative': *film noir*, in the forties, for example, has been consistently defined in terms of its pessimistic and fatalistic ethos. This, however, is less of an exception than it might at first seem: for it is precisely the attenuation of 'classic' narrativity, in the form of convoluted, non-linear plots, and the deployment of a partly 'European' aesthetic, in the form of expressionism, that accounts for *film noir*'s characteristic pessimism. It is also the use of expressionist conventions in *The Informer* (1935) which makes it's representation of Ireland an exception to the typical American model.

12. Andrew Tudor, *Image and Influence: Studies in the Sociology of Film*, London: George Allen and Unwin, 1974, pp. 213–14. This does not mean, of course, that each and every act of violence is endowed with positive connotations. The meaning of the violent act will also vary

according to genre conventions of character (as with the cowboy or Indian in the western, or the gangster and FBI man in the crime film).

13. Charles Barr, 'Opening the Drama Archives', *The Listener*, Volume 96, No. 2484, 18 November 1976, p. 651. As with Elsaesser's model of American cinema, Barr is dealing with typical characteristics rather than providing an exhaustive description of the British cinema. For a discussion of British films which appear to defy this general designation, see Julian Petley, 'The Lost Continent', in Charles Barr (ed.), *All Our Yesterdays: 90 Years of British Cinema*, London: British Film Institute, 1986.

14. Thus, by a peculiar alchemy, even British war movies made during World War II were often marked by a remarkable passivity and lack of aggression. For a discussion, see Ivan Butler, *The War Film*, London: Tantivy Press, 1974, Chapter 5, and Raymond Durgnat, *A Mirror For England: British Movies From Austerity to Affluence*, London: Faber and Faber, 1970, espec. pp. 84–5.

15. Liam O'Flaherty, *The Informer*, London: New English Library, 1980 (orig. 1925), p. 14. There is a similar absence of motivation in O'Flaherty's 'political thriller', *The Assassin*, Dublin: Wolfhound Press, 1983 (orig. 1928). Undoubtedly influenced by Dostoevsky's *Crime and Punishment*, the novel obscures the reason for the assassin's actions and, thus, like *The Informer*, pre-empts the possibility of their political explanation.

16. This is despite the fact that the film is also more specific than the novel in setting the action during the War of Independence (it introduces the Black and Tans, for example). Although O'Flaherty's novel is set in the 1920s it does not specify the year (1921 in the film) while most indications are that it is actually set after the War of Independence and that the revolutionaries are fighting the Free State government. O'Flaherty himself went further and suggested that the novel was not about the 'Irish revolution' at all but based on 'happenings in a Saxon town, during the sporadic Communist insurrection of about nineteen twenty-two or three'. See, Liam O'Flaherty, *Shame the Devil*, London: Grayson and Grayson, 1934, p. 191.

17. The Dublin Trilogy consists of *Juno and the Paycock*, *The Shadow of a Gunman* and *The Plough and the Stars*. These are collected in Sean O'Casey, *Three Plays*, London: Macmillan, 1972. For a discussion of the issues which they raise, see Seamus Deane, 'Irish Politics and O'Casey's Theatre', in Thomas Kilroy (ed.), *Sean O'Casey: A Collection of Critical Essays*, Englewood Cliffs, NJ: Prentice-Hall, 1975; also Francis Mulhern, ' ''Ideology and Literary Form'' — a comment', *New Left Review*, No. 91, May–June 1975.

18. F. L. Green, *Odd Man Out*, London: Ace Books, 1961 (orig. 1945), p. 95. In the novel, Granny is not a relative but a neighbour whom Agnes (Kathleen in the film) visits.

19. James De Felice, *Filmguide to Odd Man Out*, Bloomington and London: Indiana University Press, 1975, p. 47.

20. Ernest Lindgren, *The Art of Film*, London: George Allen and Unwin, 1963, p. 169.

21. See, for example, the complaints of Colin MacCabe in 'Memory, Phantasy, Identity: Days of Hope and the Politics of the Past', in Claire

Johnston (ed,), *History/Production/Memory*, Edinburgh Film Festival, 1977.

22. Bhiku Parekh, *Marx's Theory of Ideology*, London: Croom Helm, 1982, p. 6.

23. Liam McGabhann, *Irish Press*, 10 March 1974, p. 4.

24. However, the fact that the League were also prepared to offer 'all honour' to the film's director, Carol Reed, does suggest something of the ambivalence of the film's approach towards its subject. For while it may be opposed to Johnny's violence, its employment of a tragic structure does, nonetheless, make him a figure of sympathy (as, in all likelihood, does the casting of James Mason). And, as Richard Kearney has suggested, it is precisely this ability to solicit sympathy and support through suffering (as in the hunger-strike) which has historically been one of republicanism's strongest weapons. See, 'The IRA's Strategy of Failure', *The Crane Bag*, Volume 4, No. 2, 1980/81. The film's employment of a decontextualising aesthetic strategy does, however, work against sympathy for Johnny in political, as opposed to more general 'human', terms (although it could, of course, be argued that it is this more general form of human sympathy which republicanism itself has sought to cultivate, particularly in its appeal to the symbols of Christian martyrdom).

25. Tom Nairn, *The Break-Up of Britain*, London: New Left Books, 1981, pp. 222 – 4.

26. As Philip Elliot points out, it is a common characteristic of British ideology to claim an 'opposition to violence' which, in fact, refers only to anti-state or 'unconstitutional' violence rather than all violence (including that employed by the state itself). See, 'Reporting Northern Ireland: a study of news in Great Britain, Northern Ireland and the Republic of Ireland', in *Race, Ethnicity and the Media*, UNESCO, 1977.

27. Anon., 'Laurels Go to Irish Stars', *Irish Independent*, 10 March 1947, p. 2.

28. Robin Cross, *The Big Book of British Films*, Bideford: Charles Herridge, 1984, p. 85. See also Charles Barr's comments on Ealing's 'horror of violence' in *Ealing Studios*, London: Cameron and Tayleur, 1977, p. 147.

29. Although set in 1941, by which time the English campaign was over, the film is clearly based on the London underground bombings of February 1939. For the details of these, and the campaign more generally, see J. Bowyer Bell, *The Secret Army*, London: Sphere, 1972; also Tim Pat Coogan, *The IRA*, London: Fontana, 1971. Reviewing the film in *The Irish Press*, Liam McGabhann complained that the film-makers had seized on this specific campaign as 'a chance to paint the Irish anti-partition picture all black' ('Gunman Effort a Freak', 9 February 1953, p. 4).

30. Although the emphasis of the discussion is on the film's treatment of the Irish 'character', the way that this is seen to 'grow out' of the landscape (as in the introduction of Shinto and Johnny taking target practice in the mountains) would also appear to confirm Luke Gibbons' discussion of romanticism elsewhere in this volume.

31. Durgnat, *A Mirror For England*, p. 108.

32. Raymond Durgnat, 'Dearden and Relph — Two on a Tandem', *Films and Filming*, July 1966, p. 27.

33. The speech is undoubtedly based on the Covey's argument in *The*

Plough and the Stars that 'there's no such thing as an Irishman, or an Englishman, or a German or a Turk; we're all only human bein's.' See Sean O'Casey, *Three Plays*, p. 143.

34. Jean-Paul Sartre, *Portrait of the Anti-Semite*, London: Secker and Warburg, 1948, p. 45.

35. In so far as mainstream cinema has conventionally conceived of homosexuality as a form of 'castrated' masculinity, so there may also be a suggestion of homosexuality about the film's ending. And, it is, of course, the same actors — Dirk Bogarde and John Mills — who play out a drama of repressed homo-erotic desire in the later British film, *The Singer not the Song* (1960). For a discussion of Bogarde's screen persona, and its relationship to homosexuality, during the 1950s, see Richard Dyer, 'Victim: Hermeneutic Project', *Film Form*, No. 2, 1977; also Andy Medhurst, 'Dirk Bogarde', in *All Our Yesterdays*, op. cit.

36. This, to a large extent, is inherited from Rearden Connor's original novel. As he explains, in his semi-autobiographical *A Plain Tale From the Bogs*, London: John Miles, 1937, he intended to write in a way that would 'not shield the brutalities nor the courage of the men on either side' and how this resulted in the book pleasing neither 'the Imperialists' nor 'the extremist Irish' (see pp. 237–41). Although Leslie Halliwell classifies the film as Irish (see *Halliwell's Film Guide*, London: Granada, 1979) and Clark and Lynch regard it as American (see *The Kaleidoscopic Lens*, op cit.), *Shake Hands With the Devil* was, in fact, made by the British director, Michael Anderson's own production company, Troy Films, and was registered with the British Board of Trade as British. In designating films as British, I have been following the Board of Trade's lead.

37. The idea of Irish violence as a sublimation of sexual drives may be traced, once again, to the writings of Sean O'Casey. In *The Plough and the Stars* there is a discomfiting juxtaposition of the down-to-earth prostitute, Rosie Redmond, lamenting the loss of custom inside the public house, and the 'voice of the man' outside (Padraig Pearse), inciting Irishmen to bloodshed. John Ford's film version downplays this implication by toning down Rosie's speeches and substituting Pearse's 'Coming Revolution' speech with a much more 'moderate' declaration by Connolly of the Irish people's right to national sovereignty.

38. Sexual repression is linked with 'authoritarian character' in T. W. Adorno *et al.*, *The Authoritarian Personality*, New York: Harper and Row, 1950, and Wilhelm Reich, *The Mass Psychology of Fascism*, Harmondsworth: Penguin, 1983 (orig. 1946). Both works, of course, suggest a connection between social structure and individual personality which is entirely absent from *A Terrible Beauty*'s representation of McGinnis.

39. Puritanism and sadism are conventionally linked in Freudian theory in terms of their shared 'anality'. For a discussion, see Paul Hoch, *White Hero Black Beast: Racism, Sexism and the Mask of Masculinity*, London: Pluto, 1979. It is this link which forms the basis of Liam O'Flaherty's novel *The Puritan* (1931) in which a religious fanatic murders a prostitute. A more recent variant may be found in Dervla Murphy's suggestion that 'Irish Christianity's anti-sex complex' may be connected to republican violence. See, *A Place Apart*, Harmondsworth: Penguin, 1980, p. 20.

40. Len Mosley, *Daily Express*, 29 May 1959. Although a number of

British reviewers commented on this aspect of the film, it went largely ignored by the Irish press. Ironically, it appears that the version released in Ireland was incomplete and excluded the most sexually explicit scenes (such as the beach scene).

41. Thomas Szasz, *The Second Sin*, London: Routledge and Kegan Paul, 1974, p. 95. For a more general statement, see the same author's *The Manufacture of Madness*, London: Paladin, 1977. The labelling of political violence in terms of 'psychopathic tendencies' is also discussed in Philip Schlesinger *et al.*, *Televising 'Terrorism': Political Violence in Popular Culture*, London: Comedia, 1983.

42. This is one of the most noticeable of a number of departures which the film makes from the original novel which contains no reference to the Treaty. Unlike the film, the IRA's hostage *is* executed and it is this which, in turn, prompts Kerry to inform. However, once the Black and Tans have attacked the IRA hide-out and uncovered their arms factory, they tie Kerry up and leave him for dead. The novel ends with Kerry waiting for the landmine which they have set to explode. See Rearden Connor, *Shake Hands With the Devil*, New York: Literary Guild, 1934.

43. Michael Mills, *Irish Press*, 25 May 1959, p. 6. Included in the opponents of the Treaty, it might be noted, was the founder of *The Irish Press* and future Taoiseach and President, Eamon de Valera. Cagney himself seemed totally unaware of the damaging consequences of his IRA portrait, claiming that, while he wanted 'to get away from violence', he accepted the role in *Shake Hands With the Devil* because of its concern with the 'dedicated men who fought the battle to bring peace and freedom to Ireland'. See Patrick McGilligan, *Cagney: The Actor as Auteur*, London: Tantivy Press, 1975, p. 148.

44. For a discussion of the border campaign and the Irish government's use of internment and military tribunals, see Bowyer Bell, *The Secret Army*.

45. For a consideration of the Lemass years, see, for example, Terence Brown, *Ireland: A Social and Cultural History 1922–79*, Glasgow: Fontana, 1981. For a discussion of 'the convergence between North and South' during this period, see Belinda Probert, *Beyond Orange and Green*, London: Zed Press, 1978.

46. To this extent, the film does, at least partly, anticipate the subsequent split in the IRA in 1970. For the details, see Bowyer Bell, *The Secret Army*; also David Reed, *Ireland: The Key to the British Revolution*, London: Larkin Publications, 1984.

47. An interesting sidelight on this theme is provided by the doyen of 'swinging sixties' British pop movies, *A Hard Day's Night* (1964). Paul's grandfather, Tommy McCartney (Wilfred Brambell), is arrested and taken to the local police station. Denouncing the British police as 'paid assassins', he announces that he is a 'soldier of the republic' before bursting into a rendition of 'A Nation Once Again'. A perplexed but genial sergeant (Deryck Guyler, no less) decides to offer him a cup of tea while Ringo looks on in bewilderment.

48. Like Maureen in *The Gentle Gunman*, Hannah is the daughter of an IRA man who employs her sexuality as a means of encouraging violence. Indeed, on receiving his first kiss, Rogan has to ask whether it was for him or 'the legend'. Although she subsequently comes to recognise the futility

and 'meaninglessness' of the factory explosion, she is nonetheless condemned to loneliness, like Maureen before her, by virtue of her earlier approval of violence.

49. Malachy Magee, 'Political Dynamite in Ireland', *Evening Herald*, 5 July 1969, p. 6; Anon, *Monthly Film Bulletin*, August 1969, p. 178.

50. Milton Schulman, *Evening Standard*, 23 October 1952.

51. Quoted *Daily Mail*, 23 June 1975.

52. For the details, see Sophie Balhetchet, 'The Long Good Friday', *A.I.P. and Co.*, No. 28, September 1980.

53. Dutch-produced, but shot in English, *The Outsider* was itself the subject of controversy when it was refused a screening at the 1979 London Film Festival (partly, it was suspected, because of its explicit illustration of the use of torture by the security forces in Belfast). Although critical of the British presence in Northern Ireland, the film is equally disenchanted with the machinations of the IRA and concludes on the despairing note of 'a plague on both your houses'.

54. Tom Nairn, *The Break-Up of Britain*, p. 223.

55. Robert Stam and Louise Spence's discussion of how the point-of-view conventions of the Western rule out 'sympathetic identifications with the Indians' would apply equally to *The Long Good Friday*'s treatment of the IRA. See 'Colonialism, Racism and Representation', *Screen*, Vol. 24, No. 2, March–April 1983, p. 12.

56. Quoted *Guardian*, 16 February 1981.

57. Raymond Durgnat, *A Mirror for England*, p. 23.

58. John Ford began the shooting of the film but only completed 20 minutes of material before falling ill. The rest of the film was directed by Jack Cardiff. Apart from some distinctively Fordian scenes, such as the brawl involving the hurley players, the film more closely conforms to a pattern laid down by the British 'new wave' (the sickly Sean O'Casey, for example, is transformed into a tough working-class hero of the type made fashionable by Albert Finney in *Saturday Night and Sunday Morning*). For a discussion of the film's connections to the British 'new wave', see my *Sex, Class and Realism*.

59. Philip Schlesinger, *Putting 'Reality' Together*, London: Constable, 1978, p. 243. For a more wide-ranging discussion of British news coverage of Northern Ireland, see Liz Curtis, *Ireland: The Propaganda War*, London: Pluto Press, 1984.

60. This is, of course, also true of the British cinema's treatment of other colonial groups. The representation of Malaysian rebels in such films as *The Planter's Wife* (1952), *Windom's Way* (1957) and *The Seventh Dawn* (1964), for example, is equally adroit at highlighting, quite often psychopathic, violence while ignoring its social and political determinants. For a general discussion of Britain's 'cinema of Empire', see Jeffrey Richards, *Visions of Yesterday*, London: Routledge and Kegan Paul, 1973.

61. Richard Cook, 'Angel of Death', *New Musical Express*, 13 November 1982, p. 27.

62. See Philip French, 'Avenging Angel', *Observer*, 31 October 1982, p. 30.

63. Quoted Chris Peachment, 'Bad Day Near Black Rock', *Times*, 27 October 1982.

64. The quote is taken from Blake Lucas, 'Point Blank', in Alain Silver and Elizabeth Ward (eds.), *Film Noir*, New York: Overlook Press, 1979, p. 230.

65. Neil Jordan quoted in Chris Peachment, 'Bad Day'.

66. Richard Kearney, 'Avenging Angel: An Analysis of Neil Jordan's First Irish Feature Film', *Studies*, Autumn 1982, pp. 297–302.

67. Margaret Hinxman, *Daily Mail*, 5 November 1982.

68. It is also the idea of 'madness' which characterises Edward Bennett's treatment of Northern Ireland in *Ascendancy* (1982). Set in Belfast in 1920, the film is unusual in its focus on the Protestant community — a group conspicuously absent from most films about Ireland — but fails to offer much more than the conventional view of a 'human tragedy' by virtue of its use of the central female character, Connie (Julie Covington) — and her affliction of hysterical paralysis — as a metaphor for the political situation more generally.

69. Donald Hounam, *In Dublin*, 7 April 1983, p. 6. Neil Jordan has himself argued that the film deliberately deals with an 'individual' whose violence is 'apolitical'. (See his interviews in the *New Musical Express*, 13 November 1982, p. 27 and 13 September 1986, p. 14.) However, this is to ignore the effect of setting this 'individual' violence in a recognisable political situation. For, despite the attempt to avoid political detail, the film's choice of a specifically Northern Irish setting will inevitably encourage an interpretation of events not in terms of 'pure' violence but the actual violence which is occurring in Northern Ireland. A good example of this is provided by Hugh Hebert's description of Pat O'Connor's television adaption of Neil Jordan's short story, *Night in Tunisia*, as '*Angel* . . . without the IRA'. (See *Guardian*, 3 February 1984, p. 14.) In fact, in so far as *Angel* does identify the paramilitaries, they are not (with one possible exception) members of the IRA at all but, rather, a gang of Protestants led by a member of the police. Hebert's assumption, nonetheless, that the film was dealing with the IRA was not simply an individual misreading of the film but a fairly predictable response given the film's refusal to deal with political specifics.

70. It is, of course, a recurrent characteristic of the crime film that its conventions do not normally allow a satisfactory embodiment of the superior values of a system of criminal justice. Thus, when James Cagney changed from gangster to G-Man (i.e. Federal government agent) in the thirties his means and methods did not alter, only the side of the law which he was on. His success as a law enforcer continued to depend on violence, rather than the back-up of the legal process. As Eugene Rosow suggests, legal authority was confirmed but 'depended ultimately on firepower'. See, *Born To Lose: The Gangster Film in America*, New York: Oxford University Press, 1978, p. 226.

71. The film does, of course, suggest that the gang of assassins is led by a police detective but this does not undermine the film's general faith in law enforcement: it is, after all, his police superior who calls the detective to account. Donald Hounam, *In Dublin*, op. cit., argues that this concurs with 'the standard political line of liberal Anglo-American cinema' that 'the institutions are themselves fine: it is just occasional individuals within them who are corrupt'.

72. Richard Kearney, 'The Nightmare of History', *Irish Literary Supplement*, Vol. 2, No. 2, 1983, p. 24. This is a review of the original novel.

73. One of the less appealing aspects of the film's relentless concentration on the suffering and deprivation of its characters is the way that this, in the absence of any political challenge to the spectator, presumes and encourages the moral and emotional superiority of the audience, who are less 'alongside' the characters than 'above' them 'looking down'. A similar element of 'class voyeurism' is noted in Pat O'Connor's earlier RTE productions, *The Four Roads — Ballinasloe* (1973) and *Stolen Years* (1975), by Martin Dolan in *The Irish National Cinema and its Relationship to Irish Nationalism*, Ann Arbor: University Microfilms, 1979, pp. 331–4.

74. Pat O'Connor quoted in Michael Dwyer, 'New Directions' (*sic*), *Sunday Tribune*, 9 September 1984, p. 16.

75. Joe McMinn, 'Fighting the Past: Myth and the "Troubles" in Contemporary Irish fiction', Paper delivered to the Symposium on 'Myth and Reality in Irish Literature', University of Ulster, 1986 (unpublished). See also Joe McMinn, 'Literary Clichés Out of Chaos', *Fortnight*, No. 213, 4–17 February 1985.

76. The representation of Skeffington clearly echoes Rearden Connor's original characterisation of Lenihan in *Shake Hands With the Devil* where the IRA man is a puritanical village schoolteacher, rather than, as in the film, a Dublin surgeon. Such was the familiarity of this literary type that it had already become an object of satire in the fifties in Brendan Behan's *The Hostage* (1958). In a sort of bawdy re-working of O'Casey, the IRA officer — a teetotal schoolteacher, who works for the St Vincent de Paul Society and justifies this service by quotes from Pearse — is cast among the eccentric inhabitants of a Dublin lodging house/brothel. See Brendan Behan, *The Hostage*, London: Methuen, 1964, Act One.

77. Joe McMinn, 'Fighting the Past'.

78. As Laura Mulvey explains, 'sadism demands a story, depends on making things happen, forcing a change in another person, a battle of will and strength, all occurring in linear time with a beginning and an end'. See, 'Visual Pleasure and Narrative Cinema', *Screen*, Vol. 16, No. 3, Autumn 1975, p. 14.

79. Bernard MacLaverty, *Cal*, Belfast: Blackstaff Press, 1983, p. 170. This is, in fact, the concluding line of the novel.

80. Julian Moynahan, 'The Deceiving Conscience', *New York Review of Books*, Vol. XXI, No. 2, 16 February 1984, p. 41.

81. Richard Kearney, 'The Nightmare of History', p. 24.

82. This need for the reinstatement of authority is underlined by the film's suggestions of oedipal upset. As in Freud's model of the Oedipus complex, Cal's crime may be related to a desire to kill the symbolic 'father' in order to possess the 'mother'. Accordingly, Cal dons the dead man's clothes for his initial attempt at seduction while the connection between his successful consummation and the act of murder (or 'patricide') is laboriously stressed by cross-cutting between the two different forms of 'shooting'. Social and sexual order so flouted, it is inevitable that punishment must follow. In a world empty of father-figures (Cal's real father has relapsed into madness, Skeffington's father and

Morton Sr are both cripples), it is up to the police and the army to call Cal to task and so reinstate the 'law of the father'.

83. They are not entirely alone, however. Many of the same features also reappear in Kieran Hickey's version of William Trevor's short story, *Attracta* (1983), where the social and political complexities of the 'troubles' are simply reduced to grotesque atrocity (mass rape and, rather improbably, a decapitated head in a biscuit-tin). As Barbara O'Connor suggests, 'violence . . . is represented *in vacuo* . . . thereby denying its existence in social and political terms'. See 'Aspects of Representation of Women in Irish Film', *Crane Bag*, Vol. 8, No. 2, 1984, p. 82.

84. Although it is important that Irish film-makers should address an international audience, it is also important that this does not exact too high a price. On the one hand, the enthusiasm for international appeal may encourage an acceptance of the conventional images of the Irish as the quickest route to commercial success, irrespective of whether these images work to the advantage or disadvantage of the film-producing nation. On the other hand, the desire to address an international audience may encourage an approach to film-making, exemplified by *Angel*, which tries to sacrifice the merely 'parochial' in favour of more 'universally' relevant themes and images. But, as the references to O'Flaherty, and, to some extent, O'Casey, suggest, the understanding of a particular political situation is not necessarily well served by too self-conscious a concern to 'transcend', or generalise out from, the particular experience. Despite these temptations, it does not seem impossible for another type of Irish film — one which challenges, queries and destabilises taken-for-granted assumptions about Ireland — also to be commercially successful, just as the history of other national cinemas suggests that a genuine international, or 'universal', appeal does not derive from a denial of local difference but rather an emphasis on and examination of it.

85. There has, however, been a history of documentary, rather than fiction, film production which has, with varying degrees of success, attempted to 'correct' or balance the representations of mainstream film and television output. These include *People of Ireland* (Cinema Action, 1973), *Ireland Behind the Wire* (Berwick Street Collective, 1974), *The Patriot Game* (Arthur MacCaig, 1978), *Ireland: The Silent Voices* (Rod Stoneman, 1983), *The Cause of Ireland* (Chris Reeves, 1983) and *Too Long A Sacrifice* (Michael Grigsby, 1984).

7
Romanticism, Realism and Irish Cinema

Luke Gibbons

In Mrs S. C. Hall's Victorian melodrama *The Groves of Blarney* (1838), an ingenuous Cockney visitor, Peter Swan, has no sooner landed in Ireland for the first time than he exclaims: 'Well! such a set of savages, I never did see! all real origonal *Hi*rish; the haborigines of the soil . . . Well, here I am at last, so far safe on my *tower* [i.e. tour] in search of the picturesque in this dangerous country.'[1] The outsider's instant familiarity with the finer points of Irish life and character is subsequently explained when he drops his portfolio of sketches while taking leave of his Irish cousin Flo:

Flo: Why, cousin Peter, what are all these?
Peter: My *hin*valuable stock of sketches, and descriptions of *Hi*rish scenery, and *Hi*rish people.
Flo: What, just arrived, and done all these already?
Peter: Bless ye, no; I did 'em all afore I set out, *tower*ists always lay in a stock aforehand — saves a deal of trouble and travelling.[2]

The hapless Peter Swan is hardly alone is saving himself 'a deal of trouble and travelling' by coming to Ireland with an imagination well furnished with preconceived images. Due to both its colonial history and its position on the Celtic periphery of Europe, representations of Ireland over the centuries have been enclosed within a circuit of myth and romanticism. With the spread of popular imagery in the Victorian periodical and the mass circulation press,[3] and more particularly with the advent of film and television, this tradition of caricature and stage Irishry reached wider audiences than ever before. Faced with these alienating images, it is not surprising that cultural apologists within Ireland should seek an alternative body of imagery which addressed itself to the realities of Irish life, free from the straitjacket of stereotypes and misrepresentation. Underlying this belief is an assumption that stereotypes are somehow rebutted by a simple recourse to truth, as if, like the incarcerated remains of Egyptian tombs, they have only to be exposed to the harsh glare of reality to disintegrate before our eyes.

The view that truth can only win out in the struggle against myth and prejudice manifested itself in film debates in the call for greater realism in Irish cinema. This assumption is clearly evident, for example, in the enthusiastic critical reception accorded to *Man of Aran* during its Irish première in May 1934. It was taken immediately to heart as an evocative portrayal of the harsh realities of life on the west coast of Ireland. As Dorothy Macardle, the reviewer most sympathetic to official government thinking, expressed it, here we had an alternative to the traditional caricature of the stage Irishman:

I have never seen a film which produced so complete an illusion; the taste of brine came on one's lips . . . we had a real share in their [i.e. the Aran Islander's] pride: real because these are our countrymen and their actual, constant achievements are no less than these . . . We have become almost resigned to being traduced in literature, whether under the guise of the comic 'Paddy' of Victorian music halls, or the drunken swindler of some Irish farces or the 'gunman' of more sombre writers to-day. Not three generations of pro-testing could do as much to rehabilitate the Irish people in the imagination of the peoples of other countries as this faithful and beautiful motion picture will do.[4]

The subtle equation of beauty and truth at the end of this quota-tion should perhaps alert us to the possibility that what passes for realism may often be little more than romanticism in disguise. This is in fact the version of realism which informs a recent article by Robert G. Lowery on Irish cinema in which the Samuel Goldwyn production *Beloved Enemy* (1936) is taken to task for its portrayal of the War of Independence on the grounds that it conveys 'an overly-romantic portrayal of life with almost no relevance to the real situation'.[5] Lowery proceeds to administer a breathalyser test of truth to what he terms the 'Hollywood poitín' of John Ford, singling out for particular criticism 'the calendar art of *The Quiet Man*, where everyone seemed to gather at a Norman Rothwell type pub to sing and call each other "mate" '. Ford, he writes, 'creates a world and a code which never existed'. By way of contrast, and as an example of authentic Irish cinema, Lowery cites David Lean's *Ryan's Daughter* (1970) in which Irish people are shown warts and all, 'with faults as well as good points':

> In *Ryan's Daughter*, there is jealousy, rage, squalor, gossip, back-biting, but also heroism, by individuals and by the townspeople . . . Here is reality, tough-minded and hard to bear at times.[6]

In making a distinction of this kind between the romanticism of films like *Beloved Enemy* and *The Quiet Man* (1952), and the realism of *Ryan's Daughter*, Lowery is subscribing to a common misconception according to which romanticism is primarily concerned with emphasising the 'good news', highlighting the bright side of the landscape.[7] John Ford's moonshine is taken as being particularly illuminating in this regard, but is basically no different from the numerous 'Oirish' films which depict Ireland as a primitive Eden, a rural idyll free from the pressures and constraints of the modern world. As against this, realism is considered a powerful demystifying force, tearing away the veils of deception which distort or obscure the more unpalatable social truths. To this end, poverty, hardship and other forms of human suffering are brought to the fore, demonstrating that all is not sweetness and light in the countryside or indeed in society generally. It is in this sense, presumably, that *Man of Aran* and *Ryan's Daughter* were welcomed as providing a much needed break with the escapism and mythology which has vitiated so much Irish cinema.

Yet the matter is not as clear cut as this, for underlying the opposition between romanticism and realism outlined above is an assumption that romanticism is precluded from dealing with misery, suffering and horror, from attending to the dark side of the landscape. Nothing, however, could be further from the truth. 'Romance', Sean O'Faoláin reminds us, 'is not made of pretty things. As a movement, it began in France out of dissatisfaction and despair . . . romance comes out of blood and toil and tears and sweat'.[8] In approaching films such as *Man of Aran* and *Ryan's Daughter*, it is useful to bear in mind Walter Benjamin's argument that nothing in Western culture is immune from the romantic impulse, if by that we mean the urge to embellish and beautify even the most disturbing and intolerable aspects of reality. As a case in point, Benjamin cites the development of photography in the early twentieth century, at that time perhaps the medium best equipped to assert the sovereignty of truth over beauty:

> What do we see? It has become more and more subtle . . . and the result is that it is now incapable of photographing a tenement or a rubbish-heap without transfiguring it. Not to mention a river dam or an electric cable factory: in front of these, photography can now only say, 'How beautiful' . . . It has succeeded in turning abject poverty itself, by handling it in a modish, technically perfect way, into an object of enjoyment.[9]

Benjamin's strictures are equally applicable to Irish culture. It was not the idea of a bucolic nature but rather the bleakness and austerity of the countryside which drew cultural nationalists such as Patrick Pearse, Douglas Hyde and Canon Sheehan to the west of Ireland during the Literary Revival, allowing them to re-create the harsher aspects of rural life in the image of an ascetic, elemental Christianity.[10] Thus we find J. M. Synge, before his eventual rift with this strand of nationalism, finding an aesthetic dimension in the very poverty of the people whom he meets on his travels in the Irish countryside: 'In a way it is all heartrending, in one place the people are starving but wonderfully attractive and charming'.[11] Related sentiments found their way into discussions of film in Ireland. Comparing the relative merits of film industries in other countries as possible models for the development of Irish cinema, T. J. M. Sheehy wrote in 1943:

> Of all the nations probably our greatest affinity is with France . . . Their directors have shown that delicate beauty can be portrayed in ordinary lives, and even in slums, as easily as in luxury surroundings.[12]

It is this desire to redeem hardship and squalor in the interests of aesthetic experience which runs through *Man of Aran* and *Ryan's Daughter*, rather than the realist imperatives ascribed to them by Macardle and Lowery. Despite the desolate, windswept locations, and the evident destitution of the people, both films conform to one of the key conventions of the *pastoral* genre which has underpinned idealisations of rural life in literature and the visual arts since antiquity. This involves the absence or elimination of the principal source of rural poverty and degradation: the experience of work and exploitation, the social reality of labour in the face not only of material scarcity but also of profound political and economic divisions. It is misleading, however, to think on this account that the pastoral genre consists entirely in an image of a primitive Arcadia, where people enjoy a life of unlimited leisure and sensual indulgence. As the art historian Erwin Panofsky points out, not least of the ironies of the pastoral vision is that the original Arcady, an actual region in central Greece, was seen by writers in antiquity 'as a poor, bare, rocky, chilly country, devoid of all the amenities of life and scarcely affording food for a few meagre goats'.[13] This belies the commonly held view that idealisations of rural life always portray the countryside in glowing terms, and leads Panofsky to make an important distinction between two versions of pastoral, one of which he terms 'soft primitivism', the other 'hard primitivism'. We will look at each of these in turn.

Soft primitivism, Panofsky informs us, 'conceives of primitive life as a golden age of plenty, innocence and happiness — in other words, as civilised life purged of its vices'.[14] In this idyllic world, labour and exertion are rendered obsolete in the presence of an opulent, bounteous nature which simply yields itself up to human requirements. In its more whimsical — and self-parodying — Irish variants, as popularised in films such as *Finian's Rainbow* (1968), nature directly intervenes in the economy in the form of what might be called 'the rainbow mode of production', whose discovery we owe to the advanced monetarist theories of one Finian McLonergan (Fred Astaire). Why has America not only so many rich people, but also 'the best ill-housed and the best ill-clad in all the world?' he asks his daughter Sharon (Petula Clark), and proceeds to answer his own question by citing no greater authority than himself:

Finian: Why? . . . I'll tell you — quote myself. Quote: 'Didn't the Americans rush to dig gold from the ground in California in 1849 . . . and didn't they plant it in the soil at Fort Knox a hundred years later?'

Sharon: Granted.

Finian: Well, that's it. You see, there's something about the soil in and around Fort Knox that gives that magical quality to gold. It causes the gold to radiate a powerful influence throughout America. It activates the assembly lines in Detroit, it makes skyscrapers sprout up from the gutters in New York city, and it produces a bumper crop of millionares. And that (*Finian takes a swig from a jar of whiskey*) is the McLonergan theory of economics.

It is precisely the assembly line mentality of American industry, and its obsession with 'lousy money', which drives Sean Thornton (John Wayne) back to the idyllic Ireland of *The Quiet Man* — 'Another name for Heaven', as Sean himself describes his homeplace, Inisfree. Here we encounter what seems to be a rural world divested of material cares and the struggle for survival, in which people spend their time singing, drinking and fighting, and in which even horses minister to their owner's constant need of refreshment by stopping, Pavlovian fashion, outside public houses. When labourers do appear, as in the case of Red Will Danagher's (Victor McLaglen) farmhands, they are engaged in conspicuous consumption, eating him, in his own words, 'out of house and home'. Farm technology seems to be redundant — 'dirty, smelly things', Mary Kate (Maureen O'Hara) says of tractors — yet later on in the film we see that Red Will has tractors on his farm, thus associating them with the grasping acquisitive outlook which he embodies. Such transgressions of the traditional pastoral idiom — there are also cars, telephones and even sleeping bags — suggests that there is not just one but several versions of reality competing for our attention in *The Quiet Man*. The one scene in which manual labour is prominently featured turns out in fact to be a parody of Red Will's progressive farming, for even though, as Mary Kate says, there is not 'a turnip or a cabbage or a potato' in the fields, Sean is occupied in planting roses, inscribing on nature, as it were, his mother's lasting memory of the family homestead, White O'Morn:

> It was a lovely little house, Seaneen, and the roses! Your father used to tease me about them but he was that proud of them too!

These words reverberate in voice-over through Sean's mind when, early in the film, he first apprehends his ancestral cottage, bathed in sunlight in the midst of luxuriant verdure. Yet the fact that the cottage is revealed to us in a point-of-view shot through Sean's eyes, and that little effort is made at maintaining spatial continuity between Sean's position and the countryside surrounding the cottage, throws into relief the possible fictive status of his vision. This articulation of Sean's world through point-of-view shots is carried forward to the next scene in which his eyes alight on Mary Kate Danagher for the first time. Here, in John Ford's most memorable evocation of the pastoral ideal, we see a radiant Mary Kate driving sheep through a primeval forest in luminous sunlight, a perfectly realised image of woman at home with nature. Such is the visual excess of the spectacle that Sean is led to question its authenticity: 'Hey, is that real? She couldn't be.' It is this ability of certain strains in Irish romanticism to conduct a process of self-interrogation, to raise doubts at key moments about their own veracity, which cuts across any tendency to take romantic images as realistic accounts of Irish life. This suggests that it is not so much realism which offers a way out of the impasse of myth and romanticism, but rather a *questioning* of realism or any mode of representation which seeks to deny the gap between image and reality.

This becomes clear if we turn to a consideration of 'hard primitivism' which, as Panofsky describes it, 'conceives of primitive life as an almost subhuman existence full of terrible hardships and devoid of all comforts — in other words, as civilised life stripped of its virtues'.[15] It is in hard primitivism, rather than soft primitivism, that the drift towards realism can be detected, not as a means of challenging romanticism but, on the contrary, as a way of authenticating it, of adding credibility to what are otherwise characteristically romantic situations. Thus for all its bleak locations, and the emphasis on some of the more squalid aspects of rural life, one of the most striking features of *Ryan's Daughter* is that nobody in the film appears to work for a living. 'Doing nothing is a dangerous occupation', the local priest, Fr Collins (Trevor Howard) warns Rosy Ryan (Sarah Miles) in one of the opening scenes, and as if to bear out his oracular pronouncement, the young men of the village spend most of their time hurling on the street, conspiring in pubs or engaging in mob violence, whereas the women pass the time gossiping or else making life miserable for the village idiot.

Man of Aran presents a more complex relationship to work and production, in that it purports to deal directly with the struggle of the Aran Islanders to eke out a living. As the opening credits express it:

In this desperate environment the Man of Aran, because his

independence is the most precious privilege he can win from life, fights for his existence bare though it may be. It is a fight from which he will have no respite until the end of his indomitable days . . .

In one stark, if rather drawn out sequence, we see the Man of Aran, Tiger King, isolated against the horizon as he breaks rocks with a sledge hammer in order to prepare the ground for a meagre potato plot. The titles inform us: 'The land upon which Man of Aran depends for his subsistence — potatoes — has not even soil!' Yet far from constituting a 'realistic' depiction of life on the western seaboard, it should be apparent that this represents the hard primitivist ideal at its most powerful, elemental level. All technology, even the plough, is redundant, as Yeats put it, on 'those grey islands where men must reap with knives because of the stones'.[16] This echoes Rousseau's reconstruction of an imaginary 'state of nature' before the eventual fall from grace brought about by civilisation, and, in particular, the invention of metallurgy: 'It was iron and corn', wrote Rousseau, 'which first civilized men, and ruined humanity'.[17] In this respect, contemporary critiques of the film which charged that 'romanticism and . . . "the noble savage" pervades the whole'[18] would appear to be nearer the mark than those reviews which praised it on account of its fidelity to the 'stern and brutal realities' of social conditions on the islands.

The mythic element in *Man of Aran* is best exemplified by the manner in which the everyday grind of work and production is desocialised and transformed into a heroic struggle between humanity and nature. Though the process of making 'artifical soil' was spurred on in the early years of the state by such humdrum exigencies as government subsidies and the need to cope with the parasitic 'eel worm',[19] it is elevated by the dramaturgy of the film into an epic commentary on the human condition: 'It was Man breaking Nature to his will' enthused Dorothy Macardle, 'human history since the world began'.[20] Nature on these terms is a formidable enemy, an agency of immense power and a continual source of pain and danger testing human endurance to its limits. Soft primitivism, as we have seen, is pre-eminently a *social* vision, a form of communion with nature 'which transcends the individual and forges a link between many men'. It places its hopes on a communal ideal, 'an idyllic peace in which all beings will live together in friendship and fraternity'.[21] By contrast, hard primitivism corresponds to what Peter Marinelli refers to as 'romantic pastoral', a view of nature

> which begins with the individual figure, concentrates upon his hard lot in life, and then magnifies him, almost insensibly, into a figure of titanic proportions, an emblem of general Humanity.[22]

It is, ironically, this tendency to decant away social and economic relations, an aspect of the film much commented on by hostile critics during its intital reception, which impels *Man of Aran* towards a realistic mode of representation. In soft primitivism, nature is not apprehended in a raw primeval condition but it is rather overlaid with social accretions, attesting to the intervention of culture and community. In the absence of any attempt to posit a pure, authentic nature beyond the reach of artifice, and in its insistence on a socially mediated vision, it is not surprising that soft primitivism often runs the risk of exposing its own fabrication, proclaiming its status as an imaginary construct rather than as a realistic 'slice of life'. Hard primitivism, on the other hand, with its emphasis on an encounter between the solitary individual and nature, strives for a clear transparent vision free from all traces of mediation, particularly, as we shall see, that of language. According to Frances Hubbard Flaherty, the film-maker's wife, the most important feature of Robert Flaherty's style 'was that it was purely visual. Words played no part in it; it went beyond words. It was simply a degree of seeing'.[23] Or as Dorothy Macardle expressed it more dramatically with regard to one of the storm sequences in *Man of Aran*:

> Words, if one endeavoured with them to describe that conflict would seem as weak as the pulings of the sea gulls where the rocks and caverns of Aran meet the Atlantic in its power.[24]

Though *Man or Aran* was warmly received during its first run in 1934 as a welcome departure from the 'comic Paddy' of traditional stereotypes, there is a sense in which its devaluing of language and community is equally at odds with what is perhaps the most important strain in Irish romanticism, that which seeks to combine the collective vision and sensual abandon of soft primitivism with the disorder and violence of its darker, hard primitivist counter-part. Indeed, in one of the more perceptive contemporary Irish reviews, G. F. Dalton was led to observe that certain Irish films may be 'quite free from stage-Irishism: but only at the cost of being quite free from Irishism of any kind'. 'Flaherty has certainly avoided sentimentality', Dalton went on to remark, 'But has he brought to the filming of his fellow Flahertys in Aran any attitude which differs from his attitude to the Eskimos of *Nanook* or the South Sea Islanders of *Moana*?'[25] It is clear, however, that in its emphasis on a spartan lifestyle in wild inhospitable surroundings, and in its adoption of the *family* rather than the individual as the adversary of an implacable nature, *Man of Aran* did take stock to some extent of the more austere, rigorist elements of Irish romanticism which were reasserting themselves in the grim economic conditions of the 1930s. It was, no doubt, the affirmation of the resourcefulness and fortitude of the Irish family in this harsh social climate which recommended the film to the then President Eamon de Valera, and the other members of his Cabinet who attended the Irish première. The ease with which the bleak landscape and ascetic ideology of works like *Man of Aran* passed into popular political rhetoric during this period points to the dangers inherent in taking romantic images at face value, as truthful representations of reality. As Ivor Montagu wrote in what was perhaps the most forceful contemporary critique of the film:

> No less than Hollywood, Flaherty is busy turning reality to romance. The tragedy is that, being a poet with a poet's eye, his lie is the greater, for he can make the romance seem real.[26]

Language, nature and Irish romanticism

Landscape has tended to play a leading role in Irish cinema, often upstaging both the main characters and narrative themes in the construction of Ireland on the screen.[27] To a considerable extent, this preoccupation with landscape dates from the emergence of a romantic sensibility which, in the late eighteenth and early nineteenth centuries, sent the urban middle classes and an enervated aristocracy back to nature to escape the effects of the Industrial Revolution and the machinations of an unrestrained market economy. In the case of Ireland, however, this primitivist impulse had far reaching consequences, for lacking the advanced social and political structures of the new economic order, it came to embody, along with other similar regions on the European periphery, all the attributes of a vanished pre-industrial era — if not of a society entirely beyond the pale of civilisation. As Raymond Immerwahr states in his comprehensive study of the origins of European romanticism:

> Beginning about 1755, the picturesque landscape really comes into its own in descriptions of Ireland and the English lake country. The adjective is applied a number of times to the environs of Lake Killarney in Charles Smith's book on *The Antient and Present State of the County of Kerry*. A castle is 'pleasantly and boldly situated in a romantic manner on a high cliff, inaccessible from the sea, commanding . . . a bay . . . environed with craggy stupendous mountains'.[28]

At this early stage, Ireland shared its reputation for rugged, uncultivated scenery with the Lake District of England — and, of course, with the more remote areas of Wales and the Scottish Highlands. At the turn of the nineteenth century, this situation was to change as the deteriorating political situation in Ireland, and the development of a new, assertive form of cultural nationalism helped to redefine and accentuate the differences between Ireland and the more temperate irregularities of the British landscape. By 1806, it was possible for the romantic Irish novelist Lady Morgan, one of the more spirited precursors of Sir Walter Scott, to damn with faint praise the artificial decor of English scenery in her novel *The Wild Irish Girl*, all the more to contrast it with the wild intractable fastnesses of the Irish countryside. While the 'glowing fancy' could dwell 'enraptured on the paradisal charms of English landscape', this is hardly comparable to 'those scenes of mysterious sublimity, with which the wildly magnificent landscape of Ireland abounds':

> To him who derives gratification from the embellished labours of art, rather than the simple but sublime operation of nature, *Irish* scenery will afford little interest; but the bold features of its varying landscape, the stupendous attitude of its 'cloud capt' mountains, the impervious gloom of its deep embosomed glens, the savage desolation of its uncultivated heaths, and boundless bogs, with those rich veins of a picturesque champaigne, thrown at intervals into gay expansion by the hand of nature, awaken in the mind of the poetic or pictorial traveller, all the pleasures of tasteful enjoyment,

all the sublime emotions of a rapt imagination.[29]

The version of wild landscape which emerges in the course of Lady Morgan's pioneering novel is of interest in that it presides over the visit of a young Englishman, Mortimer, to his father's estate on the west coast of Ireland. To a stranger such as Mortimer, seeking to escape the artifice and decorum of polite society, Ireland appears as a haven of natural plentitude, a source of raw unprocessed experience or, as Roland Barthes might put it, of 'an experience without a code'. The call of the wild in this sense is obviously dependent on the outsider's ability to penetrate the mysteries of an alien, unchartered region, and it is for this reason that at key moments in the novel — e.g. confrontations with awe-inspiring scenery or with the inscrutable native inhabitants — Mortimer's narration strives for *realist* effect, for the direct clarity of *vision* rather than the coded responses and mediating influence of *language*. As he is drawn ineluctably into the vortex of life 'on the wildest shores of the greatest ocean of the universe', he is gradually confronted, he tells us, by 'that vehement excess which forbade all expression, which left my tongue powerless'.[30] The renunciation of language for the greater immediacy of images is assured when Mortimer's eyes first light on Glorvina, the eponymous Wild Irish Girl, in the suitably exotic surroundings of a ruined chapel, complete with the compulsory bard and dispossessed chieftain (her father, the Prince of Inismore):

> What a *picture*! . . . all that I had lately seen revolved in my mind like some *pictured* story of romantic fiction. I cast around my eyes; all still seemed the *vision* of awakened imagination . . . But how cold — how inanimate — how imperfect this description! Oh! could I but seize the touching features — could I but realize the vivid tints of this enchanting *picture*, as they then glowed on my fancy![31]

The appeal to graphic clarity evident in this passage, the belief in the superiority of vision over language as a vehicle of truth is, of course, inspired not simply by aesthetic imperatives of realism but by a desire to subject a refractory body of experience to the controlling gaze of the outsider. Yet even in this initial encounter, it is clear that there are forces present which are working against this process of pictorial entrapment. Though Mortimer is intent on establishing the primacy of perception, there is nonetheless a signal resistance to vision, for even though he frequently shifts his position in the chapel to get a better view of the enigmatic beauty of the Wild Irish Girl, an 'envious veil intercepted the ardent glance which eagerly sought the fancied charms it concealed'.[32]

This scene, and the familiar romantic motif of the veil, points to an underlying ambivalence in Irish romanticism, or at least in that variant of it popularised in the nineteenth century by Lady Morgan and, as we shall see, the playwright Dion Boucicault. While the external observer pursues the lucidity of a realist perspective to impose order and intelligibility on a potentially disturbing set of experiences, an 'envious veil', metaphorically speaking, is continually thrown across his line of vision. The outsider attempts to bring the wildness of a strange, disconcerting environment under control by seeing in it a manifestation of 'authenticity' and 'the real', as if some kind of stable, enduring essence lies behind the superficial — and deceptive — world of social appearances. However, the raiments of culture — in the form of language, politics, local customs, folklore and antiquities — repeatedly interpose themselves between the outsider and a pristine vision of nature.

In denying instant access to a different culture in this manner, it is not so much that the essence of Irishness eludes the visitor (as traditional nationalism would have it) but that there is no essence at all behind the veil of appearances. 'There is nothing behind the curtain', Hegel once said, 'other than that which is in front of it.'[33] It is the outsider in Lady Morgan's novel, not the native, who is caught up in the pursuit of essences and the cult of the natural. In marked contrast to Flaherty's Man of Aran, Glorvina is a poor candidate for the role of noble savage: in fact she turns out to be that rarity in world literature, a noble savage who actually *reads* Rousseau and is quite prepared to immerse herself in the master's texts rather than endure the insufferable advances of his disciple.[34] Again, while Mortimer, true to form, is concerned to expose the blatant posturing of Macpherson's counterfeit Ossian, Glorvina prefers the forgery to the 'ridiculously grotesque' original.[35] In an ironic reversal, those points in the novel at which nature is expected to impinge most forcefully on human experience — wild landscape, primitive society, the 'innocent eye' — became precisely those points at which direct, unmediated access to nature is denied. It is as if one strand in Irish romanticism contains within itself its own destabilising moment, insisting on its own contrivance in the face of any attempt to mistake it for reality. The search for authenticity, for an experience without a code, is only successful when one code is substituted for another, and the outsider is accepted into the local community.

The basic premise of the outsider's approach to both nature and 'primitive' society in *The Wild Irish Girl* is a drive towards transparency, a desire to lift the veil and penetrate the strangeness and recalcitrance of 'the Other'. This willingness to risk the hazards of the wilderness (all the more to conquer it) received perhaps its most exemplary and influential expression in the puritan tradition of American romanticism, establishing the basis of a great push westwards which led to the opening up of the frontier. In its most characteristic form, the American puritan imagination sought, in the words of Perry Miller, 'to confront face to face' the 'physical universe . . . without the intermediacy of ritual, of ceremony, of the Mass and the confessional'[36] — and, he might have added, language. Nature was to be experienced in a raw elemental condition, more or less in the state in which God had left it at creation. As one nineteenth-century commentator put it in his advice to an aspiring artist:

> No history or legendary interest attached to landscape could help the landscape painter . . . he must *go behind all this* to nature as it had formed by the Creator and find something there which was superior to man's work, and to this he must learn to give intelligible expression.[37]

What we have here is the prospect of a rugged uncharted wilderness, devoid of any symbolic associations with history or legend, undefiled, as it were, by the encrustations of language and society. In these circumstances, *silence* and *solitude* become central to the pioneering, romantic quest. Thus one observer in a meditative mood could describe the area around Fort Laramie as 'a sublime waste, a wilderness of mountains and pine-forests, over which the spirit of loneliness and silence seemed brooding'.[38] Or in the words of the writer Fitz Hugh Ludlow, confronting the Valley of the Yosemite: 'Not a living creature, either man or beast, breaks the visible silence of this inmost paradise'.[39] As the nostalgia for the blissful moment of creation indicates, there is a sense in which this pursuit of a 'visible silence' seeks to recreate 'Adam's dream', the perspicuous vision of the solitary individual who achieves direct communion with nature without the intervening clutter of langauage and culture. At its most ascetic, as in the writings of Ralph Waldo Emerson, this version of romanticism is akin to a form of religious ecstasy which cleanses the self of all social and material accoutrements:

> Standing on the bare ground, — my head bathed by the blithe air and uplifted into infinite space — all mean egotism vanishes. I become a transparent eyeball; I am nothing; I see all . . . The name of the nearest friend sounds then foreign and accidental; to be brothers, to be acquaintances, master or servant, is then a trifle and a disturbance.[40]

It is interesting to compare this to the view of nature which has informed an Irish romanticism shaped in different ways by Catholicism, a semi-feudal Ascendancy and an overriding colonial situation. Unlike its American counterpart, Irish romanticism, though no less concerned with the celebration of wildness and natural disorder, is from the outset characterised by an aversion to individualism and the clarity of vision required by the puritan ideal. Perception is accorded no primacy over language, so that there is little evidence of any wish to apprehend nature in a pristine unadulterated state, free from any symbolic or linguistic contamination. A comment made by Dorothy Wellesley about Yeats' poetry is instructive here:

> The matter of Yeats' visual life is deeply interesting. To an English poet it appears at times incredible . . . I have come to the conclusion that [his] lack of 'visualness', this lack of interest in natural beauty for its own sake, may originate in the fact that most of the Celtic poets are not concerned with nature at all.[41]

This refusal to acknowledge the sovereignty of vision does not mean, of course, that nature is of no concern to a poet such as Yeats: it means that nature, and more particularly landscape, can never be reduced to mere scenery but always bears some traces of meaning, exuding in Elizabeth Bowen's words, 'a pre-inhabited air'.[42] As Thomas Flanagan remarks, highlighting the difference between the idea of landscape in Lady Morgan's *The Wild Irish Girl* and the preoccupation with the prairie in the early American romanticism:

Before we have done [with Lady Morgan's novel], the reader is likely to have become quite bored with ruins, just as studies of early American novels weary us with prairies — and for the same unavoidable reasons. Ireland is a country of ruins. They do not so much define the landscape as exist as part of its being . . . The prairie suggests a culture which has yet to create its forms, while the ruin implies a culture whose forms have been shattered. But the fallen stones bear hieroglyphs which the artist tries to read.[43]

It is as if a grid of language, history and social relations is placed between the observer and the natural world in Irish romanticism, even at those points where nature seems at the furthest possible remove from all contact with civilisation. For the romantic historian Standish O'Grady, the course of Irish history itself is like the countenance of the landscape in that it is impossible to achieve 'a clear and definite' view, that 'verisimilitude and underlying harmony' which is the pre-condition of a literal minded, historical realism. The past, for O'Grady, is rather like 'the dawn of the day' in which 'changing . . . empurpled mist [and] vapours'

conceal the solid face of nature, the hills, trees, streams, and the horizon, holding between us and the landscape a conceal-ing veil, through whose close woof the eye cannot penetrate, and over all a weird strange light.[44]

If the recourse to the wilderness in American romanticism is motivated by a flight from society, and a pursuit of individualism, the reverse situation would seem to hold in Ireland. In its most typical form, whether it be a novel such as *The Wild Irish Girl* or a film such as *The Quiet Man*, an individual, usually an outsider, tries to gain access to a tightly-knit community and, by extension, to the natural unspoilt landscape which the native community inhabits. This desire to discover (or renew) a sense of communal identity through an affinity with nature was one of the primary considerations which drew Yeats to the west of Ireland in search of suitable themes for his early poetry:

I sought some symbolic language [he writes] reaching far into the past and associated with familiar names and conspicuous hills that I might not be alone amid the obscure impressions of the senses.[45]

The contrast with Emerson could not be sharper. Whereas the senses of the American are heightened through clarity ('I am a transparent eyeball'), Yeats tries to avoid the 'obscure impressions of the senses'. Likewise, while Emerson is exhilarated by the experience of the individual at one with nature and its Creator, Yeats seeks refuge among 'the familiar names and conspicuous hills' in order to escape the loneliness of the self. Yeats is interested in nature, not for what lies behind it but for what lies in front of it. As Richard Ellmann remarks: 'Yeats used . . . symbols primarily to hide this world rather than to reveal another one.'[46]

The point of drawing attention to this interpretation of nature as a symbolic field is to underline the case for treating landscape in romantic images of Ireland not merely as a picturesque backdrop, but as a layer of meaning in its own right, a thematic element which may reinforce or cut across the other levels of meaning in a text. Indeed, as Lady Morgan's fiction shows, it may often be the case that landscape is operating on two levels, one which conforms to a realist, pictorial aesthetic and which represents the vantage point of the outsider, and the other which refuses instant or immediate access and the kind of transparency which is integral to the tourist or colonial vision. With the demise of the romantic novel in the 1830s these competing perspectives on landscape transferred their energies to Victorian melodrama which, in certain important respects, acts as the prehistory of Irish cinema — without incurring, it is hoped, the nebulous, ethereal quality of Irish prehistory as seen by imaginative historians such as O'Grady.

Landscape and character in Irish romantic melodrama

Victorian melodrama lent itself particularly to the type of pictorial aesthetic which was to dominate romantic representations of Ireland. Throughout the late eighteenth and early nineteenth centuries, technical advances in lighting (e.g. gaslight and limelight) and stage machinery (the picture frame stage, sliding traps, the diorama and panorama) brought about a revolution in visual realism and scenic illustration. Dramatic character and action were increasingly circumscribed by an elaborate scenic environment so that the stage came gradually to resemble, in Michael Booth's words, 'a painting that moved'.[47] Given this vogue for romantic spectacle, it is not surprising that playwrights in search of the exotic or picturesque began to quarry the Irish landscape for their materials, looking particularly to Ireland as the setting for some of the more Gothic and violent excesses of melodrama. It was at this point, however, that the requirements of good theatre and vivid spectacle began to merge directly with the outlook of colonial administration which was, for obvious reasons, favourably disposed towards any 'explanation' of agrarian violence in Ireland which diminished or even suppressed its social and political causes. The overpowering effects of stage scenery on dramatic action provided a useful, popular support to the view that political violence and 'agrarian outrages' were not a product of colonial misrule, or any social conditions, but emanated instead from the inexorable influence of landscape and climate on the Irish character. The fact that Irish landscape was defined in terms of wilderness and disorder, and that the weather was gloomy, turbulent and subject to fitful changes, made any suggestion of a strange osmosis between climate and character all the more attractive. As a travel book in the 1830s expresses it:

> We imagine we can trace in the chequered character of the Irish people a reflection of the varied aspect of the country. Their exuberant gaiety, their deep sadness, their warm affections, their fierce resentment, their smiles and tears, their love and hatred, all remind us forcibly of the lights and shadows of their landscapes; where frowning precipices and quiet glens, wild torrents and tranquil streams . . . are all blended by the hand of Nature beneath a sky, now smiling in sunshine, now saddening in tears.[48]

It is from this perspective that we must view the proliferation of wild mountain scenery, overcast skies, desolate cottages and, of course, the abrupt contrasts between sunshine and thunderstorms, which came to signify 'Irishness' in the romantic canon. Of crucial importance here is the fact that since *character* was at the mercy of the landscape and hence was, to all intents and purposes, non-existent, the Irish peasant or rebel tended to be depicted as part of an undifferentiated community or criminal gang, lacking the psychological complexity which distinguishes the individual personality.

Conventionally, these figures are seen as the type of cardboard cut-outs or stereotypes which give rise to repeated demands for greater realism and individual depth of character in representations of Ireland on the stage or screen. In the context of Victorian

theatre, the Irish dramatist Dion Boucicault is commonly perceived as being the first to make this breakthrough by bringing a
new naturalistic dimension to his otherwise highly coloured
romantic treatment of Irish life.[49] Boucicault's achievement is
regarded as twofold: firstly, he is considered as having toned down
significantly the wildness of his stage scenery and hence its impact
on dramatic action; secondly, a direct consequence of this, his
peasant characters acquire distinctive personalities and are con-
stituted as separate 'individualized and humanized being(s)' in
marked contrast to the communal self of the peasantry in previous
plays.[50] Indeed, so forceful was Boucicault's contribution to
Victorian drama that in the opinion of some commentators, he
deserves the credit for being the first to put the Irish rural poor on
the stage with any degree of sympathy or fidelity to life. It is
interesting to note, moreover, that this accords with Boucicault's
estimation of his own work. Inveighing against the stereotypes of
his predecessors, he wrote:

> The fire and energy that consist of dancing round the stage in
> an expletive manner, and indulging in ridiculous capers and
> extravagancies of language and gesture, form the materials of
> a clowning character, known as 'the stage Irishman,' which it
> has been my invocation, as an artist and as a dramatist, to
> abolish.[51]

It must certainly come as news to a modern audience that
Boucicault set out to *abolish* the stage Irishman! Yet his declaration
is highly revealing in that it demonstrates clearly the cyclical (and
self-defeating) nature of 'realist breakthroughs' from the enclosing
myths and 'distortions' of romanticism in Ireland. For it was
precisely Boucicault's 'realism' that the Abbey Theatre was later
to dismiss as 'the home of buffoonery and easy sentiment', and of
course it is now the Abbey and the general legacy of the Literary
Revival which is seen, with revisionist hindsight, as the repository
of 'ancient idealism' and other forms of romantic self-deception.

The general agreement among critics that Boucicault's work
represents a significant advance on the previous history of misrepresentation would appear to be justified, but it is questionable
whether his strength lies in the direction of realism and artistic
truth. For one thing, the assertion that scenic illustration was
subordinated to the psychological development of individualised
peasant characters seems hardly warranted. Quite apart from the

fact that Boucicault wrote his most famous play *The Colleen Bawn* (1860) around a specific set of steel engravings of Killarney, and that the elaborate scenery was commissioned in advance of the text, contemporary observers had little doubt that with Boucicault, visual spectacle in theatre had reached new, unprecedented heights (or depths, if we are to take into account the introduction of a giant aquarium to simulate the Lakes of Killarney in a revival of *The Colleen Bawn*). In a contemporary review, *The Era* magazine praised the special effects used in the sensational drowning scene in *The Colleen Bawn* and described the play as

> little short of being the first of the sensational dramas, that is to say, the first drama in which a striking mechanical effect was the principal attraction, and the first serious drama in which the actor became of secondary importance to the machinist and the scene-painter.[52]

With this in mind, A. Nicholas Vardac can say with some conviction that in Boucicault's work 'his setting was always his most important actor'.[53]

It would on reflection be surprising to find, in an Irish context, scenic illustration and landscape succumbing to the development of the kind of rounded, self-contained individuals who stalked the pages of Adam Smith or the market-places of liberal capitalist economies such as Great Britain or the United States. Boucicault uses wild landscape not to accentuate the individual psychology of his characters, but to displace both the individual and violence on to a *collective* and ultimately political plane. Nature still looms large but it does not infiltrate the personalities of Boucicault's rogues and political malefactors: rather they redefine the landscape as *social* terrain, transforming it from scenery into bandit territory, the jurisdiction of 'the proclaimed district'. 'The place is full of you', the faithful Arte O'Neal says to the Fenian rebel, Robert Ffolliott, in *The Shaughraun* (1874), when they arrange a clandestine meeting in the ruins of the old abbey — to which Robert replies later on: 'I can reach the ruins by the seashore; the rocks will conceal me'.[54] The disposition of a colonial ideology to deprive the agrarian rebel of his personality is in Boucicault's plays turned to the rebel's advantage as it allows them to *politicise* the landscape, to organise collectively under the subterfuge of scenery. This is brought out amusingly in the first act of *Arrah-na-Pogue* (1864), when Beamish Mac Coul, the elusive rebel, accosts the snivelling process-server Feeney at a pass in the Wicklow mountains (later to feature prominently in films about Ireland). Beamish warns Feeney: 'At every fifty paces there's a man stationed behind either a rock or a bush', and then turns, as it were, *sotto voce* to his fellow bandits: 'There he goes; we need fear no alarm from him. I have turned every stone and every bush on his road into a sentinel, ha ha!'[55] It is difficult not to suspect here that Boucicault is having one over on those members of his English audiences for whom Ireland afforded a prospect of release and wild passions, mingled with feelings of fear and apprehension. Awe-inspiring, elemental landscape is not à manifestation of natural, still less supernatural forces, but of *political* incomprehension: the deceptive ease of access to Irish life provided by Boucicault's apparent realism is offset by his insistence on making both landscape and character more impervious to the gaze of the outsider.

It is of course true that Boucicault's extravagant scenery and stage devices were to some extent striving for naturalistic effect, and were even intended to reproduce reality with photographic accuracy.[56] To this end, he was not above introducing a real fire engine in *The Poor of New York* (1857) to quench a 'real' tenement fire; a hydraulic castle tower in *Arrah-na-Pogue*; an almost life-size train in *After Dark* (1868); and a live race-horse in *The Flying Scud* (1866). Yet these attempts to pull out all the stops and maximise scenic effects culminated not in the narrative economy of realism, but in a form of visual excess and surplus energy which all but upended the progression of the narrative in his plays. Boucicault's 'sensation scenes' were so spectacular that in some cases it was clear that they were all that contemporary audiences went to see. In the final analysis, his tendency to overload the realism of his plays only succeeded in drawing attention to the contrived nature of his stagecraft, thus stretching dramatic credibility to its limits. By the 1890s a reviewer could complain of his unintentional, Brechtian effects:

> When, therefore, in one act we have as many as six changes of scene, it requires more than the usual amount of make-believe to ignore the flitting figures of gas-men and scene-shifters, and the various contumacies of the scenery, so as to concentrate one's attention on the acting and the play.[57]

As if the visual inundation of his scenic effects were not sufficient to dispel the semblance of illusion, there was another element in Boucicault's plays which cut across any aspirations towards pictorial realism. Unusually for a dramatic form which depended on gesture, heightened actions and visual choreography, *language* played a vitally important role in Boucicault's Irish melo-dramas, the verbal raillery and word-play of his peasant characters proving almost as engaging to audiences as the theatrical stunts which made his reputation. In fact, it would seem that a large part of the strength and resourcefulness of characters such as Myles in *The Colleen Bawn* and Shaun and Arrah in *Arrah-na-Pogue* derives not so much from their 'psychological complexity' or 'depth of character' as from their verbal proficiency, their ability to deploy language as a political weapon. There is a certain historical irony here, for given the absence of any obvious *visible* marks of 'inferiority' (such as racial traits or skin colour), colonial stereo-types of the Irish were forced traditionally to rely on auditory rather than visual discrimination: the brogue, the 'Irish Bull' and the blarney became the signs of cultural retardation. But while degradation on physical grounds such as skin colour seeks to locate inferiority in a stable and ineradicable biological sphere, language is a highly volatile instrument of racial stigma and may just as easily be reappropriated and turned against the oppressor.[58]

This is what happens in Boucicault. Repeatedly throughout his plays, verbal sparring or feinting is used as a form of disguise and misrecognition to throw representatives of the colonial regime (military officers, legal dignitaries, process servers) into confusion and disarray. In the opening scenes of *The Shaughraun*, Molineaux, an army officer in search of the Fenian Robert Ffolliott, flounders in a wilderness on the west coast of Ireland due to his inability to pronounce Irish place-names or understand the brogue (the fact that it is an incognito Ffolliott who eventually saves him only adds to the sense of bewilderment). In *Arrah-na-Pogue*, the intimate relationship between language and politics is taken a stage further when the eponymous heroine Arrah uses the pretext of a kiss to transfer a concealed written message to the mouth of the imprisoned Beamish Mac Coul — hence the derivation of her name.[59] This use of language as deception, as a means of sowing *mis*understanding between the Irish and their imperial masters, is seen to telling effect in the extraordinary courtroom sequence in *Arrah-na-Pogue* in which the appropriately named Shaun the Post, the bearer of letters, seeks to disrupt the smooth, linear function-ing of legal discourse through his evasive word-play. 'I'm aquil to botherin' a regiment of the likes of them', he says, 'I'll keep on

215

saying nothing all the while'. The breakdown of communication is signalled on the way to the court when Shaun and a Cockney sergeant fail to agree on even the meaning of the word 'alibi', let alone its relevance to Shaun's particular predicament. This is only the prelude to a display of equivocation and repartee which ensures that the proceedings of the court can hardly get past identifying Shaun as an individual:

Major: Your name?
Shaun: Is it my name, sir? Ah, you're jokin' . . .
Major: Will you give the Court your name, fellow?
Shaun: Well, I'm not ashamed of it.
O'Grady: Come, Shaun, my man.
Shaun: There, didn't I tell ye! he knows me well enough.
Major: Shaun (*writing*), that's the Irish for John, I suppose.
Shaun: No sir; John is the English for Shaun.[60]

When Shaun is finally asked whether he is guilty or not he replies with disarming innocence: 'Sure, Major, I thought that was what we'd all come here to find out.' Such is the frustration of the due process that O'Grady, an Anglo-Irish military officer, colludes with Shaun by suggesting that he be let off, if only on the grounds of 'the eloquence of his defence'. No wonder the exasperated Secretary at Dublin Castle is driven to exclaim later in the play: 'Shall I ever be able to understand this extraordinary people?'

There is an additional edge to the subversive thrust of language in Boucicault, since the brogue is firmly established as a point along an axis which links landscape and nature to both class and political identity. The comparison of the brogue with nature or with natural forces is a familiar motif in descriptions of Irish character. 'Elusive as running water is the brogue of the Irish peasant', write Somerville and Ross, 'hardly attained even by those who have known its tune from childhood'.[61] In social terms, this alignment of the brogue with nature is translated into an opposition between the unrestrained verbal energy of the primitive 'lower classes' and the rigid linguistic protocols of polite society. In *The Colleen Bawn*, the unreconstructed brogue of Eily O'Connor is a clear embarrassment to her prospective clandestine liaison with the upper-class Hardress Cregan: 'I'm gettin' clane of the brogue', she says, 'and learnin' to do nothing — I'm to be changed entirely'. To which Myles, her jilted vagabond admirer, can only reply: 'Oh! If he'd lave me yer own self, and only take away wid him his improvements'.[62] The underlying vitality of the brogue, and its identification with the 'real' (Irish) self, is brought out forcefully in another exchange in which the aristocratic Anna Chute loses her veneer of good breeding and exclaims: 'When I am angry the brogue comes out, and my Irish heart will burst through manners, and graces, and twenty stay-laces.'[63]

What is interesting here is the suggestion that the 'authentic' self is not some kind of inner psychological entity, hovering, as it were, 'behind' language, but is rather inscribed in a deviant, linguistic idiom. By the same token, the brogue in Boucicault does not come across as some kind of 'natural' unpremeditated speech, existing outside the codes and conventions of a signifying system as in a Rousseau-type 'naturalised' language.[64] Instead it must be seen as a generalised application of the principle which governs the comic contradictions of an Irish bull, i.e. an *excess* of linguistic expression over intended meaning.[65] The self-conscious equivocation and inflated diction of the brogue in these plays is the linguistic equivalent of the visual overkill of Boucicault's sensation scenes: the subversion of dominant 'transparent' or self-effacing modes of communication is achieved not by stepping outside existing codes but by *intensifying* them to the point of making them opaque. The paradoxical implications of this strategy are captured with characteristic acumen by Synge in *The Playboy of the Western World* (1907) when Pegeen rebukes the obsequious Shawn Keogh on the grounds that, unlike the garrulous Christy, he has 'no savagery or fine words in him at all'.[66] For Pegeen, savagery and the unleashing of semantic violence is produced by refinement, or more precisely *over*-refinement, and not by a relapse into some primitive, mythic state of nature. As Charles Maturin wrote in the preface to his historical novel *The Milesian Chief* (1812), a work largely inspired by Lady Morgan's example:

> I have chosen my own country for the scene, because I believe it is the only country on earth, where . . . the extremes of refinement and barbarism are united, and the most wild and incredible situations of romantic story are hourly passing before modern eyes.[67]

Georg Lukacs noted in relation to Walter Scott that the role of the outsider as principal figure in his historical novels is to bring various warring factions, or hostile forces, together. The detached, neutral hero provides a kind of middle ground, usually by means of a love affair or a 'human interest' angle, which brings about a reconciliation of opposites.[68] In Lady Morgan's *The Wild Irish Girl* and Boucicault's political melodramas, there is a different denouement: the happy ending is assured (albeit forced and contrived even by melodramatic standards) but this is achieved through the absorption of the outsider into the local community. Common ground does not exist: there is either assimilation or confrontation.[69] In Boucicault's plays, the middle course is negotiated not by an outside individual but by a partisan, lawless rogue, whose personality is fused with that of his community and, through them, with his native landscape. Typically, Boucicault's political Irish melodramas end with a crowd scene ('enter omnes') in which alien British army officers at last prove their worth by recognising (in so far as they can) the enemies' point of view — in *The Shaughraun*, for instance, Captain Molineaux discovers that the idealised Fenian Robert Ffolliott is not really a villain after all. There is a hint that, notwithstanding the whimsey, this late conversion is fortunate on Molineaux's part, for just before the final communal resolution, the frenzied mob ('D'Ye see that wild ould woman, wid the knife?') have forced the devious informer Harvey Duff to jump over a cliff to his death. That this rapid alternation between 'savagery' and social 'refinement' is still a source of confusion to the outsider is evident in Molineaux's last words when he expresses bafflement at the ease with which an Irish funeral (Conn the Shaughraun is believed to be dead) is transformed into a wedding (Conn disrupts his wake and 'comes back from the dead' to marry Moya): 'Turn the ceremony into a wedding', Molineaux exclaims, 'I really don't see you Irish make much distinction'.[70]

This abrupt transition from barbarism to community, from grief to joy, is a clear indication of the absence of any happy medium or middle ground, and attests to one of the most pervasive traits of Irish character as seen by travel-writers and other visiting observers in the nineteenth century. As L. P. Curtis notes:

> The stereotypical Irishman was a kind of Celtic Jekyll and Hyde: he oscillated between two extremes of behaviour and mood; he was liable to rush from mirth to despair, tenderness to violence, and loyalty to treachery.[71]

Or as Mrs S. C. Hall put it, borrowing liberally from Thomas Moore: 'The tear and the smile, as regards Ireland, seem really twinborn'.[72] It was this tendency to veer from one extreme to another, in effect a celebration of instability and unpredictability, which presented the greatest challenge to the organising perspective of a realist aesthetic which was appropriated by colonial ideology in its attempts to make Ireland 'intelligible'. It was not just extremes of violence but any kind of extremism which transgressed straitlaced Victorian ideals of high seriousness, and which emphasised the irreconcilable differences between the Irish and British way of life. Boucicault did not so much replace Gothic violence with comic bathos as run the two together, combining, as it were, terror and beauty, 'hard primitivism' and 'soft primitivism', in one precarious narrative. Violence was retrieved from an underworld of pre-social brutish instincts and invested with a sense of collective release and abandon — the end-point on a continuum of lawlessness and unrestrained behaviour which included revelry, drunkenness (especially due to illicit distilling), passionate rhetoric, gushing sentiments, patriotic fervour, in general, what Yeats was later to call in a different context, 'the emotion of multitude'. Inverting a stereotype in a manner which prefigured Synge, violence became an affirmation rather than a negation of community.

The constant swerves brought about by the stark juxtapositions and numerous dramatic reversals in Boucicault's plot structures placed immense strains on his theatrical ingenuity. The need to maintain escalating tension and a rapid pace drove him to increase the number of scene shifts in an act to the point where, as we have seen, the physical capacities of the stage were stretched to their limits. In his attempts to cope with these pressures, Boucicault was forced to develop what was in effect a rudimentary cinematic syntax, rather than adhering to the conventions of theatre as traditionally conceived. The number of sudden scene shifts, for instance, pointed to the techniques of editing and cutting, which played such an important role in the evolution of episodic film narratives. Indeed, such was Boucicault's mastery of these techniques that he introduced an elementary form of cross-cutting by developing three simultaneous lines of action on the stage in the run-up to the sensational escape scene in *Arrah-na-Pogue*, the focus of attention switching by means of alternating scenic flats, and lighting effects akin to cinematic fades and dissolves.[73]

It was, however, his desire to enhance the impact of his sensation scenes, to discharge the energy produced by their dislocating effects on the main narrative, which brought out the showman in

Boucicault. In the famous escape scene in *The Shaughraun*, the action 'cuts' from the interior of Conn the Shaughraun's prison cell where the wily hero is escaping through a window, to an 'exterior shot' of the same scene by means of an elaborate pivotal stage. In *Arrah-na-Pogue*, a similar breathtaking escape is further heightened by showing Shaun clinging valiantly to the ivy of the outside wall as he attempts to scale the lofty prison tower. At this point, the wall begins to sink gradually through the floor, 'simulating' a vertical tracking shot in order to chart Shaun's progress to the top. Then the lights are dimmed and the action cuts almost a full 180 degrees, as we see Shaun finally making it to the safety of a rocky ledge where the loyal Arrah is waiting for him.

Boucicault's obsession with stagecraft was such that there is a sense in which he would have deployed his innovative stage devices for their own sake, regardless of their thematic relevance. Yet it is clear that his interest in Irish subject-matter, above all his commitment to taking on board the formidable problems of staging a narrative of extreme situations, drove him to a form of theatrical excess and dramatic barn-storming which eventually undermined the very basis of scenic illusion in theatre, and paved the way for a whole new departure in the art of motion pictures. Nor was Boucicault's influence confined to the pre-history of cinema. There is a certain irony in the fact that when the burgeoning American film industry first attempted to move out of studios and simulated scenery for non-American themes, their search for 'authentic' regional locations brought them to Boucicault's Killarney. In 1910 Sidney Olcott and the Kalem Company arrived in Killarney to shoot a series of films on Irish themes, and by 1912 *The Colleen Bawn*, *Arrah-na-Pogue* and *The Shaughraun* were born again on the screen, accompanied once more by claims of 'realist breakthroughs' and greater fidelity to nature. As a contemporary reviewer of *The Colleen Bawn* wrote:

> The scenes which are presented on the screen have a highly educative value, being photographic reproductions of the exact spots mentioned in the original work of Dion Boucicault. In this respect the moving picture loving public will see the ideas of the great dramatist portrayed with a fidelity and a realism which neither have been, nor could possibly be achieved on the stage.[74]

Boucicault, no doubt, would have had mixed feelings had he lived to see his dramatic thunder being stolen by the realistic pretensions of a new visual medium. According to Walter Benjamin:

> The history of every art form shows critical epochs in which a certain art form aspires to effects which could be fully obtained only with a changed technical standard, that is to say, in a new art form. The extravagancies and crudities of art which thus appear, particularly in the so-called decadent epochs, actually arise from the nucleus of its richest historical energies.[75]

Boucicault's melodrama, straining at its theatrical leash, is a perfect example of his favourite theme of one extreme leading to another, of extravagance and crudity preparing the way for the refinement of a new cultural form.

Romanticism and Irish cinema

At one point in *The Colleen Bawn*, the seemingly lighthearted atmosphere of the play is disrupted by a short scene which foreshadows the impending darkness and near tragedy of the attempted drowning in the 'sensation scene'. Myles, the noble poacher, comes across Anne Chute (a true 'wild Irish girl', according to Robert Hogan)[76] in a wood on the verge of a lake. Anne's horse has taken fright at a clap of thunder, and as she speaks the thunder starts up again:

Anne: The storm is coming down to the mountain — is there no shelter near?

Myles: There may be a corner in this ould chapel. (*rain*) Here comes the rain — murdher! ye'll be wet through. (*Music — pulls off coat*) Put this round yez.

Anne: What will you do? You'll catch your death of cold.

Myles: (*taking out bottle*) Cowld is it. Here's a wardrobe of top coats. (*thunder*) Whoo! this is a fine time for the water — this way, ma'am.[77]

This scene is duplicated, albeit to different dramatic effect, in *The Quiet Man* in the strange sequence where Sean and Mary Kate finally break away from their marriage broker, Michaeleen Og Flynn (Barry Fitzgerald), and take to the freedom of the open countryside in the radiant sunshine. Suddenly, the whole tenor of the film changes as they find themselves in a derelict graveyard, replete with ruins and Celtic crosses, under an overcast sky. This signals the release of pent-up emotion, for as they kiss the heavens open in a cloudburst of thunder and lightning. The music swells, and Sean leads Mary Kate to a corner of a ruined chapel. There he puts his coat around her as if to seal in their new-found intimacy in the act of protecting her from the rain.

Apart from the obvious incongruity in choosing a graveyard as an appropriate location for the expression of sexual passion, the most striking juxtaposition in this sequence would appear to be the contrast between the social world of 'soft primitivism' — the rigid conventions associated with courting and 'going out' — and the sense of escape from social inhibitions provided by 'hard primitivism', the irruption of natural forces as Sean and Mary Kate embrace. Nature as an outlet for energy and sexual licence seems to be pitted in confrontation with the stultifying constraints of culture. Many commentators have drawn attention to the manner in which, from her first appearance in an idyllic pastoral setting, Mary Kate is associated with nature and the fluctuating moods of the Irish landscape.[78] Rain streaming down the window-pane distils her longing and disappointment when Sean is first turned away as a prospective suitor by her brother Red Will, and in the race episode, her susceptibility to natural influences is shown when the wind blows off her bonnet, in effect forcing her to enter it in the stakes as a garland for the winner of the race. The most notable opposition between the social and the natural in this regard occurs when Sean first meets Mary Kate in his cottage, the scene which introduced E.T. to some of the stranger encounters among humankind. The action shifts from the conviviality and unison of the village pub, where Sean gains his first tentative admission into the community (if not the local male choir), to his windswept desolate cottage, shrouded in darkness. The restlessness of the elements hints at the forces which are stirring beneath the outward composure of Sean's personality, so that when Mary Kate makes her startled appearance and they kiss passionately in the doorway, all nature breaks loose. The sequence ends with a long shot of Mark Kate scurrying through the storm in the darkness, as if fleeing from the forces she has unleashed. There is a clear contrast with an earlier long shot of Mary Kate gambolling among her flock of sheep in the brilliant sunshine, which suggests that her personality rests on an uneasy alliance between the social and the natural, between the bright and dark side of the landscape. As Mary Kate and Sean succeed in throwing their chaperone Michaeleen off their trail, Mary Kate removes in an almost ritualistic fashion her stockings and her bonnet, as if shedding the last vestiges of culture in order to reveal a more authentic, 'natural' reality beneath the proprieties of social convention.

It is not surprising that in the intitial critical response to *The Quiet Man*, Irish reviewers singled out the landscape, and the 'healthy naturalness' of the photography,[79] as being one of the few concessions to realism in what was otherwise a dream-world of stage-Irishry and nostalgic sentiment. As we have observed above, it was precisely the pursuit of 'authentic locations' and 'life-like scenery' which brought the first film-makers to Ireland, and which was the subject of the earlier critical accolades. The inclusion of scenery was so important in establishing the realist credentials of these early Irish films that in some cases shots of well-known beauty spots were inserted for their own sake, to authenticate, as it were, the setting for the main storyline. Thus in Sidney Olcott's costume drama *Rory O'More* (1911), the second feature film produced by the Kalem Company in Ireland, the narrative ostensibly deals with the daring adventures of the rebel Rory O'More (Jack Clarke), as he attempts to escape the clutches of English justice. In the time-honoured romantic tradition which associated banditti with wild landscape, Rory conveniently chooses Killarney and its environs as the base of his one-man resistance movement against the British Empire. Rory and his sweetheart Kathleen (Gene Gauntier) are repeatedly framed against rugged mountainsides to get the most out of the picturesque locations, but just in case the action obscures the scenery, the narrative is punctuated by shots of various beauty spots, accompanied by appropriate captions: 'Lakes of Killarney', 'Gap of Dunloe', or whatever. These inserts, totally unmotivated by the plot, only succeed in throwing the action off course to the point of ruling out any possibility of developing a coherent, realist narrative. That the scenery of Killarney could override the main narrative in this manner is borne out by the fact that even in melodrama, a poster for the original London run of *The Colleen Bawn* could list in bold capitals virtually the same beauty spots — 'Act I — The Lake of Killarney; The Gap of Dunloe' and so on — as if these were the main components of the story.[80]

In *The Quiet Man* the desire to enhance the authenticity of the Irish landscape is also achieved at the expense of character and action. In a perceptive comment, a contemporary reviewer in *The*

Irish Independent noted that while the 'exaggerations' of the plot gave cause for complaint

> there can be no quarrel with Ford's fine treatment of the scenery he found in the West. It is a lovely background, caught in soft shades of technicolour and as real as one could wish. The camera lingers on it lovingly, almost reluctant one would imagine at times, to be getting on with the story.[81]

By dwelling unduly on the landscape, the camera tends to go above the heads of the characters and to draw attention to its own intrusive presence, hence denying the very transparency and invisibility of the medium which realism seeks to attain. One way out of this dilemma is to integrate the characters more completely with their environment. In a romantic context, this may carry with it the suggestion that somehow the influence of natural surroundings brings out 'the true self', the deeper, more recondite aspects of one's personality. This accords with the traditional primitivist view that nature, and particularly wild, unsubdued landscape, represents a more profound and permanent reality than the fleeting world of social appearances. In romantic landscape painting, the Ruskinian view that 'The heights are where society is not'[82] tended to take the form of a series of contrasts between foreground and background, human figures occupying the former, while the overpowering presence of mountains, the ocean or some other imposing natural spectacle loomed large in the background. As Thomas MacGreevy expresses it in relation to Jack Yeats' colourful romantic evocations of life on the west coast of Ireland:

> It was against that mountain background, so suggestive of unchanging, extra-human, transcendent things, and, by implication, of the precariousness of all human achievement, that he painted the people of Ireland, men, women, and children, at work and play, farmers, labourers, car-drivers, jockeys, ballad singers, tramps, women old and young, barefooted boys in rakish looking caps — 'men with the eyes of people [who] do be looking at the sea'.[83]

To travel back then in pictorial space is to pursue a higher, albeit more elusive plane of truth, as when at the end of *Finian's Rainbow*, *The Luck of the Irish* (1948), or *Ryan's Daughter*, the various protagonists head towards a distant, hazy mountain horizon, the Irish equivalent of riding off into the sunset.

It is the prospect of a fusion with nature in this sense, with a more fundamental order of things, which brings the emigrant Sean Thornton back to Inisfree and which accounts for the enchanting spell which Mary Kate casts over him. Yet there is an inherent paradox in the depiction of landscape in *The Quiet Man*, a serious difficulty which detracts from any attempt to identify nature with a deeper, more authentic mode of existence. This has to do with the blatant unreality of the studio sets and fake backdrops which are inserted at key moments in the film, often indeed at precisely those points where nature is meant to impinge most forcefully on the action. This 'flaw' in the visual style of the film was a source of some concern to contemporary reviewers, and particularly those who valued the film for its use of outdoor locations. According to Lindsay Anderson

> Some scenes (particularly towards the beginning of the picture) have a distinctly rough-and-ready, first-take air about them. And production difficulties — largely, one imagines, occasioned by bad weather on location — have necessitated a number of studio inserts in exterior sequences which are particularly regrettable in other Ford films which elsewhere gains so immensely from the freshness and vividness of its sense of locality.[84]

It is doubtful if these lapses in pictorial realism can be attributed solely to the vagaries of the Irish weather, if only because there are similar stylistic 'breaks' in other Ford films such as *The Searchers* (1956), which also relies heavily on what Andrew Sarris refers to as 'cosmic' landscape compositions.[85] In *The Quiet Man*, the first significant use of a false backdrop occurs in the scene, described in the opening section above, in which Sean, sitting on a bridge, is captivated by the discovery of his family cottage, White O'Morn. Here we are presented with a sharp juxtaposition between soft and hard primitivism, as in a shot/reverse shot sequence Sean's view of the cottage is contrasted with the dark landscape behind him. But there is a further opposition here, for while the shots of White O'Morn, suffused in sunlight and surrounded by greenery, are clearly outdoor locations, the sombre landscape behind Sean, with mountains dominating the background, is flat, poorly-lit and so obviously contrived that one expects Sean's shadow to fall upon it.

It would be a mistake, moreover, to see the 'real' outdoor locations as yielding a perspicuous vision of pure nature, unalloyed by subjective or human considerations. Though Michaeleen tells Sean that 'it is nothing but a wee humble cottage', language, in the form of his mother's words in voice-over, intercepts Sean's line of vision and shapes his point of view. By contrast, the one part of the landscape that is not invested with significance and which can claim with some justification to be unadorned nature, is shown to be fabricated and unreal.

In the graveyard episode, the convulsions of the climate and Sean and Mary Kate's passionate embrace may be taken, at one level, as a vindication of suppressed, natural vitality over the artificial milieu of social proprieties and observances. Yet the thunderstorm and the surrounding Celtic crosses and Gothic ruins are themselves so artificial and theatrical as to rule out any semblance of wild, uncontrolled nature. In the depiction of landscape, the 'social', it would seem, is given the full benefit of outdoor locations (as in the preceding communal courtship ceremony), while the 'natural', paradoxically, is relegated to a twilight zone of props and studio sets. Several critics have pointed to this scene as being one of the most erotic sequences in John Ford's work, with some commentators even suggesting that it 'is as close to a nude scene as Ford has ever come'.[86] The interesting point here, however, is that notwithstanding Mary Kate's discarding of her stockings and bonnet earlier on, the erotic charge derives from the fact that their flesh is not shown directly but is rather seen through the clinging, semi-transparent fabric of their clothes. It is as if, like the obvious stylisation of the sets, some form of mediation or cultural process must always come between the human and the natural world. As C. S. Peirce wrote in a different context of attempts to push aside 'the veil' of language to reveal a more fundamental, non-linguistic source of meaning:

> The meaning of a representation can be nothing but a representation. In fact it is nothing but the representation itself conceived as stripped of irrelevant clothing. But this clothing can never be stripped off; it is only changed for something more diaphanous.[87]

In Nicholas Poussin's famous painting *The Arcadian Shepherds* (1629–30), one of the great meditations on the paradise theme in Western art, a group of shepherds is shown, registering surprise and dismay at finding a tomb in their edenic setting bearing the inscription (presumably enunciated by Death): 'Et in Arcadia Ego' [i.e. 'I too am in Arcadia']. It would seem at first glance that the shepherds are startled at having discovered death within the precincts of Arcadia, but as Erwin Panofsky ingeniously suggests, it could also be that their consternation derives from the fact that *writing* has invaded their idyllic existence (one of the group is shown tracing the letters out with his forefinger).[88] For romantic theorists ranging from Rousseau to Emerson, the loss of paradise was inevitable as soon as Adam named the animals: the acquisition of language, and more particularly the advent of writing, was taken as one of the crucial stages in the transition from nature to culture. In his idealisation of the primitive American wilderness, Rousseau could even fantasise that the American Indian moved around in a virtual state of silence:

> The American savages hardly speak at all except outside their homes. Each keeps silent in his hut, speaking to his family by signs. And these signs are used infrequently, for a savage is less disquieted, less impatient than a European.[89]

The contrast with the verbose 'noble savages' of Synge and Boucicault — or for that matter John Ford — could hardly be more striking, notwithstanding the soubriquet of *The Quiet Man*. In *Finian's Rainbow*, the mere presence of Finian McLonergan and his daughter, Sharon, or more precisely the leprechaun Og (Tommy Steele), in the American west is sufficient to restore the power of speech to the mute, 'natural' girl, Susan the Silent (Barbara Hancock). In *The Luck of the Irish*, there is a more complex play on this theme. The film deals with the moral crisis confronting an Irish-American, Stephen Fitzgerald (Tyrone Power), who is forced to choose between the ruthless pragmatism of a successful business career in America, or a more sincere, unaffected way of life in Ireland. The opening images establish Ireland as a peaceful Arcadia — that is, until the roar of Stephen's car disturbs the drowsy tranquillity of the sheep and the cattle. When a bridge collapses tendentiously under the weight of the car, Stephen announces that he will 'scout up the road a bit' since 'it must lead somewhere'. His friend Bill (James Todd) replies: 'Don't be too sure about Irish paths. Irish paths are whimsical — like the Irish character'. The film seems to be preparing us for another variation on the old Victorian theme that Irish character is indistinguishable from the wayward native landscape. When Stephen's reconnaissance takes him into a mysterious wood and he encounters a rather oversize leprechaun (Cecil Kellaway) beside a waterfall, our suspicions appear to be justified. True to form, Stephen subsequently meets up with Nora (Anne Baxter), a wild Irish girl ('Don't waste your fiery Irish temper, my dear', Bill says to her at one stage) who acts as his conscience, the embodiment of the life he is denying by returning to America. In one sequence, Stephen and Nora venture into the woods and come to the edge of an ocean, a characteristic romantic scenario for coming to terms with the 'real' self. The unusual feature of this episode, however, is that the inner character Nora is seeking to bring out in Stephen is his vocation as a *writer*. Stephen is temporarily attracted by the lure of power and wealth in New York, even if it means acting as a yes-man and selling his services to the corrupt, aspiring politician Augur (so corrupt he appears to forget his daughter's name). But Nora, with a little help from Horace the leprechaun, finally convinces Stephen that it is precisely the trappings of American capitalism which are preventing him from realising his true potential, the self which is expressed through his mastery of language.

In the hard primitivist environment of *Ryan's Daughter*, we encounter a different attitude towards writing and the world of books. Early in the film, Rosy meets the crotchety parish priest Father Collins as she is wandering aimlessly on the open expanses of a windswept beach. 'What do you do Rose, mooning about all day by yourself?' the priest asks. 'Read', Rosy answers defensively, showing him the lurid cover of a romantic pot-boiler *The King's Mistress*. She then corrects herself: 'Well, I wasn't really reading it'. 'You're doing nothing then', the priest replies and adds his ominous parting shot: 'Doing nothing is a dangerous occupation'. When the action cuts back to Rosy on the beach we see her hurtling the book onto the crashing waves, in effect throwing caution to the winds. Rosy will now choose the actual world as the site for her fantasies so that, like the film itself, her problem is that she doesn't know where romance ends and reality begins. When Charles (Robert Mitchum), Rosy's cultured husband, is shown at one stage pressing flowers between the pages of a book, Rosy remarks that she prefers her flowers growing. Deprived of any mediating vision, it is not surprising that she offers little resistance to the encroachments of nature on her personality. The attitude shown towards nature by the Colleen

Bawn's mother in the filmed musical of Boucicault's play, *The Lily of Killarney* (1934), would seem to be equally applicable to Rosy Ryan: 'Don't you forget that one touch of nature would make the whole world sin.'

Ryan's Daughter has been accurately described as 'a work divided against itself'.[90] At one level, the overriding emphasis on authentic outdoor locations, and the meticulous care taken in constructing period detail (sepia postcards were actually sold of the fake village, simulating the 'real Ireland'), pushes the film in the direction of visual realism. Added to this is the fact that unusually for an Irish film, it attempts to chart the psychological turmoil of an individualised Irish character, Rosy Ryan, who is not so much outside as at odds with her community. To Rosy's romantic temperament, society appears entirely a matter of prohibitions and constraints. True freedom, as she sees it, is only to be found in nature, a point underlined in one exchange where she tells Fr Collins that she expects the sexual pleasures of marriage to transform her into a different person. 'Child, what are you expecting . . . wings is it?' the priest replies, as the camera follows Rosy's gaze to a flock of seagulls overhead. Seagulls for Rosy are the embodiment of a carefree, untramelled existence. What she does not seem to realise is that, controlled by their instincts and buffeted by the wind, seagulls live completely at the mercy of nature. Rosy's clichéd conception of freedom can only pose immense problems for her credibility as a character, since translated into narrative terms, it has the effect of removing all traces of psychological development from her personality. Subject to the play of natural forces, she becomes little more than a barometer, a sensitive register of atmospheric change.

If the critics were agreed on any one issue in their initial response to *Ryan's Daughter*, it was that the sweep of the photography and the breathtaking scenery totally swamped the development of plot and character. According to Nigel Andrews, the film presents 'nature, fate and emotions in symbolic harness' to such a degree that the

> plethora of eye-catching backcloths not only dwarfs the characters — as it did in *Zhivago* and *Lawrence* — but dilutes the pastoral-tragic idiom to produce a mere escapist dream, tragedy and moral conflict alike dissolving in the aesthetic euphoria of the scenery.[91]

That Rosy's personality is susceptible to natural influences is established in the opening sequence which shows her chasing an umbrella after it has been blown over a cliff by a gust of wind. Fate in the guise of nature again intervenes to bring Rosy and Charles closer together when a sudden rush of wind blows off his hat and her bonnet on the beach — thereby striking an interesting contrast with a similar scene in *The Quiet Man* where Sean and Mary deliberately remove their headgear in the open countryside after their escape from Michaeleen. The contrasts with *The Quiet Man* are again evident in the love-making scene, which also begins with a meeting at a ruin. Rosy and Major Doryan (Christopher Jones) then retire to a gloomy wood where they make love to the accompaniment of nature as the wind rises, trees creak and flashes of sunlight punctuate the dark foliage. In *The Quiet Man* the love scene seems to intrude suddenly on the narrative, like the abrupt outbreak of thunder and lightning. In *Ryan's Daughter*, by contrast, there is a slow ponderous build-up to the scene and, as if to highlight the staged look of *The Quiet Man*, the camera lingers on various natural phenomena — two intertwined webs of gossamer, the wind stripping the petals off two flowers — which, like the lovers' nudity, accords with Rosy's idea of freedom as a surrender to nature. In *The Quiet Man*, language literally comes between Sean and Mary Kate in the form of Michaeleen Og, their loquacious chaperone, but in *Ryan's Daughter*, it is the mute, grotesque Michael (John Mills) who is the unwelcome guardian, stalking the movements of the ill-fated couple like a portent of doom.

Ryan's Daughter may be seen as a reversion to the darker, more fatalistic treatments of the Irish in early Victorian melodramas. In these plays, the absence of any psychological dimension to the Irish character did not pave the way, as it did in Boucicault, for a social conception of the self, but instead tended to reduce Irish character to the operation of landscape and climate. The incapacity — or reluctance — to understand the complexity of agrarian crime or political unrest (for even understanding, as Conor Cruise O'Brien says, is complicity)[92] meant that *collective* violence in particular was seen as mindless behaviour, as nature running out of control. In H. P. Grattan's *The White Boys* (1836), an agrarian criminal gang ambushes an English regiment at, suitably, a picturesque 'mountainous and rocky pass' which leads one of the characters to exclaim: 'How can this wild work end but in ruin and defeat? No one to control — no one to advise — nothing but their own mad wills to lead them'.[93] This seems like a commentary on *Ryan's Daughter* where a spectacular storm provides the setting for an attempted arms landing by the IRA, the entire village community surging like a wave down the rocky sea-shore to help 'the boys' in a paramilitary version of *Man of Aran*. (The pervasiveness of the 'mob mentality' is indicated by the fact that *every* member of the community — except, of course, Rosy and Charles — rushes to the aid of the rebels.) When the arms party is intercepted by Major Doryan and his troops — at which point, the weather unexpectedly changes to sunlight — the community seek to exact tribal revenge and in a second manic rush, attack and humiliate Rosy by stripping off her clothes and cutting her hair. At the end, we see Charles, Fr Collins and Michael waiting in the sunshine at a bus-stop with Rosy, who is trying to hide her shame by concealing her chopped hair under a bonnet. 'Ah, it's brightness for you', Fr Collins observes, and adds, 'A grand day for a journey'. 'A sign of good luck', Rosy whimpers, but no sooner has she uttered this remark than a gust of wind whips the bonnet off her head, leaving her exposed to the gaze of Michael who, in fact, she has now come to resemble.

In accordance as politics, or indeed any kind of social dimension, is removed from the representation of violence in films about Ireland, we find nature stepping in to fill the breach. At the end of *A Terrible Beauty* (1960), the stunted IRA leader McGinnis (Dan O'Herlihy) waits in the darkness during a thunderstorm to gun down Dermot O'Neill (Robert Mitchum), who has turned his back on the movement. Literally blinded by the rain, McGinnis shoots at a passing cyclist whom he takes to be Dermot but is in fact Bella (Marianne Benet), Dermot's sister. As McGinnis looks down in horror at the crumpled body of his innocent victim, a loud crash of thunder attests to the forces which have driven him on his tragic course of destruction. There is a similar denouement at the end of *Shake Hands With the Devil* (1959) in which a young woman is again at the receiving end of a psychotic IRA leader's bloodlust. The promiscuity of Kitty Brady (Glynis Johns), a local barmaid, is seen by Lenihan (James Cagney), the misogynistic IRA leader (who also happens to be one of Ireland's leading surgeons!) as the weak link in the IRA's covert operations. Kitty tempts fate by deciding to go for a midnight swim on a moonlit beach the night before a major IRA raid. In a sequence which fell foul of the censor in Ireland, the camera lingers alluringly on Kitty's legs as she caresses herself while lifting her clothes off the ground. At this point the menacing figure of Lenihan appears on the scene. 'We're alone with only the wind and the sea', Kitty says defiantly, 'so what's to stop you, Commandant?' Lenihan takes Kitty at her word and proceeds to let nature take its course by attempting to strangle her with a viciousness which suggests that the likelihood of her being an informer is at most incidental to the assault.

One of the main casualties in any simplistic reduction of political violence to natural or irrational forces is *history*. For this reason, it is interesting to contrast the recourse to nature in films such as *Shake Hands With the Devil* and *Ryan's Daughter* with a view of communal violence which seeks to reinstate history and culture, albeit within the confines of another version of romanticism. In an early scene in the film *Captain Boycott* (1947), the local unit of the Fenians is shown drilling and organising clandestinely under the cover of a foreboding ruined castle. No sooner has Hugh Davin (Stewart Granger) joined the group than an argument develops as to the relative merits of peaceful methods and violence in achieving their political ends. One of the disgruntled men voices the classic liberal opposition of *language* (and by extension reason and parliamentary procedures) to violence: 'If you ask me we'd be a sight better off talking over our troubles with the Land League. They haven't got guns — but they've got Mr Parnell.' 'When we get the guns', the rabble-rousing schoolmaster McGinty (Noel Purcell) replies, 'they'll listen to something a sight more powerful.' Though Hugh castigates the men for treating a military organisation as 'a debating society', it is clear that McGinty sees violence, not as the negation of language but as a more forceful, if crude, form of communication. As Hugh's mother (Maureen Delaney) puts it in the preceding scene when she suspects that Hugh is going over to non-violent politics: 'Your father appealed to the landlords *in the language they understood*. And it's not so different today . . . I've heard tell of 'em gathering together again — organising and drilling ready for the moment to strike . . .' (my emphasis).

This ambivalent relationship between language and violence is given an additional twist in Douglas Sirk's baroque foray into Irish romanticism, *Captain Lightfoot* (1955). True to form, the secret agrarian society chooses an imposing ruined abbey as their headquarters, and again the discussion reverts to a heated confrontation over the merits of physical force and non-violent means. 'I'm tired of all this soft talk', the impulsive Michael Martin, alias Captain Lightfoot (Rock Hudson) declares, having announced that he has just robbed the local landlord's agent: 'It's time we took real action.' He is opposed by the 'moderate' leader Regis O'Donnell (Denis O'Dea), who, proclaiming that he is on 'the side of reason', asks Martin to return the money. 'You think courage and violence are the same thing,' he says, but 'a word is often more powerful than a blow.' Martin sneers contemptuously in reply: 'Words, words, words. A mask for a coward to hide behind.'

Not least of the ironies in both of these exchanges is that the vigorous debates over language and violence take place within the interiors of *ruins* which, in the canon of Irish cultural nationalism, are already inscribed with the historical resonance of a written text. Discussing the various sources of Irish history in his *Lectures on Faith and Fatherland*, the influential nineteenth-century preacher Fr Thomas Burke pointed to the obvious importance of ancient manuscripts and written records. 'But', he continues,

> besides these more direct and documentary evidences, the history of every nation is enshrined in the national traditions, in the national music and song; much more, it is *written* in the public buildings that cover the face of the land. These, silent and in ruins, tell most eloquently their tale . . . This is the volume which we are about to open.[94]

The fact that the proponents of violence invariably win out over the advocates of 'talk' and dialogue does not mean that they have stepped outside language. On the contrary, they are, quite literally, already situated within an elaborate signifying system; one, moreover, which provides the very rationale for their activity. It was precisely the invocation of an ancient Irish civilisation, exemplified as we have seen by ruins and antiquities, which brought about a convergence between cultural nationalism and the separatist tradition which sought a complete break with England, outside the limited horizons of parliamentary reform.[95] To place an argument about language and violence within the precincts of an ancient ruin is, therefore, to see its outcome as a foregone conclusion, in the sense that the environment itself represents a synthesis of both sides, a kind of spatial language which culminates in violence. If one type of romanticism, as in *Ryan's Daughter* and related films, portrays violence as a manifestation of raw nature, another form of romanticism, that espoused by cultural nationalism, sees landscape (and by extension violence) as a cultural creation, a mask which, in Fr Burke's words, 'covers the face of the land'. The consequences of this latter view are seldom spelled out, however. It means that cultural identity can no longer claim the permanence or authenticity of nature, but becomes a kind of masquerade, a pursuit of artifice akin to the artistic process itself. Sirk, for one, had no reservations in teasing out the implications of this approach to culture. At one point in *Captain Lightfoot*, Michael Martin is fitted out in a new suit of clothing, thus completing, as Aga (Barbara Rush) his girlfriend says later, the transformation from 'bogtrotter' to 'gentleman'. Captain Thunderbolt (Jeff Morrow), the master of disguise, compliments the tailor — 'Man, you're an artist' — and then, in what is virtually direct address to camera, congratulates the civilised rebel, Captain Lightfoot:

> Now you're a gentleman. Most people are born gulls and judge a man by his dress. We live in a world of phantasmagoria, false forms and false faces. Each man wears a mask against his fellows . . .[96]

Character, community and Irish cinema

In a contemporary review of *Shake Hands With the Devil*, Kathleen Rowland remarked that given the weaknesses in plot and characterisation 'it is some consolation that location sequences give glimpses of Dublin beauties, and that for most of the time the action takes place under the wide skies of the West'.[97] Landscape, in other words, once more predominates at the expense of plot and character. Lest it be thought that this problem arises from a lack of realism, from an emphasis on beauty rather than truth, some critics took the argument a step further by suggesting that the upstaging of character by the environment may often be accentuated rather than diminished by adding to the realism of a film's locations. Thus in a sustained and acute analysis of *Odd Man Out* (1947), Donat O'Donnell (alias Conor Cruise O'Brien) wrote that notwithstanding the claims at the start of the film that the Belfast locations were not directly relevant to a story which addressed itself to 'the human condition',

> In actual fact the environment stole a good piece of a much-stolen picture. Mr. Carol Reed's cameramen did not, as they might well have done, take refuge in dense fog, like that which shrouded, for example, the 'Dublin' of *The Informer*. They actually photographed Belfast, beginning with an aerial view showing Harland and Wolff's, the Cave Hill, and the

Albert Memorial . . . Belfast haunted and overshadowed
every out-of-door scene; its formidable presence lent . . . life
to the film as a whole by distracting attention from the
inadequacies and improbabilities of the story and the long
dreariness of the dialogue.[98]

For O'Donnell, this kind of topographical realism ensures that
Belfast stands as a place apart, disengaged from the narrative and
the action. As a result 'the social reality at which the visible
physical presence of the city is continually pointing' recedes from
view, and the action is 'precipitated back into the Limbo of
absolute untethered destiny'. The character of the main
protagonist Johnny (James Mason), an IRA man on the run, is
accordingly flattened out and deprived of individual depth: 'he has
become one to whom, around whom, things happen'.

To remedy this situation, O'Donnell argues that character and
action should be integrated more with the environment, so that the
'objective' locations might connect with the 'inner drama of
Johnny's destiny'. Yet there is a problem with this approach, for
while it may help us to understand Johnny's *private* world as an
individual, it does little to illuminate the *social* world which he
inhabits and which defines his role in the film. 'For', as O'Donnell
himself puts it:

the story of Johnny is not, like the story of, say, *Brief
Encounter*, a private affair. Johnny is leader of an organization
at war with the rulers of the city. His natural immediate
environment is the people that make up, support or tolerate
that organization. If he is to live convincingly these people
must live too. Therefore, as the city chosen is Belfast, an
attempt must be made to portray Republicans and Catholics
in that city, and the city's deeply divided, suspicious, almost
racialistic life.[99]

The charged political environment of a city like Belfast cannot be
treated as simply an expressive foil for individual characters, however much this may lend itself to narrative cohesion. Still less can it
step outside the action, functioning as an inert, 'authentic'
location. Rather, it subordinates both individuals and their
natural environment from the outset to a sense of place, to a social
engagement with the landscape as historically contested terrain.

It is interesting that O'Donnell should cite the establishing shots of Cave Hill (the country) and Harland and Wolff shipyards (the city) in *Odd Man Out* as examples of topographical realism, for these are of course not just familiar landmarks in Belfast but constitute hallowed ground, imbued with the resonance of their respective political traditions. Thus in a film such as *Jacqueline* (1956), the opening shots of the cranes and gantries of the shipyards signify not only Belfast but Protestantism — and, as the film sees it, a particularly dour version of Protestantism which is unable to cope with what would in a John Ford film be seen as a strong point in someone's character, their tendency to engage in bouts of ribald drunkenness. Mike McNeil's (John Gregson) job in the shipyards is jeopardised by his 'dizzy spells', induced by alcoholism, and on returning home he is ostracised by his prim, self-reliant neighbours (but not by his adoring daughter Jacqueline (Jacqueline Ryan)). In a remarkable pivotal scene, set ironically during street celebrations for the Coronation, the impulse towards community temporarily asserts itself over individualism when the neighbourhood joins in a display of Irish dancing. As soon, however, as the women resume their bickering, Mike takes the 'henpecked' Mr Flanagan (Cyril Cusack) off on a drinking spree. When they return, Flanagan is singing a garbled version of the 1798 Republican ballad 'The Shan Van Vocht', and then to the horror of all the neighbours, dances an irreverent Irish jig under the insignia of the Queen. At this stage, no doubt straining under the narrative excess, the proceedings are disrupted by a thunderstorm (the only way, it would seem, of clearing the streets in an Irish film), but this hardly dampens Flanagan's ardour as he outdoes Gene Kelly by giving a virtuoso performance singing — and dancing — in the rain.

The resolution of Mike's problem is in keeping with the narrative incoherence of this scene, for Jacqueline, through her winsome ways, gets her father a job as a farm labourer on an idyllic, rustic farm (owned by his ex-shipyard boss Mr Lord!). Here it emerges that even Mike's mastery of the brogue is inimical to the Protestant spirit. In an unusually pointed exchange which brings together themes of language, nature and drunkenness Mr Lord (Liam Redmond) remarks to him, while attending to his car: How does a man like you come to have a child like that [i.e. Jacqueline] born to him?

Mike: How does a man like you come to be born at all?
Mr Lord: Oh! You have a glib tongue like the rest of your

generation, all wind and water. (*At this point Mr Lord discovers he has a puncture.*)

Mike: Wind's a pretty useful thing, Mr Lord, when you're short of it.

Mr Lord: A pity you don't feel the same way about water.

From the realist topography of the shipyards, we are brought in *Jacqueline* to the pastoral charms of a story-book farm. What is striking here is not so much the unreal settings, but the total break-down, in both visual and dramatic terms, of a narrative which seeks to integrate the 'Irishness' of language, landscape and community into the working-class 'social problem' film. The individualist work-ethic of puritanism is not easily reconciled with the excesses of Irish romanticism.

When Sean Thornton returns to Ireland in *The Quiet Man*, and is forced to run a gauntlet of rituals and courting customs to win the hand of Mary Kate Danagher, he initially mistakes these for puritan regulations and a regime of social repression. 'I don't get it', he says, voicing the sentiments of American individualism when he is forced to 'walk out' with Mary Kate under a chaperone, 'why, back in the States, I'd drive up, honk the horn, and a girl would come running up . . .' — to which Michaeleen replies as if gloating over another's misfortune: 'America . . . PRO-HI-BITION!'[100] To Michaeleen, it is America which is the home of austerity and prohibitions, and Sean's increasing identification with the social world of Inisfree is bound up with his growing awareness of this element of repressive individualism in his American past. Sean is in fact trying to put aside the memory of an *individual* act of violence, and a form of self-interest which drove him into a ring in America to kill an opponent — 'For what? The purse, a piece of the gate, lousy money'. As the film progresses, it becomes clear that it is not the social aspects of the dowry and courting traditions which Sean objects to but the fact that they have been corrupted by an Irish version of the killjoy mentality and market economy which he associates with the United States.

While the dowry system was a general feature of rural marriage in Ireland over the centuries, its equation with money rather than possessions or personal goods is largely a post-Famine develop-ment.[101] This change was prompted by the gradual accession to power of the medium-sized farmer who, intent on consolidating his holdings, tended to see marriage, if not all emotional relation-ships, in terms of economic calculation. In *The Quiet Man*, Red

Will Danagher, the 'jumped up' progressive farmer (as is clear from his tractors and farm labourers) who passes himself off as a squire, is the embodiment of this acquisitive ideology, and as such is the Irish equivalent of the American pursuit of 'lousy money'. Sean and Mary Kate obviously feel greatly restrained by the formal protocols of match-making, and it is this frustration which prompts their escape from Michaeleen's surveillance during their courtship. Yet in no sense can their relationship be seen as a search for private space, for a kind of romantic love in which 'isolation from society . . . leads to the shedding of sexual inhibitions'.[102] It is not the private self which is compromised by economic imperatives, but rather the social, public self. Thus the shadow is lifted from Sean's boxing past when violence is not so much renounced as redefined in social rather than in private, profit-seeking terms — a transformation which is neatly effected during the showdown between Sean and Red Will when Michaeleen's advice to follow the Marquis of Queensberry rules is ignored, as a private match becomes a free-for-all Donnybrook.

That the success of Sean and Mary Kate's relationship might lie in a similar public direction is clear from the explicit connection which Michaeleen makes between the opposing extremes of love and communal violence. 'Easy now, easy now', he says before Sean and Mary Kate manage to elude his supervision, 'is this a courting or a Donnybrook?' When Sean and Mary Kate fail to consummate their marriage on their wedding night, Mary Kate's main concern the next morning is not the personal aspects of their problem but the fact that the neighbours might see Sean's sleeping bag in the kitchen, and realise that all is not well between them. Mary Kate's preoccupation with the dowry is similarly motivated in that it is not so much the money as a social recognition of her independence which ensures that she comes to Sean on an equal footing. When they eventually consummate their relationship, Sean takes this to be the end of their difficulties, and strides into the kitchen the next morning expecting to find Mary Kate beaming at the prospect of living happily ever after. To his astonishment, Mary Kate has left him, for again the physical expression of their love in the privacy of their bedroom is not sufficient to secure the relationship.

Mary Kate does not finally pledge herself to Sean until he has publicly redeemed himself by burning Red Will's dowry, and by completing his initiation into the community through engaging in a ritual of collective violence. In this, Sean is no different from

Fitz in *The Luck of The Irish* who also wins his Irish sweetheart through a rejection of 'lousy money', and an American life-style dominated by the profit motive. Fitz's commitment to Nora also comes about as a result of a riotous Donnybrook which he causes at an Irish wedding in New York. When he comes to in an inside room, Nora is nursing his wounds and they kiss in a tender embrace. At this point, the camera pans slightly to the right to reveal the community looking on with evident approval through the door at the back! Contrary to romantic individualism, social structures and a communal presence are seen not as constraints or external impositions but as enabling mechanisms, necessary conditions of emotional fulfilment. The fact that this sense of community manifests itself through a breakdown of self-control, whether in the form of sensuality, drunkenness, garrulousness, gambling, violence or even the presence of the IRA ('So the IRA are in this too', Red Will says before the Donnybrook), only adds to its efficacy. In a perverse reformulation of Bernard de Mandeville's famous dictum about the workings of a market economy, communal or public vices make private virtues.

Lindsay Anderson has written of *The Quiet Man* that it evokes a 'landscape in which soft and rugged cordially combine, as they do in the whole personality of the picture'.[103] It is true that the film features both soft and hard primitivism, but it is not clear that they always blend in a harmonious manner. It is difficult to think of any way of reconciling opposing extremes in a film which moves rapidly from sunshine to thunderstorm, from personal love to communal violence, and in which scenes of comedy and intimacy are frequently offset by ominous undertones of death. In the love scene, we have noted the startling juxtaposition of death and sexual passion, as Sean and Mary Kate release their suppressed feelings in the surroundings of a run-down graveyard. This macabre contrast is carried over into the next scene as Sean and Mary Kate's wedding celebrations turn sour and Red Will floors Sean with a punch. There is a sudden transition from the levity of singing 'The Humour Is On Me Now' to an eerie dreamlike flashback which recalls the full horror of Sean's murder of an opponent in the ring. Death even intrudes at a more humorous level into some of the incidental cameos by various actors, as when Red Will's toady Feeney (Jack McGowran) moves Mary Kate's piano into Sean's cottage, a candle placed at both ends, and intones with mock solemnity as if carrying a coffin: 'God bless all here'. Death does not have the last laugh, however. In one of the final scenes, a set-piece borrowed from Boucicault's *The Shaughraun*, an infirm old man rises from his death bed and can hardly wait to put on his trousers as he rushes out the door to join in the communal brawl at the end. The elixir of collective violence can even bring people back from the dead.

So far from resolving the various contradictions which are thrown up in the course of the story, the ending of *The Quiet Man* casts doubt on everything that has gone before. In the opening shots of the final scene, Fr Lonergan's (Ward Bond) voice-over changes into present tense as if reality has finally caught up with his first person narration — 'Well then, so peace and quiet came once again to Inisfree . . .' At this moment, the flashback structure of the film is set aside, and we expect the higher level of truth revealed *directly* by the camera, as in the kind of conventional denouement exemplified by the classic Hollywood narrative, to wrap up all the loose ends and reconcile the competing versions of 'reality' in the film. In fact, the opposite happens. The Rev. Playfair (Arthur Shields), the local vicar, is receiving a visit from his Protestant bishop who is about to transfer him from Inisfree because of the lack of Protestant parishioners. No sooner has Fr Lonergan ceased his narration than he enjoins the crowd still lingering on after the Donnybrook to put on a *semblance* of community for the visiting bishop. Fr Lonergan and his curate hide their collars and all wave to the gullible outsider. This masquerade is followed by a 'curtain call' in which the leading members of the cast wave directly to the audience, as if to remind us both of the presence of the camera and the fact that we too are in the position of the bishop, viewing a mere pretence, a *representation* of community.[104] Though central to the film, community is not presented as being 'natural' or 'organic' but it is instead a construction, a result of organised human endeavour (or in this case, human ingenuity). By the same token, 'truth' in the film is not a given, a point at which the medium becomes objective or transparent, but in fact draws attention to its own contrivance at the very moment reality — whether it takes the form of 'authentic' nature, the 'real' self, or the omniscient camera — impinges upon the screen. To Sean Thornton's question on first beholding Mary Kate, the incarnation of his dream Ireland: 'Hey, is this real?' the answer lies firmly in the negative.

New departures: Irish cinema in the 1980s

Since the late eighteenth century, it is possible to identify at least two dominant strains in popular romantic representations of Ireland. The first aspires towards realism and authenticity, but in its eagerness to make Ireland palatable for external consumption, merely succeeds in lending credibility to the darker aspects of romanticism or hard primitivism. In an Ireland divested of social or political 'complications', it is not surprising that landscape overshadows character, and that nature seems to be the greatest adversary of individuals, whether as an internal or an external force. By contrast, there is an alternative approach which, while recognising important motifs such as landscape, violence, language and community, tries to render these problematic by refusing to press recalcitrant Irish subject-matter into the convenient moulds of realism and romanticism. In keeping with an approach which places considerable weight on social mediation, this view does not seek to posit some kind of 'essential' or 'natural' Irishness, but instead sees cultural identity as a construct, a construct moreover whose artifice becomes apparent in proportion as it attempts to cancel social difference. It follows from this that controlling myths are challenged not by having recourse to an essential, indubitable truth which underlines false appearances, but rather by showing the contrived, *imposed* nature of these myths. If the narrative excesses of Boucicault or John Ford seem at times to strain our credulity, then this may be precisely because we are forced to question some of our most sedimented beliefs about fiction and Irish identity. This is not to say that contemporary film-makers should devote themselves to remakes of *The Quiet Man*, as if endlessly quoting from the past could ever meet the needs of present-day film production. However, these destabilising images do show the potential there exists for reworking, undercutting or transgressing received ideas, even at a highly popular level.

If John Ford's westerns are often vitalised by an infusion of Irish themes — collective violence, family ties, rituals of solidarity, a longing for community — then *Eat the Peach* (dir. Peter Ormrod, 1986), the first fully commercial indigenous production in Ireland, seeks to reverse this trend. Here the landscape seems to question Seamus Heaney's claim that Irish bogland cannot hope to emulate the vast American prairies which 'slice a big sun at evening'. For Heaney, Irish bogs are compressed layers of history, forcing the eye inwards rather than drawing it towards the horizon.[105] In *Eat the Peach* the bleak industrial bogs of the Irish midlands (albeit relocated near the Northern Ireland border) stretch towards an endless skyline, offering no relief or let-up to the observer. The landscape is stripped by mechanisation of all its cultural striations, and for those trapped within its prairie-like vistas, there is a corresponding absence of cultural identity. In the opening scene, a local high-tech factory is closed down by its Japanese owners, their departing helicopter framed by a row of international flags on the industrial estate as it disappears from view.

Not surprisingly, this fly-by-night cosmopolitanism lends itself to the ersatz culture of country and western music, Irish style. It is in the sprawling interiors of 'The Frontier' singing lounge that Arthur (Eamon Morrissey), recently laid off by the factory, and Vinnie (Stephen Brennan), an employee on the local industrial bog, hit on a scheme to inject some sense into their lives. As if to escape the oppressive weight of the landscape, Vinnie proposes building a Wall of Death in which he will be able, quite literally, to lift himself off the ground on his motorcycle. 'Amigos', the local country and western huckster Boots (Niall Toibin) exclaims, 'it's great to see somebody in this crazy goddamn country get off their asses, and show a bit of enterprise'. Vinnie, looking at the incomplete structure, interprets this in his deadpan way as defying gravity: 'It's a long way to go yet. The strength is not there. The G-Force will tear it apart. Needs more posts.'

Vinnie's attempt to raise himself above his limited horizons succeeds as far as it goes, but the problem is that it does not go far. Instead of following a 'road to God-knows-where' (the name of a nationalist ballad sung by the rebel-rousing group, the Wolfe Tones, in the background in one scene), Vinnie finds himself going around in circles, a fate captured visually in one striking long shot of a bog road heading towards infinity while Vinnie speeds around endlessly in his shaky edifice on the roadside. Following his dream, Vinnie at different points in the film loses his family and is deserted by his community (who flee the ramshackle Wall during the grand opening). In a series of recurrent images drawn from westerns, he strums his guitar in the twilight while an Irish version of a lonesome whistle blows as a bog train rumbles by. In a final descent into individualism (which he mistakes for freedom),[106] he burns the Wall, an act as capricious as the building of the structure in the first place.

Vinnie in one sense conforms to the traditional stereotype of the imaginative, impractical Celt, a small-time Fitzcarraldo who expends all his energy on impossible dreams. But at a more important level, he has not even the advantage of being imprisoned within an overpowering tradition. His inspiration for the Wall comes from watching a video of a ponderous Elvis Presley movie *Roustabout* while the rest of the community are attending mass. Throughout the film, the trappings of modernity and technology do not replace but rather mimic and cash in on the symbols of traditional Ireland: a ghettoblaster with appropriate sound effects substitutes for a truckload of pigs; a tanker of smuggled oil passes itself off as a milk container; sheep escape from a crashed consignment of alcohol (one concession at least to *The Quiet Man*); and a tractor-load of hay explodes when activated by British army counter-insurgency technology. Even stereotypes of Irish women are taken over by the western genre, as in the conventional opposition between Nora, the domesticated wife (Catherine Byrne), and Nuala (Bernadette O'Neill), the saloon girl. The venal politician (Tony Doyle) who hightails it at the first sign of catastrophe and who is identified through his insistent loudhailer, seems like a stray from Robert Altman's *Nashville*, as indeed is Nuala, the blonde barmaid, hoping to hitch a ride to stardom on her equivalent of the road to God-knows-where. In the character of Vinnie, the traditional association of the Celt with 'the triumph of failure' is reduced, like the landscape itself, to a flat, one-dimensional level, a pastiche of the original myth. In the final scene, he farcically re-enacts a more powerful myth when his makeshift do-it-yourself helicopter is uncovered by the astonished Boots. This latter-day Stephen Dedalus owes more, however, to the designs of Heath Robinson than to the liberating vision of his original artificer.

The physical beauty of the photography in Cathal Black's third film *Pigs* (1984), set in the down-and-out world of an inner city squat, runs the risk of aestheticising poverty which, as we have seen,[107] underlies some of the darker aspects of romanticism. But there is a point in hinting at traces of beauty in the midst of a run-down Georgian tenement, for Georgian Dublin in the eighteenth century was the heyday of the Anglo-Irish aristocracy, the nearest the city ever came (at least in retrospect) to a form of urban pastoral. It was the lingering aura of this golden age which redeemed Dublin in the eyes of Anglo-Irish writers such as W. B. Yeats (and still redeems it in the eyes of the Irish Tourist Board). In the opening scenes of the film, we get a faint sense of a world which was lost as a meditative camera moves over the ruins of a

Georgian building, fixing on the conflagration of a burning car while a horseman passes by.

In *Pigs* a new leisure class inhabits these buildings, the rejects of the welfare state. A social worker calls on the main character Jimmy Gibbons (Jimmy Brennan) early in the film, checking up on his claim that he is supporting a wife. 'It's well for you people,' she says. 'Why?' he asks. 'Nothing to do.' 'That's the hardest part of all,' he replies. Just as the enforced leisure of unemployment is far removed from the arcadian vision, so also are urban ruins the antithesis of their romantic predecessors. Ruins in cultural nationalism represent a triumph of history over nature: by contrast, the derelict buildings of the inner city are a denial of history, depriving their immediate environments of any sense of identity. In *Pigs*, the ill-adjusted inhabitants of the squat try to restore some life to the decaying tenement, to the point even of allowing classical music to drift again through the rooms (albeit from a stolen ghettoblaster). Yet the apparatus of the state — the police, the welfare system — succeeds where nature had failed in the past, that is, in reclaiming the ruined building for its own anonymous ends.

Robert Wynne-Simmons' film *The Outcasts* (1982) might be seen at one level as an attempt to bring the rural idyll of *The Quiet Man* down to earth. Set in a pre-Famine era in which marriage is gradually succumbing to market forces, it deals with the harsh effects of the dowry system on those who, like Maura (Mary Ryan), the lame and simpleminded daughter of a small farmer, were not considered viable marriage propositions. The smooth operation of this new emotional regime is disrupted, however, by a mysterious fiddler, Scarf Michael (Mick Lally), who appears disguised as a Strawboy at the wedding of Janey, Maura's sister.[108] Maura is entranced by Scarf Michael and in an escape scene reminiscent of *The Quiet Man*, they take refuge in a graveyard on the night of the wedding, waking the next morning to find nature out of control (except this time it has snowed in early summer). The morbid setting is all the more appropriate for their relationship when it transpires that Scarf Michael is believed to have come back from the dead, having survived an attempt to drown him.

To the romantic sensibility of the local priest, Fr Connolly (Paul Bennett), Maura's flight to the woods and mountains with Scarf Michael is a return to nature, as if in the classic romantic scenario, only nature awaits those who turn their back on the community. The priest recognises the challenge posed by the magic of Scarf

Michael to the Church's desire to regulate belief in the supernatural, but depicts him as an outsider, an isolated individual: 'He
is a wild and ungodly man,' he warns Maura. 'His power is rooted
in evil . . . He is without friends, without a home. Now you have
both of these.' As the story develops, however, it is clear that Scarf
Michael does not embody natural, or even supernatural forces,
but is rather the representative of a residual, pagan *culture* which
threatens the stability of the new post-Famine moral economy. It
was the prospect of revitalising pagan beliefs and superstitions as a
means of combating the increasing dominance of the Catholic
Church which led many otherwise urbane Anglo-Irish writers to
develop an interest in Irish folklore in the nineteenth century.[109]
The celebration of some of the more wayward and exuberant
traces of pre-Famine culture in *The Quiet Man* and *The Outcasts* can
be seen in a similar light, except that in the more sombre
atmosphere of the latter, this imaginative world is doomed as
Maura is forced to take her own life to finally join her enigmatic
lover.

In Thaddeus O'Sullivan's short film *The Woman Who Married
Clark Gable* (1985), set in Dublin in the 1930s, cinema occupies the
place of the magical world of Scarf Michael, offering to Mary
(Brenda Fricker) both the promise and the denial of a release from
the constraints of Irish family life. Mary's marriage to George
(Bob Hoskins), an Englishman, has come to a point where a gulf
has opened up between them on account of her inability to live up
to an idealised self-image of motherhood. Early in the film she is
pictured in a mirror while dusting a sideboard, the routine
domestic chore disturbing the trinkets as in a minor earth tremor.
The action cuts immediately to her bathing the dog in front of the
fireplace, a surrogate for the void in her life.

A night out at the cinema watching Clark Gable in *San Franciso*
provides an outlet for her unfulfilled desires. Whereas George's
pleasure in the film derives from his fascination with the special
effects deployed in the earthquake scenes ('I still can't work out
how they did that earthquake business . . .'), the dividing line
between the imaginary and the real becomes more problematic for
Mary when she notices a resemblance between George (who has
just grown a moustache) and the famous screen idol. Carried away
by this 'discovery', the emotional plenitude of life on the screen
spills over in her everyday existence, acting, as Christian Metz
would have it, as a 'psychical substitute' for her maternal desire.[110]
Their love life is revitalised to the extent that George finds her new

persona as inexplicable as the special effects which exercised his curiosity in the first place.

The underlying ambiguity in their relationship gradually works its way through as George becomes more childlike in her eyes, exemplified in one scene in which he imitates a young boy hanging over a balcony in the Botanic Gardens. Mary goes to confession to assuage her guilt about her fantasy life, only to find it accentuated as the priest reminds her that the primary role of a woman in a Catholic marriage is to produce children, to act as a mother rather than a lover. The undermining of her fantasy goes deeper than this, however, for the confessional box itself parodies the experience of cinema-going: the enveloping darkness, the expectation of inner release, the male figure hovering behind a rectangular aperture. When the shutter is pulled over, Mary is shown leaving a cinema rather than a church.[111] It is as if cinema and religion are competing for the same emotional space in her life. Cinema does not win out on this occasion (as befits perhaps the stifling cultural climate of the 1930s) but the possibility is nevertheless opened up that film may be in a strategic position to challenge some of the dominant self-images of Irish people.

On the evidence of these films alone, it is clear that some of the most important developments in Irish cinema at present derive their impetus from an attempt to engage critically with, rather than simply to disown, the often disfiguring legacy of the past: landscape, history, family and community, escapism and oppression. Few film-makers have explored the intricate connections between these themes, and placed them in the overall context of nationalism and romanticism. The work of Pat Murphy represents one such project, and shows how even the most familiar romantic motifs may be revitalised by releasing the latent energy which is trapped in any incarcerated image. In *Maeve* (1981), we find the traditional theme of an emigré, Maeve Sweeney (Mary Jackson), returning to her native community in Belfast, except in this case, the point of the exercise is not to escape reality but to confront it. Instead of giving way to the kind of generalities which smooth over the complexities of the Northern conflict, *Maeve* focuses on the social and political issues, locating them in their precise historical and territorial contexts. Landscape is not reduced to a series of romantic interludes, at one with the psychic travails of its inhabitants. Rather, it forces its way into the action at key moments, usually by way of 'unmarked' flashbacks from Maeve's past which interrupt her father's repeated attempts to control the narrative through his endless storytelling. The countryside is scarred with ruins and antiquities, bearing the imprint of history, myth and legend. The far-reaching nature of *Maeve*'s reworking of some of the key themes in cultural nationalism is captured in one striking scene, set in an ancient ring fort, in which the young Maeve (Nuala McCann) searches for a foothold in the stone walls of the ruin while her father (Mark Mulholland) dominates the foreground, immersed in one of his long, rambling stories. As she reaches the centre of the frame Maeve alights from the wall, just before her father delivers the punchline to his story: ' "Do you know who I am," says he. "I am Tomas O'Mahony, the last of the Irish bards." ' This is spoken in direct address to camera, as if there is no one left to listen. For Maeve, this is her point of departure from a male narrative tradition, whether secreted in stones or in oral history.

In another sequence on Cave Hill, language cuts across both landscape and the flow of the narrative as the camera pans slowly, giving a commanding view of Belfast and the surrounding countryside while Maeve's voice, off-camera, intones a series of fragmented word-associations. This voice-over, and the subsequent non-naturalistic exchange between Maeve and Liam (John Keegan), her republican boyfriend, as they argue about nationalism, disengages language from its subsidiary role to the image in cinema, and invests the landscape with a sense of place. Cave Hill, renowned for its United Irishman associations,[112] is not just a topographical landmark (as in *Odd Man Out*) but becomes a historical site, a point of intersection for various issues relating to language, vision, history and landscape. At the end of the film, Maeve comes to terms with her fractured identity by going on a drinking session with her sister and mother at the great antiquarian shrine of the Giant's Causeway, solidarity replacing community as they set their face firmly against the landscape on their way home.[113]

In *Maeve*, there is a sustained critique of the means whereby myth coalesces with reality, and particularly of the ways in which 'nature' and 'the past' are invoked to confer legitimacy — and permanence — on specific political and gender relations. In Pat Murphy's recent film, *Anne Devlin* (1984), this process would appear to be reversed with the reinstatement of nature (and its human equivalent, biology) as a space outside language, a source of authenticity and integrity behind the façade of social and symbolic practices. The film deals with Anne Devlin (Brid

Brennan), the faithful 'servant' who retreated into silence, the denial of language, in order to withstand the attempts of her British captors to force her to inform on her 'master', the rebel leader Robert Emmet (Bosco Hogan). In one scene, Julia (Bernie Downes), Anne's sister, is shown sitting on a gate, framed against the landscape while she unties her hair before brushing it out with slow, deliberate strokes. This would seem to be a 'letting the hair down', getting back to nature, as it were, but in fact it is the opposite, an elaborately contrived *sign* to indicate to a band of insurgents, taking refuge in the landscape, that the coast is clear for them to emerge from hiding.[114] This reinscription of the body (and by implication nature) into language, is carried over into the portrayal of Anne herself. Rather than attempting to cancel out the powerful myth of the silent, suffering heroine, the 'Mater Dolorosa' figure which has exerted such a deep influence on popular representations of women in Irish culture, the film seeks to rework this image and to display its operations as a stereotype. Anne's withdrawal into an impenetrable silence during her confinement is accompanied by a relapse into the biological functions of her body such as hunger and menstruation. As if to bear out the view that anatomy is destiny, we see her gradually merge with the role of mother-figure, a process which culminates in a scene near the end in which she is depicted, grief-stricken, holding her dead brother in her lap. Yet so far from vindicating nature, it is precisely at this point that the film reverts to the painterly tableau-like composition of the *Pieta* in Western art, drawing attention to its own status as a representation. In many scenes in the film, the visual style takes over from dialogue and action, but always in such a heightened artificial way as to dispel any semblance of realism, emphasising the fact that images also form part of a coded system of meaning. In marked contrast to the tendency in American romanticism to equate silence and nature, there is nothing 'natural' about silence, suffering or indeed the role of mother in Anne Devlin. As is often the case with stereotypes, what appears to be a sign of weakness — silence, passivity, endurance — on Anne's part, turns out to be a source of hidden strength, a calculated act of resistance.[115]

According to Edward Said, a stereotype belongs to a category of 'knowledge' which

is not so much a way of receiving new information as it is a method of controlling what seems to be a threat to some established view of things. [By means of the stereotype] the threat is muted, familiar values impose themselves, and in the end the mind reduces the pressure upon it by accommodating things to itself as either 'original' or 'repetitious'.[116]

In an Irish context, it is important that myths and stereotypes, with their obsessiveness and their need to coerce experience, are not seen simply as negative or derogatory but are recognised for what they are: stress points in a system of representation which is unable to cope with difference and the unintelligible, which evinces, in Wallace Stevens' words, 'fear before the disorder of the strange'.[117] The desire to make a refractory culture clear and instantly accessible to a casual (external) observer, as in a convergence between romanticism and realism, arises not so much from a wish to understand that culture but to control it, to provide a privileged vantage-point while remaining apart from, rather than a part of, a given community. The most important contemporary Irish film-makers are intent on following a different course, cultivating an indigenous rather than innocent eye. Instead of cleansing the medium of perception, independent film-makers like Pat Murphy, Thaddeus O'Sullivan, Bob Quinn, Cathal Black and Joe Comerford are seeking in various ways to prise open the cracks in the distorting glass, exposing the political and cultural pressures which gave rise to the fissures in the first place. In Thaddeus O'Sullivan's recent film *The Woman Who Married Clark Gable* we have noted how an Irish woman tries to patch up her difficulties with her English husband by recreating him in the image of Clark Gable in the film *San Francisco*, searching for his true love amid the ruins in the aftermath of the great earthquake. This film, with its images of a world rent asunder, is perhaps a fitting epitaph to a tendency to look towards Hollywood (or its equivalents) as the solution to cultural differences, not least those between Ireland and England.

Notes

1. Mrs S. C. Hall, *The Groves of Blarney*, Dicks' Standard Plays no. 453, John Dicks, London, n.d., p. 3.
2. Ibid.
3. See L. P. Curtis Jr, *Apes and Angels: The Irishman in Victorian Caricature*, Newton Abbot: David and Charles, 1971, and R. N. Lebow, *White Britain and Black Ireland: The Influence of Stereotypes on Colonial Policy*,

Philadephia: Institute for the Study of Human Issues, 1976. For a recent short historical account of anti-Irish stereotypes, see Liz Curtis, *Nothing But the Same Old Story*, London: Information on Ireland, 1984.

4. *Irish Press*, May 7 1934. Dorothy Macardle was a confidante of the then President Eamon de Valera and was the author of a monumental 'official' history of the War of Independence, *The Irish Republic*, London: Victor Gollancz, 1937.

5. Robert, G. Lowery, 'The Silver Screen and the Emerald Isle', *Workers Life*, Vol. 3, No. 4, August 1982, p. 26.

6. Ibid., p. 29.

7. Though it is hardly necessary to go into the considerable controversy which has been waged over definitions of romanticism, romanticism in this chapter will be taken to mean, among other things, a concern with imagination (rather than truth), a tendency to idealise (or simplify) the world, an emphasis on the 'organic' as against the 'mechanical' and a desire to return to nature or the past. (For a useful collection of different perspectives on romanticism, see A. K. Thorlby (ed.), *The Romantic Movement*, London: Longmans, 1969.) Realism is even a more problematic concept than romanticism. In terms of subject-matter, it entails a commitment to exposing the harsher sides of social life, particularly having to do with work and poverty (see Linda Nochlin, *Realism*, Harmondsworth: Penguin, 1971, pp. 33 – 40). At the level of form and style, it seeks to convey a sense of *illusionism* (usually by attempting to make the medium of representation invisible or 'transparent') and lays emphasis on a coherent plot and fully rounded 'convincing' characters (to facilitate identification with the fictive world of the story). These definitions will be expanded in the course of the article.

For an interesting recent discussion of the relationship between romanticism and realism, see Charles Rosen and Henri Zerner, *Romanticism and Realism: The Mythology of Nineteenth Century Art*, London: Faber and Faber, 1984.

8. Sean O'Faolain, 'Romance and Realism', *The Bell*, Vol. 10, No. 5, August 1945, p. 382.

9. Walter Benjamin, 'The Author as Producer', in *Understanding Brecht*, trans. Anna Bostok, London: New Left Books, 1973, pp. 94 – 5.

10. See John Wilson Foster, 'Certain Set Apart: The Western Island in the Irish Renaissance', *Studies*, Vol. 66, No. 264, Winter 1977, and Terence Brown, *Ireland: A Social and Cultural History 1922 – 79*, London: Fontana, 1981, Ch. 3.

11. J. M. Synge, *Collected Works, II (Prose)*, Alan Price (ed.), London: Oxford University Press, 1966, p. 283. Elsewhere Synge wrote that 'it is part of the misfortune of Ireland that nearly all the characteristics which give colour and attractiveness to Irish life are bound up with a social condition that is near to penury' (ibid., p. 286). Though frequently found in Irish culture, this theme is not by any means unique to Ireland as can be seen from the homiletic tone of an anthology devoted to the uplifting nature of poverty, *The Pleasures of Poverty*, Anthony Bertram (ed.), London: Hollis and Carter, 1950.

12. T. J. M. Sheehy, 'What Kind of Films Should We Make'?, *Irish Cinema Handbook*, Dublin: Parkside Press, 1943, p. 54. A facility for

finding beauty in poverty and slum districts was also a characteristic
feature of the British documentary movement associated with John
Grierson. 'Can we romanticise our industrial scene,' Grierson asks,
'when we know that our men work brutally and starve ignobly in it? . . .
We might make an English cinema . . . if we could only send our creators
back to fact. Not only to the old·fact of the countryside which our poets
have already honoured, but to the new fact of industry and commerce and
plenty and poverty which no poet has honoured at all.' ('Flaherty', in
Grierson on Documentary, Forsyth Hardy (ed.), London: Faber and Faber,
1979, pp. 30, 32).

13. Erwin Panofsky, '*Et in Arcadia Ego*: Poussin and the Elegiac
Tradition', in *Meaning in the Visual Arts*, New York: Doubleday Anchor
Books, 1955, p. 298. Panofsky derived this distinction from A. O.
Lovejoy's and G. Boas's pioneering work, *Primitivism and Related Ideas in
Antiquity*, Baltimore, 1935.

14. Ibid., p. 297.

15. Ibid.

16. W. B. Yeats, *Essays and Introductions*, London: Macmillan, 1961,
p. 299.

17. Jean-Jacques Rousseau, 'A Discourse on the Origin of Inequality',
in *The Social Contract and Discourses*, trans. G. D. M. Cole, London: J. M.
Dent, 1975, p. 83. For an interesting discussion of some forerunners of
Rousseau in literature, see James Turner, *The Politics of Landscape*,
Oxford: Basil Blackwell, 1979, pp. 164 – 8.

18. See David Schrire, 'Evasive Documentary', *Cinema Quarterly*,
Autumn 1934, pp. 7 – 9. Comparisons with Rousseau feature regularly in
descriptions of Flaherty's work, as in Siegfried Kracauer's reference to
Flaherty's 'Rousseauan conviction that primitive cultures are the last
vestiges of unspoiled human nature.' (Siegfried Kracauer, *Theory of Film*,
Oxford: Oxford University Press, 1960, p. 247).

19. John C. Messenger, 'Man of Aran Revisited', *University Review*,
Vol. III, No. 9, p. 45.

20. Macardle, *Irish Press*.

21. Bruno Snell, 'Arcadia: The Discovery of a Spiritual Landscape', in
The Discovery of the Mind: The Greek Origins of European Thought, trans. T. G.
Rosenmeyer, New York: Harper and Row, 1960, pp. 301, 293.

22. Peter Marinelli, *Pastoral*, London: Methuen, 1971, p. 6. Marinelli
contrasts this with 'classic pastoral' which corresponds roughly to soft
primitivism.

23. Frances Hubbard Flaherty, *Odyssey of a Film Maker*, Princeton, New
Jersey: Beta Phi Mu Chapooks, 1960 (cited in Christopher Williams,
Realism and the Cinema, London: British Film Institute, 1980, p. 90).

24. Macardle, *Irish Press*.

25. G. F. Dalton, 'The Irish Film', *Ireland Today*, Vol. 4, September
1936, p. 64.

26. Ivor Montagu, Review of *Man of Aran* in *New Statesman and Nation*,
April 28, 1934, p. 638.

27. See, for example, Patrick Carey's comment on his film *Errigal*
(1968) which celebrates the beauty of the Donegal mountain of that name:
'The mountains are the characters in the story. The drama is in the battle

of the elements. I have tried to convey this feeling of personality in a land-scape by picture, supported only by music and natural sound.' (Quoted in Liam Miller, 'Yeats Country', *Ireland of the Welcomes*, Vol. 17, No. 3, August–September 1968, p. 20.)

28. Raymond Immerwahr, ' "Romantic" and its Cognates in England, Germany and France before 1790', in Hans Eichner (ed.), *Romanticism and its Cognates: The European History of a Word*, Manchester: Manchester University Press, 1972, p. 33.

29. Lady Morgan, *The Wild Irish Girl: A National Tale*, New York: P. M. Haverty, 1872 (first published 1806), Vol. 1, p. 30.

30. Ibid., p. 91.

31. Ibid., pp. 84, 85, 88 (my italics).

32. Ibid., p. 82.

33. Cited in Dudley Young, *Out of Ireland: The Poetry of W. B. Yeats*, Cheadle, Cheshire: Carcanet Books, 1975, p. 57.

34. Lady Morgan, *Wild Irish Girl*, Vol. 2, pp. 27–8, 36.

35. Ibid., Vol. 1, p. 191.

36. Perry Millar, *Errand into the Wilderness*, Cambridge, Massachussets: The Belknap Press of Harvard University Press, 1956, p. 185. (Cited in Bryan Jay Wolf's brilliant analysis of American romanticism, *Romantic Re-Vision: Culture and Consciousness in Nineteenth-Century American Painting and Literature*, Chicago and London: University of Chicago Press, 1982, p. 37.)

37. Sanford Robinson Gifford, cited in Barbara Novak, *Nature and Culture: American Landscape and Painting 1825–1875*, London: Thames and Hudson, 1980, p. 152 (my italics). Along with Wolf's study, Novak's book is an invaluable survey of American romanticism.

38. Ibid., p. 149.

39. Ibid., p. 152.

40. 'Nature', in *Selections from Ralph Waldo Emerson*, Stephen E. Whicher (ed.), Boston: Houghton Mifflin, 1957, p. 24.

41. Cited in Young, *Out of Ireland*, p. 92.

42. See Elizabeth Bowen, *Bowen's Court and Seven Winters*, London: Virago Press, 1984 (first published 1942), p. 15: 'It will have been seen that this is a country of ruins . . . ruins feature the landscape — uplands or river valleys — and . . . give clearings in woods, reaches of mountain or sudden turns of road a meaning and pre-inhabited air . . . Only major or recent ruins keep their human stories; from others the story quickly evaporates. Some ruins show gashes of violence, others simply the dull slant of decline.'

43. Thomas Flanagan, *The Irish Novelists 1800–1850*, Westport, Connecticut: Greenwood Press, 1976 reprint of original 1959 edition, p. 123.

44. 'Irish Bardic History', in *Standish O'Grady: Selected Essays and Passages*, Dublin: Talbot Press, n.d., pp. 28, 26–7.

45. Yeats, *Essays and Introductions*, p. 349. Comparing Greek and Irish legends, Yeats wrote that we in Ireland have 'legends which surpass, as I think, all legends but theirs in wild beauty, and in our own land, as in theirs, there is no river or mountain that is not associated in the memory with some event or legend' (ibid., p. 205).

46. Richard Ellmann, *Yeats: The Man and the Masks*, London: Macmillan, 1949, p. 165. I have analysed some of the differences between Irish and American romanticism in my article 'Synge, Country and Western: The Myth of the West in Irish and American culture', in Chris Curtin, Mary Kelly and Liam O'Dowd (eds), *Culture and Ideology in Ireland*, Galway: Galway University Press, 1984.

47. Michael Booth, 'Irish Landscape in the Victorian Theatre', in Andrew Carpenter (ed.), *Place, Personality and the Irish Writer*, Gerrard's Cross: Colin Smythe, 1977, p. 160.

48. Ibid., p. 164–5. (From the introduction to N. P. Willis and J. Stirling Coyne, *The Scenery and Antiquities of Ireland*, London: 1846, I, iii.)

49. Allardyce Nicoll, *A History of English Drama 1666–1900: Vol. 5, Late Nineteenth Century Drama 1850–1900*, Cambridge: Cambridge University Press, 1959, p. 85.

50. Annelise Truninger writes that 'psychological rather than external characterization' was 'taken up and brought to perfection by Dion Boucicault' (*Paddy and the Paycock*, Berne: Francke Verlag, 1976, p. 51. See also pp. 54–5). According to Frank Rahill, what distinguishes Myles in *The Colleen Bawn* is that for the first time the peasant character 'develops as a personality in the course of the action' (*The World of Melodrama*, University Park and London: Pennsylvania State University Press, 1967, p. 189).

51. Cited in Robert Hogan, *Dion Boucicault*, New York: Twayne, 1969, p. 81. On Boucicault's treatment of the rural poor, see Truninger, *Paddy and the Paycock*, p. 59.

52. Cited in A. Nicholas Vardac, *Stage to Screen: Theatrical Method from Garrick to Griffith*, Cambridge: Harvard University Press, 1949, pp. 41–2.

53. Ibid., p. 53.

54. Dion Boucicault, 'The Shaughraun', in *The Dolmen Boucicault*, David Krause (ed.), Dublin: Dolmen Press, 1964, pp. 210–17.

55. Dion Boucicault, 'Arrah-na-Pogue', in Krause, *Dolmen Boucicault*, p. 115.

56. Rahill, *World of Melodrama*, p. 184.

57. Vardac, *Stage to Screen*, p. 44.

58. This is not to say, of course, that racialist schemes based on biological considerations cannot be successfully challenged and overthrown. On this point, see Homi Bhabha, 'The Other Question: the Stereotype and Colonial Discourse', *Screen*, Vol. 24, No. 6, Nov.–Dec. 1983.

59. 'Pogue' means 'kiss' in the Irish language.

60. Krause, *Dolmen Boucicault*, p. 150.

61. Edith Somerville and Martin Ross, 'Children of the Captivity', in *Some Irish Yesterdays*, London: Longman, Green, 1936, p. 244.

62. Dion Boucicault, 'The Colleen Bawn', in Krause, *Dolmen Boucicault*, p. 64. On the use of the brogue in Boucicault, see Krause, pp. 29–32, and two valuable articles on the playwright: Stephen M. Watt, 'Boucicault and Whitbread: The Dublin Stage at the End of the Nineteenth Century', *Eire–Ireland*, Vol. 18, No. 3, Fall 1983, pp. 23–43, and James Malcolm Nelson, 'From Rory and Paddy to Boucicault's Myles, Shaun and Conn: The Irishman on the London Stage 1830–1860', *Eire–Ireland*, Vol. 13, No. 3, Fall 1978, pp. 91ff.

63. Krause, *Dolmen Boucicault*, p. 73.

64. For a sustained and influential critique of Rousseau's attempts to naturalise language, see Jacques Derrida, *Of Grammatology*, trans. Gayatri Chakravorty Spivak, London & Baltimore: Johns Hopkins University Press, 1977, part II.

65. For some interesting comments on the linguistic basis — and extravagance — of Irish humour, see George Townshend, 'Irish Humour', in *The Genius of Ireland and Other Essays*, Dublin: Talbot Press, 1930.

66. J. M. Synge, 'The Playboy of the Western World, in *Collected Works, IV (Plays)*, Ann Saddlmyer (ed.), London: Oxford University Press, p. 153.

67. Charles Maturin, Dedication to *The Milesian Chief*, New York and London: Garland Publishing, 1979 (originally published 1812), p. v.

68. Georg Lukacs, *The Historical Novel*, trans. Hannah and Stanley Mitchell, Harmondsworth: Penguin, 1976, Ch. 1.

69. For a discussion of the way in which the Irish historical novel deviates from Lukacs' 'model', see James Cahalan, *Great Hatred, Little Room: The Irish Historical Novel*, Dublin: Gill and Macmillan, 1984.

70. Krause, *Dolmen Boucicault*, p. 238.

71. L. P. Curtis Jr., *Anglo Saxons and Celts: A Study of Anti-Irish Prejudice in Victorian England*, Bridgeport, Connecticut: Conference on British Studies, 1968, p. 51.

72. Ibid., p. 55. Mrs S. C. Hall borrows the paradox from Thomas Moore's poem 'Erin! The Smile and the Tear in Thine Eyes'.

73. Vardac, *Stage to Screen*, pp. 25 – 31. My discussion of Boucicault's contribution to the prehistory of cinema is greatly indebted to Vardac's pioneering work and also to John L. Fell's account of Boucicault in *Film and the Narrative Tradition*, Norman, Oklahoma: University of Oklahoma Press, 1974, pp. 18 – 22.

74. Cited in Anthony Slide, 'The Colleen Bawn', *Vision*, Vol. 3, No. 2, Spring 1967, p. 22.

75. Walter Benjamin, 'The Work of Art in the Age of Mechanical Reproduction', in *Illuminations*, trans. Harry Zohn, London: Collins/Fontana, p. 239.

76. Hogan, *Dion Boucicault*, p. 83.

77. Krause, *Dolmen Boucicault*, p. 81.

78. Brandon French, 'The Joys of Marriage: *The Quiet Man*', in *On the Verge of Revolt: Women in American Films of the Fifties*, New York: Frederick Ungar, 1978, p. 16; Marilyn Campbell, 'The Quiet Man', *Wide Angle*, Vol. 2, No. 4, p. 45.

79. Aidan Pender, *'Hand of Maestro in The Quiet Man'*, *Evening Herald*, 17 May 1952, p. 4.

80. *New York Daily Tribune* (March 30 1860) could also single out for particular praise the 'beautifully appropriate' stage-sets of 'The Lakes of Killarney' and 'The Gap of Dunloe', during its première in New York (Vardac, *Stage to Screen*, p. 43).

81. Anon., 'An Eye on the U.S. Market', *Irish Independent*, 19 May 1952, p. 8. For a valuable discussion of the conflict between 'spectacle' and the flow of the narrative in depictions of landscape in cinema, see Andrew Higson, 'Space, Place, Spectacle', *Screen*, Vol. 25, Nos. 4 – 5, July – October 1984.

82. See George Levine, 'High and Low: Ruskin and the Novelists', in U. C. Knoepflmacher and G. B. Tennyson, *Nature and the Victorian Imagination*, Berkeley: University of California Press, 1977.

83. Cited in 'The Heroic Energy of Cuchulain', editorial in *Apollo*, October 1966, p. 259.

84. Lindsay Anderson, 'The Quiet Man', *Sight and Sound*, Vol. 22, No. 1, July–September 1952, p. 25.

85. See Dave Lusted, ' "The Searchers" and the Study of the Image', *Screen Education*, No. 17, Autumn 1975, p. 25; Andrew Sarris, *The John Ford Movie Mystery*, London: Secker and Warburg, 1976, p. 173.

86. Joseph McBride and Michael Wilmington, *John Ford*, London: Secker and Warburg, 1974, p. 123.

87. Cited in Umberto Eco, *A Theory of Semiotics*, Bloomington and London: Indiana University Press, 1976, p. 69.

88. Panofsky, in *Meaning in the Visual Arts*, p. 312.

89. Cited in Derrida, *Of Grammatology*, p. 253.

90. Gordon Gow, 'Ryan's Daughter', *Films and Filming*, Vol. 17, No. 5, February 1971, p. 48.

91. Nigel Andrews, 'Ryan's Daughter', *Monthly Film Bulletin*, Vol. 38, No. 444, January 1971, p. 13.

92. See Conor Cruise O'Brien's review of Seamus Deane's collection of essays, *Celtic Revivals*, in *The Observer*, 18 August 1985, p. 18.

93. Cited in Booth, in *Place, Personality and the Irish Writer*, p. 166.

94. Rev. Thomas N. Burke, 'The History of Ireland, as Told in Her Ruins', in *Lectures on Faith and Fatherland*, London: Burns, Oates & Washbourne, n.d., pp. 78–9 (my emphasis).

95. The best short account of the fusion between antiquarianism, cultural nationalism and the separatist tradition is in Oliver MacDonagh, *States of Mind*, London: George Allen & Unwin, 1983, pp. 108–13. See also F. S. L. Lyons, *Culture and Anarchy in Ireland 1890–1939*, Oxford: Clarendon Press, 1979, Ch. 2.

96. Though quintessentially Sirkian in tone, it is interesting to note that these sentiments are taken almost word for word from the novel on which the film was based, W. R. Burnett, *Captain Lightfoot*, New York: Alfred A. Knopf, 1954, p. 23. In his comments on the filming of *Captain Lightfoot*, Sirk makes a revealing throwaway remark: 'When we started shooting we were standing in one of those things you must know very well, having lived in Ireland — an Irish ruin.' (Jon Halliday, *Sirk on Sirk*, London: Secker & Warburg in association with the British Film Institute, 1971, p. 104.)

97. Kathleen Rowland, 'Fast-Moving Tale of Ireland's days of Trouble', *Universe*, 29 May 1959, p. 15.

98. Donat O'Donnell, 'Beauty and Belfast: A Note on *Odd Man Out*', *The Bell*, Vol. 14, No. 2, May 1947, p. 57.

99. Ibid., p. 61.

100. Michaeleen's attitude to the work ethic is shared by the barman in Cohans who, on hearing the crowd gather for the final Donnybrook, exclaims: 'Oh what a day for industry! On a day like this I can say only one thing — Gentlemen! Drinks are on the house.'

101. J. J. Lee, 'Women and the Church Since the Famine', in Margaret

MacCurtain and Donncha O Corráin (eds), *Women in Irish Society: the Historical Dimension*, Dublin: Arlen House/The Women's Press, 1978, pp. 38–9.

102. Campbell, p. 47. As against this, however, Campbell notes astutely that 'The Ireland depicted in *The Quiet Man* is anything but a natural state' (p. 45).

103. Anderson, 'The Quiet Man', p. 25.

104. For Christian Metz it is the mutual recognition of actors and audience in theatre, as in the final bow, which prevents theatre from relapsing into the kind of voyeurism which characterises the detached spectator in the cinema: 'The cinema's voyeurism must (of necessity) do without any very clear mark of consent on the part of the object [of the audience's attention]. There is no equivalent here of the theatre actors' final ''bow''.' (C. Metz, *Psychoanalysis and Cinema: The Imaginary Signifier*, London: Macmillan, 1982, p. 63.) It is as if, unlike the visiting bishop, the audience in *The Quiet Man* are not treated as outsiders but are let in on the act, sharing the secret of the masquerade.

105. See Heaney's remarkable poem 'Bogland' in *Door into the Dark*, London: Faber and Faber, 1969. Heaney's exploration of bogland as a metaphor for Irish history is a central theme in his next collection of poems, *North*, London: Faber and Faber, 1975.

106. As the press kit which accompanied the film on its release expresses it: '*Eat the Peach* is a film about losers who are authentic heroes. The wall is a metaphor for an attempt to assert identity and to express individuality. The film is about a search for a sense of freedom and resilient courage . . .'

107. See pp. 196–7 above.

108. According to S. J. Connolly, the success of marriage customs such as those involving Strawboys derived from the sinister manner in which 'they combined a request for hospitality or gifts with an element — sometimes symbolic but in other cases all too real — of menace and hostility' (S. J. Connolly, 'Marriage in pre-Famine Ireland', in A. Cosgrove (ed.), *Marriage in Ireland*, Dublin: College Press, 1985, p. 94). As we have seen, it is precisely this precarious juxtaposition of hospitality with violence which characterises communal identity in Irish romanticism.

109. See Mary Helen Thuente, *W. B. Yeats and Irish Folklore*, Dublin: Gill and Macmillan, 1980, esp. Chs. 1 and 2.

110. In Metz's psychoanalytic terminology, 'The subterranean persistence of the exclusive relation to the mother, desire as a pure effect of lack and endless pursuit . . . All this is undoubtedly reactivated by the play of that *other mirror*, the cinema screen, in this respect a veritable psychical substitute . . .' (Christian Metz, *Psychoanalysis and Cinema*, p. 4). For Metz the failure to distinguish between the imaginary and the real on the screen is analogous to a reversion to a pre-Oedipal fusion with the mother.

111. In an earlier scene, George tells a joke to Mary about an inebriated woman who woke up in a confessional box thinking she was in the snug of a public house rather than in a church. Mary is not amused at George's humour, as if anticipating that the joke will be on her.

112. In 1795, Wolfe Tone, Henry Joy McCracken, Thomas Russell

and a number of other members of the republican United Irishman climbed to the summit of Cave Hill where 'surveying the vast panorama that stretches in every direction . . . they "took a solemn obligation . . . never to desist in our efforts, until we have subverted the authority of England over our country, and asserted her independence" ' (Mary McNeill, *The Life and Times of Mary Ann McCracken*, Dublin: Allen Figgis, 1960, p. 105). For a wide-ranging discussion which seeks to relate the representation of landscape in *Maeve* to developments in contemporary avant-garde cinema, see Paul Willemen, 'An Avant Garde for the Eighties', *Framework*, no. 24, Spring 1984.

113. For a more extended discussion of *Maeve*, see Claire Johnston, '*Maeve*: Interview with Pat Murphy', *Screen*, Vol. 22, No. 4, 1981, and my article ' "Lies That Tell the Truth": *Maeve*, History and Irish Cinema', *The Crane Bag*, Vol. 7, No. 2, 1983.

114. Discussing the associations between the landscape of Co. Wicklow and the guerrilla leader Michael Dwyer, one of Emmet's co-conspirators, James Plunkett, writes: 'At the farthest end of the glen, just across the river, the ruins of a cottage are another reminder of Dwyer. A woman lived there who had the habit now and then, of coming out onto the roadway in front to comb her hair. If she did so, the look-out post high up the mountain knew the military were up to something and took precautions.' (*The Gems She Wore: A Book of Irish Places*, London: Arrow, 1978, p. 78.)

115. I discuss *Anne Devlin* at a greater length in 'The Politics of Silence: *Anne Devlin*, Women and Irish Cinema', *Framework*, Nos. 30–31, 1986.

116. Edward Said, *Orientalism*, London: Routledge and Kegan Paul, 1980, p. 59.

117. Wallace Stevens, 'Mr. Burnshaw and the Statue', in *Opus Posthumous*, New York: Alfred A. Knopf, 1957, p. 48.

Bibliography

Cinema and Theatre Annual Review and Directory of Ireland 1947, Dublin: The Parkside Press, 1947

Fr Richard Devane, SJ (ed.), *Irish Cinema Handbook*, Dublin: The Parkside Press, 1943

Martin Dolan, *The Irish National Cinema and its Relationship to Irish Nationalism*, Ann Arbor, Michigan: Xerox University Microfilms, 1979 (Ph.D. thesis)

Green on the Screen, Dublin: Irish Film Institute, 1984 (booklet)

Louis Marcus, *The Irish Film Industry*, Dublin: The Irish Film Society, 1967 (booklet)

Liam O'Laoghaire, *Invitation to the Film*, Tralee: The Kerryman, 1945

Liam O'Leary, *Cinema Ireland 1895–1976*, Dublin: Dublin Arts Festival, 1976 (booklet)

Proceedings of the Public Hearing of Bord Scannán na hÉireann/Irish Film Board, Dublin: Irish Film Board, 1982 (booklet)

Proinsias Ó Conluain, *Ár Scannáin Féin*, Dublin: Foilseacháin Náisiunta Teoranta, 1954 (booklet)

——, *Scéal na Scannán*, Dublin: Oifig an tSoláthair, 1953

Report of the Film Industry Committee, Dublin: The Stationery Office, 1968 (booklet)

Kevin Rockett, *Film and Ireland: A Chronicle*, Dublin: A Sense of Ireland, 1980 (booklet)

Index

Abbey Players 96, 104–5, 106–7
Abbey Theatre 17, 24, 38, 45, 79, 96, 98, 103–11, 212
ABC 84, 114
Abraham, J. Johnston 59
Acceptable Levels 140
After Dark 214
Afton, Richard 101
Age of de Valera, The 90
Aiken, Frank 61, 81–2, 88, 97
Aiséirghe 76
Alexander, Frances 25
Alfie 112
Algar, Michael 120
Allgood, Sara 59
Algongin Trilogy, The 125n59
Allen, Ira 37
Allen, Ted 113
Alpha Picture Company 7
Altman, Robert 114, 243
Ambush in Leopard Street 114, 123n19
Amharc Éireann (A View of Ireland) 86
Anderson, Kevin 121
Anderson, Lindsay 225, 239
Anderson, Michael 111
Andrews, Nigel 229, 255n91
Androcles and the Lion 96
Angel 119, 125n59, 178–81, 184
Anglo-Irish Treaty 16, 29, 30, 38, 39, 40, 42, 63, 88, 127, 167, 168
Anne Devlin 121, 125n59, 140, 143, 247–8
Annes Lumières, Les (Light Years Away) 114
Another Shore 111
Anti-Partition of Ireland League 82, 158
Aran Islands 71–2, 195, 200–3
'Arcadian Shepherds, The' 226
Arden, John 137–8
Ardmore Studios 98–114, 168
Ardmore Studios International

(1972) 102
Armstrong, Kathleen 41
Army film unit 80
Arrah-na-Pogue 8, 9, 213, 214, 215, 219, 220
Art of Reception, The 92n24
Arts Act (1973) 128
Arts Council 116, 121, 128, 129, 135
Ascendancy 191n68
Ashe, Thomas 21
Assassin, The 186n15
Associated Communications Corporation 172
Association of Cinematograph, Television and Allied Technicians (ACTT) 100–1, 124n47
Association of Independent Film-Makers 116
Association of Independent Producers of Ireland 116, 117, 119, 120
Astaire, Fred 198
At a Dublin Inn 111
At the Cinema Palace: Liam O'Leary 48n44, 125n59
Atlantean 125n59
Attracta 125n59, 193n83
ATV 172
Auxiliaries (see Black and Tans)

Bairéad, Colm 129
Baker, Robert S. 113
Ballad in Blue 100
Bank Holiday 45
Barr, Charles 152
Barry, David 73
Barry, Tony 122
Barthes, Roland 205
Bates, Paul 121
Battleship Potemkin, The 50n91
Baxter, Anne 228
Baxter, John 58
Beatty, Robert 155, 165

Begley, Ed 168
Behan, Brendan 112, 192n76
Bell, Tom 168
Beloved Enemy 195, 196
Ben Hur 7 – 8
Benet, Marianne 166, 231
Benjamin, Walter 196 – 7, 221
Bennett, Paul 244
Bergin, Emmet 136
Berman, Monty 113
Berwick Street Collective 193n85
Bewitched Castle 5
Bhabha, Homi 253n58
Big Birthday, The 107
Binstock, Judah 101
Bioscope, The 23
Birmingham, George 57
Birth of a Nation, The 19, 23
Black and Tans 13, 27 – 8,
  42 – 4, 62, 63, 65, 68,
  108 – 10, 165, 177
Black, Cathal 130, 131, 136,
  243, 249
Black, Donald Taylor 48n44,
  49 – 50n84
Blarney 57 – 8
Blarney Stone, The 57
Blue Lamp, The 152
Blue Max, The 113
Blythe, Ernest 40, 98, 105
Boas, G. 251n13
Bodenstown Film, The 33
Boer War 42
Bogarde, Dirk 160
'Bogland' 256n105
Bohemian Cinema, Dublin 14,
  17, 27
Bold Emmet, Ireland's Martyr 8, 9
Bonar Law 34
Bond, Ward 240
Boorman, John 102, 114, 118,
  119, 120, 178
Booth, Michael 210
Bord Fáilte (Irish Tourist Board)
  85, 90
Borzage, Frank 55
Boucicault, Dion 8, 9, 54, 206,
  212 – 21, 227, 229, 240, 241,
  253n50,n51,n62
Bowen, Elizabeth 208, 252n42
Box, Muriel 108

Boyd's Shop 98, 107
Boyne Cinema, Drogheda 35 – 6
Brambell, Wilfred 189n47
Breatnach, Séan Bán 138
Breen, Dan 96 – 7
Brennan, Brid 247
Brennan, Jimmy 131, 244
Brennan, Stephen 242
Brief Encounter 152, 235
Brien, Oliver 35
British Army 11, 13, 27, 30,
  32 – 3, 35, 60 – 1, 137, 171,
  172
British Cinema 147 – 84
Broadcasting Authority Act
  (1960) 118
Brogan, Harry 82, 106, 107, 108
Brooke, Rupert 53
Broth of a Boy 107
Brown, Terence 58, 250n10
Browne, Noel 77, 80
Bruton, John 120
Burger, Germain 57
Burke, Fr Thomas 233
Burnett, W. R. 255n96
Business Development Scheme
  122
By Accident 45, 72
Byrne, Catherine 243
Byrne, David 133
Byrne, Donn 57
Byrne, Dorothea Donn 57
Byrne, Sir W. P. 15 – 16, 35

Caffrey, Peter 136
Cagney, James 111, 165 – 6, 231
Cahalan, James 254n69
Cal 125n57, 181 – 4
Cambrensis, Giraldus 148
Campa 76
Campbell, Daisy 43
Campbell, Marilyn 254n78,
  256n102
Cannes Film Festival 85
Caoineadh Airt Ui Laoire (Lament
  for Art O'Leary) 137 – 9, 140
Capallology 86
Capitol Cinema, Dublin 51, 63
Capitol Tiller Girls 51
Captain Boycott 111, 175 – 6, 232
Captain Lightfoot 232, 234, 255n96

Cardiff, Jack 111
Carey, Patrick 84, 114, 251n27
Carleton, William 24–8
Carlton Cinema, Dublin 67
Carpenter, Andrew 253n47
Carr, Kathleen 41
Carr Lett, L. G. 79
Carre, J. M. 17, 19
Carstairs, John Paddy 113
Carty, Ciaran 129
Casey Millions, The 40–1
Casino Cinemas 68
Castlereagh, Lord 12, 14
Catholic Church 10, 22, 40, 51,
    53, 136, 142
Catholic Emancipation
    Centenary celebrations 51
Catholic Film Society, London 64
Cattle Drive to Galway, A 7
Caught in a Free State 90
Cauldwell, Brendan 139
Cause of Ireland, The 193n85
Cave Hill 234, 236, 247,
    257n112
Cellier, Antoinette 60
Censorship of Films Act (1923)
    36, 40, 55
Censorship of Films
    (Amendment) Act (1930) 52
Censorship of Films Appeal
    Board 59
Chaffey, Don 113
Channel Four 119, 122, 125n57
Chaplin, Charlie 58
Chapman, David 131
Chesterfield, Lord 25
Chief Secretary for Ireland 35–6
Christian   Brothers   136
Christie,   Julie   177
Cinema   Action   193n85
Cinematograph Act (1928) 39, 57
Civil War 30, 39, 42, 86, 88,
    99, 110, 167
Clancy, Nora 17, 18, 104
Clann na Poblachta 76–81
Clark, Petula 198
Clarke, Jack 9, 12, 223
Clarke, Mrs 9
Clarke, Thomas J. 33, 49n63
Clarke-Clifford, C. 45
Cleary, Fr Michael 85

Colleen Bawn, The 8, 10, 31, 34,
    213, 215, 216, 220, 221, 223,
    228–9, 253n50
Collins, David 121
Collins, Michael 24, 29, 30,
    109–10, 169
Collins, Michael (exhibitor) 114
Comerford, Joe 116, 131,
    132–3, 140, 249
Communist Party of Ireland 79
Connolly, James 156
Connolly, S. J. 256n108
Connor, Rearden 188n36
Conscription Bill 21–2
Cookson, Catherine 107
Cooper, Tom 62–8
Corcoran, Vincent 102
Corinthian Cinema, Dublin 43,
    56
Cork Film Festival 86, 88, 110,
    116, 118
Cormac OFM, Fr 97
Cosgrave, Liam 81
Cosgrave, William T. 21, 44,
    54, 88
Country Girls, The 125n59
Coutard, Raoul 85
Covington, Julie 191n68
Cox, Arthur 96
Coyne, J. Stirling 253n48
Cradle of Genius 124n30
Crichton, Charles 111
Criminal Conversation 136
Crosby, Bing 102
Cross, Robin 160
Crowe, Eileen 57, 83
Cruiskeen Lawn 41
Cu Uladh 52
Cullinane, Patrick 43
Cultural Relations Committee
    81, 84
Curran, Eileen 67
Curran, Sarah 13
Curtin, Chris 253n46
Curtis, Liz 250n3
Curtis, L. P. 218, 249
Cusack, Cyril 55, 61, 129, 159,
    165, 236
Customs House, Dublin 42, 75

Dáil Éireann 16, 28–9, 30, 36,

72, 73, 81, 99, 103, 115 – 18
Dalton, Audrey 109
Dalton, Emmet 98 – 100, 104 – 11
Dalton, Geoffrey 68, 203
D'Alton, Louis 105, 108 – 10, 124n40
Dalton Productions, Emmet 107
Dance School 76
Dancers of Arran 72
Davidson, J. N. G. (Norris) 45, 72, 73
Davies, John 139, 140
Davis, Desmond 112
Davis, Lee 101 – 2
Davis, Thomas 74
Davison, Philip 136
Dawn, The 62 – 6, 95
Days of Hope 158
Deane, Seamus 255n92
Dearden, Basil 160, 162, 177
De Buitléar, Eamon 85
De Clerq, Louis 6
De Felice, James 157
Defence of the Realm Losses Commission 16
Delany, Maureen 57
Delaney, Maureen 232
Delfont, Bernard 171
De Mandeville, Bernard 239
Department of Agriculture 92n23
Department of Education 73
Department of External Affairs 81 – 2
Department of Foreign Affairs 84 – 5
Department of Health 81
Department of Industry and Commerce 96, 98, 99 – 100, 115, 120 – 1
Department of Local Government 80
Department of the Taoiseach 89, 96, 121
Dermody, Frank 97
De Rochemont, Louis 65
Derrida, Jacques 254n64
Desecration 130
Destiny Bay 57
De Valera, Eamon 13, 21, 22, 35, 58, 64, 71 – 2, 76, 80,

96 – 7, 99, 110, 203
Devane S.J., Fr Richard S. 96
Devilled Crab 5
Devil's Agent, The 113, 123n19
Devil's Rock 57
Devlin, Alan 132
Devoy, John 33
Dewhurst, George 42
Director, The 57
Dirrane, Maggie 72
Dirty Harry 173
Doctor O'Dowd 57
Dolan, James 44
Dolan, Michael 57
Donaldson, Arthur 11
Donnelly, Deirdre 136
Donovan, Judy 132
Dowling, Vincent 107
Down the Corner 116, 131, 136 – 7
Downes, Bernie 248
Doyle, Eric 82
Doyle, Tony 243
Driefuss, Arthur 112
Dublin 3 – 6, 75, 77, 81, 83, 90, 112, 116, 128, 131 – 2, 141 – 2, 143, 154, 165, 234
Dublin Amateur Film Society 51
Dublin Castle 15 – 16, 35 – 6
Dublin Film Productions Management 98
Dublin Little Theatre Guild 68
Dublin Theatre and Television Productions 98
Duke of Bedford 27
Dunne, Lee 112
Durgnat, Raymond 161 – 2, 175
Dwyer, Michael 257n114

Eades, W. 114
Eady finance 100 – 1
Ealing 160
Early Bird, The 57
Easter Rising 1916 13, 16, 17, 21, 27, 33, 36, 43, 44, 59, 83, 89, 90, 136 – 7, 177
Eat the Peach 122, 241 – 2, 256n106
Eco, Umberto 255n87
Economic Co-operation Administration 82
Edwards, Henry 57

Edwards, Hilton 61, 94n43
Eichner, Hans 252n28
Eldridge, Michael 73
Eleventh Hour, The 18
Elliman, Abe 98
Elliman, Louis 98–100
Ellis, Brendan 130
Ellmann, Richard 6, 210
Elsaesser, Thomas 150–1, 153, 185n11
Elstree 60, 62, 64, 68, 77, 78, 79, 91
Emerson, Ralph Waldo 208, 210, 227
EMI 171–2
Emmet Dalton Remembers 123n14
Emmet, Robert 8, 9, 12–13, 257n114
Empire Marketing Board 44
Empire Marketing Board Film Unit 72
Empire Palace, Dublin 5
Empire Palace, London 3
Empire Theatre, Dublin 21
Enter Inspector Duvall 114, 123n19
Eppel, Dr Isaac 42–4
'Erin! The Tear and the Smile in Thine Eyes' 254n72
'Erin's Isle' 31
Errigal 251n27
Ervine, St. John 98, 107
ETU (I) 100
Eucharistic Congress 136
Excalibur 114, 119
Exposure 130, 135–6

Face of Fu Manchu, The 113
Fallon, Gabriel 67
Famine, The 13, 19, 22–3
Farmer, Thomas 102
Farrell, Michael 59
Farrell, M. J. 57, 113
Farrell, Paul 108
Fay, W. G. 153
Fell, John L. 254n73
Fenians, The 13, 18, 48n39, 65, 149
Festival of Film and Television in the Celtic Countries 119
Fianna Fáil 51, 52, 61, 63, 73–82, 88, 97, 110, 117

Fianna, Na 32–3
Fields, Gracie 59
Film Censor 36, 53, 55, 59, 112
Film Company of Ireland, The 7, 16–32, 36, 43, 104
Film in National Life, The 96
Film Industry Bill (1970) 115
Film Industry Committee 114–15
Film Script Award 121, 128, 130, 132, 133, 135
Fine Gael 88
Finian's Rainbow 198–9, 224, 227
Fintona: A Study of Housing Discrimination 81–2
First Great Train Robbery, The 114
First Paris Orphanage, The 5
Fisher, Terence 113
Fishing Village 76
Fitzcarraldo 243
Fitzgerald, Barry 57, 61, 107, 221
Fitzgerald, Jim 85
Fitzgerald, Michael 13
Fitzgibbon, Henry M. 16
Flaherty, Frances Hubbard 202
Flaherty, Robert 67, 71–3, 129, 202, 203, 206
Flanagan, Thomas 208
Fleá Ceoil 86
Fleischmann, George 81
Flight of the Doves 112
Flying Scud, The 214
Foley, Don 134
Food of Love 18
Foolsmate 68, 76
For Ireland's Sake 8, 9, 11
Ford, Cecil 67
Ford, John 17, 57, 59, 96, 111, 151, 154, 156, 176, 188n37, 196, 200, 226, 227, 236, 241
Ford's Cork Factory film 44
Foster, John Wilson 250n10
Foster, Preston 156
Four Roads — Ballinasloe, The 192n73
Fox Film Production Unit 55
Fox of Glenarvon, The 185n2
Freedland, George 84
Freedom to Die 123n19

French, Brandon 154n78
French poetic realism 152
Fricker, Brenda 134, 245
Friel, Brian 112
From Time to Time 98
Frontroom Productions 140
Fugitive, The 29

Gable, Clark 134, 245
Gael Linn 86 – 9, 94n43
Gaelic Athletic Association 75,
    80
Gaelic League 40, 52, 76, 89
Gageby, Douglas 85
Garnett, Tay 164 – 7
Garnett, Tony 158
Gate Theatre 61, 98
Gaumont Graphic 32, 34
Gaumont Studios 72
Gauntier, Gene 7 – 12, 223
General Film Supply 7, 33 – 8
General John Regan 57
General Strike 158
George V 53
Gentle Gunman, The 160 – 4, 165,
    171, 175
Geraghty, Tom 57
German Expressionism 152
Gibson, Catherine 133
Gifford, Sanford Robinson
    252n37
Gilliat, Sidney 175
Ginger Man, The 112
Girl of Glenbeigh, A 18
Girl With Green Eyes 112
Gleeson, James 65
Gogarty, Oliver St John 52
Golden, Geoffrey 105, 107, 108
Goldwyn, Samuel 195
Goodbye to the Hill 112
Goretti, Maria 183 – 4
Gormley, Michael 134
Gow, Gordon 255n90
Grade, Lew 172
Grafton Cinema, Dublin 32 – 3,
    63
Granger, Stewart 175, 232
Grattan, Henry 12
Grattan, H. P. 230
Green, F. L. 155
Green for Ireland 90

Greene, Roger 92n23
Gregson, John 236
Grierson, John 76, 91n2,
    251n12
Griffith, Arthur 24
Griffith, D. W. 19, 29
Grigsby, Michael 193n85
Groves of Blarney 194
Guests of the Nation 60 – 2, 121
Guillermann, John 113
Guthrie, Kevin 59
Guy Called Caesar, A 123n19
Guyler, Deryck 189n47
Gypsies in Ireland 8

Haddick, Colonel Victor 56
Hall, James 53
Hall, Mrs S. C. 194, 218,
    254n72
Haller, Daniel 112
Halliday, Jon 255n96
Halligan, Liam 131
Hampshire, Susan 169
Hancock, Barbara 227
Handmade Films 172
Hangman's House 57
Hanson, Barry 172
Happy Ever After 152
Hard Day's Night, A 189n47
Harding, Gilbert 161
Harpur, Bill 102
Harpur, Joan 131
Harris, Julie 106
Hartnett, Noel 77
Hasson, Ann 134
Hathaway, Henry 112
Hawkins, Jack 177
Hayes, Tom 103, 114, 124n30
Hayward, Richard 56 – 7, 73,
    92n23
Healy, Gerard 80, 93 – 4n43
Heaney, Seamus 241, 256n105
Heelan, Louis 102, 114, 118, 119
Heffernan, Honor 178
Hegel, G. W. F. 206
Hennessy 171 – 4, 176, 179
Hennigan, Tom 106
Henry V 113
Heritage of Ireland, The 89
Heywood, Anne 165
Hibernia Films 66

Hickey, Kieran 93 – 4n43, 130, 135 – 6, 193n83
Hickey, Tom 130, 183
Higson, Andrew 254n81
Hilliard, Michael 88
Hitchcock, Alfred 53
Hogan, Bosco 135, 248
Hogan, Robert 221, 253n51
Hollister, George 8
Hollywood 31, 39, 45, 46, 51, 55, 59, 62, 64, 66, 68, 91, 124 – 5n47, 147 – 52, 153, 172, 178, 183, 195, 249
Home is the Hero 106 – 7
Home Rule 13
Hoskins, Bob 134, 174, 245
Hostage, The 192n76
Hounam, Donald 180
Houses of Parliament 28, 172
Howard, Trevor 176, 200
Hudson, Rock 232
Hughes, Hazel 58
Hughes, Ken 112
Hungry Hill 111
Hunt, Iris 81
Hunt, Peter 81
Hurley, John 57
Hurst, Brian Desmond 59 – 60, 111
Hussein, Warris 112
Huston, John 85, 102, 112, 113, 114, 124 – 5n47
Hyde, Douglas 197

I See A Dark Stranger 111, 175 – 6, 182
I Was Happy Here 112
Images 114
Immerwahr, Raymond 204
Imperial Conference 44
In the Days of St Patrick 37 – 8
Industrial Credit Company 99 – 101, 114, 118
Industrial Development Authority 81, 99
Informer (1929), The 59
Informer (1935), The 17, 59, 96, 154, 183, 185n11, 234
Inghinidhe na h.Éireann 32 – 3
Institute of Contemporary Arts 123n28

Insurrection 90
Invitation to the Film 76
Ireland 44 – 5
Ireland a Nation 12 – 16, 35
Ireland: A Television History 90
Ireland: Behind the Wire 193n85
Ireland-Rome 81
Ireland's Call to Arms 92n23
Ireland the Oppressed 8, 9, 31
Ireland: The Silent Voices 193n85
Irish Amateur Film Society 45
Irish-America 8 – 11, 13, 20, 43 – 4, 147 – 8, 154 – 5, 156 – 7
Irish and Proud of It 57
Irish Animated Picture Company 6, 33
Irish Cinema Handbook 95 – 6, 250n12
Irish Citizens Army 177
Irish Civic Films 77
Irish Congress of Trade Unions 102
Irish Destiny 42 – 4, 50n91
Irish Events 7, 33 – 6, 37, 86
Irish Film and Television Guild 116, 117, 120
Irish Film Board 115, 118 – 22, 178
Irish Film Board Act (1980) 118 – 19
Irish Film Board Bill (1979) 116 – 18
Irish Film Centre 121
Irish Film Finance Corporation 100 – 1, 113
Irish Film Institute 121
Irish Film Society 51, 68, 76, 79
Irish Film Theatre 129
Irish Film Workers Association 115, 116
Irish Films 125n59
Irish For Luck 57
Irish Hearts 59
Irish in America, The 8
Irish Jew, The 41
Irish Labour Party 28, 36, 118
Irish Legation, Washington 73
Irish Limelight 16, 17, 22, 28, 32, 34, 104
Irish National Film Unit 92n23

Irish Parliamentary Party 13, 21, 22
Irish People, The 18
Irish Pictorial Review 86
Irish Question, The 73–4
Irish Republican Army (IRA) 24, 29, 30, 40, 42–3, 60–6, 78, 88–9, 99, 108, 111, 112, 127, 152–84, 231, 235, 239
Irish Rising 1916 90
Irish Theatre Company 24
Irish Tourist Association 73
Irish Tourist Board 85, 90
Irish Transport and General Workers Union 102, 115, 116, 117
Irish Vendetta, An 48n39
Irish Volunteers 9–10, 24, 28, 34
Irish Wives and English Husbands 7
Irish Workers League 79
Irvine, Blanaid 108
Islandman, The 66–8
It's Handy When People Don't Die 139

Jackson, Mary 139, 246
Jackson, T. A. 26
Jacobs, Lewis 31–2
Jacqueline 236–7
Jameson, J. T. 33
Jamieson, Lucy 134
Jeffs, Fred 41
Jimmy Boy 58
John Bull's Other Island 108
John, Love 125n59
Johnny Nobody 112, 123n19
Johns, Glynis 166, 231
Johnson, Fred 61
Johnson, Richard 173
Johnson, Thomas 36
Johnson-Matthey Bank 103
Johnston, Denis 59, 60–2, 68, 71, 121
Johnston, Jennifer 121
Jolly, Professor 4–5
Jones, Christopher 230
Jordan, Neil 119, 132, 178–81
Joyce, Eileen 6
Joyce, Eva 5
Joyce, James 5–6, 112, 148

Joyce, John 6
Joyce, Stanislaus 6
Juno and the Paycock 53, 186n17
Justine, R. V. 17

Kalem Company 7–12, 31, 34, 220, 223
Karlin, Marc 140
Kavanagh, John 182
Kavanagh, Seamus 105
Kay, Kwesi 131
Kean, Marie 106
Keane, Eamonn 130, 133
Keane, Molly 57, 113
Kearney, Richard 179, 180, 181, 184, 187n24
Keating, Justine 102
Kee, Robert 90
Keegan, John 139, 247
Kellaway, Cecil 228
Kelleher, John 121
Kelly, Eamonn 141
Kelly, Gene 236
Kelly, Mary 253n46
Kennedy, Arthur 106
Kennerley, Peter 123n14
Kenney, James 160
Keogh, Garret 136, 139
Kerr, Deborah 175
Kerrigan, J. M. 17, 18, 56
Kerry Electric Company 62
Kerry Gow, The 31
Kew Bridge Studios 12
Kickham, Charles 18–23, 96
Killanin, Lord 114
Killarney 7, 204, 213, 220, 223, 229, 254n80
Killester Film Studio 37
King, 'Tiger' 72
King Oedipus 153
Kinkisha, The 130, 133
Kirwan, Kitty 157
Kirwan, Patrick 108
Kiss Tomorrow Goodbye 166
Knights of the Round Table, The 113
Knocknagow 18–23, 24, 28, 29, 30, 96
Knoepflmacher, U. C. 255n82
Knott, F. 55
Kracauer, Siegfried 251n18

Krause, D. 253n62

La Scala, Dublin 41
Labour Movement 21, 22
Lad From Old Ireland, The 8, 9,
  10–11, 23
Lady Gregory 104
Laffan, Pat 132
Lally, Mick 134, 244
Lalor, Leslie 136
Lament for Art O'Leary 137–9, 140
Land of Her Fathers 57
Land War 7, 19, 22–3, 48n39,
  175–6
Launder, Frank 111, 175
Laurimore, Jon 170
Laverty, Maura 76
Lawrence of Arabia 229
League of Gentlemen, The 177
Lean, David 113, 176, 196
Lebow, R. N. 149, 249n3
Lee, Joseph 90, 255n101
Legacy of the Land League, The 90
Lehners, John 124–5n47
Lemass, Sean 96–100, 106,
  110, 127, 168
Lennon, Peter 85
Leonard, Hugh 107, 120–1
Levine, George 255n82
Lewis, J. Gordon 37, 92n23
Lies My Father Told Me 113,
  123n19
Life of Michael Flaherty, The 73
Life of Saint Patrick, The 37
*Life on the Great Southern and
  Western Railway* 6
Light Years Away 114
Lily of Killarney 229
Lindgren, Ernest 158
Linehan, Fergus 85, 88, 110
Literary Revival 197, 212
Little and Company, Arthur D.
  116–17
Lives of a Bengal Lancer, The 53
Lloyd George, David 13
Loach, Ken 158
Loder, John 60
Lodge, John 60
Logue, Cardinal 37
London High Commissioner 42,
  44

London to Killarney 7
Lonely Girl, The 112
Long Good Friday, The 171–2,
  174–5
Look at Life 84
Love, George 14, 35
Lovejoy, A. O. 251n13
Lowrey, Dan 3–5
Lowry, Robert G. 195–6, 197
Luck of the Irish, The 56, 224,
  227–8, 239
Luckwell, Bill 114
Luckwell, Michael 114
Ludlow, Fitz Hugh 207
Lukacs, Georg 217
Lumière films 3–5
Luraschi, Tony 173
Lusted, Dave 255n85
Lynch, Barry 134
Lynch, Jack 89, 114
Lynch, John 181
Lyons, F. S. L. 255n95
Lysaght, W. J. 17

McAnally, Ray 105, 179, 184
Macardle, Dorothy 22, 71, 195,
  197, 202, 250n4
McArdle, John 133
McArdle, Tommy 130, 133, 139
McBride, Joseph 255n86
MacBride, Maud Gonne 66
MacBride, Sean 77–9, 81
MacBride, Tiernan 120
MacCaig, Arthur 193n85
McCann, Donal 129, 180
MacCann, Nuala 247
McCarty, Niall 123n14
MacConghail, Muiris 119–20
McConnell-Hartley 44
McCormack, John 55–6, 57
McCormick, F. J. 57, 153
McCracken, Henry Joy 256n112
McCracken, Mary Ann 256n112
MacCurtain, Margaret 256n101
MacDonagh, John 23–7, 29,
  30, 34, 40–2, 48n44
MacDonagh, Mrs 34
MacDonagh, Oliver 255n95
MacDonagh, Thomas 24, 34
MacDonnell, Barrett 40–1, 42
MacDougall, Roger 160

MacEntee, Sean 51, 78–80, 81, 86, 88
McEvoy, Michael 102
MacFarlane, Noel 131
MacGabhann, Liam 63, 66, 67, 75, 106
McGahern, John 130
MacGarvey, Cathal 43
McGilligan, Patrick 44, 189n43
McGinnis, Niall 60, 108, 175
MacGiolla, Tomás 138
MacGowan, J. P. 11
MacGowran, Jack 161, 239
McGrath, Cornelius P. 98
McGrath, Joseph 97
MacGreevy, Thomas 224
Macken, Walter 106, 112
McKenna, T. P. 135
MacKenzie, John 174
Mackintosh Man, The 112
McLaglen, Victor 199
MacLaverty, Bernard 181–4
McLaverty, Micheál 134
MacLiammóir, Micheal 57
McMinn, Joe 182
McNally, Hubert 101
McNally, Patrick 101
MacNamara, Barbara 133
MacNamara, Brinsley 57
MacNamara, Frances (née Alexander) 43
MacNamara, Walter 12–13
MacNeill, Eoin 40, 71
MacNeill, James 42, 44
Macpherson, James 206
McQuaid, Archbishop John Charles 97
Macready, General 27
MacSwiney, Terence 13
Madame Butterfly 8
Madden, Doreen 83
Maeve 139–40, 246–7, 257n113
Mahon, Sir Bryan 14–15
Mageean, Jimmy 56
Magowan, Brian 17, 18, 19, 25, 30, 43
Making of the Land League, The 90
Man of Aran 67, 71–2, 195, 196, 197, 200–1, 202–3, 206, 231, 251n19,n26

Man Who Shot Liberty Valance, The 176
Manning, John 61
Manning, Mary 45, 54–6, 61
Marcus, Louis 86, 88–90, 100–1, 103, 114, 120
Marinelli, Peter 202
Markievicz, Countess 21, 32, 170
Marren, Martin 102
Marshall Aid Programme 82
Mason, Herbert 57
Mason, James 152, 235
Maturin, Charles 217
Mayor of Ireland, The 31
Meehan, John 57
Melbourne-Cooper, Arthur 7
Messenger, John C. 251n19
Metropole Cinema, Dublin 56
Metz, Christian 245, 256n104, n110
Michaeleen 72
Middle of Nowhere 113, 123n19
Miles, Sarah 200
Milesian Chief, The 217
Millar, Liam 252n27
Miller, Perry 207
Mills, John 160, 164, 169, 176, 230
Minister for Arts and Culture 121
Minister for Defence 61
Minister for Education 40
Minister for External Affairs 81–2
Minister for Finance 40, 51, 97, 99
Minister for Health 78, 80
Minister for Home Affairs 36
Minister for Industry and Commerce 44, 81, 96–100, 102–3, 115–18, 120
Minister for Posts and Telegraphs 43
Mirren, Helen 181
Mise Éire (I Am Ireland) 86–8, 110
Miser's Gift, The 18
Miskelly, Bill 134
Mitchel, Geraldine 57
Mitchell, Yvonne 112

Mitchum, Robert 111, 164, 176, 228, 231
Moana 203
Moby Dick 113
Moiselle, Nuala 120
Monsieur Beaucaire 8
Montagu, Ivor 203
Montgomery, William 55
Mooney, Ria 41, 59
Moore, Colleen 53–5
Moore, Thomas 8, 218, 254n72
Moran, Tom 41, 57
Morgan, Lady 204–6, 208–9, 210, 217, 218
Morley, Johnny 134
Morrison, George 86–8, 90
Morrison, Kathleen 54
Morrissey, Eamon 242
Morrow, Jeff 234
Morven, Myrette 58
Mosley, Len 166
Moss and Stoll 5
Motion Picture Company of Ireland 119
Moynahan, Julian 183
'Mr Burnshaw and the Statue' 257n117
MTM Enterprises 103
Mulcahy, General Richard 88
Mulholland, Mark 247
Mullen, Barbara 161
Mulvey, Laura 183
Murder in Eden 114, 123n19
Murphy, John A. 118
Murphy, Johnny 130, 132
Murphy, Kathleen 18
Murphy, Pat 139–40, 246, 249
Murray, Don 165
Musso, Jeff 59
Mycroft, Walter C. 57
My Life for Ireland 185n2

Nairn, Tom 159, 174
Nanook of the North 203
Nash, W. P. 15–16
Nashville 243
Nation Once Again, A 74–5, 76
National Development Corporation 103
National Film Institute of Ireland 80, 81

National Film Studios of Ireland 102–3, 112, 116, 117, 120
National Film Theatre, London 123n28
National Volunteers 24, 28, 34
National Westminster Bank 102
Nelson, James Malcolm 253n62
Nelson, Ralph 112
Nesbit, George 24
New Brighton Towers 101–2
New Description of Ireland, A 148
New Gosoon, The 106
Ní Chaoimh, Bairbre 134
Ní Conghaile, Máiréad 130
Night Nurse, The 59
No Resting Place 104, 111
Nochlin, Linda 250n7
Northern Ireland 63, 75, 82, 87, 89, 91, 111, 128, 132–3, 139–40, 152–84, 234–7, 246–7
Novak, Barbara 5–6, 252n37
Nowlan, David 88

O'Brien, Barry 12
O'Brien, Conor Cruise 85, 230, 234, 235, 255n92
O'Brien, Edna 112
O'Brien, Niall 135
O'Cahill, Donal 62–3, 65, 66–7, 68
O'Caoimh, Padraig 80
O'Casey, Sean 44, 53, 59, 111, 156–7, 161, 176–7, 186n17, 188n37
Ó Conluain, Proinsias 10, 32
O'Connell, Daniel 12
O'Connor, Barbara 193n83
O'Connor, Frank 54, 60–2
O'Connor, Jim 124n30
O'Connor, Pat 124n30, 181–4, 192n73
Ó Corráin, Donncha 256n101
Ó Dálaigh, Cearbhall 55
Odd Man Out 105, 111, 152–63, 165, 169, 170, 178, 179, 180, 181, 183, 234–6, 247
O'Dea, Denis 61, 232
O'Dea, Jimmy 41, 42, 49–50n84, 57–8, 68
Ó Díorain, Tomás 72

O'Donnell, Donat (alias Conor Cruise O'Brien) 234, 235
O'Donnell, Frank Hugh 57
O'Donnell, Marie 105, 106
O'Donoghue, Maurice 131
O'Donovan, Fred 17, 18
O'Donovan, Harry 58
O'Donovan, Rossa 34
O'Dowd, Dermot 20
O'Dowd, Liam 253n46
Ó Faoláin, Seán 82, 85, 134, 196
Of Human Bondage 100, 112
Official Sinn Féin 137
O'Flaherty, Liam 59, 154, 185n2, 186n15,n16
Ó Flathearta, Máirtin 134
O'Flynn, Phillip 106, 108
O'Grady, Standish 209, 210
O'Hara, Joan 106
O'Hara, Maureen 151, 199
O'Hara, Phyllis 57
O'Herlihy, Dan 159, 166, 231
O'Higgins, Kevin 36
Oidhche Sheanchais (Storyteller's Night) 72–3
Oireachtas Committee on Public Accounts 103
O'Kelly, Aideen 107
O'Kelly, Kevin 76
O'Kelly, Sean T. 81
O'Laoghaire, Colm 86
Olcott, Sidney 7–12, 32, 57, 220, 223
Old Mother Riley's Ghosts 149
O'Leary, Art 137–8
O'Leary, Liam 28, 48n44, 55, 68, 73, 74, 76–81
Olivier, Laurence 113
Olympia Theatre, Dublin 3
O'Mahony, Jerry 67
O'Malley, Desmond 102–3, 116–18
O'Malley, Colonel 'Kit' 43
O'Malley, Robert Emmett 43
On a Paving Stone Mounted 140–2
O'Neil, The 31
O'Neil of the Glen 17
O'Neill, Bernadette 243
O'Rahilly, Professor Alfred 80
O'Reilly, George 102

Ormrod, Peter 122, 241
O'Shannon, Cathal 123n14
O'Shannon Finola 106
O'Sullivan, Brian 65, 67
O'Sullivan, Maureen 55
O'Sullivan, Morgan 103, 121
O'Sullivan, Robin 118
O'Sullivan, Thaddeus 134, 140–2, 245, 249
Othello 94n43
Ó Tuathaigh, Gearóid 90
Our Boys 125n59, 136, 140
Our Country 76–80
Our Daily Bread 92n23
Ourselves Alone 60, 63, 65
Outcasts, The 125n59, 130, 133–4, 244–5
Outsider, The 173, 190n53

Paddy 112
Páisti Ag Obair (Children At Work) 86
Palace Cinema, Dublin 42
Panofsky, Erwin 199, 200, 227, 251n13
Parekh, Bhiku 158
Parker, Cecil 175
Parnell, Charles Stuart 90, 175
'Partition' Bill 28
Pascal, Gabriel 96–7
Passing Shower, A 18
Patch Ruadh 72
Pathé Gazette 16, 32, 34, 36
Pathé Pictorial 84
Pathetic Gazette 45
Patrick, Nigel 112
Patriot Game, The 193n85
Paul, Robert 6–7
Paying the Rent 29, 30
Peacock Theatre 45
Pearse, Padraig 24, 89, 182, 197
Pearson, Noel 120
Pedelty, Donovan 56–7
Peirce, C. S. 226
Pender, Aidan 254n79
Pender, Mrs. M. T. 17
People of Ireland 193n85
People Walking in Sackville Street 4
Performance 174
Perry, John 57, 113
Phibsboro Picture House 35

Philadelphia Here I Come 112
Phillips, Leslie 108
Photo Historic Film Company 37
Picard, Ulli 84
Pickford, Mary 8
Picturedrome, Killarney 63
Pigs 121, 125n59, 131–2, 140,
    243–4
Pint of Plain, A 140
Piperno, J. H. 114
Plain Tale From the Bogs, A
    188n36
Plant, Jim 24
Planter's Wife, The 190n60
Playboy of the Western World, The
    17, 27, 111, 114, 123n19, 217
Plough and the Stars, The 44, 59,
    96, 156–7, 165, 186n17,
    188n37
Plunkett, James 257n114
Point Blank 178–9
Poitín (Poteen) 129–30
Pollock, George 107
Poor of New York, The 214
Porter, Eric 173
Portrait of Dublin 81
Pourponnière, La 5
Poussin, Nicholas 226
Power, Charles 20
Power, Joseph A. 62
Power, Tyrone 227
Power, William 48n39
Presho, Neville 130
Presley, Elvis 243
Private Life of Henry VIII, The 53
*Proceedings of the Public Hearing of
    Bord Scannán na hÉireann/Irish
    Film Board* 125n58
Professor Tim 98, 105–6
Project Cinema Club 128–9
Promise of Barty O'Brien, The
    82–4
Provincial Theatre Company 6
Provisional IRA 173
Public Enemy, The 166
Puck Fair Romance, A 18
Pudovkin, Vsevolod 51, 64, 79,
    84
Punch 149
Purcell, Noel 58, 169, 232
Purcell, Olive 45

Puritan, The 59, 185n2
Purple Taxi, A 112
Puttnam, David 125n57

*Quackser Fortune Has a Cousin in
    the Bronx* 112
Quare Fellow, The 111, 123n19
Queen Elizabeth II 173
Quested, John 112
Question of Suspense, A 114,
    123n19
Quidnunc 84
Quiet Man, The 111, 151, 152,
    175, 196, 199–200, 209,
    221–3, 225–7, 230, 237,
    239–40, 241, 243, 244, 245,
    256n102
Quigley, Godfrey 107
Quinn, Bob 129, 137–9, 249

Rafferty's Rise 18, 30
Rahill, Frank 253n50,n56
Rank 84, 98, 114, 171
Ray, Aldo 112
Raymond, Gary 111
Rea, Stephen 178
Read, John 171
Receivers 100–3
Redmond, John 13
Redmond, Liam 161, 236
Reed, Carol 105, 111, 152–60,
    234
Reeves, Chris 193n85
Relph, Michael 162
Remembering Jimmy O'Dea
    49–50n84
*Report of the Film Industry
    Committee* 114–15
Republican Loan Bonds film 24
Return to Glennascaul 94n43, 98
Revival: Pearse's Concept of Ireland
    89
Reynolds, Albert 103
Rich, Barnaby 148
Richards, Jeffrey 190n60
Richards, Shelah 59, 61, 121
Riders to the Sea 59, 105
*Rise and Many Falls of Ardmore
    Studios, The* 123n14
Rising of the Moon, The 111, 114
Ritt, Martin 113

271

RKO 98–9
Roberts, Ruaidhri 102
Robinson, Lennox 45, 57, 98
Robison, Arthur 59
Rocky Road to Dublin, The 80, 85
Rodway, Norman 109
Rooney 107
Rory O'More 8, 9, 11, 23, 31, 65, 223
Rosaleen Dhu (Dark Rosaleen) 48n39
Rosen, Charles 250n7
Rosenthal, Joe 42
Roth, Arthur J. 111
Rotha, Paul 104, 111, 124n30
Rothwell, Norman 196
Rotunda, The 9, 14–16, 33, 34, 48n39
Rousseau, Jean Jacques 201, 206, 227, 251n17,n18, 254n64
Roustabout 243
Rowland, Kathleen 234
Rowson, Simon 122n1
Royal Cavalcade 53
Royal Irish Constabulary 27–8, 30, 35–6, 60, 65
RTE 84, 85, 90–1, 102, 119, 120, 122, 128, 136, 137
Rural Electrification Scheme 82–3
Rush, Barbara 234
Rushe, Desmond 88
Ruskin, John 224
Russell, Thomas 256n112
Ryan, Kathleen 153, 175
Ryan, Jacqueline 236
Ryan, Mary 134, 244
Ryan's Daughter 113, 176, 182, 196, 197, 200, 224, 228–31, 232, 233

Said, Edward 248
Saint Enda's 24, 26
Saint Joan 96
Saint Patrick 37–8, 140
Sally's Irish Rogue 106
San Francisco 134, 245, 249
Sands, William 101
Saoirse? (Freedom?) 86–9, 110
Sarris, Andrew 225
Sartre, Jean-Paul 162

Savoy Cinema, Dublin 44, 54–5, 58
Scallon, Brenda 134
Schell, Catherine 135
School of Film Techniques 76
Schooner, The 125n59, 134–5
Schrire, David 251n18
Schlesinger, Philip 177
Schulman, Milton 171
Schuster, Harold 57
Scott, Michael 92n23
Scott, Sir Walter 204, 217
Searchers, The 176, 225
Seat Among the Stars: The Cinema and Ireland, A 125n57
Seely, Tim 106
Sellars, Elizabeth 163
Senate 118
Seventh Dawn, The 190n60
Shadow of a Gunman, The 177, 186n17
Shake Hands With the Devil 100, 111, 164–7, 168, 175–6, 182, 231, 232, 234
Shakespeare, William 179
Shane, George 131
Sharp, Don 112, 113
Shaughraun, The 8, 34, 213, 215, 218, 220, 240
Shaw, Bernard 96–7, 108
Shaw-Smith, David 85
Sheehan, Canon 197
Sheehy, T. J. M. 197
Shepherd's Bush Film Studios 43
Sheridan, John D. 81
Sheridan, Richard Brinsley 24
Sherry, Peter 76
Shields, Arthur 240
Shiels, George 98, 106
Shiels, Una 43
Short Story: Irish Cinema 1945–1958 93–4n43
Siege of Sidney Street, The 113, 123n19
Sim, Alastair 175
Sinclair, Arthur 30
Sinful Davey 114
Singer not the Song, The 188n35
Sinn Féin 20, 21, 22, 23, 28, 29, 34–6, 40, 86, 127

Sinn Féin Review, The 34–6
Sipra, Mahmud 103
Sipra Studios 103
Sirk, Douglas 232, 234, 255n96
Sirr, Major 14
Slide, Anthony 254n74
Smiling Irish Eyes 53–5
Smith, Adam 213
Smith, Charles 204
Smith, J. 17
Smith, Sheamus 102
Snell, Bruno 251n21
Snowden, Alec C. 108
Society of Film-Makers of
   Ireland 115
Some Say Chance 57
Somerville and Ross 216
Song O' My Heart 55–6
Sophocles 153
Sparling, T. A. 13–16
Spillane, Davy 132
Spring Meeting 57
Spy Who Came in from the Cold,
   The 113
Stack, Austin 28–9
Stafford, Brendan 68, 73, 76, 84
Standing, Michael 170
Stanley, Alderman J. 43
Stanwyck, Barbara 157
Star of Erin Theatre of Varieties
   3–5
Steele, Tommy 227
Steiger, Rod 172
Stevens, Wallace 249
Stolen Years 192n73
Stoneman, Rod 193n85
Stop Thief! 92n24
Stork Talk 123n19
Storm Over Asia 51, 69n1
Storm Song 71
Stranger at My Door 111
Strick, Joseph 112
Strong, L. A. G. 57
Strongbow 122
Suedo, Julie 58
Sullivan, James Mark 16, 29
Sullivan, Owen 168
Summers, Jeremy 113
Swift, Carolyn 120
Sword of Sherwood Forest 113
Sylvester, Chris 41, 42

Synge, J. M. 17, 59, 111, 197,
   217, 219, 227, 250n11,
   253n46
Szasz, Thomas 167

Talk of a Million 105, 113
Tanner, Alain 114
Tara Productions 103
Taxi Mauve, Un (Purple Taxi)
   112
Taylor, Rod 176
Teleffs Éireann (RTE) 84, 90
Tennyson, G. B. 255n82
Terrible Beauty, A 111, 164–7,
   173, 175, 231
Terrington, Lord 16
Thames Television 90
Theatre de Luxe, Dublin 33, 56
Theatre Royal 60
They Got What They Wanted 105
Thirteenth Hussars Marching
   Through the City 5
This Other Eden 108–10, 124n40
Thompson, Kate 136
Thorlby, A. K. 250n7
Thornburn, June 107
Three Leaves of a Shamrock 111
Thuente, Mary Helen 256n109
Tibradden 76
Tine Bheo, An (The Bright
   Flame) 89
Todd, James 227
Toibín, Niall 129, 242
Tomelty, Joseph 155, 161
Too Long a Sacrifice 193n85
Tone, Wolfe 256n112
Townshend, Charles 148
Townshend, George 254n65
Trades Union Congress 22, 28
Traffic on Carlisle Bridge 4
Tragic Story of Beatrice Cenci, The
   5
Train Coming Into a Station 4
Traveller 132–3, 140
Treasure Hunt 113
Trevor, William 193n83
Trewey, Felicien 3–4
Troubles, The 90
Tudor, Andrew 151
Turner, James 251n17
Tyler Moore, Mary 103

Ulster Television 125n57
Ulysses 112, 142
Uncle Nick 66–7
Unfair Love Affair, An 18

Valentine, Fr 64
Valentino, Rudolf 8
Van Eyck, Peter 113
Van Geldern, Gerrit 85
Vardac, A. Nicholas 213
Varnell, Max 114
Vengeance of Fu Manchu, The 113
Very Edge, The 123n19
Violent Enemy, The 112, 168–71
Vitti, Monica 179
Voice of Ireland, The 56
Volta Cinema, Dublin 5–6,
  33
Voyage to Recovery 92n24

Walls, Tom 57
Walsh, J. J. 43
Walsh, J. Theobald 37
War of Independence 12, 20,
  23–4, 30, 42, 43, 58, 59,
  60–6, 68, 72, 76, 86–90, 97,
  98, 108–10, 137, 156–7,
  180–4, 177, 183
War Office Gazette 32, 36
Warrington, Ken 58
Waterbag 140
Watt, Harry 91n2
Watt, Stephen M. 253n62
Wayne, John 151, 152, 157, 199
W. B. Yeats: A Tribute 81
Welles, Orson 94n43
Wellesley, Dorothy 208
West of Kerry 66–8
Whaling Ashore and Afloat 7
Wheels 130, 133
When Love Came to Gavin Burke
  18, 31
When Reason Sleeps 122
Whitbread, J. 253n62
White Boys, The 230
White, John 76
White Heat 166

Whitehall 180
Whitten, Norman 33–8, 40, 42
Wicklow 214
Wicklow Gold 41
Widow Malone, The 18
Wild Ireland 125n59
Wild Irish Girl, The 204–7, 208,
  209, 218
Willemen, Paul 257n112
Williams, Christopher 251n23
Willie Scouts While Jessie Pouts
  48n39
Willis, N. P. 253n48
Willy Reilly and his Colleen Bawn
  23–9, 30, 38, 43
Wilmington, M. 255n86
Windom's Way 190n60
Wings of the Morning 57
Withdrawal 131
Wolf, Bryan Jay 252n36
Wolfe Tones, The 242
Woman Who Married Clark Gable,
  The 134, 245–6, 249
Woman's Wit, A 18
Woods, Arthur 57
Workers' Party, The 137, 138
World War I 32, 39, 98, 113
World War II 74, 80, 90, 111,
  164–7, 175–6
Wright, Tony 107
Wynne-Simmons, Robert 122,
  130, 133, 244
Wynter, Dana 165

Year of the French, The 90
Yeats Country 84–5
Yeats, Jack 224
Yeats, W. B. 71, 84, 104, 105,
  201, 208, 210, 219, 243, 232n45
You'll Remember Ellen 8, 11–12,
  31
Young Cassidy 111, 176–7
Young, Dudley 252n33

Zardoz 114
Zerner, Henri 250n7
Zhivago, Dr 229